CONTEMPORARY CANADIAN MARKETING CASES

CONTEMPORARY CANADIAN MARKETING CASES

H.F. (Herb) MacKenzie

Prentice Hall Canada Inc.
Scarborough, Ontario

Canadian Cataloguing in Publication Data

Main entry under title:

Contemporary Canadian Marketing Cases

ISBN 0-13-084091-2

1. Marketing—Canada—case studies. I. MacKenzie, H.F.

HF5414.12.C3C66 2000   658.8'00971   C99-931296-0

©2000 Prentice-Hall Canada Inc., Scarborough, Ontario
Pearson Education

Prentice-Hall, Inc., Upper Saddle River, New Jersey
Prentice-Hall International (UK) Limited, London
Prentice-Hall of Australia, Pty. Limited, Sydney
Prentice-Hall Hispanoamericana, S.A., Mexico City
Prentice-Hall of India Private Limited, New Delhi
Prentice-Hall of Japan, Inc., Tokyo
Simon & Schuster Southeast Asia Private Limited, Singapore
Editora Prentice-Hall do Brasil, Ltda., Rio de Janeiro

ISBN 0-13-084091-2

Publisher: Pat Ferrier
Acquisitions Editor: Mike Ryan
Developmental Editor: Sherry Torchinsky
(Senior) Marketing Manager: Ann Byford
Copy Editor: Valerie Adams
Production Editor: Sarah Dann
Production Coordinator: Deborah Starks
Permissions/Photo Research: Susan Wallace-Cox
Art Director: Mary Opper
Cover Design: Julia Hall
Page Layout: Heidi Palfrey

All cases in the book were prepared as a basis for class discussion rather
than to illustrate either effective or ineffective handling of an administrative situation.

1 2 3 4 5   04 03 02 01 00

Printed and bound in Canada.

Visit the Prentice Hall Canada Web site! Send us your comments, browse
our catalogues, and more at **www.phcanada.com**. Or reach us through
e-mail at **phcinfo_pubcanada@prenhall.com**.

Table of Contents

CASE 10: PARKER'S CLASSICS   56

Ramesh Vankat

Philip Parker, the owner of Parker's Classics, has noticed a sales decline in his upscale men's wear stores. His son, Jonathan, and one of the store managers have suggested that he should specifically target gay consumers. Philip is considering the attractiveness of this niche market, but he is also concerned with the risk it might pose for his small business. Philip has agreed to conduct a market research study.

CASE 11: EYCKLINE FARMS   59

Jane Funk and Thomas Funk

Wilhelm Van Eyck, a broiler grower, must make a buying decision. He has been using feed supplied by a large, national feed manufacturer for a number of years, but recently has become concerned about the product, the price, and the service. The case describes the process he uses to identify alternatives. The case also describes the approaches of three salespeople who call on, and try to influence him.

CASE 12: THE TRAIN TRIP   66

Rosemary Polegato

This case describes the problems a family experiences with a train trip during a vacation in Europe. It is focused on family consumption behaviour for a service, and the managerial issues involved in handling consumer complaints.

CASE 13: "GREENER PASTURES": THE LAUNCH OF STAGREEN™ BY HYDROCAN   70

Anne T. Hale

HydroCan is a new venture with a potentially profitable product called StaGreen™. Since the firm does not have a marketing representative, it has hired a consulting firm to help decide issues of market segmentation, target marketing, and product positioning. The decision must be made with the information at hand—there is no time to acquire additional market research, such as consumer or retail surveys.

CASE 14: DEPARTMENT OF HEALTH   77

James Agarwal and Dorothee Feils

Rising health care costs and budgetary constraints have led health care providers to look for additional non-government-based supplementary financing. Joan Smith, at the Department of Health, sees a tremendous potential in the marketing of health databases. However, she faces some challenging ethical and distribution-related issues.

CASE 15: RESTORED VISION INC.   83

Brock Smith

Restored Vision Inc., a clinic for laser eye surgery, is experiencing problems typical of new businesses. Monthly revenues have only begun to match expenses, and the owners now realize that they need some help to reach their business goals. The case offers interesting insight into the concepts of diffusion of innovation, services management, and economies of scale.

CASE 16: WILDERNESS NEWFOUNDLAND ADVENTURES   95

Cori-Jane Radford and H.F. (Herb) MacKenzie

Stan Cook, Jr. is reviewing the previous year's promotional expenditures for his family's eco-tourism business, and is trying to decide on the budget for the current year, and how it should be allocated.

CASE 17: SAMUEL'S FURNITURE: A FAMILY AFFAIR   110

Lindsay Meredith

Samuel's Furniture has opened a retail store just south of the Canada-US border in an attempt to capture business from the many Canadians participating in cross-border shopping. While the owners have thought through much of their marketing strategy, some promotional decisions must still be made, including media selection, scheduling, and message content.

CASE 18: UNIVERSITY OF OTTAWA INTERCOLLEGIATE SPORTS   114

David S. Litvack

Due to recent budgetary cuts, all sports teams at the University of Ottawa have to manage with less, particularly teams with male athletes. To compensate, there is a need for corporate sponsors. But potential sponsors look for exposure, and attendance records have been particularly poor. The immediate problem is to develop a promotional plan to increase attendance.

CASE 19: HEC ON THE INTERNET   122

Stéphane Bossé and Normand Turgeon

Two Masters students at École des Hautes Études Commerciales have developed a student associations Internet site that they wish to present to the Board of Directors. The case provides a forum to discuss the ethical issue of financing the site through sponsor advertising, and more generally, the role of the Internet within the marketing mix.

CASE 30: SYNDCOM LIMITED   205

Thomas Funk and Michael Atkinson

Syndcom Limited produces syndicated, business-related T.V. and radio features. Its radio division is quite new and currently features only one product, BizRap, a two-minute feature aired on 123 stations across Canada. BizRap has been distributed by Trirad Enterprises which, to date, has not achieved all of the objectives agreed upon when a distribution agreement was signed over a year ago. As a result, Debra Gray, the radio manager for Syndcom, is trying to decide whether they should distribute BizRap directly to radio stations.

CASE 31: NATURE-PLUS LIMITED: US EXPANSION?   214

Joseph J. Schiele

Brian Reis, President of Nature-Plus Canadian Operations, is struggling with the decline in the number of new distributors that were joining the firm each month. He is considering a proposal to expand the operations of Nature-Plus into the United States as a way to address this issue. He needs to decide whether this is a viable solution to his problems, and if so, how to carry it out.

CASE 32: EJE TRANS-LITE INC.   225

H.F. (Herb) MacKenzie

Paul Edison has just prepared his new sales forecast, and it is being threatened by competitive price reductions. He must decide whether to meet competitive pricing, or to hold his current price. Another option is to introduce several new models of his product, where there are no directly comparable competitive models, and price pressure would be less.

CASE 33: FORTRON INTERNATIONAL INCORPORATED   228

Marvin Ryder

The General Manager of Fortron International Inc., Steve Foxcroft, is reviewing the company's international marketing approach. When entering foreign markets, the company used a renewable sales agency agreement granting exclusive distribution rights for its unique, patented sports whistle to a country-specific distributor. The first such agreement was set to expire. Foxcroft felt the German market could be better exploited and was looking for alternate arrangements.

CASE 34: AIRVIEW MAPPING INC.   235

Kris Opalinski and Walter S. Good

Rick Tanner, the president and major shareholder of Airview Mapping Inc., is concerned about the apparent maturation of his company's primary domestic markets. He has collected a lot of market information on four foreign markets. He now must decide whether to try to penetrate any of them, and, if so, what entry strategy to use.

CASE 35: THE RIVERSIDE MOTOR INN   252

Ian Spencer

Ronald Veinot, the general manager of the Riverside Motor Inn, has just hired Heidi Smith as the senior lounge hostess for Chapters Lounge. Sales have fallen dramatically in the past year but show potential to recover. Ronald has written to Heidi outlining the situation and inviting her to provide her insights and analysis. Ronald challenges Heidi to think confidently and aggressively by posing the question, "Do you think we could hit $100 000 in the year 2000?"

CASE 36: PANTRY PRIDE STORES   256

H.F. (Herb) MacKenzie

Brenda Howley has written a letter to the president of Pantry Pride following a series of dissatisfying experiences she had at one of their stores. The case looks at the issues of retail service, customer expectations, complaint action, and service recovering.

CASE 37: TORONTO DOOR & TRIM   260

Donna Bernachi, John Blackie, and David S. Litvack

Toronto Door & Trim is a wholesaler (industrial distributor) that sells to residential construction contractors. Gerry, the owner, has moved the business to a larger location, and he is now trying to decide whether to start a retail operation to help cover his increased costs and to increase his profits.

CASE 38: TREMCO LTD.   265

Marvin Ryder

Paul Sagar, the marketing manager at Tremco Ltd., is re-examining Mono Foam. He had not been involved in the first marketing plan for the insulating foam spray, but is now trying to develop a strategy to increase sales volume and market share, improve profitability, and increase the total market for insulating foams.

CASE 39: MM BAKERS, LTD.—NOUS PLAISIR   272
Anne T. Hale

MM Bakers, Ltd., is trying to decide whether to expand the scope of the distribution of their product—packaged cookies. The decision to expand involves the leasing of new facilities, for which there is a very tight deadline. If the company wants the site next to their current facility, they must make a decision within approximately four weeks. The decision to expand distribution will be based on an analysis of the initial year of sales to supermarkets in the Montreal area. Determining the relative success of the firm's pricing, advertising, promotion, and distribution strategies employed during the previous year is the key to the expansion decision.

CASE 40: MOTUS INC.   280
Kris Opalinski and Walter S. Good

Greg Klassen and Phil Poetker, founders and principals of Motus Inc., are assessing their performance based on their overall marketing strategy, and are considering a number of changes that they could make to it.

Preface

Contemporary Canadian Marketing Cases is a collection of forty marketing cases by many of Canada's best case writers.

Two considerations helped focus my selection of cases. First, I believe that cases provide an excellent basis to build rapport among everyone involved in the case-learning environment; cases should provide fun for and be interesting to both students and instructors. I have tried to include cases on current marketing issues, in the context of a variety of Canadian industries. There are cases that involve tourism and recreation, sports, music, ethics, financial services (including database and relationship marketing), agriculture, gay markets, the Internet, co-op marketing, direct marketing, entrepreneurship, laser surgery, health care, sexual harassment in sales, hospitality, service failure, and international marketing.

Second, I believe that the best cases provide a rich environment for student learning. In that respect, I have re-written teaching notes, added topics for discussion, and included suggestions for using specific cases. The simpler cases can be used for assignments and exercises, or for class discussions; the more complex ones can be taught over two classes (for example, "Smiths Industries Medical Systems") and may be used in such a way that students can apply knowledge from an introductory course. The instructor may also attempt to increase students' knowledge by adding concepts from more senior marketing courses.

I have tried to bring together a selection of cases that provide instructors with maximum flexibility in designing and personalizing their own courses. While many cases are focused on specific marketing issues, there are also many that require a comprehensive marketing strategy/implementation focus, recognizing that many instructors prefer a variety of these types of cases for in-class discussions, for hand-in assignments, for examinations, and for group presentations.

Exhibit 1 provides a matrix of cases and topics. The primary focus for each case is provided, along with an indication of secondary case issues.

H.F. (Herb) MacKenzie
Memorial University of Newfoundland

EXHIBIT 1 Primary focus and secondary issues*

#		Primary focus	market analysis	ethics	marketing research	international marketing	buyer behaviour**	segmentation/targeting	product	price	distribution	promotion	strategy/implementation
1.	Financial Exercises	variety of financial analysis exercises											
2.	Wing and a Prayer	go / no go decision						xx					
3.	Entrepreneur's Marketing Source	evaluate strategic alternatives				x			x		x		xx
4.	Lucas Foods	evaluate strategic alternatives					xx						xx
5.	Looney School of Tennis	evaluating promotion alternatives					C	x			x	xx	
6.	Rocky Mountain House	developing marketing strategy for a co-op											xx
7.	Orangedale Whistle	tourism and recreation product launch	xx		x								xx
8.	Coco-Ricco Restaurants	marketing research needs			xx		C						
9.	Forum des Arts	segmentation and promotion decisions						xx				xx	
10.	Parker's Classics	whether to target gay consumers					C	xx				xx	
11.	Eyckline Farms	buyer behaviour, salesperson evaluation					B					x	
12.	The Train Trip	service failure					C						
13.	"Greener Pastures"	segmentation / targeting	xx				CB	xx					xx
14.	Department of Health	marketing a research database			xx						xx		
15.	Restored Vision Inc.	marketing a new innovative service					C		xx	x			xx
16.	Wilderness Nfld. Adventures	promotion budget and mix, tourism industry										xx	
17.	Samuel's Furniture	ad copy, media, and scheduling decisions				x	x				x	xx	
18.	University of Ottawa	increasing sports event attendance						x				xx	
19.	HEC on the Internet	role of Website in marketing			xx							xx	
20.	Ontario Rutabaga Council	promotion program development						x				xx	xx
21.	Health Care Corporation	personal selling simulation					B					xx	
22.	Provel	pricing and promotion decisions									xx	xx	
23.	Smiths Industries	organizational buying and selling					B	x	xx			xx	x
24.	Sue Jones	sexual harassment										xx	
25.	Some Ethical Dilemmas	several ethical situations		xx							x	x	
26.	Power & Motion	salesperson compensation and evaluation										xx	
27.	AGF	financial services marketing					BC		xx				xx
28.	Parker Instruments	channel relationships				xx					xx		
29.	Murray Industrial	channel relationships									xx		
30.	Syndcom	distribution change decision									xx		
31.	Nature-Plus	direct marketing, declining distributors				xx						xx	xx
32.	EJE Trans-Lite	price evaluation							x	xx	x		
33.	Fortron International	foreign market entry				xx							xx
34.	Airview Mapping	foreign market entry	xx			xx	x						x
35.	The Riverside Motor Inn	restaurant marketing											xx
36.	Pantry Pride	retail service failure					C						x
37.	Toronto Door & Trim	expansion decision					CB	x			xx		x
38.	Tremco	revising marketing strategy									x	xx	xx
39.	MM Bakers	expansion decision	xx					x					xx
40.	Motus	developing marketing strategy	xx		x			xx					xx

* 'xx' denotes focus of primary decision; 'x' denotes secondary decisions or topics
** 'C' denotes consumer buyer behaviour; 'B' denotes business or organizational buying behaviour

Introduction for Students

LEARNING FROM CASES

One of the most valuable experiences for marketing students is the opportunity to participate in marketing case analyses and discussions. However, if you are to benefit most from this experience, it is important to be an active rather than passive participant. Many students, particularly if their educational experiences have been focused on readings and lectures, find it difficult to do case analyses, and even more difficult to express themselves in case discussions. This is unfortunate because case analyses and discussions can add a whole new dimension to your marketing education and to your personal growth.

While lectures may be the most efficient method of transferring knowledge, case analyses and discussions foster learning through the development of independent thought and creativity, interpersonal communication, and decision-making skills. The focus changes from simple content, to both content and process. This means that students must share responsibility for their learning, while instructors must be confident in sharing power in the classroom, encouraging student views and participation. This provides a positive learning environment for everyone. Learning from case analyses and discussions should result from the initial reading of the case and individual case preparation, through small to large group discussions.

Individual Case Preparation

Cases vary in scope. Some are comprehensive cases that require a complete analysis, including consideration of the marketing environment; buyer behaviour; segmentation, targeting, and positioning strategies; and product, price, promotion, and distribution strategies. Other cases are more narrowly focused. You should quickly read through a case, paying particular attention to the opening and closing sections, to gain some idea of what the case involves and what decisions you are required to make.

Then, you should read the case more carefully. This is when you should underline important facts and make notes in the margins concerning your thoughts as you proceed through the case. Some careful thought after this reading will help you decide how to proceed: what decisions you must make, what numerical analysis is important, what alternatives may be appropriate, and what qualitative facts you must consider before making action-related recommendations. A word of caution here is to avoid focusing on one alternative too early. That will constrain your analysis. In most situations, there are several good alternatives, and effective managers recognize that different courses of action may enable an organization to meet its objectives.

Once you have completed your analysis, it is time to think about action—what you will do. It is sometimes easy to argue that more information is needed before you should act, but the reality is that many times, managers are required to make decisions with incomplete or imperfect information. You may need to make some assumptions, and you should test the robustness of those assumptions. For example, your success may depend very much on competitive reaction to your market strategy. You may need to assume that a competitor response will be to reduce its price by 10%. What effect will this have on the success of your strategy? What if the competitor reduces its price by 15%, or even 20%? How would this affect your performance? Would these competitor price reductions require additional changes in your marketing strategy?

A final recommendation when doing individual case preparation is to stay within the context of the case. While you may have information relating to events subsequent to the writing of the case, you should try to ignore this information when doing your analysis and deciding your recommendations. Cases are written concerning problems and issues at a particular point in time, and the situations that the decision maker faced at that time. You should analyze the case with the information that the decision maker had as that is the information that would have determined his or her actions. After the case discussion, or at a point where the instructor requests, you may wish to contribute additional knowledge.

While you can do too little analysis on a case, you can also do too much analysis. You need to consider what you are expected to do with your case analysis. If you are to make a formal class presentation, or to hand in a written analysis and action plan, more time and effort will be required than if you are preparing for a large group discussion. For most cases, you should spend two to four hours doing your individual analysis. Cases can, if you are not careful, take all of the time you allow them. Beyond some point, however, there is a diminishing return from working alone on a case. You need to consider participating in a small group discussion.

Small Group Discussions

In some classes, you may be assigned to a small discussion group or you may wish to consider forming your own group. Discussing your analysis and recommendations among a small group of peers allows you to refine and test your thinking. It provides additional learning opportunities for all participants. Many students feel more comfortable presenting and defending their recommendations, and the assumptions they have used, in this environment. To be effective, groups should consist of approximately four to six members committed to doing individual case analyses before the meetings and making contributions during the meetings. The duration of these small group discussions may vary depending on the case, but you should expect to spend 20 to 30 minutes for each meeting.

Large Group Discussions

In an effective case course, the most significant learning takes place in large group discussions. Even if your instructor has organized the course around formal group presentations, there is usually time for questions and discussions after each presentation.

To get the most from large group discussions, you should be committed to actively participate. You must be able to listen to what others are saying and follow where the discussion is going. That means you should limit, or eliminate, note taking. It is difficult to listen to what others are saying if you are focused on taking notes. That is a strategy you use when someone is transferring knowledge to you; for example, during a lecture. During large group discussions, you should be learning from the process, not focusing simply on the content. It is important to listen to understand what is happening if you wish to make an appropriate contribution. At the end of an effective case discussion, you should be able to review what has happened and to summarize what you have learned from the experience.

Participation is essential when working with case analyses. Some students find this process exciting and challenging, while others are intimidated and fear speaking in a large group of their peers. Small group discussions prior to class often help. Another consideration is your seating position in class. Some students gravitate to the back of the class as they find this seating position less threatening. You may wish to consider moving forward. Many students find it easier to participate from the front row. From that seating position, the size of the classroom seems smaller, and the interaction with the instructor seems more personal.

Also, participation becomes easier with practice. Like most worthwhile skills, if you do not practise, you will not improve. By partaking early on in the dialogue, it is often easier to continue making contributions as the case continues. For students less confident during discussions, another good opportunity to participate is when the direction of the discussion changes. As your confidence increases, you can increase your involvement in large group discussions.

Marketing Strategy

When developing marketing strategies, managers must consider both internal and external factors that may affect marketing decisions. A marketing strategy is a plan of action focused on developing, pricing, promoting, and distributing need-satisfying goods and services to target customers. The development of a marketing strategy requires the consideration of many aspects. It often helps to have an outline to guide your thinking. Organized around internal and external analysis and action, Exhibit 1 provides a framework of factors to consider during this development.

Exhibit 1	A Framework for Case Analysis and Action

Internal Analysis:

Objectives	Strengths/Weaknesses
Sales growth	Marketing and sales
Market share	(people and knowledge)
Increased profit	Other personnel
Product development	Financial condition
Innovation	Costs and revenues
Quality (products and service)	Marketing information systems
Reputation and image	Production capacity
Employee satisfaction	Distribution channels
	Reputation and image
	Quality (products and service)

Exhibit 1	A Framework for Case Analysis and Action (continued)

External Analysis:

Customers	Competitors
Size and growth	Relative size or market share
Segments (sizable, measurable, accessible, responsive)	Market leaders or followers
Purchase criteria (quality, price, service, etc.)	Strengths and weaknesses
Roles (initiator, user, influencer, decider, buyer, gatekeeper)	Reaction profile (aggressive or passive)
Relationship needs (transactional, or long-term orientation)	
Buying conditions (limited or extended problem solving; new task buy, straight rebuy, or modified rebuy)	
Search (extent and type)	

Opportunities / Threats	Distribution Channels / Suppliers
Competition	Relationships (power, dependence, (interdependence, cooperation)
Buyer needs (unmet, changing)	
Channels (availability, development capacity)	Availability, development, capacity
Resources (human, financial, material)	Technological capabilities
Technology	Financial condition
Market (size, growth, share)	Cost
Economic conditions	
Political and legal changes	

Action:

Product	Price
Quality (higher, competitive, lower)	Level (premium, competitive, low)
Service (superior, competitive, inferior)	Discounts (cumulative, noncumulative, trade, cash, seasonal)
Warranty or guarantee, and level	
Branding (generic, family vs. independent, manufacturer vs. distributor)	
Line (depth and breadth)	
Packaging	

Promotion	Distribution
Objectives (inform, persuade, remind)	Intensity (intensive, selective, exclusive)
Budget	Motivation (margin, support)
Mix (advertising, personal selling, sales promotion, publicity)	
Push vs. pull (or both)	

As you can see from this exhibit, there are many things to consider at the analysis stage, and many more to consider before deciding a course of action. A framework helps reduce confusion by providing a basis for beginning your analysis and for deciding action. Hopefully, you will find it useful, and the case process enjoyable and rewarding.

FINANCIAL ANALYSIS EXERCISES

H.F. (Herb) MacKenzie

Fundamental to any marketing analysis is an analysis of the financial and economic data relevant to each situation. You must understand what the numbers are telling you: where you are. This, along with more qualitative considerations, will suggest various courses of action. You must then be able to assess the effect of implementing these actions on financial performance: where you will be.

The following exercises provide the opportunity to practise sales, markup, and break-even analyses, and analyses related to each element of the marketing mix.

A. SALES ANALYSIS

Canada Controllers, Inc. manufactured electric motor starters and motor control centres, used in all types of industrial plants, including mines, pulp mills, and manufacturing plants. Motor starters were installed on or near individual pieces of equipment and usually operated only a single motor. They ranged in price from $50 to several thousand dollars. Motor control centres consisted of dozens or even hundreds of motor starters that were combined in a customized enclosure and were capable of starting motors in various locations of the plant from a centralized location. They ranged in price from less than $50 000 to several hundred thousand dollars.

Analyze the following sales data for Canada Controllers, Inc.

Year	Company Sales	Industry Sales
1994	$10 250 970	$ 74 600 000
1995	$11 844 888	$ 92 300 000
1996	$13 384 152	$111 700 000
1997	$14 722 155	$133 500 000
1998	$16 040 063	$158 900 000

Analyze the following sales data for 1998.

Product Line	Company Forecast	Company Sales	Industry Sales
Control centres	$ 2 500 000	$ 3 233 727	$ 20 250 000
Motor starters	$11 500 000	$10 406 040	$122 400 000
Repair parts	$ 2 000 000	$ 2 400 296	$ 16 250 000
Total	$16 000 000	$16 040 063	$158 900 000

Analyze changes in the following sales data from 1997 to 1998.

Product Line	1997		1998	
	Sales (units)	Sales ($)	Sales (units)	Sales ($)
Control centres	28	$ 1 766 740	38	$ 3 233 727
Motor starters	16 775	$11 041 600	18 305	$10 406 040
Repair parts	*	$ 1 913 815	*	$ 2 400 296
Total		$14 722 155		$16 040 063

* unit volume of repair parts not monitored

B. MARKUP ANALYSIS

1. Northgate Convenience store wishes to sell two cans of either Coke or Pepsi for $1.00. If the store does not sell anything at a markup lower than 25%, what is the maximum price that it can pay for a can of either brand?

2. Tom Thompson owns an apple orchard in Alberta. He was hoping to sell his apples at roadside for $0.59 per pound, and he wanted to make a 50% markup based on his total growing cost. What is the highest cost Tom can have to produce his apples and achieve his goals?

3. Harvey Hornswaggle has just left Newfoundland for a job in Cambridge, Ontario. He has decided to bring along a truck full of partridgeberry jam, and he has been busy buying it from all the people he knows who make it. He has been paying $2.00 per jar for 500 ml jars, and he hopes to sell them through grocery wholesalers around the Toronto area. According to his friend, Fred Nitney, wholesalers generally expect to make 20% markup on their cost, and retailers generally will not sell items like this unless they make 30% markup on their selling price. Harvey thinks he should make $1.00 per jar. What is Harvey's markup on his cost? What is Harvey's markup on his selling price? What

price will Mrs. Consumer have to pay in order for all channel members to achieve their desired margins?

C. BREAK-EVEN ANALYSIS

1. Moose Elbow Archery manufactures a high-quality crossbow for hunting. The company has been in business for three years, and its anticipated fixed costs for 1999 are estimated at $200 000. It sells the crossbow for $250 to retailers throughout North America. The company's variable cost to produce each crossbow is $200. Sales for 1999 are expected to be $1 250 000.

    a. What is the break-even point in units?

    b. What is the break-even point in dollars?

    c. What is the company's expected profit for 1999?

    The owner's daughter, a business student at a Western Canadian college, thought that the 1999 sales forecast was too optimistic. She forecasted sales of only $875 000.

    d. What would the company's expected profit be if her estimate is accurate?

    e. If the owner of the company believed that his daughter's forecast was correct, should he shut the company down?

2. Pooch Pullovers Inc. (PPI) has started manufacturing genuine Saskatchewan sealskin sweaters for dogs. It has 10 different designs, but has determined that the average time to manufacture each sweater is 6 hours. Saskatchewan sealskin is the most expensive cost, due to its rarity. The average cost of sealskin per sweater is $14.50, and the average cost of the rest of the materials (buttons, thread, etc.) is $1.50. The company employs a number of workers who assemble the sweaters at home and are paid a wage of $6.50 per hour. PPI sells its sweaters through craft fairs and flea markets. It has budgeted $12 000 to cover various costs associated with attending these venues (booth and table rentals, display costs, travel expenses, brochures, business cards, etc.)

    a. PPI estimated that it can produce 1200 sweaters in 1999. What is the lowest price PPI could charge in order to break even?

    b. How many sweaters would PPI have to sell at 40% markup on cost in order to break even?

    c. Comparable sweaters made from Prince Edward Island buffalo hide have appeared on the market, priced at $72.00 each. What options does PPI have? What would you recommend?

D. EVALUATING ADVERTISING EFFECTIVENESS

You are the advertising manager for a firm that manufacturers piping products for the pulp and paper, and petro-chemical industries. You have been working with a national advertising firm to develop an advertisement. You have decided to place it in trade magazines targeted at purchasing agents in these industries, and to also develop it for a more targeted direct mailing to a list of 1000 purchasing professionals that work in these industries. To control advertising expenses, you will use exactly the same ads for both advertising campaigns. The results of the two campaigns follow. Which campaign was more effective?

Campaign A

You have placed the ad in two trade magazines: *Pulp & Paper Canada* and *Canadian Oil & Chemical*. The cost to advertise in the first magazine was $4745, and to advertise in the second magazine was $4350. It was expected the ad would be read by 700 purchasing agents in the target industries. The ad generated 206 inquiries, and 105 were later qualified by telemarketing (an average of four calls per hour, and they were paid $16.50 per hour) as worthy of follow-up by a sales representative. The ad was believed responsible for 28 sales, averaging $63 344 with a 21.4% gross margin.

Campaign B

A copy of the ad was mailed to 1000 purchasing professionals on a mailing list that had been purchased for $1100 from a mailing list supplier. Other costs included printing, $1285; cover letters and envelopes, $115; and postage, $990. The ad resulted in 310 inquiries, and 164 were later qualified by telemarketing (an average of four calls per hour, and they were paid $16.50 per hour) as worthy of follow-up by a sales representative. The ad was believed responsible for 44 sales, averaging $41 445 with a 22.2% gross margin.

E. EVALUATING SALESPERSON EFFECTIVENESS

You are the sales manager for a large Canadian consumer goods company, and you are evaluating three salespeople that were hired last year. Salespeople work 230 days per year, and the average across your entire sales force was eight sales calls per day. Which of these salespeople is the most effective, and why?

Salesperson	Karen King	Bob Bishop	Anne Hand
Territory	Calgary	Toronto	New Brunswick
Calls per day	10	8	6
Direct selling costs	$72 000	$74 000	$82 000
Conversion rate (orders / calls)	22%	26.1%	29%
Average sales per call	$3 666	$4 123	$3 255
Average gross margin	21.1%	22.7%	23.3%
Average time per sales call	32 minutes	42 minutes	36 minutes

F. EVALUATING DISTRIBUTION CHANNELS

Upper Canada Clothing Company has been selling its industrial clothing across Canada for over 20 years. It has a four-member sales force: three are in Ontario and one is in Quebec. Total sales by this sales force in 1998 were $3.9 million. Total industry sales for competing products in Ontario and Quebec were $15.8 million. The company also has nine manufacturer's agents, who are paid an 8% commission on sales. Their 1998 performance follows:

Territory	No. of Agents	Sales	Market Share
British Columbia	2	$ 886 458	17.5%
Alberta	2	$ 742 458	13.4%
Saskatchewan and Manitoba	2	$1 244 553	19.5%
Atlantic Provinces	3	$ 937 887	26.3%
Total:		$3 811 356	

The agents that sell your clothing sell between three and eight other non-competing product lines. One of the agents in British Columbia has recently complained about the commission she is being paid, and has informed you that your major competitor is paying its agents a 10% commission. You have decided that it is time to re-assess your channel strategy. You are wondering whether you should continue with your current strategy, or replace all manufacturer's agents with company salespeople. The direct selling costs (salaries and selling-related expenses) for each salesperson you hire would be $90 000. You would need one salesperson for each territory. After an analysis of the situation, what would you recommend?

G. EVALUATING PRODUCT LINES

As the product manager responsible for the artificial tree line of a manufacturer of Christmas-related products, with plants in three provinces, you have been instructed to review the four items manufactured at your plant to see if one or more items could be eliminated. The company has added so many items to its product mix over the past decade that the president has decided to reduce the number of items by 20% to 40%. Each product manager has been asked to do a similar analysis. What would you recommend to the president based on the following information?

Product	Suggested Retail Price*	Projected 1999 Unit Sales Volume	Estimated Average Growth Rate, 2000–2004
Spruce	$ 90	31 000	10%
Blue spruce	$100	46 000	12%
Fir	$140	62 000	6%
Pine	$180	10 200	4%

Production overhead costs:	$800 400
Plant administrative expenses:	$140 510
Allocation of corporate overhead:	$110 500
Inventory turnover:	2.2 times per year
Inventory carrying costs:	5.25%

Direct variable cost as a percentage of manufacturer's selling price:

Spruce	75%	Fir	75%
Blue spruce	73%	Pine	80%

---

* All sales were through retailers who insisted on a markup of 50% on sales, and who expected shipments F.O.B. destination. The cost of shipping trees averaged $2.50.

The company did not have a sales force, but sold through manufacturer's agents who received a 5% commission on sales.

WING AND
A PRAYER

Marvin Ryder

Stefan Bakarich had found just the right name for his mobile bungee jumping operation—Wing and a Prayer. It was March 1994, and he had eight weeks to the May Victoria Day Weekend—the first long weekend of the summer. If he had it figured correctly, Stefan would rent a construction crane, assemble a group of friends, and tour southwestern Ontario offering bungee jumps at tourist attractions. He and his friends could earn enough money to return to university in the fall while being paid to have fun and work on their tans over the summer.

SOME HISTORY

Bungee jumping started as a ritual practised by "land divers" on Pentecost Island in the New Hebrides of the South Pacific. To cleanse themselves of wrongdoing or as acts of courage, native men constructed 30-metre towers from thin trees. Climbing to the top, they dove off with vines tied around their ankles. Their heads would just touch the ground as the vine became taut. In the 1960s, a group of Oxford University students (who called themselves the Oxford Dangerous Sports Club) brought bungee jumping to the modern world. As a commercial curiosity, the sport was born in New Zealand in 1988 where ancient vines were replaced with modern man-made fibre cords tested to withstand more than 3000 pounds (about 1360 kg), and where bamboo pole towers were replaced with bridges spanning deep river gorges.

The sport became popular on the west coast of the United States in the late 1980s and swept across the country in the early 1990s, showing phenomenal growth. In 1991, only 20 companies in the United States offered bungee jumps. In 1992, that number had grown to 200, and by 1993, more than 400 companies in the United States were in the bungee jump business. Participation in the sport had also grown. In 1992, 1.5 million Americans experienced a bungee jump, spending more than $100 million for the thrill. In 1993, 2.5 million Americans participated, spending more than $125 million.

In Canada, the first commercial bungee operation (Bungy Zone) opened south of Nanaimo on Vancouver Island on August 4, 1990. By 1993, 30 000 people had jumped at this one site. Some Bungy Zone statistics: oldest jumper 73, youngest 14; and heaviest 330 pounds. The most paid bungee jumps by one person was 30. The typical jumper was a thrill-seeking male aged 18 to 25. Ninety-nine percent of people who paid the fee completed the jump. Ten percent of jumpers took a second jump on the same day. Participation statistics were not available for Canada but, in 1993, there were about 35 companies which arranged bungee jumps off bridges, towers, cranes, and hot-air balloons. The West Edmonton Mall had introduced in-door bungee jumping. Nanaimo had even hosted bungee jumping in the nude.

Stefan had taken his first bungee jump in May 1993. He tried to describe his experience to a friend.

> I dove straight out, in my best imitation of Superman. At first, the free-fall was exhilarating. But it was also disorienting, and after a moment I panicked. I wished there were something to grab hold of. The sound of the wind was almost deafening. The ground below rushed toward me, until everything became a blur. It was hard to believe that I was feeling 3Gs—just like airforce pilots.
>
> Suddenly, the world seemed upside-down. The ground was receding, and now I was completely confused. I was up in the air again when I realized that the cord had held.
>
> I started to descend once more. This time, there was no fear, just enjoyment. I rebounded up and down four more times, with each rise becoming smaller. Finally, the bungee cord had no more bounce, and I was lowered onto the pad where my feet were untied. Friends told me I had the Look—a certain glow common to those who had just found God or had escaped the electric chair.

During the summer of 1993, Stefan took a bungee jump training course, worked for two and a half months at an amusement park in the United States, and jumped 150 more times.

OPERATIONS

Stefan's experience with a crane-based company inspired him. He had taken careful notes about its operation so that he could replicate its success in Canada. For a typical jump, a patron would be taken, in a specially designed metal cage, 130 feet to the top of a crane—a ride of 60 seconds. These jump platforms were available for $500 to $1000, though Stefan thought he could design and build one over the next eight weeks. At the top, the patron would be placed in one of two harnesses and given special instructions about jumping. One harness went around a person's ankles so that he or she would fall head first. The feet were tightly bound together with a towel and tethered to the bungee cord by a nylon strap and carabiner, a common piece of mountaineering equipment. The other harness could be strapped around a person's waist so that he or she would fall feet first. Each harness was commercially available at a cost of $150 to $300. While the patron took some time to build courage, the length of the bungee cord was adjusted to that person's weight. These "top of crane" activities could take between two and four minutes. Jumping out from the cage and away from the crane, the patron would take three seconds to fall until the bungee cord became taut and caused them to bounce. Waiting for the bouncing to stop, lowering the basket, retrieving the jumper, and removing the harness would take another two minutes.

Stefan had researched potential suppliers, so he had a firm estimate of costs. He would have to pay $100 per operating hour for construction crane rental, which included $1 million of liability insurance, fuel to run the generator, and a driver. Given the lack of office building construction, many companies had cranes parked in their compounds. These construction companies had been quite interested in Stefan's lease proposal. A crane operator would cost an additional $40 per operating hour. He felt the cost was justified as a skilled employee operating the crane would minimize the chances of something going wrong.

He and a jump assistant would be on the jump platform helping with instructions, adjusting the bungee cord, strapping on the harness, and communicating via walkie-talkie to the crane operator. On the ground, one person would use a microphone and sound system to speak to any crowd which had gathered and encourage them to participate. Two other people would assist on the ground by getting potential patrons to sign a liability waiver form, weighing jumpers to determine the proper bungee cord, collecting the jump fee, and talking personally with patrons in the crowd. While people under 18 could jump, a parent's or guardian's signature would be required on the waiver form. Excepting the crane operator and himself, all staff would each be paid $8.00 per operating hour.

Of course, a bare crane was not very attractive, so Stefan would have to invest $700 in some cloth banners which, when hung on the crane, would also be used for promotion. Some portable tables, folding chairs, walkie-talkies, and a sound system would have to be purchased for $1700. This cost also included portable "snow" fencing which would be used to limit public access to the crane, jump platform, and retrieval area. During less busy times, the sound system would play "hip hop," "dance," "house," and "rap" music to help attract and build a crowd. His major cost was an inflatable target pad that would be used to catch a jumper only if the bungee cord broke. Though pads came in many sizes, he felt it was a wise precaution to choose the largest size available at a cost of $12 000. As he thought the business would have a three to five year life, the pad and other equipment could be used year after year.

He had modelled his fee schedule on the American amusement park: $65 for the first jump and $55 for a second jump on the same day. If the patron used the waist harness rather than the ankle harness, both prices were reduced by $10.

Realistically, the company would operate for the 110-day period from the Victoria Day Weekend in late May to the Labour Day Weekend in early September. As he did not want to be bothered with portable lighting, he would start operations no earlier than a half hour after sunrise and cease operations no later than a half hour before sunset. The company would never operate during a thunderstorm or in high winds, and Stefan thought that the start of a week and overcast/rainy days would see less demand for the service.

SAFETY

Bungee jumping was not without its risks. In August 1992, a man was killed in Peterborough, Ontario, when he jumped from a crane. That same year, two people died in the United States and one in New Zealand from accidents. The Canadian Standards Association, a nonprofit agency, had not determined any rules for bungee jumping, so regulations varied by province. Some provinces had no regulations, but Ontario, working with the Canadian Bungee Association, had amended the Amusement Devices Act to regulate bungee jump operations starting in the spring of 1994.

In the legislature, Ontario Consumer and Commercial Affairs Minister, Marilyn Churley, said, "Operators can't just take a construction crane and set it up and have people jump off. We don't think that's safe. The government is committed to establishing and enforcing safety standards to minimize the risks to Ontarians who take part in this activity. Maintaining high standards of safety may also limit bungee operators' exposure to lawsuits and reduce the high cost of liability insurance."

Bungee jump operators were required to obtain a licence and permit ($310 fee) from the ministry prior to any jumps taking place. Before a licence could be issued, the operators' equipment designs first had to be approved by ministry engineers ($400 fee), after which a thorough on-site physical inspection of the bungee operation would be completed ($200 fee). The technical dossier of designs was to include: the jump height; a description of bungee cords including manufacturer, type of cord, and weight range of jumpers; an indication if the jump is static or portable; a description of the hoisting device, including name of manufacturer, year, serial number, and safe working load; depth of water or air bag; type of harnesses to be used and types of jumps offered; wind speed restrictions; and number and function of jump personnel.

A 40-page code of safe conduct for bungee jumping operations was also in place. The code had been recommended by the Task Force on Bungee Jumping, a working partnership between government and the Canadian Bungee Association. The code required a number of safety features that must be in place on bungee equipment, and technical specifications for the structure, platform, bungee cords, harness, and all other equipment used in the activity. It also outlined the qualifications for bungee jump employees, including certificates in First Aid and Cardio-Pulminary Resuscitation (CPR), and training specific to bungee jumping. Another requirement was a good first aid kit with a spinal board and speed splints, which would cost an operator an additional $500.

These changes were introduced to regulate careless operators and were aimed primarily at mobile bungee operations as they had less experienced staff and more failure-prone equipment as it was repeatedly set up and dismantled. Prior to the legislation, some operators had voluntarily introduced dual carabiners for ankle harnesses, so there was a back-up if one failed.

Stefan planned his own set of rules. No pregnant women. No people with heart conditions. No people with high blood pressure. No people who suffered from epilepsy. No people with neurological disorders. Especially no people under the influence of alcohol and drugs. He would allow no reverse jumping (anchoring and loading the bungee cord from the ground to propel the jumper upward), no sand bagging (loading excess weight with the jumper to be released at the bottom to gain more momentum) and no tandem jumping (two or more jumpers harnessed together).

A bungee cord was made from several bound strands of latex rubber, doubled back on itself thousands of times, sheathed in cotton and nylon. The cost of these cords varied from $300 to $1000. The cord could stretch to five times its original length. For safety, most operators retired a bungee cord after 150 jumps. Prior to the popularity of jumping, these cords were used by the US Air Force on aircraft carriers, so were constructed to military specifications.

SOME DECISIONS

To start his business, Stefan needed capital to acquire bungee cords, harnesses, the landing pad, and his operating equipment. He was aware of two Ministry of Economic

Development and Trade loan programs. As a returning Canadian university student, he could apply for a $3000 interest-free loan. To qualify for this loan, he had to be over 15, returning to school, and operating a business in Ontario between April 1, 1994, and September 30, 1994. Whatever loan amount he received would be payable on October 1, 1994.

He had also heard of the Youth Venture Capital Program. It provided loans of up to $7500 to help unemployed Canadian youth aged 18 to 29 start a business in Ontario. The interest rate on the loan would be prime plus one percent and he would be expected to make principal and interest payments each month. He would also be expected to contribute a minimum of one-quarter of the loan amount to the operating capital of the firm. This program was not intended to fund a summer job experience.

Neither program would provide him with all the capital he required. He approached his parents. While not completely sold on the venture, his parents thought it would be a good learning experience so they agreed to loan him $3000 interest-free, though they expected to be repaid at the end of the summer.

Needing more money, Stefan shared his plan with Zach Thompson, a friend on the university water-polo team and a recent bungee-jumping enthusiast. Zach had also worked part-time with a bungee jump operator but he had only jumped 40 times in the last year. He would act as a jump assistant. Zach proposed a partnership and a joint application for any government loan. Profits would be split 50/50. Like Stefan, he would replace a "paid" worker on the jump crew but would not draw any hourly wages. Of all people Stefan contacted, Zach asked the most questions.

Where would they operate the business? Stefan thought they could create a base of operations in Grand Bend. When special events occurred, like the Western Fair in London, Ontario, or the Zurich Bean Festival, they could pull up stakes and move to that location for a few days.

Would they only offer bungee jumps? Zach thought they could sell some complementary products. A colourful logo could be designed for "Wing and a Prayer" and applied to T-shirts and baseball caps. Selling for $20 and $10 respectively, these items would have a 100% markup on cost and could add extra revenue. Zach had also thought about selling a personalized video. That would mean purchasing a camcorder ($1800), developing some stock footage for opening and closing credits, and somehow editing/processing on site the video footage shot so the patron could quickly get his or her tape. Zach thought they could sell the videos for $25. Building on these ideas, Stefan thought about offering a colourful poster that might be especially popular among children. To produce 1000 posters would cost $800 but they could be sold for $4 to $6, generating a very healthy profit margin.

Would they make any money? That required some financial analysis, including a break-even analysis. Zach felt they needed to assess a second scenario: the likelihood that they would make enough money to return to university in the fall. These analyses would be needed along with their marketing plan when any loans were sought.

If this was going to be their summer occupation, they needed to get started right away.

C a s e

THE ENTREPRENEUR'S MARKETING SOURCE INC.

3

Barbara J. Phillips

After only nine months in business, Brent Banda, founder and owner of The Entrepreneur's Marketing Source Inc. (EMS), felt like he was facing the biggest challenge of his career. His business cards promised to provide "ideas, advice, and solutions" to other companies in Saskatoon, yet Brent wasn't sure what advice to give himself regarding the future of his company.

THE CITY: SASKATOON

Saskatoon is the largest city in Saskatchewan, with a population of 219 000. Situated along the banks of the South Saskatchewan River, the city prides itself on developing riverside parks and recreational facilities. Saskatchewan traditionally has relied on the agriculture industry, and one-third of Canada's agricultural biotechnology companies are located in Saskatoon. Recently, Saskatoon has steered its growth toward becoming a transportation and supply centre for the mining industry. It is home to mining head offices for potash, uranium, gold, and diamonds.

THE COMPANY: EMS

Brent started EMS in Saskatoon just months after he graduated from the University of Saskatchewan with his Commerce degree in Marketing. Although EMS is incorporated, Brent owns 100% of the shares and is its only employee. He has operated EMS out of his home for the past nine months and aims to break even by the end of the year.

Financial support for this case was provided by the Canadian Imperial Bank of Commerce as part of the CIBC Youth Entrepreneurship Case Project at Acadia University. The objective of the project was to develop, publish, and promote business cases that focus on a young entrepreneur and a specific problem or opportunity faced in starting up his or her business. The copyright for this case is owned by the Acadia Institute of Case Studies (AICS) at Acadia University. The CIBC cases, as well as other cases published by AICS, are available free of charge for educational purposes from the AICS Website: **http://relay.acadiau.ca/fps/business/aics/**

The mission statement of EMS is to "establish the company name as a reliable source of practical marketing information to North American small and medium-sized businesses." The idea for EMS was generated while Brent was working on projects for his university classes. He noticed many small businesses had little knowledge about, or expertise in, marketing. However, marketing was a crucial element in their continued success.

Brent created EMS to develop and sell a practical marketing workbook that could be used by small businesses in Canada and the United States. The workbook was envisioned as a general guide to help small business owners with no marketing experience create strategies tailored to their unique business situations. Brent was confident that, in the future, he could branch out and create a series of workbooks that focused on specific marketing problems, such as advertising or new product development.

The first setback occurred when Brent approached his banker for a $7000 business loan to start EMS. The banker demurred that a workbook would take some time to develop and suggested that EMS offer personalized, marketing consulting services to small business clients in Saskatoon. The consulting would furnish real-life examples that Brent could incorporate into the book and would provide EMS with steady income during the workbook's creation. Brent knew that EMS could not survive without the bank loan, so he agreed to become a consultant in the short-term while developing his long-term plans. He was worried, however, that his consulting projects would slow the progress of the workbook.

That worry turned out to be correct. Nine months after EMS was created, its consulting business is flourishing. However, Brent finds himself working 50 to 60 hours per week on personalized consulting and the workbook still is not completed. He also attends many meetings and community events in order to develop a referral network of small business consumers for his consulting activities.

THE ENTREPRENEUR: BRENT BANDA

Brent was raised in a working-class family, and worked as a waiter and in other service jobs to put himself through university. As a waiter, Brent had to talk to up to 25 strangers a day and he credits this training with giving him the confidence to approach new people when the opportunity arises. Brent does not consider himself to be a "thrill-seeking" risk taker, but feels that starting his own business is a risk that he can afford because he has nothing to lose. He is single with few assets and is just starting out in life, so even if EMS does not become successful, he can always start over working for another company.

Brent credits his education at the University of Saskatchewan for gaining business knowledge, project experience, and writing skills. The most difficult part of starting EMS for Brent was feeling confident in his ability to apply his education to practical problems. However after a short time at EMS, Brent realized that other small business owners did not possess extraordinary business skills either, and Brent learned to be confident in his strengths.

Brent is constantly involved in business planning for EMS, both for the short-term and the long-term. Early on, Brent realized that he could achieve business success by either creating an image for EMS or creating an image for himself. Because he did not have the money to launch an image campaign for EMS, Brent chose to create an image for himself as a successful entrepreneur and small business owner. He was head of the committee for North Saskatoon Business Associates, where he produced their awards banquet for two years. Recently, he had been named to the board of directors for the Provincial Exporters Association. Brent is described by others as outgoing, motivated, and hard-working.

THE CONSUMER: SMALL BUSINESS OWNERS

EMS targets small and medium-sized businesses in North America that do not have full-time marketing staff. These companies are usually managed by one owner. Industry Canada estimates that 60% of all Canadian businesses are run by one self-employed owner. An additional 30% of businesses have fewer than five employees, and this number has grown by 30% in the last ten years. The number of small businesses by province is provided in Table 3-1. In addition, over 13 million home-based businesses exist in the United States.

Compared to larger companies, small businesses often lack depth and expertise in many business functions, including marketing. While larger companies have marketing departments and operate with a marketing plan in place, many small businesses have no formal marketing plan, strategy, or objectives. In fact, many small business owners are unclear what exactly marketing is and how to apply it to their situations. Consequently, they are unlikely to seek marketing help.

To understand the small business owner better, Brent conducted a focus group interview in Saskatoon. The informants agreed that they had a poor understanding of marketing concepts and felt that a marketing plan was too theoretical and difficult to use. They were interested in learning more about how to advertise their products, however. They indicated that they were too busy to read long books about marketing, but were enthusiastic when Brent introduced a prototype of his workbook and led the group in a strategic planning seminar. Brent felt that the positive response to this workshop indicated that his marketing workbook could be a success.

Table 3-1	Number of Small Businesses by Province			
Province	**Total Businesses**	**Self-Employment**	**Total Employers**	**Small Businesses**
Canada	2 324 518	1 393 000	931 518	707 886
Newfoundland	44 274	22 000	22 274	17 854
PEI	15 732	8 000	7 732	5 684
Nova Scotia	73 678	41 000	32 678	23 689
New Brunswick	56 852	29 000	27 852	20 488
Quebec	493 680	266 000	227 680	169 812
Ontario	826 733	518 000	308 733	225 655
Manitoba	100 135	64 000	36 135	24 495
Saskatchewan	127 899	87 000	40 899	30 617
Alberta	278 771	167 000	111 771	82 162
BC	340 323	191 000	149 323	109 170
Yukon	4 247	2 700	1 547	1 011
NWT	9 154	4 000	5 154	3 455

Notes: Provinces do not sum to the total for Canada because the same companies may be counted in more than one province. This table excludes the public sector. *Self-employment* is unincorporated self-employment only. *Small businesses* are employers with less than 5 employees.

Source: Entrepreneurship and Small Business Office, Industry Canada, 1994.

EMS CONSULTING SERVICE

EMS is likely to meet its first-year objectives of breaking even and developing a consulting practice that provides a steady income to sustain the business. Table 3-2 provides EMS's financial results for the first nine months of operations. Examples of EMS's first-year clients include a husband and wife team who wanted to make their photography hobby into a full-time career, an architect who was losing clients to his competition, a real estate firm trying to attract developers, and a glass company that didn't know how to advertise. Customers like these contract with EMS to provide marketing research, create a marketing plan, and/or develop promotional strategies. Beyond marketing advice, an important part of EMS's service is the education Brent provides to small business owners. Instead of handing over a report, Brent explains the basis for his decisions and provides EMS's clients with long-range perspectives on their marketing situations.

Before any consulting work is started, EMS provides a written quote. Currently, EMS charges $75 per hour for consulting services, but Brent plans to increase this fee to $85 next year and to $100 after that. Billable hours are recorded as the work is completed and used as a guide when quoting future projects. However, if billable hours exceed the original estimate, EMS only charges the amount of the original quote. In the first year, Brent often has underestimated the amount of time a project would require, but he expects to improve this variance with experience. All clients provide a 25% deposit and are invoiced after the work is completed, with 15 days to make payment. EMS has had no trouble collecting receivables from clients.

Table 3-2	Income Statement for the Nine-Month Period Ended September 30, Year 1	
Consulting revenue	$30 425.88	
Cost of services	9 824.04	
Gross margin		$20 601.84
Operating expenses		
Accounting	$ 850.00	
Marketing	850.73	
Memberships	250.00	
Interest and bank charges	804.44	
Office supplies	1 665.95	
Phone	2 266.26	
Business meetings	588.48	
Wages	16 350.00	
Total operating expenses		23 625.86
Net operating income (loss)		($ 3 024.02)

THE COMPETITION

Many other companies offer marketing services in Saskatoon. Large consulting and research firms and advertising agencies provide specific services to larger clients with marketing departments. These consultants do not actively solicit small business clients, given that small businesses lack marketing and promotional plans, require extra time and effort, and may not be able to afford their consulting fees. In addition to large consultants, 16 small marketing consulting firms are listed in the Saskatoon Yellow Pages. Finally, many small businesses rely on media agents to help them with their marketing plans; for example, a local paper or radio station may design ads or help with strategic planning if a small business owner buys advertising space or time. Media agents provide this service free of charge.

To attract clients to EMS in this competitive environment, Brent has established a network of business contacts in the local community. A free newsletter offering practical marketing tips is mailed to these contacts each month. The newsletter is intended to build the awareness and credibility of EMS's service as well as prompting referrals and repeat business. The newsletter has a professional appearance and has been well-received by its recipients. A sample newsletter is provided in Figure 3-1.

THE OFFER

Although EMS creates promotional strategies and develops advertising plans, Brent is not a graphic designer; he relies on other local companies to create finished ads, artwork, and Web pages. One design firm he has worked with is called Imagine and is owned and operated by two young designers who quit their jobs with a large local advertising agency less than a year ago when they became "fed up" with their boss. Many of the agency's clients transferred to Imagine shortly after the split.

Brent was surprised when the partners at Imagine approached him with a business offer. They wanted to create a strategic alliance with EMS; EMS would refer all of its clients' design work to Imagine, and Imagine would send its clients in need of marketing help to EMS. In addition, EMS would share office space with Imagine; the design firm is housed on the top floor of a building in the trendy Broadway district of Saskatoon. Although rent in this district can be pricey, Imagine was willing to let EMS share the space for only $185 per month. EMS would receive one office and share the reception area and meeting room.

Brent could see the benefits of aligning EMS with Imagine. He would have access to Imagine's clients, many of whom were much larger than those he currently had. Although the partners of Imagine would not allow him to see their financial statements or discuss their operating income because Imagine would remain a separate company from EMS, Brent had a good working relationship with Imagine's partners. In addition, the partners valued Brent because he wrote clear marketing strategies that allowed them to "concentrate on the fun part of the business—making ads." However, if EMS enters into the proposed strategic alliance and receives new clients from Imagine, Brent can see that all of his time will continue to be eaten up by consulting. Publication of the workbook would be delayed for at least another year.

FIGURE 3-1   EMS Newsletter

December 1998

The Marketing Source

Marketing Tips To Build Your Business

The Entrepreneur's Marketing Source Inc.

ideas • advice • solutions

Entrepreneur's Marketing Source helps small and medium size companies plan their marketing and promotion.

adver**Tip**

Quote a satisfied customer to make your yellow page ad stand out.

This Newsletter is Published by The Entrepreneur's Marketing Source:

2nd Floor - 611- 9th Street East
Saskatoon, SK S7H 0M4
Ph: 306-343-6100
Fax: 306-244-3686
email: b.banda@sk.sympatico.ca

How To Use Direct Mail - *Effectively*

Small and medium size businesses often compete with large companies by building strong personal relationships with customers.

A salesman who looks a prospective customer in the eye leaves a powerful impression. However, this is an expensive form of promotion. A professional letter that introduces your product can increase the closure rate of your salesman.

For companies who do not use a salesman (such as a golf course), a professional offer can drum up new sales. A personally addressed envelope containing a score card and invitation for half price on a round of golf would be well received by potential customers.

To use direct mail effectively, have the following:

1. **Well-targeted list of prospects**

2. **An offer which the customer considers valuable**

3. **Interesting creative design**

Responses to direct mail vary between 0% to 100%. You can often expect a 1% to 3% average return.

Example

A small business can use a Direct Mail Letter Shop to reduce costs. The following is an example of a simple direct mail campaign by a golf course to 2000 potential golfers.

List of potential golfers (15 cents)	$300	**Letters Mailed**	**2000**
Postage (24 cents)	$480	Response Rate	2%
Print, fold, stuff,		Respondents to the letter	40
and sort letters (20 cents)	$400	Golfers (each respondent brings 3 friends)	160
TOTAL COSTS	**$1,180**	Green fees per golfer (after discount)	$20
		Sales	**$3,200**
		Cost of direct mail campaign	$1,180
		Profit on campaign	**$2,020**

The golf course makes $2,020 and attracts customers who may not have golfed at the course without the offer.

In this example, the Letter Shop did all the work. The shop provided the list, prepared the letters, and even posted the envelopes. The Golf Course supplied the letter's script.

Remember, marketing is more than placing your logo in the newspaper. It is your entire plan to get customers through your door.

Brent Banda,
Entrepreneur

FIGURE 3-1 EMS Newsletter (continued)

The Marketing
S**ource**
Marketing Tips To Build Your Business

Frequently Asked Questions About
Small & Medium Size Business

How Do I Conduct Market Research?

First, ask yourself why you feel you need market research. Do you want to prove a market exists, or find out more about your customers?

If you wish to prove that a market exists for your product (possibly to satisfy your banker), you will likely provide statistical proof of customer demand. For this, you will have to create a survey and tabulate the results.

If you want to find out more about your customers (perhaps to increase the effectiveness of your marketing), you will likely want opinions from your current or potential customers. Interviews or focus groups are useful, because your customer has the opportunity to speak freely.

Realize that there is no right way to do market research. You can often collect this information in several ways.

Before you do the work yourself, look around to see if information exists which will answer your questions. Statistical information is available from sources such as The Canada Saskatchewan Business Service Center (306-956-2323). You will likely have to dig up non-statistical information yourself.

Whatever form of research you undertake, be careful how you structure your questions. Well-structured research is useful. Poorly structured research is misleading.

Do I Need A Business Plan?

Although not every organization prepares a formal business plan, all must set goals and develop a strategy to run operations. However, a business plan would be useful for two purposes:

a. **Acquiring financing**
b. **Helping to manage your business**

A business plan simply outlines how you will tackle major issues. The plan usually contains the following:

a. **Background on you and your team**
b. **Background on the industry and your business idea**
c. **How you will handle day-to-day operations**
d. **A marketing plan**
e. **Projected financial statements**

When preparing your plan, keep in mind its purpose. If you wish to acquire financing, make sure a banker can understand it (prove cash flows can repay debts). If you will use it as a management tool, focus on developing a useful marketing strategy and operational plan.

Keep in mind that there is no correct way to prepare a business plan. Whether you prepare it yourself or use a consultant, make sure it serves its purpose well...it is the future of your business.

**The Entrepreneur's
Marketing Source Inc.**
ideas • advice • solutions
Ph: 306-343-6100
Fax: 306-244-3686
email: b.banda@sk.sympatico.ca

611 - 9th Street East, Saskatoon, SK S7H 0M4

THE WORKBOOK

If EMS does not enter into the strategic alliance with Imagine, Brent feels that he can reduce his consulting time by taking fewer clients and finish writing the workbook in the fall. He would like to begin marketing the workbook in Canada in January of Year 2 and enter the US market in Year 3. Brent is encouraged by the fact that consumers purchased over $3 billion of products through direct sales in Canada in 1994, with books, newspapers, and magazines accounting for $1 billion of these sales.

Many marketing reference books, video and audio tapes, and seminars already exist and can be found in bookstores, public libraries, and economic-development facilities like Industry Canada. However, many of these materials require a significant amount of time to read, understand, and apply. The strength of the planned EMS workbook is that it will be a practical, hands-on workbook that is concisely written for the small business entrepreneur. Brent plans to conduct focus group interviews to further refine the workbook. In addition, focus group interviews can help in the creation of a direct response campaign where small business owners can buy the workbooks by phone after reading a print ad.

The workbooks will be sold through a two-part direct response campaign. First, direct response ads will be placed in magazines that the small business owner is likely to read, such as *Home Business Report* or *Income Opportunities*. The average Canadian magazine is published quarterly, reaches 50 000 individuals, and charges $2500 per ad. The average US magazine is published monthly, reaches 300 000 individuals, and charges $5000 per ad. The planned EMS ads will be one-half page and in colour. On average, 0.2% of magazine readers order products from direct-response ads in the first month that the ad appears, and 0.15% of readers order after that.

Direct mail will also be used to generate orders. The mail piece will contain a magazine-style article on a small-business topic and a description of the workbook. Several companies sell lists of businesses that employ five or fewer employees for $0.15 to $0.45 per business name, depending on the number of names purchased. In the future, when more than one type of workbook is available from EMS, past workbook customers will receive updated product lists through direct mail as well. On average, 3% of individuals who receive a direct mail solicitation respond; the response rate increases to 15% for individuals who have ordered from the company in the past.

Customers responding to the ads will order through a toll-free number. All orders will require payment in advance, which is standard with low-cost, direct-response products. A message service will take the order, including shipping information and credit card number. This information will be faxed daily to EMS and the order will be mailed through Canada Post the next day. EMS is able to take both Visa and Mastercard orders. EMS will include a postage-paid survey with all orders to gather information on its customers.

Brent estimates that the workbooks will cost between $6.12 and $6.39 to produce and mail, depending on whether they are sent to Canada or the United States. Table 3-3 provides workbook cost information. EMS will sell each workbook for $29.95 (Canadian) which includes shipping, but does not include taxes. The type of marketing activity planned and the estimated number of workbooks sold in Year 2 and Year 3 are presented in Table 3-4. Brent also has estimated the amount of income he expects in Years 2 and 3 from workbook sales, given the above assumptions, which is shown in Table 3-5.

Table 3-3 Workbook Cost Information (in Canadian Dollars)

Cost	Canada	United States
Printing of workbook	2.37	2.37
Printing of survey	0.10	0.10
Postage	0.90	1.17
Envelope	0.15	0.15
1-800 number and answering service	2.00	2.00
Credit card fee	0.60	0.60
Total	6.12	6.39

Table 3-4 Marketing Activities and Estimated Workbooks Sold— Years 2 and 3

	Year 2	Year 3
Marketing activities in Canada		
Direct mail to list	3000 pieces	—
Direct mail to previous customers	615 pieces	1050 pieces
Magazine ads	3 ads	6 ads
Marketing activities in the US		
Direct mail to list	—	—
Direct mail to previous customers	—	8400 pieces
Magazine ads	—	8 ads
Number of workbooks sold in Canada		
From direct mail to list	90	—
From direct mail to previous customers	92	157
From magazine ads	525	1050
Number of workbooks sold in the US		
From direct mail to list	—	—
From direct mail to previous customers	—	1260
From magazine ads	—	8400

Notes: *Direct mail to list* is sent to the names purchased from list providers.

Direct mail to previous customers is sent to individuals who have purchased the workbook in previous months either from the direct mail to list or through the direct response ads.

Table 3-5	Estimated Income from Workbook—Years 2 and 3			
	Year 2		**Year 3**	
Sales (Workbook)	$21 174.65		$325 466.65	
COGS (Workbook)	4 326.84		69 114.24	
Gross margin		$16 847.81		$256 352.41
Marketing expenses				
Ad design	1 000.00		1 000.00	
Ad placement (Canada)	7 500.00		15 000.00	
Ad placement (US)	0.00		40 000.00	
Direct mail design	2 000.00		2 000.00	
Mailing list	450.00		0.00	
Printing of mailer	723.00		1 890.00	
Postage of mailer	1 265.25		4 147.50	
Total marketing expenses		12 938.25		64 037.50
Operating income		$ 3 909.56		$192 314.91

THE DILEMMA

Brent likes consulting and working with Imagine. The offer to form a strategic alliance with Imagine is tempting, given their larger client base. However, Brent's true dream is to complete and market the workbook. He is worried that another company may publish a similar product aimed at the same market. A tremendous amount of potential profit would be lost. Given the time that consulting currently takes, Brent is sure that he will only have time to pursue one option: the strategic alliance with Imagine or completion of the workbook.

LUCAS FOODS

John Fallows and Walter S. Good

Bib Martin was marketing manager of Lucas Foods, a diversified food manufacturing and wholesaling company based in Edmonton. The company had recently had some success with a new product, Gold Medal Crumpettes. Jerry Lucas, the president of Lucas Foods, asked his marketing manager to recommend an appropriate strategy for the new product, which would best capture the available opportunity and support the mission of the company.

THE INDUSTRY

Lucas Foods was in the food manufacturing and wholesaling business, marketing a broad product line that included frozen egg products, shortening, flour, baking mixes, spices, and bulk ingredients. Its primary customers were the five major national food wholesalers, with smaller regional wholesalers and independent grocery stores accounting for a smaller portion of its sales.

Gold Medal Crumpettes was a recent entry in Lucas Foods' bakery products group. It fell into the class commonly known as biscuits. Competitive products in this class included crumpets, scones, English muffins, and tea biscuits. Competition also came from a variety of substitute items, such as toast, doughnuts, and muffins. Biscuit producers included such prominent names as Weston Bakeries and McGavin Foods Ltd. domestically, as well as the American firm of S.B. Thomas, which concentrated on English muffins and dominated that market.

Prepared by John Fallows under the direction of Walter S. Good of the University of Manitoba as a basis for classroom discussion, rather than to illustrate either effective or ineffective handling of an administrative situation. Copyright by the Case Development Program, Faculty of Management, University of Manitoba. Support for the development of this case was provided by the Canadian Studies Program, Secretary of State, Government of Canada. Reprinted with permission.

Lucas Foods estimated that the product life cycle for specialty bakery goods was from five to seven years. Generally, if a new product was going to be successful, it enjoyed quick acceptance in the marketplace. Introduced in 1984, Gold Medal Crumpettes had had limited distribution. They had been sold in Alberta and Saskatchewan and had been recently introduced in Manitoba, Montana, and Minnesota. Safeway was the only major chain to carry the item in Canada, but sales growth had been steady to date.

HISTORY OF LUCAS FOODS

The company was originally formed under another name over 50 years ago. It specialized in frozen egg products and later diversified into cabbage rolls and frozen meat products. The company was purchased by a major brewery in 1972, but the frozen egg portion of the business was sold back to the original owners six years later. They sold the business to Jerry Lucas in 1979. Since then, sales have doubled to their present annual level of $12 million.

The company followed a "portfolio approach" to its product line, regularly adding or deleting items according to established criteria with respect to the marketing cycle. With the single exception of frozen egg products, no specific product or product family dominated its overall product offering. (An exception was made for frozen egg products because of their unique life cycle and recession-proof qualities).

In its statement of business mission, Lucas Foods indicated a desire to grow to an annual sales level of $50 million and to become a major national food manufacturer and wholesaler, as well as an exporter. Its major competitive weapons were believed to be its excellent reputation, product knowledge, marketing expertise, and level of customer service.

MARKETING GOLD MEDAL CRUMPETTES

Lucas Foods believed that the consumption of biscuit items was uniform across age groups, seasons, and geographic locations. It is a mature market. The merchandise itself was targeted toward the "upscale buyer." Package design, pricing policy, and product ingredients positioned Gold Medal as high-priced and high-quality relative to the competition. Therefore, the primary variables for segmenting the market were socio-economic: Gold Medal Crumpettes were a luxury item.

The Crumpettes were designed to incorporate the taste and texture of scones, English muffins, and biscuits, and could be eaten with or without butter, either toasted or untoasted. They were available in four flavours: plain, raisin, cheese, and onion, and the company had plans to add three more flavours, including pizza. The product could be stored frozen. The name Gold Medal Crumpettes was specifically selected to imply quality.

Since wholesale food distribution in Canada was dominated by relatively few firms, management felt that it had little choice in the distribution of its products. Lucas Foods did not own a large warehouse to store its finished baked goods but manufactured Gold Medal Crumpettes to order. The merchandise was then transported by common carrier to various customers under net-30-days credit terms.

The goal of the company's promotional efforts was to stimulate and encourage consumer trial of the product. There was some radio advertising when the item was first introduced. Although Lucas suggested the retail price, the distributor, especially in the case of Safeway, did most of the promotion. Typical promotions included:

- hostesses distributing free samples in supermarkets
- crossover coupon promotions with jam companies
- mail-out coupons to consumers
- free products to stores
- temporary price reductions for distributors.

So far, $50 000 had been spent on the promotion of Gold Medal Crumpettes. To complement these promotional efforts, Lucas Foods had three salespeople who, along with the marketing manager, regularly called on all major accounts.

Gold Medal's high price was consistent with its positioning and was arrived at after evaluating consumer surveys and the company's production costs. The expected price sensitivity of the market was also considered. A package of eight biscuits retailed for $1.89. The product was sold to supermarket chains in cases of 12 packages, with a factory price of $12 per case. Manufacturing costs, including allocated overhead, were $8.40 per case. This provided a contribution margin of $3.60 per case, or 30 percent. Production capacity was available for up to 16 000 cases per month.

CAPTURING THE OPPORTUNITY

For an estimate of the potential market for Gold Medal Crumpettes, see Exhibit 4-1. Bib Martin judged that Lucas Foods held a 16 percent share of the Alberta market.

The Alberta consumer had been very receptive to the product, but outside Alberta the company had only a limited reputation and was not well known as a wholesale food supplier. This lack of awareness made it more difficult for the product to obtain the acceptance of retailers. Also, the company faced an almost total lack of consumer awareness outside the province.

If Gold Medal succeeded in obtaining quick acceptance in new markets, competitors might view the development of a similar product as an attractive proposition. This could be particularly distressing if the competitor taking such an action was a major producer with an existing broad distribution system. Therefore, the speed with which Gold Medal Crumpettes could be introduced and developed into a dominant market position was very important to the long-term survival and profitability of the item. There was also the question of whether or not the degree of consumer acceptance the product had achieved in Alberta could be repeated in other areas.

Pricing research conducted by the company indicated that consumers were not prepared to cross the $2 price level at retail. If production costs were to rise and force an increase in selling price, sales might decline. Also, while the current exchange rate allowed Lucas to be

EXHIBIT 4-1	**Total Potential Market for Gold Medal Crumpettes (Yearly Sales)**	
	Cases	**Volume ($)**
Alberta	43 000	520 000
Canada	960 000	11 500 000
United States	9 660 000	115 000 000

quite competitive in the American market, a strengthening of the Canadian dollar could damage the company's export position.

SELECTING A STRATEGY

Bib Martin had to propose a marketing strategy to Jerry Lucas that he considered would best take advantage of the opportunity available to Gold Medal Crumpettes. He was considering three alternatives:

1. Maintenance of the product's existing market coverage and strategy. This implied limiting distribution and focusing the company's efforts on the Prairie provinces and the states of Montana and Minnesota.

2. Phased expansion. This would involve expanding across Canada, region by region, to become a major force in the Canadian biscuit market and begin selective entry into the American market.

3. Rapid expansion. This approach would involve an attempt to expand rapidly in both countries, to precede and preferably pre-empt competitive products in all markets, and to seek a dominant position in the North American biscuit market.

During their early discussions, Jerry had pointed out that the company had the financial capacity to undertake any of these options. It was a question of how to best focus the available resources.

Before evaluating his alternatives, Bib drew up the following criteria to guide him in coming to an appropriate decision:

- The alternative should be feasible.

- The alternative should be profitable.

- The market opportunity should be exploited as far as possible, while still meeting the first two criteria.

- The alternative should fit into the activities of the company.

- The alternative should be consistent with the mission of the company.

- The alternative should be consistent with Lucas Foods' portfolio management approach concerning return, risk, and diversity.

- There should be early evidence to support the alternative.

THE LOONEY SCHOOL OF TENNIS

Andrea Gaunt and David S. Litvack

THE SITUATION

Craig Smith, President of the Looney School of Tennis, had some difficult decisions to make. The Looney School of Tennis had only been incorporated for nine months and although demand for the company product had been high, the president realized that attention was needed in several areas.

The Looney School of Tennis had two "arms" to the company: School Tennis Programs and Summer Club Management. During the school year, the Looney School of Tennis focused on running low-cost tennis programs throughout local private and public primary and elementary schools. Although this was not the most profitable arm of the company, it was nonetheless extremely important as it served to provide a broad base of customers for the second more profitable arm of the company, Summer Club Management. While Craig was generally pleased with the level of success his company had reached in such a short time span, two problem areas needed his immediate attention.

First, in order to attract new primary and elementary schools, Craig had initiated a free promotion to interested schools. This involved providing a demonstration lesson to every gym class in the school, which took, on average, two full days of instruction. While this promotion had proved very successful in attracting new customers, it was also very costly, and Craig was unsure if he could continue on with this promotional effort.

Second, Craig also had to resolve the dissatisfaction level of his Tennis Director, Justin Mondoux, who was unhappy with his current level of compensation.

Craig was hoping to reach some decisions and to implement "solutions" to these problem areas in time for the upcoming 1999 season.

BACKGROUND

In 1994 Craig Smith was thinking about tennis. As a competitive player and high-performance tennis coach for over 11 years, he was concerned about the overall decline in participation in the sport. In the 1970s, the tennis industry went through a dramatic growth period. John McEnroe and Jimmy Connors became sports heroes, cities were building more public courts, and racquet sales soared to over $30 million in the United States. However, in the 1990s, the industry was hurting. McEnroe and Connors had retired, the public courts had become cracked and under-used, racquet sales had dropped, and the North American Tennis Federation marketing committees had fallen asleep. The sport was simply not capturing the imagination of youngsters, and this had resulted in a decline in tennis club membership and interest in competitive tennis events.

As a result of his increasing concern over this industry "recession," Craig decided to volunteer his time to local private and public schools to run children's tennis programs in order to introduce children to the sport of tennis and hopefully increase awareness and interest in the sport. This volunteer program was met with overwhelming success. Feedback from both parents and school teachers alike was excellent, and as a result of this success, membership in local tennis clubs increased. Due to the success of these volunteer programs, Craig decided to incorporate the Looney School of Tennis, an innovative grassroots company aimed at promoting the sport of tennis by offering low-cost, quality tennis lessons throughout the Ottawa-Carleton area.

The industry decline had also caught the attention of major tennis sporting good manufacturers, such as Wilson, Nike, Head, and Prince, that had initiated massive promotional campaigns to spark greater interest in the sport. This bodes well for the Looney School, whose greatest challenge is to capture the interest of children who tend to find the sport dull and "uncool."

THE COMPANY

The Looney School of Tennis was originally founded in January 1995 by Craig Smith. The company has one product: tennis lessons. The lessons are tailored to meet the needs of various purchasers by offering lessons at various times and locations. The company further differentiates itself by emphasizing to children, in particular, the fun aspect of the sport through grassroots school programming and by offering a very innovative promotion strategy. The objective is to sell a high volume of top-quality, yet reasonably priced tennis lessons to both children and adults. Although children are the main target of Looney School lessons, adult programs are also offered in the summer club programs.

During the school year, Craig focuses his attention on running tennis programs through the private and public schools in the Ottawa-Carleton region. These programs introduce groups of approximately 20 children, at $3 per child per lesson, to the fun, athletic, and positive dimensions of the sport. Lessons are held in the school gymnasium, or weather-permitting, in the school yard (see Appendix 5-1).

Once the school year is complete, the company shifts its focus towards community tennis club management. More specifically, summer clubs, particularly those concerned with low membership levels, hire the Looney School of Tennis to completely design and oversee their summer programs. This involves the recruitment, supervision, and compensation of certified tennis professionals, as well as the complete design, promotion, and implementation of all club programs, leagues, children's camps, and private lessons.

The two arms of the company are very complementary. A large percentage of children or their parents are interested in having the students continue on with the sport after being introduced to it through the school system. Parents traditionally contact the Looney School for information on tennis programs/camps offered nearby. The Looney School is then able to direct the children to the nearest community club managed by the company. The school programming offered by the Looney School is therefore an excellent platform to direct interest sparked by the school programs to the second focus of the company, summer club management.

The company was started with a low capital investment. Other than the computer purchased subsequent to incorporation, the yearly liability insurance fee, and the business telephone expense, the only expenses to the company are its variable costs which consist of office supplies, photocopying, and the hourly wages paid to the instructors.

Specialized Wilson Sporting Equipment was provided under a sponsorship arrangement to the Looney School subsequent to incorporation. The equipment, such as mini-tennis racquets and tennis nets, is provided to all students for their use, free of charge, during Looney School lessons. This specialized equipment is easier for the children to handle and provides them with better control in playing the sport. This in turn results in higher success and self-confidence while taking part in the lessons.

Since the Looney School's goal is high-volume sales, the need for a large part-time staff is critical. Through his coaching activities, Craig Smith has personal contact with many high-performance, provincially ranked tennis players who are interested in getting involved in teaching to gain experience and to work towards their coaching certification. These individuals are dynamic, energetic, and very good with children, and are placed in the Looney School "hierarchy" according to their age, experience, and interpersonal skills. The five levels of the hierarchy are as follows:

- Looney Trainees: 15 hours of volunteer lessons
- Looney Assistants: $6 per hour (uncertified) or $8 per hour (certified)
- Looney Pros: $10 per hour (certified only)
- Tennis Director: $12 per hour (Justin Mondoux)
- President: Craig Smith

Looney assistants will generally become promoted to Looney Pros after one full year. During the summer months, Looney Pros become community club head pros. This, of course, is flexible and subject to change depending on the assessment of their progress by Craig Smith. All staff is continually trained and supervised by Craig Smith.

The satisfaction level from the schools and parents alike has been very high. Feedback has indicated that the schools are very impressed with the high quality of the lessons and are particularly shocked at their low cost. In fact, the company has recently captured the interest of a local television station, CJOH-TV, which has hosted two segments on the company, aired during the six o'clock news This has directly increased school bookings and has resulted in increased awareness about the company.

The main challenge for the Looney School is to capture the interest of children, the main users of the Looney School product, who currently find the sport dull and "uncool." Fortunately for the Looney School, the massive promotional efforts launched by tennis sporting good manufacturers appear to be paying off as latest industry reports forecast an improvement in participation rates and racquet sales. Although the children are the principal users of the lessons, and hence the prime initiators in the decision-making process, it is critical that the Looney School is successful in reaching the schools in order to gain access to this large pool of children. The Looney School must convince the Ottawa-Carleton school boards that Looney lessons will be of value to the students, parents, and teachers. School boards are looking for convenient low-cost services that provide diversity in school programming, interest in students, and satisfaction of parents. After-school programs are particularly appealing to parents who prefer to have their children take part in a healthy, low-cost, after-school activity as opposed to straight supervision.

The main problem currently facing the Looney School concerns the two-day free promotions offered to interested Ottawa-Carleton schools. As many of the schools when approached by the Looney School are unsure of the success of running tennis programs in a gymnasium, the Looney School of Tennis decided to offer demonstrations to every gym class in the school, free of charge. This promotion appealed greatly to the schools and resulted, on average, in the booking of three schools for every ten demonstrations provided. The majority of schools would book three sessions of tennis programs, with each program offering five lessons to a particular class.

Although the promotions were in great demand, unfortunately, the related expenses were high. For each demonstration the Looney School provided, a salary expense of approximately $120 (or 6 hrs × 2 days × $10/hr), in addition to a photocopying expense for flyers provided to students of approximately $35 (350 flyers × $0.10), was incurred. This resulted in a total promotion expense of $155 per demo, with no guarantee of a future sale. Craig felt this situation required further attention. Several options were being considered prior to making the decision on whether or not it was worthwhile to change the current setup.

The first option being considered was to request a voluntary contribution of one or two "loonies" (dollars) from the students. In this scenario, a flyer would be sent home with the children (see Appendix 5-2) prior to the demonstration, requesting that a contribution be provided in order to defray the costs to the company. On average, 350 students attend each two-day demonstration. Craig felt that it would not be unreasonable to expect that half of the people would make some sort of contribution.

Craig decided to approach four schools booked for upcoming demonstrations, to obtain feedback on this option. None of these schools had any objection to soliciting a voluntary contribution from the students. As a result, Craig decided to go ahead with a trial run on these schools to assess the reaction of the parents. Results from this trial are provided in Appendix 5-3. He was also contemplating the possibility of simply charging each child a flat fee for the demonstration; however, he had not yet approached the schools on this option as he was unsure what their reaction would be.

The second problem area that required his attention was the compensation package for his Tennis Director, Justin Mondoux. Justin had been complaining about only working one or two hours at a time at his hourly wage, and was looking for an improvement in his compensation package. As a result of Justin's dissatisfaction level over his Looney School earnings, Craig was seriously considering changing Justin's compensation from an hourly wage to a commission structure. In this scenario, Justin would be responsible for making contact and visiting with all the schools and booking/conducting all free demonstrations on his own time. In return he would receive 35% of the profits for each school booked for follow-up lessons. This way, the company would only be incurring a "salary expense" upon a sale. Not only would this address the concern of the costly demonstrations, but it would also serve to resolve the staffing problem previously discussed, and free up valuable time for Craig Smith, who very much needed to devote time to other areas of the business. On the other hand, Craig was concerned he would lose personal contact with the schools if he implemented this option.

Craig needed to give some serious thought to the various alternatives outlined above, prior to deciding what changes, if any, he should make, and the likely effect these changes would have on the satisfaction level of his customers and staff alike.

APPENDIX 5-1

THE PRODUCT—SCHOOL PROGRAMMING

After School / Lunch-Time Lessons

Programs are offered in packages of five lessons at $3 per lesson per child and lessons are offered either during lunch hour or as an after-school program. The lessons are given in the school gym or, weather-permitting, in the school yard.

End of School Tennis Fair

Towards the end of the school year, the Looney School offers to local private and public Ottawa-Carleton schools the option to book an "end of school tennis fair." This allows the children to finish their school year "with an ace." Children from a local primary school are bussed to a nearby tennis club managed by the Looney School of Tennis. Here the children experience playing on a "real" tennis court. The fair demonstrates to the children how accessible tennis can be and how it can be played in their own neighbourhood. Each child who participates in the Tennis Fair receives a certificate that he or she is a "100% tennis fanatic." The certificate also provides a phone number for more information on how to get involved in summer Looney lessons/camps at a club nearby.

APPENDIX 5-2

LOONEY SCHOOL OF TENNIS

Date of tennis day: _____

Agassi SMASH!
Seles Squeal!!
Boris Becker Dive & Jive

Graduation Certificates!
Win Prizes!
Equipment Discount Cards!
Tons of FUN & EXERCISE

LOONEY CONTRIBUTION

The tennis promotion is free to the school however the Looney School asks if you could <u>CONTRIBUTE A LOONEY OR TWO</u> to ensure this type of positive program can continue ! Should you wish to receive information on how and where to get your family registered into summer tennis, please return the below questionnaire to your child's school. Information will be sent to you in April / May.

✂ -

Summer Tennis Information

Name: _____

Address: _____

Phone #: _____

City: _____

Postal Code: _____

Thank you for CONTRIBUTING to the promotion
of the sport of a lifetime
TENNIS!!

tape
LOONEY
here

tape
LOONEY
here

tape
LOONEY
here

APPENDIX 5-3

TRIAL DEMONSTRATIONS

School A

The first school that was visited is located in an upper-middle-class suburb of Ottawa, where the average home is valued at approximately $205 000 and municipal taxes average $3200. This area consists exclusively of single-family homes, where approximately 80% of the occupants in the district own their own home. The majority of families are dual-income professionals in their mid-40s. There are no public courts within a 1-km radius of the community.

Of the total 239 students in this school who attended the demonstration, 177 provided a contribution, with the average contribution being $1.67. The average age of the children was 10, with only 15% having ever played the sport previously.

School B

The second school that received a free demonstration is located in a working-class area of the city, with the average home valued at approximately $123 000 and municipal taxes running at approximately $1700. Here only approximately 40% of the families, which are predominately single-income families, own their own homes. The dwellings are a mixture of semi-detached and town houses with several apartment complexes nearby. There are two public courts within a 1-km radius of the community.

Of the total 305 students who attended the demonstration, 189 contributed with an average contribution of $0.41. Here the average age of the children was 12, with only 8% having ever played the sport before.

School C

The third school that was visited is also located in a working-class district, not far from the second school. The area consists mostly of garden homes, valued at approximately $112 000 and municipal taxes at $1500. Here only 35% of the families own their own homes. These households consist mainly of blue-collar workers in their mid-30s. There are no public courts within walking distance of the community.

Of the total 347 students in this school, 208 returned with an average contribution of $0.38. Here the average age of the children was 8, with 12% having ever played the sport.

School D

The last school visited is located in a middle-class district, with the average home valued at approximately $175 000 and municipal taxes of approximately $2500. The majority of families in this area are dual-income young professionals, with approximately 75% owning their own home. There is one public court within walking distance of the community.

Of the 198 students who attended the demonstration, 127 contributed an average of $1.42. The average age of the children was 10, with only 5% having ever been exposed to the sport.

Summary

School District	A upper-middle class	B working class	C working class	D middle class
Home Value	$205 000	$123 000	$112 000	$175 000
Taxes	$3200	$1700	$1500	$2500
% Homes Owned	80%	40%	35%	75%
# of Public Courts	0	2	0	1
# of Students	239	305	347	198
# Contributed	177	189	208	127
Ave. Contribution	$1.67	$0.41	$0.38	$1.42
Ave. Age	10	12	8	10
% Played Before	15%	8%	12%	5%

ROCKY MOUNTAIN HOUSE CO-OP

Thomas Funk

Frank Gallagher, General Manager of Rocky Mountain House Co-op (RMHC), was sitting in his office reviewing the performance of his organization when Milt Zirk, Petroleum Manager of the company, hurried into the room. "Frank, I'm afraid I've got some bad news," exclaimed Milt. "The word is out that United Farmers of Alberta (UFA) is planning to open a new petroleum outlet in Rocky Mountain House. The petroleum end of our business has been going fairly well for us over the past couple of years. This could really mess things up! You know they are very aggressive marketers, and because they are a co-op like us, they could really eat into our market share. Frank, I'm worried! We're going to have to make sure we're ready for them. We've got to develop a plan to minimize their impact on our sales and profits."

ROCKY MOUNTAIN HOUSE CO-OP

Rocky Mountain House Co-op is a retail outlet located in Rocky Mountain House, Alberta, approximately 80 km west of Red Deer, on Highway 11. Rocky Mountain House is a community of approximately 6000 people with both an agricultural and commercial economic base. The area is characterized by mixed farming with most farms being relatively small and having at least some livestock. Industry in the area includes general business, trucking, construction, oil exploration, and logging.

This case was prepared by Thomas Funk of the Ontario Agricultural College, University of Guelph, Guelph, Ontario, Canada. It is intended as a basis for classroom discussion and is not intended to represent either correct or incorrect handling of administrative problems. Much of the data in the case has been disguised to protect confidentiality. Copyright ©1997 by Thomas Funk. This case may not be reproduced without permission of the author. Reprinted with permission.

The trading area served by RMHC is much larger than Rocky Mountain House itself and contains the following communities: Alder Flats, Alhambra, Caroline, Condor, Leslieville, Nordegg, Rocky Mountain House, and Stauffer. The trading area has an approximate population of 16 000 people and a radius of 50 km, although the trading area on the west extends nearly 100 km to the Rocky Mountains. Exhibit 6-1 shows the Rocky Mountain House trading area.

EXHIBIT 6-1 Rocky Mountain House Trading Area

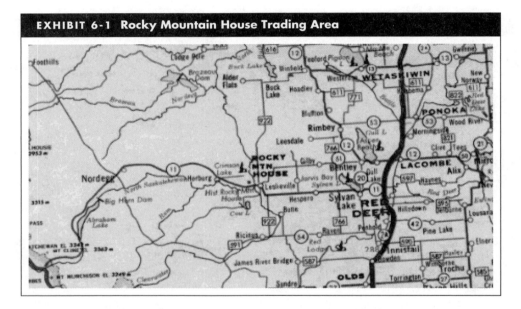

RMHC is a co-operative type business. Co-operatives are like regular businesses except they are owned by their users who purchase shares in the business. Instead of earning "profits" co-operatives earn "savings," which can be returned to members through "patronage dividends." RMHC is owned by 7332 active members. For the most part, these "owners" are people in the trading area who have become members by purchasing shares in the organization. Each share is valued at $1.00 and a minimum of five shares must be purchased to become a member. The main reason for being a member is to share in the savings of the business through patronage dividends. Patronage dividends are based on the amount of business a member does each year and have amounted to about 5% of purchases at RMHC over the past several years. In addition, members have a voice in the affairs of the co-op through their right to elect a Board of Directors to represent their views.

RMHC is involved in a number of retail businesses that they classify under three divisions: Home Centre, Shopping Centre, and Petroleum. The Home Centre consists of building materials, hardware, animal health products, livestock feed, livestock equipment, and twine; the Shopping Centre consists of food, hardware, clothing, and a cafeteria; and the Petroleum Division consists of bulk fuels, propane, oil/lubes, cardlock, and a gas bar. Despite the fact that Rocky Mountain House is in a significant grain-producing area of the province, RMHC has elected so far not to sell crop supplies. Sales, cost of goods sold, and gross margins for each division for 1995 are shown in Exhibit 6-2. Exhibit 6-3 shows the operating statement of RMHC for the same year.

EXHIBIT 6-2   Product Line Breakdown

	Home Centre	Shopping Centre	Petroleum
Sales	$4 620 000	$11 044 000	$2 550 000
Less: Cost of Goods Sold	$3 536 000	$ 8 418 000	$2 294 000
Gross Margin	$1 084 000	$ 2 626 000	$ 256 000
Less: Operating Expenses	$ 931 000	$ 2 106 000	$ 189 000
Contribution	$ 153 000	$ 520 000	$ 67 000

EXHIBIT 6-3   Operating Statement

Sales	$18 214 000
Less: Cost of Goods Sold	$14 248 000
Gross Margin	$ 3 966 000
Less: Operating Expenses	$ 3 226 000
Contribution	$ 740 000
Less: Indirect Interest Expense	$ (96 000)
Less: General Overhead	$ 432 000
Savings	$ 404 000
Patronage Dividends from Federated Co-ops	$ 683 000
Retained Savings	$ 1 087 000

In 1995, RMHC received patronage dividends of $683 000 from Federated Co-operatives Limited in Saskatoon, the large wholesaling co-operative owned by several hundred local co-ops like RMHC across Western Canada. Like most other local co-ops, RMHC used Federated Co-op as their main source of supply for all products they sold. The patronage dividend they received from Federated was based on a percentage of purchases. In the same year, RMHC allocated $614 000 in patronage dividends to local owners. This, together with current savings, left RHHC with retained savings of slightly more than $1 million. This represented funds the organization could use for future expansion.

PETROLEUM DIVISION

The petroleum division of RMHC has always been a tough business. Margins in the petroleum division are much lower than in other areas of the company largely due to intense competition and the commodity type products being sold. In the Rocky Mountain House trading area alone there are six major oil companies competing for a total fuel market of approximately 26.9 million litres. Exhibit 6-4 lists the major petroleum companies with facilities in Rocky Mountain House and their approximate fuel sales.

Most of the 26.9 million litres of petroleum sold in the Rocky Mountain House trading area went to commercial accounts. Commercial accounts purchased 18.3 million litres in 1995,

EXHIBIT 6-4   Competitive Petroleum Suppliers

	Estimated Litres
Co-op	5 900 000
Esso	7 500 000
Shell	4 000 000
Petro Canada	3 500 000
Turbo	3 500 000
Husky	2 500 000
Total	26 900 000

compared to 6.1 million litres to farm accounts and 2.5 million litres to consumers. Although precise market shares were not known, Milt estimated that Co-op and Esso were the major petroleum suppliers in the area, followed by Shell, Petro Canada, Turbo, and Husky. Exhibit 6-5 shows approximate market shares for each company by type of account.

EXHIBIT 6-5   Approximate Market Shares by Type of Account

	Farm	Commercial	Consumer	Total
Co-op	34%	17%	30%	23%
Esso	31%	27%	27%	28%
Shell	13%	15%	16%	15%
Petro Canada	6%	17%	4%	13%
Turbo	12%	13%	13%	13%
Husky	4%	11%	10%	9%
	100%	100%	100%	100%

RMHC currently sells four product lines in petroleum: bulk fuels, propane, oil/lubes, and gas bar (self-service pumps at the Shopping Centre). Sales, cost of goods sold, and gross margins for these products in 1995 are shown in Exhibit 6-6. Exhibit 6-7 shows the petroleum department expenses for the same year.

EXHIBIT 6-6   Financial Summary for Petroleum Products

	Fuels	Propane	Oil/Lubes	Gas Bar	Total
Sales	$2 016 000	$41 000	$126 000	$367 000	$2 550 000
Cost of Goods	$1 829 000	$34 000	$106 000	$325 000	$2 294 000
Gross Margin	$ 187 000	$ 7 000	$ 20 000	$ 42 000	$ 256 000

EXHIBIT 6-7 Petroleum Department Expenses

Depreciation	$ 5 600
Utilities	$ 500
Insurance	$ 4 900
Repairs & Maintenance	$ 9 000
Taxes & Licences	$ 4 600
Total Standby Costs	$ 24 600
Employee Benefits	$ 18 000
Staff Discounts	$ 1 600
Training	$ 1 800
Salaries & Wages	$ 99 000
Uniforms	$ 1 500
Total Staff Costs	$ 121 900
Advertising & Promotion	$ 5 600
Delivery Trucks	$ 29 000
Other Expenses	$ 7 900
Total Operating Costs	$ 189 000
Contribution	**$67 000**

Like most petroleum suppliers in the area, RMHC sells five types of petroleum products: premium gasoline, regular gasoline, clear diesel, marked gasoline, and marked diesel. Exhibit 6-8 shows 1995 sales of the five products in each of the major markets, while Exhibit 6-9 shows current pricing for each product in each major market. Marked gasoline and marked diesel are dyed a purple colour to distinguish them from clear product. This is done to identify the product as tax-exempt because it is used for off-road purposes and not subject to normal fuel taxes. At the moment, this means marked fuels sell for approximately $0.09 per litre less than clear fuels, which are intended for on-road use and subject to a road tax. The prices established by RMHC are very similar to other petroleum suppliers in the area. Only Turbo and Husky sell petroleum at lower prices than other companies in the area and, in both cases, the differences are very small.

EXHIBIT 6-8 Petroleum Sales by Market

	Farm	Commercial	Consumer	Total
Premium Gasoline			16 500	16 500
Regular Gasoline	200 000	1 173 000	666 500	2 039 500
Clear Diesel		1 154 000	63 000	1 217 000
Marked Gasoline	949 000	50 000		999 000
Marked Diesel	937 000	736 000		1 673 000
Total	2 086 000	3 113 000	746 000	5 945 000

EXHIBIT 6-9 Petroleum Prices by Market

	Farm	Commercial	Consumer
Premium Gasoline			$0.540
Regular Gasoline	$0.495	$0.480	$0.500
Clear Diesel		$0.390	$0.420
Marked Gasoline	$0.403	$0.390	
Marked Diesel	$0.300	$0.300	

Margins on petroleum products do not vary by type of product, but do vary by type of customer. Current margins in the farm market are $0.049 per litre; in the commercial market are $0.034 per litre; and in the consumer market are $0.063 per litre.

In the petroleum end of the business, RMHC deals with three main types of customers: farm accounts, commercial accounts, and consumers.

At the moment, RMHC has about 350 farm accounts which purchase 2 086 000 litres of fuel. Although the average farm account purchases about 6000 litres of fuel each year, some purchase much larger amounts and many purchase much smaller amounts. The largest RMHC farm account purchases nearly 20 000 litres of fuel a year. Farms in the RMHC trading area are somewhat smaller than typical Alberta farms. A very high proportion of these farms have livestock as their principle operation.

Commercial accounts represent the major proportion of RMHC petroleum business. At the moment, RMHC has 175 commercial accounts which together purchase approximately 3 113 000 litres of fuel and range in size from 5000 litres per year to as much as 300 000 litres per year. The average commercial account buys 18 000 litres. Exhibit 6-10 provides a breakdown of commercial accounts into various types of businesses.

EXHIBIT 6-10 Types of Commercial Accounts

Type of Account	Percent
General Business	29%
Loggers	11%
Truckers	18%
Construction	17%
Oil Company Contractors	22%
Institutional	3%

The final category of customer is individual consumers, which currently purchase 746 000 litres of fuel. About 80% of consumer sales are through the gas bar at the Shopping Centre and the remaining 20% are through the cardlock system described below.

Although all three types of accounts (farm, commercial, and consumer) can use the cardlock system, it is very popular among commercial accounts. The cardlock system allows approved buyers to have 24-hour access to bulk fuels at the main RMHC petroleum outlet. To obtain fuel, the buyer inserts a card into a metering device which then pumps the requested amount of a certain type of fuel into the user's tank. The user's name and the amount of the purchase are recorded electronically for future billing. Use of this system is growing very rapidly among farm and commercial accounts because of convenience and cost savings. The price of fuel purchased through the cardlock is generally $0.008 per litre less than bulk delivery. Although RMHC has a good, very clean cardlock operation, there are two problems that make it less than ideal. One problem is the fact that currently it does not sell marked gasoline and does not have the capability of adding this product into the existing system. This undoubtedly prevents some potential customers from using the RMHC cardlock. Another problem with the cardlock is that access to the facility is a little more difficult than some customers would like.

At the moment, the marketing program used by RMHC is fairly similar to that used by other petroleum suppliers in the area. In 1995, less than $6000 per year was being spent on advertising petroleum products. Most of this was for ads placed in local papers highlighting special deals on oils and lubricants (see Appendix 6-A for a sample ad). In addition to advertising, a substantial amount of selling is done by Milt on the farm, at the offices of commercial accounts, and on the phone. Milt maintains contact at least four times a year with most customers, and more often with larger customers. Some very large customers are contacted on a weekly basis. In addition, he spends a considerable amount of time calling on prospective customers. Milt's philosophy is that regular contact with prospects will put him in contention for their business if there is ever a reason for a customer to switch. History shows this to be a good strategy as RMHC has picked up a number of new customers each year when they became dissatisfied with their present supplier. Customer loyalty in petroleum, however, is very high. Milt figures that less than 10% of customers change suppliers each year. Milt also follows the practice of driving the delivery truck himself, on occasion, so he can have more contact with customers.

Frank and Milt have long thought that the success of RMHC in the petroleum business was due to a number of factors:

- The company provides excellent service. All people working for RMHC are top-notch individuals committed to providing good service. In addition, the company prides itself on clean, modern facilities and prompt attention to detail. Any customer who needs fuel can expect to receive it the same day an order is placed. RMHC currently spends more than its competitors on staff training.

- Co-op products are quality products that are produced under strict quality-control measures.

- Patronage refunds provide customers with "cash back" at the end of the year, based on their volume of business. For many customers, this is a real incentive to do business with a co-op.

- The company has an excellent highway location in Rocky Mountain House. This provides excellent visibility in the community.

- RMHC offers a very wide range of products making "one-stop shopping" possible for customers.

UNITED FARMERS OF ALBERTA

United Farmers of Alberta (UFA), like RMHC, is a member-owned co-operative. UFA has approximately 30 outlets in Alberta, in which they sell petroleum and a complete line of farm supplies. In addition, they operate approximately 90 outlets in which only petroleum products are sold through bulk plants, cardlocks, and gas bars. UFA has shown considerable growth in recent years through very aggressive marketing. This growth has come both from an increase in the number of retail distribution points, as well as an increase in the volume sold through existing outlets.

Recently, UFA was granted a development permit to build a farm supply facility in Rocky Mountain House. The permit allows UFA to construct a facility that contains a 2200 square foot building, bulk petroleum plant, gas bar, cardlock, and farm supply distribution facility. It is expected that UFA will sell a complete line of both crop and livestock farm supplies through this facility. It is also expected that UFA will construct a cardlock facility that is larger than any other in the area and will sell a compete line of fuels.

The entry of UFA into this market has the potential of causing significant problems for RMHC for a number of reasons:

- UFA is a co-op like RMHC and therefore very similar in structure and philosophy. As a result, they might be considered a good alternative for many current RMHC customers.

- The fact that they are building a complete farm supply outlet might be attractive to many current RMHC customers who would like to purchase crop supplies where they buy petroleum.

- UFA's facility will be much newer than that of RMHC. This is of particular concern for the cardlock.

- UFA currently has a number of commercial accounts on the fringes of the RMHC trading area. This gives them a foothold into the market.

- UFA has demonstrated a willingness in similar situations to enter new markets in a very aggressive manner. Often this entails aggressive pricing, introductory advertising in local media, a direct mail campaign targeted to larger potential customers, and special introductory deals.

- UFA traditionally supports its marketing efforts with a high level of excellent service. This includes the availability of skilled technical experts who can answer questions and help customers make informed buying decisions, attention to detail in all aspects of the business, and frequent sales calls (either by phone or in person) with key customers.

DECISION

Although at first Frank was not overly concerned about the situation, as he considered it in more detail, he began to worry about the potential effects it might have. RMHC had worked hard over the last ten years to build a strong customer base and some of this investment in time and marketing dollars appeared to be at risk. To determine the seriousness of the situation, and to develop some plans to counteract it, Frank called a meeting with Milt for early the next week.

The meeting began with Frank raising the issue of what impact the entry of UFA might have on RMHC. After some discussion, the two men agreed that if RMHC did nothing to soften the impact, it was conceivable they could lose a significant portion of both their farm and commercial business, especially the larger accounts that were more price-sensitive. Although it was hard to come up with specific numbers, they felt that up to a quarter of their present volume might be at risk. What was even more alarming was the fact that RMHC had three very large commercial customers who each purchased 300 000 litres of fuel a year. Losing these people alone would result in a very large sales decline. Although these large commercial accounts had been with RMHC for a number of years, and Milt provided a high level of personal service through almost weekly contact, it was conceivable they could switch allegiance if they perceived greater value in an alternative supplier.

Given the seriousness of the situation, they then began to discuss alternative courses of action they might pursue to counteract the problem. A number of possibilities were identified and briefly discussed.

1. The first idea that came to mind was to pursue a pre-emptive pricing strategy. Under this strategy, RMHC would begin immediately cutting prices and margins to existing customers. The idea behind this strategy, of course, was to solidify business relationships with customers to the point that it would make it very difficult for UFA to be successful in taking customers from RMHC.

2. A second strategy they discussed was to match UFA's promotional programs dollar for dollar and engage in a substantial amount of local advertising and direct marketing themselves. Although neither Frank nor Milt had a precise idea of what UFA would spend entering the Rocky Mountain House market, they felt $30 000 was not an unrealistic amount. They considered stressing two main points in the promotion: their excellent staff and their outstanding record of providing patronage dividends. Frank envisioned ads and direct mail pieces with pictures and human interest stories about the staff, as well as charts showing the steady growth in patronage dividends over the past few years.

3. Another idea they considered was to develop a program in which the rate of patronage dividends would vary by department. Under such a scheme it would be possible for the petroleum division, for example, to announce a patronage dividend of 8%, where some other division's dividend might decline to 3%. They felt this might be particularly effective in the short run to meet a competitive challenge.

4. Yet another alternative they were considering was to get into the fertilizer and agri-chemical business. On the assumption that some RMHC customers might be attracted to UFA because they had a complete line of crop and livestock supplies, this might provide existing customers with enough reason to stay with RMHC. It would, however, be a major investment for RMHC in a business they knew little about. Frank estimated it would require an investment of approximately $600 000 in facilities and working capital. In addition, two new full-time people would be required to run the business and work with farm customers. An additional five seasonal employees would be needed for a couple of months each year to help during peak sales seasons. Total additional labour costs would amount to approximately $150 000 plus another $50 000 in administrative costs. Margins on fertilizer were typically in the 15% to 20% range on product which sold for an average price of $250 per ton. Although an average farmer in the Rocky Mountain House trading area currently used only 25 to 30 tons of fertilizer a year, use appeared to be growing fairly rapidly as more farmers started using fertilizer and those already using fertilizer were increasing application rates. Agri-chemicals were not widely used in the Rocky Mountain House trading area, so this would be considered a break-even business which simply provided a complementary service to farmers who purchased fertilizer. Presently there are three fertilizer suppliers serving the 1200 farmers in the Rocky Mountain House trading area. One of these suppliers is a large independent farm-supply outlet specializing in crop inputs, while the other two are smaller operations, one of which is the local Esso dealer.

5. The final alternative Frank identified was to move up construction of a new bulk petroleum facility. The current facility was old and starting to show its age. Of particular concern was the fact that the cardlock system had reached its capacity and could not add a tank and pumping system for marked gasoline. Frank knew that the new UFA facility would be "state

of the art" and have ample capacity for the present and for future expansion. Although Frank hoped to get another five years out of the present facility, he felt one option was to invest immediately in new facilities so they would be ready at least by the time the UFA facility was built. A new facility, which would include a new bulk plant, an expanded sales area, and a new and expanded cardlock, would cost $300 000 to construct.

Frank and Milt concluded the meeting wondering what to do. They agreed to consider the options more fully and do some real thinking about the consequences of each option and then meet again in a week to make a decision.

APPENDIX 6-A

ROCKY MOUNTAIN HOUSE CO-OP AD

ATTENTION
FARMERS &
CONTRACTORS

Plan to Attend the
FUEL &
LUBE CLINIC

Tuesday, February 4, 1 p.m.
to be held at the
TAMARACK MOTOR INN
Rocky Mountain House
EVERYONE WELCOME!

Brought to You By:
Rocky Mountain House Co-op
PETROLEUM DEPARTMENT
Phone 845-2845

CO·OP

7

THE ORANGEDALE WHISTLE

Ian Spencer

On a hot sunny day in August 1998, Todd MacEachern sat in his office in The Creamery, a restored building on the Port Hawkesbury, Nova Scotia, waterfront, trying to decide how to launch *The Orangedale Whistle*. The proposed new venture was a scenic recreational train ride which would depart from the Cape Breton and Central Nova Scotia (CB & CNS) tracks just outside his office, travel to the Orangedale Railroad Station Museum about 30 miles away, and arrive back about three hours later. Todd had received permission to call the ride *The Orangedale Whistle* from the Rankins, a popular music group, who had recently written and recorded a ballad, "Orangedale Whistle" in honour of their great grandfather, the first station master at the Orangedale station. Todd, the 23-year-old Marketing Director of the Strait Area Waterfront Development Corporation (SAWDC), had to have a draft action plan ready for presentation at the next meeting of his Board of Directors. As he stared at the piles of information in front of him, he wished he had an assistant who could take the raw data, analyze it, and write the launch plan so he could spend his time dreaming up other ideas for the development of the Port Hawkesbury waterfront. So far, all he had done was prepare this brief summary.

Visioning *The Orangedale Whistle* had not been a problem for Todd. In his mind's eye he had seen it depart dozens of times. At the start of the summer, prior to the collection of most of the information, Todd imagined it would look something like this:

- It would operate from June to October, with a combination of about 80 scheduled trips and an unknown number of special customer bookings. The 80 trips would be scheduled: 36 on Saturdays and Sundays in July and August; 26 on Saturdays and Sundays in June, September, and October; and 18 on week-nights throughout the season. Special customer bookings, Todd thought, might average one per week.

This case was prepared by Ian Spencer, Professor of Marketing at St. Francis Xavier University. Copyright ©1998 by Ian Spencer. The research assistance of Kelly Bonvie, BBA, is gratefully acknowledged. Reprinted with permission.

- The capacity of one restored ViaRail passenger car would be 55 people.
- The car would be pulled by a CB & CNS locomotive. CB & CNS, a commercial/industrial short line, had agreed to discuss waiving its normal commercial per-mile rate for pulling a car.
- The trip would pass through several scenic areas, take about an hour to reach Orangedale, include a one-hour tour of the museum (complete with oat cakes and tea if desired), and take another hour to return to The Creamery.
- Each ride would be hosted by an interpretive guide who would provide historical, geological, genealogical, ecological, and other educational information as the group wished.
- Passengers could be families who lived within an hour or so of Port Hawkesbury, their summer guests, vacationers staying overnight in the Strait Area, vacationers travelling through the area but not staying over, bus tour groups, conventioneers and their families, school groups, and other organized groups based in the area.
- Normal fares would be $15 for adults and $7.50 for children.
- A gift shop, if typical of the industry, might generate 20 to 30 percent of total revenue.
- The initial, tentative estimates of costs were $350 per trip (for two CB & CNS operators, diesel fuel, the interpreter, and a ticket seller), plus $15 000 per year (for advertising, insurance, and maintenance), plus $40 000 one-time-only start-up costs (for purchasing and restoring a used ViaRail passenger car, signage, railroad safety improvements, uniforms, speaker systems, and interpretive research/writing).
- Advertising costs were: local radio—$30 per 30-second spot; local newspaper—$150 for a ¼-page ad; wall posters—$1.00 each; 4-colour brochures—25¢ each; and 1-colour flyers—10¢ each. The Board would be responsible for obtaining the $40 000 from various development agencies. Todd, the champion of the idea, would have to make a profit, or at least break even, on the rest.

Todd also envisioned possible theme rides, different destinations and durations, and an adults-only evening trip. Possible theme trips included Canada Day, Thanksgiving, Halloween, and other holidays. Possible destinations included heading west to the mainland (about one hour) or further east to the Highland Village at Iona (about five hours), or even to Sydney (a full day). The adults-only trip would include refreshments and entertainment on board and would conclude with a nice meal back at The Creamery.

SAWDC AND ITS INFORMAL PARTNERS

The Strait Area Waterfront Development Corporation's mandate was primarily economic development, and secondarily, the development of civic pride. It had a strong Board of Directors dominated by professionals and a track record of success. Recent projects included constructing and expanding the Granville Green Bandshell, creating the Customs House Gift Shop, upgrading the marina, creating a boardwalk, restoring The Creamery, and constructing a Pirate Ship Playground.

The Orangedale Railroad Station Museum operated from mid-June to mid-October, from 10:00 a.m. to 6:00 p.m. Monday to Saturday, and 1:00–6:00 p.m. on Sundays. It was run by a group of retired railroaders and their families, all working as volunteers. The group hired students via summer grants to help operate the museum. The museum consisted of a restored two-storey station with some of the stationmaster's quarters on the second floor converted into a tea room. The grounds included a restored caboose, a boxcar gift shop, and a restored snow-plow car. Normally visitors arrived one car at a time and received a guided tour by one of the retired railroaders. Capacity of the museum, including the outbuildings, was about 50. Admission was by donation. In 1997 the museum hosted just over 5000 visitors. Martin Boston, the leader of the group, realized the proposed recreational train ride would require adjustments in the museum's operations but observed to Todd, "Anything is possible."

The CB & CNS Railroad had been most cooperative, both in agreeing to supply an engine and operators, and in expressing a willingness to waive its normal $45 per mile fee for pulling a car. Daily except Sunday, a train left Sydney west-bound for Truro. The train attempted to leave between 10:00 and 10:30 a.m., but waiting for coal and technical/mechanical problems caused departure times to vary substantially. The speed varied as well depending upon the number of full cars. If a train left on schedule, it tended to pass Orangedale at about 2:00 p.m. and Port Hawkesbury at about 3:00 p.m. Daily except Sunday, another train headed east and passed through Port Hawkesbury at about 9:30 a.m. and Orangedale at about 10:30 a.m. This train also was somewhat unpredictable. The railroad maintained several spurs and sidings, including ones at both Port Hawkesbury and Orangedale. CB & CNS owned a diesel locomotive which, part of each workday, shunted freight cars for major industrial clients in the Port Hawkesbury area. This was the locomotive to which Todd was hoping to have access. An old but functional steam engine owned by a nearby gypsum company also might be available to pull the passenger car.

Todd and his Board had begun negotiations with ViaRail to acquire one of the dozens of retired passenger cars in storage at its yard in Halifax. Given the objectives of SAWDC, Todd was hopeful they could purchase one for a token $1. The normal price would be more like $25 000.

THE RECREATIONAL RAILROADING INDUSTRY

In July Todd asked his summer intern to research the recreational railroad industry in North America. The intern discovered there were about 60 such operations and interviewed about 20 by telephone. The interviews revealed the following facts:

- Capacity ranged from 70 to 500 and averaged 325.
- Adult prices were $8 to $12 for rides typically lasting 45 to 90 minutes.
- All offered special theme rides that seemed to be very popular and many, including some in cooler climates, operated year-round. Many were linked to other attractions such as the Rocky Mountains or the Grand Canyon.
- A steam engine seemed to be a real drawing card and gift shops were seen as mandatory.
- Most relied heavily on volunteers.
- Budgets for advertising averaged about 12% of revenue. All interviewees felt aggressive marketing was a key to success.

AN OVERVIEW OF THE MARKETPLACE

Todd also had undertaken an initial examination of the potential market. He discovered that 26 000 people lived within approximately 30 minutes of the waterfront, 38 000 lived 30 to 60 minutes away, 179 000 lived 1 to 2 hours away, and 400 000 more lived 2 to 3 hours away—most in the Regional Municipality of Halifax. The average household contained 2.9 people. Each year, from May to October, 500 000 vacationers crossed the Canso Causeway at least twice (into and out of Cape Breton). Including vacationers and locals, 150 000 people stopped each summer at the Visitor Information Centre at Port Hastings, a 5-minute drive from the Port Hawkesbury waterfront. From May to October 1997, the Strait Area's seven motels accommodated 22 000 visitor parties (about 64 000 people) in their 350 rooms. The provincial government estimated an out-of-province visitor party spent $284 per day in Nova Scotia, while visitor parties from within the province spent $158.

To obtain a feel for local interest, Todd conducted a telephone survey among 50 residents using a systematic sampling approach (every n^{th} listing in the "625" telephone exchange). The survey revealed nearly 50% awareness of the proposed ride despite only one short radio interview Todd had given in June. Almost all respondents (84%) said they would take a ride on the train and, on average, considered $14 a reasonable price for an adult ticket. Key reasons for locals' interest were the scenery, the kids would love it, its uniqueness, nostalgia, and the allure of trains. Most (60%) were also interested in the adults-only evening ride. Half said they typically had summer guests who would be interested in riding *The Orangedale Whistle.*

Other market segments Todd had identified were tour buses, school children, conventions, and local organizations. He discovered about 1000 tour buses came to Cape Breton every summer, each with about 40 passengers. About 300 tour buses spent one night, or sometimes two nights, at a Strait Area motel. Most buses arrived between 4:00 and 6:00 p.m. and left between 7:00 and 9:00 a.m. the next morning. Bus tour patrons and operators were very package-oriented ("do this ... do that ... eat here ... see this ... leave") and somewhat price-sensitive. The Strait Regional School Board has about 8500 elementary students (350 homerooms) and 4200 secondary students (160 homerooms). Almost all lived within one hour of Port Hawkesbury. Normally students would be available from 8:00 a.m. to 3:00 p.m., Monday to Friday. Principals loved the idea but were concerned about safety and price. Most felt $5 would be the maximum price for a student ticket. Some suggested area businesses might consider sponsoring (subsidizing) student trips. Todd quickly discovered the conference market was very small. Most delegates did not travel with their families and most were not in the area to sight-see. Several hundred organizations (business, educational, labour, community groups, government) existed in the Strait Area, but Todd had not yet contacted them about their interest in special bookings or to assess their needs and interests.

COCO-RICCO RESTAURANTS: MEXICAN CHICKEN

Stéphane Bossé and Normand Turgeon

Albert Cantin is the marketing director and principal partner of Coco-Ricco Restaurants: Mexican Chicken, a new restaurant chain with locations in Montreal, Laval, Longueuil, and, most recently, Quebec City. All of the restaurants in the Montreal metropolitan area are company-owned; that is, owned by Cantin and his partner. The restaurant in Quebec City is a franchise, where the Coco-Ricco concept is being tested to determine whether there is an opportunity to expand operations in the rest of the province through franchising.

The chain has an excellent reputation for the quality of meals, for fast and courteous service, and for its *fiesta* atmosphere. The walls of the restaurants are painted in warm colours, and reflect Mexican beach scenes, complete with sombreros and other Mexican items. During the winter, the cheerful atmosphere helps customers forget the harsh Quebec weather.

The menu is composed mainly of chicken dishes, but it also includes a variety of other typical Mexican items. The concept of Mexican chicken is a winning combination: the demand, both for chicken and for Mexican cuisine, has been increasing in recent years. The popular combination promises to continue to increase in demand both in Canada and internationally.

Mr. Cantin studied the sales reports provided to him by the various locations. All locations showed sales increases of at least 25%, but one location did remarkably better; location 4 reported a 45% increase in revenue. It had been reporting better than average results for some time. Demand there was very high; on Thursdays through Saturdays, there were often line-ups of people waiting to be seated.

This case was written by Stéphane Bossé, under the supervision of Normand Turgeon. Copyright 1995 by École des Hautes Études Commerciales (HEC), Montréal. This case was prepared as a basis for class discussion and is not intended to illustrate effective or ineffective handling of a management situation. Translated from the original French version by Susan Baker and H.F. (Herb) MacKenzie. Reprinted with permission.

However, this increase in sales came at a price. Many customers started to complain about the wait to be seated, the slowness of the service, and the general atmosphere that was less pleasant under crowded and rushed conditions. Mr. Cantin began to fear the loss of regular clients to other restaurants in the area. He contacted the manager of location 4, Mr. Martin, to get additional information.

The manager was also surprised at the results of the restaurant. "That doesn't mean anything; the regular clients greatly exceed the capacity of the restaurant and the ability of the kitchen to prepare meals. This situation has a direct effect on service." Mr. Martin informed Mr. Cantin that the customer-base was strong, but changing. There had been an increase in the number of students and young couples, with or without children, visiting the location.

Following the discussion, Mr. Cantin continued to think about the situation. The location seemed to respond perfectly to the demands of the area. A study that was done before the opening had clearly defined the population of the neighbouring areas (mostly commercial and industrial areas). Residents of these areas were particularly important at lunchtime, when they were looking for a fast and pleasant lunch experience. However, the fact that there was an increasing number of young children surprised Mr. Cantin. The original research study mentioned an educated, mobile, and aging population, and not a population of young couples and students.

Mr. Cantin contemplated making a call to a marketing research firm in order to study those closest to location 4 and to identify the potential problem(s).

The following day, Mr. Cantin consulted his partner, Mr. Marco, and told him about the problems connected with location 4. Mr. Marco, responsible for supplies, wasn't surprised by the news. The food orders that came from that location had increased considerably in the preceding months. The two partners agreed they needed to meet directly with Mr. Martin concerning his location. Mr. Martin advised that he was available, and the they all agreed to meet the next day.

After he looked over the available information (sales, purchases, advertising expenditures, salaries, etc.) and evaluated the situation more thoroughly, Mr. Martin suggested hiring a marketing research firm to conduct additional research.

Mr. Marco was concerned that such a study would cost approximately $15 000. He suggested it was possible that the relevant information already existed within the company and that the research could be conducted internally.

Mr. Martin, however, maintained that they should not make any hasty decisions, but should defer action until more information was available. He proposed they hire the firm that had originally conducted the research prior to opening location 4, as it was already familiar with Coco-Ricco.

Besides considering the cost, Mr. Macro also wondered what the research objectives should be. Should client satisfaction be evaluated? Should there be a survey of people in the areas surrounding location 4? Mr. Marco realized that the problem wasn't a lack of customers, it was the inability of the location to satisfy current demand. In reality, they needed to know why there was such a sudden increase in customers.

Mr. Martin still wasn't convinced and suggested again that they hire a marketing research firm. However, Mr. Marco persisted that they should be able to solve the problem without having to pay an external firm.

FORUM DES ARTS

Marvin Ryder

"Denis, it has to be your call. This show matches our mission statement and exposes Forum des Arts to a young audience. I'm all for it," said Cassie Tichbourne, Director of Marketing. "In my heart, I'm for it too. But I have a responsibility to watch how we spend taxpayer dollars. This show could lose twenty or thirty thousand dollars. At that level, we might be better off cancelling the performance." These sentiments came from Henri Robillard, Director of Finance and Administration. Both viewpoints were being weighed by the Chief Executive Officer of Forum des Arts, Denis Fournier. The future of the Taylor Dayne concert had come up at the weekly Monday morning management meeting of November 29, 1993. The concert was scheduled for December 6, so he had to make a decision quickly.

THE DEAL

On Tuesday, November 9, 1993, a major Canadian promoter called with an offer to book Taylor Dayne for a concert at Forum des Arts on Monday, December 6, 1993 at 8:00 p.m. He believed he could get the show for Ottawa while booking a second show in Montreal at the Stage du Musique for December 7. This promoter often booked stadium or arena acts like Pink Floyd, the Eagles, Billy Joel, Phil Collins, and Madonna. As another division booked smaller acts, this call had come "out of the blue" and he required an answer within twenty-four hours.

Staff were quite pleased with the offer. Taylor Dayne was a name they easily recognized. She had made several television appearances, most recently on an American television network special dealing with the music of the seventies. To get further information, staff called a couple of record stores and radio stations. These sources confirmed that Taylor Dayne appealed to a younger audience (18 to 30) but that her music crossed many boundaries. Fans could view her work as Dance, Rhythm & Blues, Adult Contemporary, Pop, or Rock. Her latest album was selling well and one record store employee speculated on a response from students attending Carleton University, the University of Ottawa, and Algonquin College. A radio station employee had noted that Taylor Dayne had been asked to sing the National Anthems at the NHL All-Star game in New York City in January, 1994.

While these data were gathered, staff from the Finance Department began to calculate a break-even point for the event (see Table 9-1). Forum des Arts could seat 2191 patrons, including ten positions for people in wheelchairs. Past experience suggested two ticket prices: one price for the orchestra section, first balcony, and the first rows of the second balcony (1909 seats); and a second price for the rear part of the second balcony and wheelchair locations (282 seats). Ticket prices were quoted to the public with the federal Goods and Services Tax (G.S.T.) and a capital improvement fund (C.I.F.) surcharge included. The latter was a $1.00 per ticket surcharge which was accumulated to pay for capital improvements to the Forum des Arts building. While the promoter had suggested a top ticket price of $30, staff felt more comfortable with prices of $25.50 and $22.50.

Table 9-1	Taylor Dayne Concert—Break-Even Analysis	
Revenue	1909 seats @ $25.50	$48 679.50
	282 seats @ $22.50	6 345.00
	Less: C.I.F.	2 191.00
	G.S.T.	3 600.00
Net Revenue:		$49 233.50
Total Fixed Expenses		$32 150.00
Variable Expenses:		
SOCAN		671.54
Credit Card Fees		755.48
Total Variable Expenses		$ 1 427.02
Total Expenses		$33 577.02

Break-Even Point is $33 577.02 / $49 233.50 = 68.2 % of seats

THE ACT

Taylor Dayne was born March 7, 1962, on Long Island, New York, an area she still called home. According to a press release, her childhood influences were Stevie Wonder, the Temptations, the O'Jays, and Undisputed Truth. By 18 she was performing with a series of club bands. She studied music theory, composition, and theatre in college and then joined The Next, a new wave group. Shortly after, she set out on a solo career, signing with BMG/Arista Records for an album to be released in late 1987.

Her debut single was "Tell It to My Heart" which shot to #7 on Billboard's Hot 100 chart in 1988, and to #4 on the dance chart. It went on to sell over a million copies worldwide, hitting #1 in five countries. Her next single, "Prove Your Love," also went to #7 and to the top of the dance charts. On the same album, she showed her versatility with a #1 Adult Contemporary hit, "I'll Always Love You," which revealed a more romantic side. Her fourth consecutive Top Ten hit, "Don't Rush Me," solidified Taylor's popularity. The album containing these songs, *Tell It to My Heart,* reached Gold status in Canada and Double Platinum status in the United States.[1] In 1989, Taylor won five New York Music Awards and was honoured with three Grammy nominations for the album. She also won the Tigre Award, West Germany's equivalent of the Grammy for Best New Artist.

After a sold-out world tour, including dates opening for Michael Jackson, Taylor released a second album *Can't Fight Fate* in late 1989. She had three more Top Ten hits with "I'll Be Your Shelter," "Love Will Lead You Back," "With Every Beat of Your Heart" and the title cut. Taylor once again toured in support of the album bringing her live show to sold-out audiences worldwide. The second album once again reached Gold status in Canada and Double Platinum status in the United States.

After a three-year hiatus, Dayne released a third album on the BMG/Arista label, *Soul Dancing,* in 1993. For the first time, Taylor wrote some of her own material and collaborated with new producers and writers, some of whom worked for Madonna, Whitney Houston, and C&C Music Factory. The first single was "Can't Get Enough of Your Love," a remake of a classic Barry White song. By November 1993, the album had reached Gold status and could reach Platinum status by Christmas in Canada. The first single reached the Top Ten and stayed there for five weeks.

THE BOOKING DECISION

All of this information was presented by Cassie Tichbourne to Denis Fournier on November 10, 1993. The two talked about the act, the potential for ticket sales, and the local market. The act fulfilled three mandates as specified in the corporate mission statement (see Exhibit 9-1). Satisfied that the risk was worth taking and that Forum des Arts would likely break even on the concert, Cassie received direction to confirm the booking with the promoter.

EXHIBIT 9-1 Forum des Arts Corporate Mission Statement

1. To maintain, operate, manage, and promote Forum des Arts on behalf of the City of Ottawa.

2. To positively impact the economic health of the area through the increased use of hotels, restaurants, retail shops, and services, by using the facility as the catalyst to retain local spending, and attract people from outside the region.

3. To maximize the use of the facility, while providing programming that reflects local interests, and contributes to the quality of life.

4. Via effective, efficient management, to constantly work towards maintaining the 1993 subsidization by the corporation of the City of Ottawa at or below the current rate of inflation.

5. All of this is to be achieved while pursuing excellence of management and service, in a manner that fosters local pride and enhances the City's reputation and image.

As the next day was Remembrance Day, Cassie contacted the promoter on November 12. A preliminary copy of the contract was forwarded. While each contract was different in some of its details, nothing in the twenty-five pages seemed out of the ordinary. The price was stipulated in the contract with half due when the contract was signed and the other half due on the night of the performance.

On Monday, November 15, an opening act was found. Vivienne Williams was born and raised in Burlington, a city in southwestern Ontario. She had released her first album under the Sony label in 1993. Her debut single "My Temptation" was the most added track on programmers' playlists, outperforming even Whitney Houston. The song reached #7 on the Adult Contemporary charts in Canada, was in the Top Ten for five weeks, and stayed on the charts for a total of 24 weeks. Her second release, "You May Be Dancin' With Me (But I'm Making Love to You)," entered the Pop Adult chart at #54 with a bullet and remained on the chart for eight weeks. The third single was "Let Love Speak." On November 19, she was scheduled to appear as co-host of specialty cable station MuchMusic's *Soul in the City* program. The presence of a high-profile Ontario artist could only enhance the concert, even though her reasonable performance fee was an unbudgeted extra cost.

Also on November 15, the details of the advertising budget were confirmed. Three media were to be used. Ads would be placed in *The Ottawa Citizen*—the local daily newspaper. This paper published two special entertainment sections: *City Lights* on Thursdays and *Weekend* on Sundays. As can be seen in Table 9-2, these special sections would be used for maximum profile for the event.

Radio would also be used. MAJIC 100, an adult contemporary Ottawa-based station, had a package of promotional spots. For $1200, the station would "present" the concert. In return, the station would provide extra unpaid advertising. Forum des Arts staff also identified a local dance radio station, KOOL-FM, and agreed to supply it with 24 tickets for "giveaways" in return for promoting the show.

Finally, Forum des Arts staff identified six local night clubs/discos: Topaz, The Pit, Ozzie's, Roxanne's, Woody's, and The Watering Hole. Forum des Arts agreed to supply each club with four tickets to "give away" in return for promoting the show. In addition, 5000 flyers were to be printed for $145. Some were to be placed in record stores. Some more would

Table 9-2   Newspaper Advertising for Taylor Dayne Concert in *The Ottawa Citizen*

Date	Columns × Lines	Cost per Column-Line	Cost	Section
Thu. Nov. 18	3 × 100	$2.98	$ 894	City Lights
Fri. Nov. 19	3 × 100	$1.655	$ 497	Entertainment
Sun. Nov. 28	3 × 100	$3.61	$1 083	Weekend
Mon. Nov. 29	3 × 100	$1.655	$ 497	Entertainment
Sun. Dec. 5	2 × 65	$3.61	$ 469	Weekend
Mon. Dec. 6	2 × 65	$1.655	$ 215	Entertainment
			$3 655	

be sent to each of the six local dance clubs, while the remainder were to be placed under the windshield wipers of patrons' cars parked in each club's parking lot.

With these details confirmed, the contract was signed on Tuesday, November 16. Tickets for both the Ottawa and Montreal shows were to go on sale on Thursday, November 18.

THE FIRST WEEK OF SALES

At both the Forum des Arts box office and at Ticketmaster outlets, sales the first day were disappointing. Forum des Arts staff contacted the promoter and were surprised to find Ottawa's sales figures to be slightly ahead of Montreal's. With the Christmas season moving into full gear, information about the concert might not yet have reached the intended audience. Both groups decided to avoid passing judgment on ticket sales until after the weekend.

By Monday, November 22, the concert appeared to be in trouble. Over 1400 seats needed to be sold for the event to break even, and sales had not yet reached half that number (see Table 9-3). Forum des Arts staff decided to increase publicity for the event.

Lynn Saxberg, the pop music critic for *The Ottawa Citizen,* agreed to do a feature story about Taylor Dayne in the December 2 edition of *City Lights.* MAJIC 100 agreed to do telephone interviews with Taylor Dayne and Vivienne Williams during the week of November 29. MAJIC 100 had also agreed to "give away" a pair of tickets during each of the last seven days before the concert. CJOH-TV was willing to do interviews with Taylor Dayne and Vivienne Williams. The latter would be interviewed on November 30 and the interview would include her video and a live performance. Management for Taylor Dayne was not certain about the live interview and felt it could be organized no earlier than the day of the concert. A press release was sent to all print, radio, and television media in Eastern Ontario and the Outaouais region in Quebec, in the hopes of generating news stories and free publicity.

THE MEETING

Every Monday morning, there was a Forum des Arts management meeting attended by the CEO (Denis Fournier), the Director of Finance and Administration (Henri Robillard), the Director of Marketing (Cassie Tichbourne), and the Director of Operations (Nikolai Litau). The first topic of the November 29 meeting was the Taylor Dayne concert.

Table 9-3 Day-by-Day Ticket Sales for Taylor Dayne Concert	
Date	**Number of Tickets Sold**
Nov. 18	165
Nov. 21	280
Nov. 22	326
Nov. 23	363
Nov. 24	381
Nov. 25	414
Nov. 28	453

"How are the ticket sales for the concert?" Denis asked.

"As of Sunday, November 28, we had sold 453 tickets, not including any complimentary tickets given away as part of our promotional effort," Cassie responded.

"Wow. That's nowhere near our break-even point." Denis paused and thought for a second. "What are our options here?"

Henri Robillard was the first to speak. "We could cancel the show. The management for Taylor Dayne already has half the money from us and I think we could negotiate with them on the remaining monies so that our loss could be kept to less than the performance fee. Think of the money they could earn from doing nothing! And I doubt they would want Taylor Dayne to play to a near-empty house."

"I agree," Nik Litau said. "I thought this show was better suited to a dance club. Forum des Arts has too many rules for the crowd she attracts. You know what I mean? They have to sit in their seats—no dancing in the aisles. There is no alcohol or smoking in the theatre itself. And thank goodness we have those restrictions as you can imagine the damage the audience could do to our upholstered chairs and carpets. This rap/hip-hop/dance music is just not appropriate to our venue. I don't know why she was booked in the first place."

"I disagree with Henri's scenario. Legally, we haven't got a leg to stand on. The contract specifies a talent fee and they don't have to take anything less. Also we have committed advertising dollars and staff time to this project which would be lost. Cancelling would also require more advertising to tell patrons about the cancelled date and to inform them about ticket refunds. As Marketing Director, I would prefer a different approach."

"Continue," Denis said.

"Ottawa has the reputation of being a 'walk-up' city. Translation—patrons just don't like to buy tickets in advance. You remember that NBA exhibition game last year. The Ottawa Civic Centre sold 7000 of 13 000 tickets on the day of the game, and I am sure you remember the hassles at the ticket windows. I believe our promotional strategies are working. We are in the Christmas season and people may not be willing to commit to this show until they are sure they have the time. I bet we will have a big day-of-sale walk-up. All of our publicity work is supporting the last-minute walk-up, what with the newspaper, radio, and television interviews, ticket give-aways, and promotions at dance clubs."

"Sure. And if the walk-up doesn't materialize we are stuck with little box office revenue, talent fees, and the costs of mounting the show," added Henri. "Also imagine the newspaper reviews of the show. We have been stung before by poor attendance. And you know how the aldermen react to being called bush league. We are already receiving a subsidy from the City of Ottawa of over $800 000. If we blow a bundle here, we are guilty of fiscal mismanagement."

"Cassie does have a point, Henri. We're obligated for the talent fees. About 40% of the production costs are items over which we have some control. As we won't use the entire theatre, I can cut back on ushers and maybe there are a few other costs we can manage. The current box office revenue covers these expenses. Any additional revenue could go toward the talent fees. Even a poorly attended concert might be a better financial proposition than one which is cancelled," Nik said.

"I hate to muddy the water but I just had another brainstorm," Cassie interrupted. "What if we paper the house?"

"You know my opposition to giving away blocks of free tickets," Henri retorted. "It can cause a lot of ill will and complaints when paying customers find out they are sitting beside people who did not pay for their tickets. Some patrons demand a refund and when we don't give one, there are letters to aldermen and the local newspapers."

"Sure, that's one possibility," added Cassie. "But my records show that the average patron spends $3.00 at the concession areas in the lobby. They purchase liquor, wine, beer, soft drinks, or the gourmet cookies and ice cream we stock. Our markup on cost is 100% so we stand to clear $1.50 per patron even if they haven't purchased a ticket. That could be a couple thousand dollars toward our bottom line. Unfortunately, we don't get any revenue from T-shirts or promotional programs sold by the act. But if we target an audience that rarely visits Forum des Arts, these free tickets could be an investment in audience development."

"Generally, I would agree," said Nik. "But remember the time of the year. If we have a snowfall or freezing rain, all those people could really mess up the place. The additional cleaning costs and the lack of savings from having a full complement of ushers on hand could completely use up the additional revenues you just found!"

Denis had been quiet during the discussion. A good CEO lets his staff debate the merits of the options before him. Cassie turned to Denis. "There may be some other options we haven't considered, but there you have the most likely scenarios. The concert is a week away and we should act today if any adjustment to our plans is to be made. How do you want to proceed?"

ENDNOTE

1. In Canada, Gold and Platinum status is reached when an album sells more than 50 000 and 100 000 copies respectively. In the United States, the same standards are 500 000 and 1 000 000 copies respectively.

PARKER'S CLASSICS

10

Ramesh Venkat

Philip Parker is the proprietor of Parker's Classics, a men's wear store with three branches in Vancouver. During the last few years, Parker's Classics had been experiencing a slight decline in sales. Philip felt that this was attributable to a high level of competition in the Vancouver market. In addition, Holt Renfrew and other upscale stores in the suburbs of Vancouver, together with Eaton's and the upscale Bay in downtown Vancouver, presented a major challenge.

Philip had over 20 years of experience in the men's wear market, having worked in some of Canada's leading department stores for several years. He had also had a two-year stint with a French designer of men's wear. In 1985, at the age of 46, he decided to be his own boss and opened the first of the Parker's Classics stores in the west end of Vancouver. Within four years he had three more stores: one in Vancouver, one in West Vancouver, and one in Coquitlam, a Vancouver suburb.

Parker's Classics quickly established a name for itself in upscale men's wear. Philip prided himself on being able to completely dress an upscale man. Parker's carried a wide range of clothing from casual to semi-formal and formal wear. In addition, the stores had a large selection of male accessories and colognes. Parker's carried such well-known names as Hugo Boss and Armani, as well as its own Parker's Classic suits, specially designed by a New York-based designer.

Growing competition and a slowing economy in the early 1990s had put a stop to the frenzied growth that Parker's experienced in the late 1980s. Sales and profits continued to show a steady decline in 1994 and 1995. Philip knew that he had to do something to reverse this trend. In mid-July 1995, Philip, together with his 27-year-old son Jonathan, who has an

Prepared by Ramesh Venkat, Saint Mary's University, Halifax, Nova Scotia, as a basis for classroom discussion. ©1995. Reprinted with permission.

MBA degree, and Christine Delaney, the manager of the downtown Vancouver store for the last eight years, met to review the second quarter and devise a strategy for the firm's future.

During the course of the meeting, Christine remarked that she had come to know some of the regular clients well, and that she was surprised to find out that many of them were gay. Philip knew that many of his clients were leading lawyers, bankers, businessmen, and doctors. He too was surprised by this revelation and found it somewhat disconcerting. He expressed his discomfort and asked Jonathan and Christine how this might affect the firm.

Jonathan had some gay friends and immediately saw a business opportunity. His view was that Parker's Classics, in specific locations such as the west end of Vancouver, should openly target gay consumers. Jonathan felt that such a market niching strategy would ensure continued growth for the company. The major competitors, he felt, would be unwilling to go after this market segment. Jonathan asked Christine if she knew what percentage of the customers in her store were gay. Christine did not have a definite answer, but she thought it would be less than 20 percent.

Philip was uncomfortable with his son's idea. He felt that as more gay customers came into his stores, he was, perhaps, losing many of his heterosexual clientele—and maybe this was the reason for the declining performance in the stores. Philip was of the view that openly targeting gay consumers would antagonize other customers. Furthermore, he was not comfortable with the idea of associating Parker's Classics' image with gay consumers.

Jonathan felt that "upscale" was not a homogenous market and that there were several sub-segments. Christine agreed that going after one smaller segment, the gay market, would give Parker's the edge over its more traditional rivals. Jonathan and Christine felt that the stores that currently attracted gay consumers could specifically target gays without antagonizing other customers. The other stores in the suburbs would not have any specific promotions targeted to the gay market and would continue to go after a broader clientele. Philip disagreed. After a heated exchange of views, all three agreed that further market research was required to determine the percentage of gay customers, as well as social attitudes and possible competitive reaction which might affect such a market niching strategy.

That same evening, Jonathan arranged a meeting with David Gower, a management consultant with considerable experience in lifestyle-based market segmentation. The next day Philip, Jonathan, and Christine had a lunch meeting with David Gower. First, Gower asked Philip if he had considered opening stores in smaller markets in the east as a growth strategy. Philip replied that he wanted to be based on the west coast and did not want to be national at this stage. Philip then voiced his concern over his son's proposal and asked Gower what he knew about the gay market.

Gower then gave a lengthy discourse on how marketers were dealing with the gay market. He pointed out that members of the gay community were often young, well-educated, in high-paying jobs, and had a taste for fine living. Gower talked about how consumer product giants like Procter & Gamble and Toyota were seeking detailed demographic information on the gay community. Gower thought that it was only a matter of time before such companies had specific brands and promotions targeted to the gay market. In fact, Toyota had recently placed an ad in an Australian gay magazine.

Philip, still not convinced, asked Gower if there were any companies specifically targeting the gay market, and if so, how they were performing. Gower readily provided some examples. For instance, the Nordstrom department store chain had placed ads in *Washington Blade*, a gay newspaper, and Calvin Klein had run several ads with nude or partially clothed men. Other clothing stores like Banana Republic and The Gap had run ads featuring well-known gay people. In Canada, Gower said, IKEA, the Swedish furniture manufacturer, had run television ads featuring gay consumers. Gower also mentioned that more information was now available on the gay market, through market research firms such as the Chicago-based Overlooked Opinions, who were specializing in this market.

Philip, as well as Jonathan and Christine, were surprised that some of the leading clothing stores were openly targeting gay consumers. Based on in-store customer surveys, Philip had determined that his clientele was mostly in the 24 to 45 age group and he felt that the older of these consumers might be more conservative in their views. He was still worried about a possible backlash from these people. He probed Gower further about problems and failures associated with targeting the gay market.

Gower narrated the experiences of California-based Levi Strauss, which is considered to be a gay-friendly company. Levi Strauss had to face a boycott, as well as a lot of unwanted publicity, when the Family Research Council, a Washington-based conservative advocacy group, joined boycotts of gay-supportive companies. Other companies, like Kmart, pulled an ad featuring two men after only a few airings, because some people believed it portrayed a gay couple and protested. Gower then said, "I'm not sure if such protests have any long-term implications. I don't think the average heterosexual consumer cares if a company sells its products to gay people. There seems to be a growing tolerance and acceptance."

After mulling over this comment for a few minutes, Philip asked how big the gay market was in Vancouver and the rest of Canada. Philip pointed out that from what Gower had indicated, it appeared that it was only large companies who were taking the risk of going after that particular market. He wanted to know if a small company like his could withstand any negative publicity or protest as a result of targeting the gay market.

Gower said that he would have to do some secondary research and conduct some focus groups to be able to provide answers to such questions. Gower went on to say that the gay market was a growing segment, to which not many companies had paid any attention, and that it was a segment with few dependents. Consequently, this segment had more disposable income to spend on items such as expensive clothes. As the meeting concluded, Jonathan and Christine were convinced that there was tremendous potential in the gay market. Philip still had lingering doubts, but he agreed to commission a market research study.

EYCKLINE FARMS

Jane Funk and Thomas Funk

Wilhelm Van Eyck turned his pick-up into the lane of Eyckline Farms and stopped at the mail-box. Pulling out the day's mail, he found the usual collection of advertisements, magazines, and personal letters. He noted that his wife would be pleased to get her latest *Good Housekeeping* and that he had received a letter from cousin Charlie in British Columbia. Wilhelm and Charlie had corresponded regularly since their immigration to Canada thirty years ago. They had gone through public school together and then worked on a local farm while taking evening courses at a Dutch agricultural college. When they left the Netherlands and came to Canada, Charlie settled in British Columbia and Wilhelm came to Ontario. Wilhelm and Charlie spent most of their yearly visits in heated debates about the relative importance of various inputs in their broiler operations, and Wilhelm had little patience with Charlie's belief that he would increase his profits once he found the "magic feed" formula. Wilhelm always answered that no grower would ever have consistently outstanding crops: "too many variables, Charlie. Better trust your own judgment, not some magic formula. You need healthy chicks and proper management as well as good feed." Charlie never listened, of course. That's what made their yearly visits so interesting.

Wilhelm had done well for himself and was quite pleased with his operation, which included capacity to produce 100 000 broilers a year, a 300 sow farrow to finish operation, and 2000 acres of crops. Wilhelm was also pleased because his two sons, Harold and Martin, were actively involved in the operation. Although Wilhelm made most of the key management decisions on the farm and was mainly responsible for the broiler operation, Harold had primary responsibility for the swine operation and Martin looked after the crops and the maintenance of all equipment. Harold's wife, Marcia, was very skilled in computers, so she looked after keeping records, ordering supplies, and paying bills. Harold and Marcia lived just a half-mile from the main operation of Eyckline Farms, while Martin, who was not married, lived at home. Harold graduated from the Ontario Agricultural College at the University of Guelph four years ago with a degree in Animal Science. Although Martin had no formal education past high school, he had taken a number of equipment mainte-nance courses at a local community college and was considering applying for the Diploma in Agriculture program at the University of Guelph.

Eyckline Farms also employed Adrian Vandenburg as a full-time employee who helped in all the operations, but spent most of his time with the broilers. This gave Wilhelm enough time to look after general farm management issues. Prior to joining Eyckline Farms, Adrian had a small broiler operation of his own, so he was very knowledgeable in this field of agri-culture. Wilhelm liked Adrian and often sought his opinion on decisions relating to the broiler operation. While Wilhelm felt diversifying into crops and hogs was a good busi-ness decision and spread his risk, he was always partial to the broiler operation, perhaps because it was how he got started.

As Wilhelm climbed back into his pickup, he tossed the mail onto the seat beside him and continued down the lane. No doubt about it, he had come a long way in the thirty years since he and Charlie stepped off the boat. He surveyed the orderly spread of Eyckline Farms and admired the new siding on the house and the new broiler barn built this year. "Yessir, if you make a dollar you sometimes do well to put it back into the business," he said to himself. He appreciated the advice the building representative had given him on ventila-tion for the new facility. Of course, it seemed a bit extravagant given Wilhelm's budget, but once he adapted it to his own operation, it worked out fine. He appreciated good advice. Brushing a speck of dust off the steering wheel of his new pick-up, Wilhelm gathered the mail and went into the house where Polly Van Eyck was preparing lunch.

"Here's your *Good Housekeeping*, Polly," Wilhelm said, "and I got a letter from Charlie, too."

"Anything from my sister?" asked Polly.

"No, just advertisements. These guys never give up. Wait, here's one from Master Feed. I wonder what they want. I just saw Jim yesterday and he didn't seem to have anything to say—seemed in a hurry, as usual."

Master Feed was Van Eyck's current feed supplier for his broiler operation. He had been with Master Feed for two years despite two price increases. The last price increase had annoyed him somewhat since it seemed designed to cover an increase in extra salesman ser-vices which Van Eyck did not use. However, he had stayed with Master Feed because results were reasonably good. He had to admit that the last crop had not been up to par, but he decided he would wait until he got the next results before considering a switch. All the same, he thought, as he looked at the letter, it would have been appreciated if Jim Sellars, the Master Feed salesman, had stopped by to check up on his last results. "I guess he's too busy carting the neighbour's birds to the vet," Wilhelm thought to himself. Since Jim knew Wilhelm pre-ferred to take his own birds to the vet, he rarely stopped by except to take an order.

Although Eyckline Farms purchased broiler feed from Master Feed, they purchased hog supplement from Smith Feeds. Chuck Hustead, the Smith Feed rep, and Harold had become very close friends at university, so Harold was anxious to do business with Chuck. In addition, Smith Feed had an excellent reputation in the swine industry for products that would deliver high performance under superior management conditions.

Wilhelm gave no more thought to the letter from Master Feed until later that afternoon when he, Harold, Martin, and Marcia met in the farm office for their weekly management meeting. Marcia had just finished summarizing the results from the last broiler crop which she presented to the others. Much to Wilhelm's disappointment, feed conversion had slipped again for the third crop in a row. The decline was not great, but there appeared to be a consistent trend. Harold suggested that they might do better with something less expensive. Then Wilhelm remembered the letter. Opening it, he discovered a form letter explaining Master Feed's new policy which required their contract growers to assign proceeds from the processing plant to the feed supplier, who then deducted the cost of feed and chicks before sending the balance to the grower. Wilhelm had never contracted with Master Feed, though he bought both feed and chicks from the company. He preferred to choose his own processor, and it annoyed him that he should have received a form letter meant only for contract producers. He put down the letter and glanced again at the performance results. It was irritating that Jim Sellars had not taken the time to make sure his non-contract customers did not receive the letter. "Too busy giving out expensive advice about medication and high brooder temperatures," muttered Van Eyck. Even more alarming was the policy itself, which seemed almost an insult and further evidence to Wilhelm that the producer who contracted with an integrated firm lost much of their independence. "I don't want anybody telling me what to pay for feed or chicks or when to ship my crop," Wilhelm said to the others.

During the meeting, Marcia also mentioned her growing frustration with billing problems from several suppliers, especially Master Feed. Marcia prided herself on always getting cheques prepared and in the mail in enough time to earn early-payment discounts. The fact that occasionally these were not properly handled was becoming annoying. "It makes me wonder how good their products are when companies are sloppy in how they handle administrative matters like accounting," she noted. "In addition, it causes me a lot of unnecessary work. I have enough to do without having to check every statement that comes in. In an operation like ours, we get over 30 every month."

The next morning Van Eyck was on his way to the barn when his neighbour Fritz Lonsdorf stopped by. Lonsdorf was one of the larger broiler producers in the area and Wilhelm enjoyed comparing notes with him. They chatted for a while about the weather, and then Wilhelm mentioned the new Master Feed policy and their carelessness in sending him the form letter. They had discussed the price increase earlier, and Wilhelm's disappointing crop.

Fritz suggested trying Domar, the brand he had been using for a number of years. "My cockerels weighed over 2.1 kilograms at 38 days on the last crop," exclaimed Fritz.

"I remember you telling me," said Wilhelm, lighting his pipe. He also remembered checking with the processor and finding that Fritz's cockerels had actually been killed at 42 days and averaged 2.07 kilograms. "Nice fellow, Fritz, but you have to take what he says with a grain of salt," Wilhelm told Harold at the time. "Dad," Harold laughed, "you say that about everybody. Fritz does brag a little, but you and I both know 2.07 kilograms is a darned sight higher than our last average, even with our more expensive feed."

He and Fritz continued chatting about John Stern's new farrowing house and the best cure for "bent beak syndrome." Fritz mentioned a new remedy which he had seen advertised in *Canada Poultryman*. Wilhelm remained skeptical: "I wouldn't take a chance, Fritz. I'd get my birds to the vet as fast as I could if I were you. Maybe take them to the university. See what they think of your idea before you try it." Fritz said he would consider it and the two of them made further plans to visit the London Poultry Show later in the month. "Always look forward to seeing the new displays and talking with the other producers," Wilhelm said as Fritz left.

That evening, Wilhelm spread the reports Marcia had prepared on the kitchen table and noticed again the poor results of the last crop. Not drastic, he thought, but he would hate to see it continue, especially given the higher price he paid for Master Feed. Fritz's results kept running through his mind. He thought Master Feed was much the same as other quality feeds, but the latest price increase and the poor results made him wonder. He considered the other major variables in his operation to see if they could be responsible for the disappointing performance. His buildings and equipment were the latest design and he handled the management himself, with Adrian doing most of the work. In the past, Adrian had been a little careless—failing to clean the waterer or some other little thing, but lately he was really shaping up. The chicks, also purchased since he started his operation from a Master Feed affiliate, were top quality. Wilhelm personally rushed them to the university or the lab at the slightest sign of disease. Lately, Jim Sellars seemed anxious to do this for his customers, but Wilhelm preferred to be right there to give the vet the benefit of his own ideas. He found the vet's advice sound, though he never followed it without first airing his own idea. "Nobody knows my operation as well as I do," he remarked to the vet.

Chicks, management, and equipment were all checked out. That left feed. With the latest price increase, the slightest rise in feed conversion could cause a significant decrease in return per bird. "Beyond a certain price, quality isn't that different," Wilhelm often told cousin Charlie. He looked at the entries in the record book, which detailed his feed purchasing history from the beginning of his operation:

Feed Company	Purchase History
Starlight Feeds	Five years until the company was purchased by Supersweet
Supersweet Feeds	Three years
Chance Feeds	Two years until the company was purchased by P & H
P & H Feeds	One year
Full-O-Pep Feeds	Three years until the company was purchased by Master Feed
Master Feed	Current supplier

Wilhelm remembered how he had been quite happy with Starlight Feeds and stayed with them even after they were purchased by Supersweet. Soon Supersweet discontinued the Starlight brand and tried to switch customers to their Supersweet brand by offering an initial price reduction. Wilhelm had used Supersweet for three years, even as the planned price increases were implemented, because he was reluctant to switch. Finally, he could not agree that there was a quality difference worth the $8–$10 a ton premium that Supersweet was charging. When the Chance Feeds salesman came around and offered $10 a ton less, Wilhelm gave their feed a try and found it was every bit as good as the higher priced Supersweet product. Not only was it less expensive, the feed conversion was equally good.

Wilhelm stayed with Chance Feeds for two years, even after they were purchased by P & H Feeds. Once again the price started to go up about $2–$3 per ton. "Seems to be the story of my operation," Wilhelm muttered to himself. P & H was now at the same price level as Full-O-Pep, and Wilhelm had heard about Full-O-Pep results from other growers, so he decided to give it a try. The results were good and Wilhelm stayed with them even after their operation was purchased by Master Feed. Soon Master Feed phased out the Full-O-Pep line, replacing it with their own brand. Since Master Feed was competitively priced, Van Eyck made the change and had been satisfied. Then Master Feed began to raise their price. After two price increases they were one of the most expensive brands in the industry, priced in the range of Supersweet. Neither price increase had been announced and Wilhelm had noticed it only after the feed bills arrived. Though not immediately alarmed, Wilhelm had become uneasy when his latest crop results were less than spectacular. "And here I am," Wilhelm said. "Every time one of those big fellows takes over, price goes up and service goes down."

Wilhelm felt he was pretty realistic about his feed expectations, unlike cousin Charlie. He also appreciated that Jim Sellars didn't pressure him to sign a contract but wished he would stop by every now and then for a chat just to see how things were going. Wilhelm enjoyed chatting with salesmen about market changes, growers' results, and disease problems, but he became annoyed when they brought out their "outstanding grower results." He also disliked paying (through price increases) for services which he did not use. It seemed that Jim Sellars was too busy running around the country taking birds to the vet and dispensing "free" advice on feeder space, temperature, and ventilation, all areas where Wilhelm relied on his own experience. When he wanted advice, he'd ask for it, thank you, and he'd ask somebody who knew what they were talking about.

Wilhelm put down the performance report and wandered into the living room. Polly was at a church meeting and Martin was at a ball game, so he picked up the day's mail, turned on the radio, and sat down. Glancing through *Canada Poultryman*, he noticed the ads for Chance Feeds and Ralston Purina. Both featured a testimonial by an "outstanding poultry producer," neither of whom was known to Wilhelm. "Sure they get great results," Wilhelm thought. "They probably have two million dollars worth of equipment!" An ad for new feeding equipment caught his eye and he made a note to ask Harold, Martin, and Adrian what they knew about it. Continuing on, he saw the medication mentioned by Fritz and made another note to ask the vet about it next time he was at the clinic. Then he heard a car drive in the lane and, looking out, saw Dave Crawford, the salesman for Domar in Elmira, walking toward the house. Crawford was a pleasant fellow, not much older than Martin. He had been with Domar for about a year and had been trying to get Wilhelm to consider their broiler feeds. It would be pleasant to pass some time with Crawford.

"Hello, Dave. Good to see you. Come on in and have a coffee."

"Thanks, Wilhelm. I was in the neighbourhood and thought I'd stop by to give you this article on a new feeding system. I saw it in *Ontario Farmer* and thought you would enjoy reading it."

"That's real thoughtful of you, Dave. I was considering a new system," Wilhelm answered, thinking how Jim Sellars had never even bothered to stop by to see the new broiler barn, let alone bring a bit of unsolicited information.

"My pleasure, Wilhelm. I figured you'd be alone tonight with the women off at the church meeting and Martin at the ball game. Of course, I also wanted to see that new broiler barn. It's the talk of the neighbourhood."

They chatted for awhile about local events, the latest marketing board activities, and Fritz Lonsdorf's problem with bent beak syndrome. Then Dave said, "Wilhelm, the mill is taking a group of growers to the London Poultry Show and I thought you might be able to join us."

Wilhelm thanked him but explained that he and Fritz had already planned to go. Dave then casually remarked, "I hear Master Feed upped their prices again."

Wilhelm acknowledged that this was so. "Well," Dave went on, "They've got a good feed there, no doubt about it. Are you still pleased with the results?"

Wilhelm hesitated, then admitted his last crop was a little disappointing.

"I can understand your feelings, Wilhelm. I really believe Domar can give you equal or better results. You know our quality and feed conversion ratios are competitive and our price is a good $5 a ton lower. Someone who is as experienced as you are knows we have to offer a quality product to stay in business. Why not let us feed the next crop and see how our feed performs in your barn?"

"Dave, I'm just not ready to make a change yet, but I sure will give your offer some thought," Wilhelm answered. "Adrian is encouraging me to try Smith Feeds because of his past experience with their brand and the fact that Harold likes it for the hog operation. I'll let you know in a week or so."

"Sure, Wilhelm. I understand. I appreciate your considering us. I remember that Adrian used Smith Feed when he had his own operation. I thought he was disappointed with their performance."

"Is there anything I can do to help you better understand the value of our Domar product?" asked Dave. "I would be pleased to bring our company nutritionist out in a couple of days to discuss your situation in more detail and provide a professional opinion."

"Thanks, Dave," Wilhelm said, "but I don't think that will be necessary right now. I have a pretty good feel for my own operation."

"Fine, Wilhelm, talk to you later," Crawford said as he rose to go. "Better get on, the women will be home soon."

The next day Wilhelm took a load of birds to the vet. He drove past the P & H dealer but didn't stop, remembering that their prices were at least as high as Master Feed. Besides, not one of their salesmen had stopped by since he had switched several years earlier. While at the vet, Wilhelm mentioned his dissatisfaction with Master Feed and asked the vet's opinion about Domar. The vet agreed that above a certain price range, quality was quite comparable and results would probably be much the same using either feed.

Driving home, Wilhelm passed Chuck Hustead, the sales rep for Smith Feeds. Hustead pulled over and asked if Wilhelm had a few minutes to spare. Wilhelm glanced at the birds in the back, but said he could give Hustead a few minutes. Hustead climbed into the truck, dropping his portfolio in the process and scattering papers. Wilhelm sighed and glanced at his watch and the chicks sitting in the sun in the back, while Hustead tried to rearrange the papers.

"I was just by your place, Wilhelm. That's some broiler barn you have there. I was a little surprised at the ventilation, though."

Wilhelm filled his pipe and looked at Hustead pointedly. "Is that right, Chuck? Well, I did what I thought best."

"Sure, Wilhelm, but I thought those reports I showed you gave some pretty good suggestions," Hustead said.

"They were a little too experimental for me, Chuck. Now what can I do for you?"

"Well, I thought I would stop by and explain our new program. You know we're quality and price competitive, especially after that latest Master Feed price increase. And Harold is very pleased with the performance of our hog feed. Did Marcia show you how the average number of pigs per litter has increased since you started using our new sow ration?"

Wilhelm's pipe went out and the chicks seemed to be getting more restless. Chuck didn't seem to notice as he continued. "Look at these broiler reports! I'll bet you've never seen better results than these."

"My results aren't so bad, Chuck. Besides, I told you before, I don't hold with these consistently outstanding results. You know as well as I do that excellent crops are as much the result of chance and good management as they are of feed."

"Well, have it your own way Wilhelm, but these figures don't lie."

Wilhelm looked at him silently. "Besides we'll deliver whenever you want and take your birds to the vet so you don't have to waste your time running around," Hustead continued.

Wilhelm's pipe went out again. "Speaking of birds, Chuck, you may have noticed mine are getting nervous, so I'd best be getting on."

"Oh—sure, sure! I'll leave these results with you. Once you look them over I'm sure you'll be impressed. By the way, have you considered doing business with Fairview Hatcheries? They have good quality chicks. Hardly ever get sick. Probably save you in the long run. Not nearly as nervous as yours."

"See you later, Chuck," said Wilhelm, closing the door and driving away.

"I'll be hearing from you soon," shouted Hustead. Wilhelm drove on.

Smith Feeds had a good reputation, especially in swine, and they were price and quality competitive, but Wilhelm was annoyed at Hustead's continual harping on "excellent grower results." It was the same every call. Besides, "the ventilation is fine in my new chicken house and it's my business which hatchery I choose!" At least Jim Sellars never pushed him to try a new hatchery! Wilhelm knew that Harold was very happy with the performance of Smith Feeds in the hog operation. Harold often urged Wilhelm to at least give them a try in the broiler operation. So far, Wilhelm prevailed with the argument that Smith Feeds does not have a comparable reputation among broiler producers. Not having seen any performance results, Harold could not argue otherwise.

When he arrived home, Wilhelm put the chicks in the chicken house and went into the kitchen, dropping Hustead's reports on the table. Polly came over with the dishes and, glancing at the reports, said, "Do you need these, Wilhelm?"

What? Oh, those. No, Polly, throw them away," Wilhelm said as he opened the evening paper.

In the days that followed, Wilhelm continued thinking about his feed situation but made no move to change suppliers, as he still had a couple of bins of Master Feed product on hand. He knew he would have to decide soon. Crawford stopped by several times and so did Hustead. Jim Sellars came by once, but Wilhelm was out. He left a message to have Wilhelm call if he had any problems. Wilhelm knew there were other feed suppliers in the immediate area and he was not opposed to travelling a few miles further, though he thought local feed was probably fresher. Their prices were all pretty competitive with Smith Feeds and Domar, and the quality was similar, at least in his view. There were also several large companies with prices similar to Master Feed and P & H, but he suspected the price difference went into their flashy advertising and not the quality of their feed. "Maybe it isn't worth it to change," he thought. Just then Jim Sellars passed him on the road and waved. Wilhelm thought he might be coming for a chat, but Jim drove on. Wilhelm turned in to Eyckline Farms. He had made his decision and would place the call after dinner.

THE TRAIN TRIP
Rosemary Polegato

On July 21, 1993, Marianne and Robert relived their annoyance as they composed a letter to the French National Railway concerning a recent bad experience with the train system. It had been the only blight on a two-week family holiday in Europe in May/June 1993.

PLANNING THE FAMILY HOLIDAY

Marianne Ricci (aged 41 years) and Robert Dupuis (aged 48 years) were a typical professional couple, with one son, Michael (10 years). They lived in a small town in Northeastern Nova Scotia. They usually took their family vacation at the same spot on the Gaspé Coast of Quebec. The summer of 1993 would be special, however. Marianne had a special leave from work, Robert was flexible in his job as an independent consultant, and Michael was now old enough to go with the flow of a "big trip."

The family initially contemplated going across Canada, going to Europe, or Marianne taking a trip to Japan by herself. However, she had not been to Europe since 1978 and had always wanted to visit France with Robert because he spoke French fluently. At this point, Michael would also appreciate a different cultural setting. Robert was less keen on going to Europe; he saw it as an expensive holiday with the risk of not accommodating the whole family in a truly holiday way. (One of his sisters did not have a good time travelling in Europe in the 1970s. It just might be an expensive two-week nightmare!) Michael was keen and became increasingly enthusiastic as Mom described her trips to Europe and what he might take with him and what he might see and do. After discussion off and on from November 1992 to February 1993, they came to a consensus and decided to take a trip to Europe. One of the deciding factors was that a trip to Europe would cost about $1400 more than going across Canada, accounted for by being able to stay with friends or family in various parts of Canada. As usual, they would work within a pre-determined budget.

The family narrowed down their range to France and Italy. Since Marianne had taken two holidays in Europe in the late 1970s, she felt that Robert and Michael should have first choice for places to visit. Her only requests were that they spend time in Florence, Italy, and that she visit, however briefly, a friend who had moved to Milan, Italy. Michael wanted to see the Eiffel Tower, the Leaning Tower of Pisa, and Venice. Robert wanted to see the heart of Paris, Venice, and Florence. So they decided to visit Paris, Venice, Florence (with a side trip to Pisa), and Milan, spending about four days in each of the first three cities. They worked out in detail what they would like to see and do.

Marianne investigated travel arrangements with the airlines. The travelling was complicated because they lived two and a half hours from the airport (in Halifax, NS) and would have to fly to Montreal or Toronto where virtually all international flights originated for travellers in Atlantic Canada. The return trip would involve staying overnight at the Airport Hotel in Halifax. They bought their tickets from Canadian Airlines who could fly them into Paris on May 26th and out of Milan on June 9th for a reasonable price. The rest of the travel would be by train, since they were not interested in driving in Europe. The routes seemed direct and Marianne's experience on the European trains was very positive; she said they were comfortable, ran on time, and had frequent departures and various routes.

Robert was particularly concerned about accommodations and how they might get from one place to another at reasonable times and at reasonable prices. To enjoy the experience everyone would need adequate sleep and time to rest. Thus, Robert spent a lot of time gathering information on where to stay and how to get around. He spoke to friends and family members, collected brochures from tour companies, talked to travel agents, and spent over $100 during April phoning hotels in Europe. Marianne assisted with gathering this information, but Robert took primary responsibility for it. He wanted to be thorough and to have as few surprises as possible. They spent nearly $150 on travel guides, such as *Let's Go to Europe* and the Fodor's guides, purchasing most of them in March during a business trip to Halifax by Marianne.

Robert wanted to know more about how the train schedule would work, so a month prior to the trip he called the French Embassy for the train schedule leaving Paris for Italy. The Embassy forwarded his call to a Canadian agency which looked after train passes for Canadians travelling abroad. He determined that the best route to follow would be a stay in Paris, followed by a 12-hour daytime train trip to Florence via Lausanne, Switzerland (with a bonus stopover of two hours), through Milan to Florence. After a few days in Florence, they could go up to Venice and then have a day in Milan before flying home. He carefully noted the times of arrivals and departures and took this information with him to Europe. Hotel reservations for each city were made and confirmed with deposits.

THE TRIP

The trip went very well except for the train trip between Paris and Florence on May 31st. On the previous day, Robert went to the International Travel desk at Gare de Lyon (a major train station in Paris) and presented the schedule he had brought with him. The agent informed him that they had just been computerized and that Robert's schedule was incorrect. The agent had problems getting the tickets from the computerized set-up, but finally printed them out after numerous attempts and working with various manuals. Robert paid 1754

French francs for the tickets and three reserved seats (optional, unless you want your seats guaranteed). Although the agent seemed experienced and seemed to know what he was doing, Robert left still having doubts about the schedule.

The train arrived in Lausanne on time, giving the family an opportunity to have lunch and walk around Lausanne. Upon returning to the train station in plenty of time to catch their next train, however, they discovered that they had tickets and reservations for a train departure which did not exist! (In fact, the agent told Robert that the schedule obtained while in Canada was correct and that the agent in Paris had been working off the old schedule.) An unsettling chain of events unfolded.

They were able to use their tickets to get another train to Milan, but did not make their original connection to Florence because the Lausanne train arrived five minutes late. In Milan, after spending nearly one and a half hours speaking to personnel at three different desks, Robert finally learned (through a half-French, half-Italian exchange) that the choice was to take a train which would arrive at 00:30 hours in Florence or to buy tickets for the next train out of Milan, which was first-class only, but would get them there at 22:00 hours. They chose to take the first-class train and called the pension (hotel) in Florence to say that they would be late. The tickets cost 170 500 lire plus an additional 33 360 lire for the high exchange rate at the train station. The clerk would not refund the tickets bought in Paris because he insisted that there was no error in the system. However, he did stamp the tickets to indicate that they were not used.

The first-class service offered no consolation. The car was filled with fashionably dressed Europeans, many working on lap-top computers and doing business. Two attendants served dinner and generally looked after the passengers. Neither the other passengers nor the attendants seemed particularly pleased at the presence of the family dressed very casually, carrying backpacks and duffel bags, and asking for extra water to quench their thirst. They were hot (from August temperatures in May), tired, and annoyed. As they approached Florence, they realized that the train stopped only at the other end of the city from their pension. They had chosen to stay at that particular pension because it was a short walk from the downtown train station where they were originally supposed to arrive. They managed to find a taxi quite easily, however, and the fare they paid the skillful driver was worth it in comic relief. The three passengers found themselves in a very small automobile travelling at what seemed incredible speed through very narrow streets in a strange city late at night. They were impressed and laughing by the time they reached their pension, where they were greeted as expected guests. After a good night's sleep, they were determined to put the train ordeal behind them and enjoy the rest of the trip—which they did.

THE TRIP REVISITED

When they returned home, they were reminded of the train incident each time they shared the news of their trip with friends and family. As well, the extra expense showed up in accounting for the budget for the trip. The amount was significant to Robert in particular, who looked after the family books. Both Marianne and Robert became increasingly annoyed over time. Although Robert was doubtful that anything would be achieved from such a long distance, Marianne convinced him that they should at least try to appeal for some compensation by writing a letter to the French National Railway. They composed a registered letter (Exhibit 12-1) on July 21, 1993, in English, since it would be too complicated for them to try to explain the situation in French. They felt good about having documented the events as best they could along the way and about stating their case.

EXHIBIT 12-1   Letter to the French National Railway

12 Pinevale Drive
Smalltown, Nova Scotia
Canada B0Z 4X2
July 21, 1993

French National Railway—SNCF
Departement Apres-Vente
10 Place Budapest
Paris, France

Dear Sir or Madam:

On Saturday, May 29, 1993, my wife, my young son, and I made reservations and bought tickets at Gare de Lyon (in Paris) to go from Paris to Florence (Italy) on Monday, May 31. Our trip required that we change trains in Lausanne and Milan.

While waiting for our train in Lausanne, we became alarmed when Train #323 leaving at 12:55 did not appear on the Departure Notice Board. We immediately spoke to a ticket agent and were informed that our train no longer existed, that a new schedule had recently come into effect, and that the train we should have been on had departed Lausanne for Milan at 11:13. The ticket agent told us to take the next train (#327) at 13:32 to arrive in Milan at 17:45. This was a second-class train and reservations were not required. The agent doubted that we would be able to catch Train #541, for which we had reservations, which was leaving Milan for Florence at 17:50. We were told to take Train #511 leaving Milan at 19:40 to arrive in Florence at 22:08 if we missed Train #541.

Unfortunately, Train #327 was late, arriving in Milan at 17:50, and although we tried, it was impossible for us to catch Train #541 for Florence.

The ticket agent we spoke to in Milan stamped our reservation card (Milan to Florence) as not having been used. However, the agent also informed us that Train #511 from Milan to Florence at 19:40 would cost us an additional 170 500 lire. Naturally, we protested, but were forced to pay the additional fee to get to our destination.

The ticket agent at Gare de Lyon made a mistake when he issued our tickets and reservations. This mistake resulted in lost time, a great deal of frustration, and additional costs to us of 170 500 lire. We hold the SNCF responsible and hereby request a refund of our additional costs.

You will find enclosed with this letter photocopies of our tickets, reservations, payment receipt, directions we were given in Lausanne, and our ticket from Milan to Florence with the costs indicated. Should you require the original copies I would be happy to forward them to you.

I look forward to hearing from you.

Sincerely,

Robert S. Dupuis

Robert S. Dupuis

"GREENER PASTURES"

The Launch of StaGreen™ by HydroCan

Anne T. Hale

Stone Age Marketing Consultants was founded five years ago by Cari Clarkstone, Karen Jonestone, and Robert Sommerstone. Their target clients were small, start-up firms as well as medium-sized firms looking to expand operations. Their newest client, HydroCan, had a meeting scheduled for the following afternoon, and the three founders were discussing the results of their market analysis. HydroCan was a start-up company that was obtaining patents in both the US and Canada for a new type of lawn-care product. Since the company was comprised of four agricultural engineers and a financial accountant, they were in need of marketing advice concerning their new product, StaGreen™. This product, when applied to most types of grass, enabled the root system to retain water longer, thus reducing the need for both extra watering as well as frequent fertilizing. They were anxious to take this product to market; however, they desperately needed answers to several questions, including which segment to target, how to position their new product, and what type of launch strategy they should use. They approached Stone Age Marketing Consultants approximately four weeks ago with their needs. The marketing consultants had analyzed the markets, costs, prices, and communications options. Their last task was to formulate a comprehensive strategy for the launch of StaGreen™.

INITIAL MEETING WITH HYDROCAN

During the initial meeting between HydroCan and Stone Age, the engineers outlined the product and its potential benefits. The product was very similar in appearance to most brands of common lawn fertilizer. In fact, StaGreen™ was classified as a chemical fertilizer with one very important difference. Its primary benefit was its effect on the root system of most

---

This case was prepared by Anne T. Hale, Visiting Assistant Professor of Marketing, Faculty of Business, University of Victoria, Victoria, British Columbia, as a basis for class discussion. Copyright ©1996 by Anne T. Hale. Reprinted with permission.

of the common types of grasses used for lawns. The small pellets attached to roots and attracted and retained moisture. Extensive laboratory testing demonstrated that StaGreen™ reduced the need for manual watering on most types of grass by up to 40%. Obviously, such a product would have high demand. The first question that HydroCan needed addressed was what market to target, initially, with this product. Gary Gillis, CEO of HydroCan, wanted to target the consumer lawn and garden market as their initial target segment. Carla Humphreys, on the other hand, was more inclined to target the commercial lawn and garden market. Since these two markets required very different launch strategies, selecting the appropriate segment was the primary concern. And, due to the fact that both Mr. Gillis and Ms. Humphreys were extremely biased towards their position, the consultants knew that they would have to present strong reasons to support their recommendation. To make this task manageable, they divided the research and analysis along the following lines: Cari Clarkstone was to investigate the viability of a consumer launch, Karen Jonestone investigated the viability of a commercial launch, and Robert Sommerstone was to obtain all necessary financial information.

THE CONSUMER MARKET

In 1995, Canadians spent nearly $2.3 billion, at the retail level, on gardening. This figure includes $945 million for grass (both sod and seed), trees, and plants; $620 million on lawn maintenance (with fertilizers accounting for 52% of the total); and $815 million on hand tools, pots, window boxes, books, magazines, landscaping services, etc. In other words, gardening is big business in Canada. Lawn care is, however, a highly seasonal business, with 70% of sales occurring in the 2nd and 3rd fiscal quarters (i.e., April to September).

According to Cari Clarkstone's research, if HydroCan was to target this segment, they would be competing primarily with fertilizers. The consumer fertilizer market is extremely competitive, with the top two firms, Scotts Co. and Ortho Chemicals, controlling approximately 50% of the total consumer market. Both firms are headquartered in the US (with divisional offices in Canada), and both have extensive international operations. The market share leader is Scotts Co., with their two powerful brands, Turf Builder and Miracle-Gro (acquired in May of 1995 from the privately held Stern's Group). Turf Builder is a slow-release fertilizer that reduces the number of applications required for a healthy lawn. This slow-release technology is relatively new—having been available to the consumer market for less than two years. Slow-release simply means that the fertilizing chemicals are released gradually over a number of months. Thus one application of slow-release fertilizer could last for a maximum of two years (although most manufacturers recommend applications every year).

Turf Builder is priced slightly lower than most Miracle-Gro products, which are advertised as maximum growth products, and not specifically (i.e., exclusively) aimed at lawn care. Ortho's products are priced competitively with Turf Builder—their added value comes from the inclusion of pesticides within the fertilizer that prevents most common lawn infestations. See Exhibit 13-1 for pricing information on the major branded fertilizer products.

Market research has shown that four out of ten consumers in this market have no concrete brand preferences. They rely heavily on in-store advertisements and sales staff for information and recommendations. Many consumers cannot recall a brand name or a manufacturer of fertilizer. The product with the highest brand name awareness is Miracle-Gro;

EXHIBIT 13-1 Competitor Prices for the Consumer Market

	Size(s)	Retail Prices(s)
Scotts Turf Builder	10 kg	$24.50
Scotts Turf Builder	25 kg	$59.99
Scotts Turf Builder	5 kg	$14.75
Miracle-Gro—Plant/Crystals	200 grams	$ 8.50
Miracle-Gro—Lawn/Garden	2.5 kg	$12.95
Miracle-Gro—Liquid	1 litre	$ 7.99
Ortho (with pesticide)	10 kg	$23.99
Ortho (with pesticide)	30 kg	$68.79

however, most associate this brand name with their plant foods rather than their lawn fertilizers. Because of consumer behaviour and attitude towards this product category, most manufacturers relied on a strong push strategy.

Most lawn care products are sold by three distinct types of retailers: discount stores, such as Canadian Tire, Wal-Mart, and Sears; specialty stores, including nurseries; and home improvement stores. The discount stores, who buy direct from manufacturers, place strict requirements on their orders and expect price concessions and special support. Marketing expenses for both Scott and Ortho went up by approximately 10% between 1994 and 1995, with the bulk of the increase devoted to promotions to discount retailers. This indicates the relative importance of this channel—it is estimated that 60% of all consumer fertilizer sales are made in discount stores, compared to approximately 30% of sales being made in specialty stores, and 10% of sales being made in home improvement stores. Discount stores have, in fact, been spending millions in renovations in order to accommodate larger lawn and garden areas within their stores. The same is true with home improvement stores, such as Home Depot, which has 21 locations in Canada.[1]

Specialty stores, the vast majority of which are nurseries, tend to be independently owned and thus much more numerous. While the nine top discount chains across Canada control over 89% of all sales from discount stores, the top 50 specialty garden stores account for less than 28% of all sales from this store type. The most recent research indicates that there are over 1000 specialty garden stores in Canada. Most of these stores purchase from large horticulture wholesalers, and receive little, if any, promotional assistance from the major manufacturers. Home improvement stores are growing in numbers, and tend to be large, powerful chains, such as Home Depot. While these stores do not represent a large portion of current sales, they are expected to grow in importance. Like discount stores, home improvement stores buy direct from the manufacturers and require price concessions and promotional support.

The large manufacturers of fertilizer products generally spend approximately 20% of sales on marketing activities. The bulk of this money goes towards the sales force, and selling in general, and trade promotions. Due to the three different channels in which their product is sold, most fertilizer manufacturers recognize the importance of a strong sales force. In terms of trade promotions, they provide in-store literature, displays, and sales training—especially to the large discount stores and the home improvement stores. Less important is advertising. Miracle-Gro is the most heavily advertised brand on the market, and they generally spend 4% of sales on advertising (which probably accounts for the high brand name awareness). Scotts advertises Turf Builder, but only during the early spring when demand for lawn fertilizers is at its peak. Most companies run their advertisements for their existing brands and any new brands they may be launching during the spring and early summer months. Thus, advertising expenditures are generally at their highest in March, April, May, and June, and zero at all other times. Only Miracle-Gro is advertised year-round, with different messages at different times of the year. For example, Miracle-Gro advertises its benefits for house plants during the winter months, and its benefits for fruits, vegetables, and flowers during the spring and summer months.

THE COMMERCIAL MARKET

The commercial market consists primarily of Canada's 1800 golf courses, but also includes commercial properties such as office complexes and apartment buildings. The most lucrative market, however, is golf courses. Currently under fire for being a major source of ground water pollution, due to the high and frequent levels of fertilizers used to keep courses green, most owners are actively looking for ways to cut both water and fertilizer usage. Course owners spend, on average, $300 000 to maintain their golf course during the year, of which 42% represents water usage costs and 24% represents fertilizer purchases. For extremely large, complex courses, this figure can run as high as $800 000, and for smaller inner-city public courses, as low as $104 000. Tests have indicated that StaGreen™ will reduce water usage by one half and fertilizer usage by one third. This is the primary reason why Ms. Humphreys was so adamant that the company select the commercial market as their primary target market.

The game of golf has been enjoying a renewed popularity after a drastic decrease in participation during the 1980s. The growing number of public courses with reasonable fees, the continued aging of the Canadian population, and the development of better equipment have all contributed to this growth in popularity. It is estimated that the number of golf courses will increase by 22% to 2200 by the end of this decade. Most golf courses are independently owned and operated. Only 4% of all courses are owned by a company that owns more than one course. Courses are dispersed throughout Canada, but British Columbia, and Vancouver in particular, boast the highest number of courses.

Currently, golf courses purchase maintenance supplies from wholesalers who specialize in products uniquely designed for the type of grasses used. Manufacturers of these fertilizers tend to be small firms, or divisions of the larger chemical companies. The market share leader in golf course fertilizers is Sierra Horticultural Products, a subsidiary of Scotts Co. Scotts purchased Sierra in 1993 and it represents only about 2.2% of Scotts total sales. Their biggest competitor in Canada is Nu-Gro Corporation—an Ontario-based horticultural products company founded in 1992. Unlike the firms competing in the consumer lawn maintenance market, these firms spend only about 9% of sales on marketing activities. These firms engage in little advertising, preferring to spend their marketing funds on sales calls to golf courses. They provide free samples of their products to non-users and try to build solid, long-lasting relationships with course owners. They know that it takes a tremendous selling effort to get a golf course owner to switch brands. If satisfied with their current brand, many course owners are unwilling to risk switching to a new product that may not perform as well. Since the condition of the course is the most important attribute in a consumer's selection of a course to play, course owners tend to be highly brand-loyal.

Course owners, however, have two overriding concerns. The first problem concerns the growing public debate on the ground water pollution caused by golf courses. Heavy use of fertilizers and constant manual watering results in a chemical buildup in nearby reservoirs. In fact, according to the US Environmental Protection Agency, golf courses are the major source of ground water pollution in the United States. More and more negative publicity, in the form of newspaper and magazine articles, has resulted in golf course developers being denied permits to construct new courses. Thus, addressing the issue of ground water pollution is a major concern with course owners.

Their second problem is that of shrinking profits. While golf is growing in popularity, and more courses are being built to accommodate demand, the actual number of golfers that can be accommodated on any one course cannot be expanded. With some courses engaging in green-fees price wars, profit margins for many of the public courses have become strained. Thus, while loyalty may play a role in fertilizer purchases, these difficult problems will also influence purchase behaviour.

Estimated to be about one eighth the size of the golf course market is the balance of the commercial lawn care market, consisting of apartment and office complexes. Their needs are much less complex than golf courses, resulting in purchasing behaviour that mirrors that of the consumer market. Little concrete information is available concerning the number of office complexes and apartment buildings, although estimates have put the total figure around 2900, of which 16.5% represent multiple holdings by one corporation. These commercial real estate property firms spend a disproportionate amount on lawn maintenance—they account for nearly 26% of the total dollars spent in this sector of the commercial maintenance market. This sector of the commercial market tends to purchase in bulk through wholesalers—generally the same wholesalers who service the specialty stores in the consumer market.

HYDROCAN

HydroCan was incorporated nearly one year ago. They have leased their production facilities, and have purchased and/or leased all of the equipment and machinery necessary for use in the production of StaGreen™. Their production facility has the capacity to produce 180 000 kilograms of StaGreen™ per month. The owners of HydroCan have suggested a quality/value-added pricing strategy. They believe that they have a superior product that will save the end user both time and money, due to the reduced need for fertilizer products and reduced need for manual watering. The founders of HydroCan outlined their ideas for the launch year marketing strategy for both the consumer and the commercial lawn-care markets.

If HydroCan elects to target the consumer market, they will package StaGreen™ in a 10 kilogram bag, which market research indicates was the most popular size with consumers. They will set their price to trade (i.e., wholesalers and retailers) at $22.50, with their variable costs representing 52% of sales. On average, the large discount stores and home improvement stores take a 25% markup on lawn maintenance products. The smaller specialty stores take a larger markup of $35%. Wholesalers (if used) take a 15% markup. Fixed production costs include $700 000 in annual rental (for the site and the equipment), general and administrative expenses of $80 200, research and development expenses of $20 650, and miscellaneous expenses of $12 350. Distribution costs (including freight, warehousing, and storage) represented a significant yearly expense due to the seasonal nature of demand. Production of StaGreen™ would be continuous year round; however, sales would be highly concentrated in the months of April through September. This means that the company would have relatively high distribution costs, estimated to be $426 000 per year. Not yet included in any of their financial statements are the salaries for the four founding partners of HydroCan. They would like to earn $50 000 per year (each), but are willing to forego their salary in the launch year.

Their marketing budget has been set at $ $555 000, and HydroCan has suggested this amount be allocated to the various tasks, as shown in Exhibit 13-2. Seasonal discounts are price discounts offered to retailers and wholesalers as an incentive to purchase well in advance of the peak selling season. HydroCan plans to offer these discounts, estimated to be 20% off the trade price for each bag purchased, to wholesalers and retailers in the months of November and December as a method to reduce warehouse and storage costs. The displays will cost approximately $250 each (which includes promotional materials, such as brochures), and will be furnished to discount stores, home improvement stores, and as many nurseries as possible. The sweepstakes is used to increase awareness and interest in StaGreen™. Consumers will have the chance to win several valuable prizes, including a year of free lawn maintenance, lawn and garden equipment and supplies, and other related prizes.

In terms of the sales force, HydroCan has planned on hiring 20 sales reps at an average cost of $25 000 per rep (salary and commission). The sales reps will be responsible for selling the product to the various channels, as well as offering sales training seminars.

If HydroCan elects to target the commercial market, then the size of the product will be increased to a 50 kilogram bag, which they will sell to wholesalers or end users at a price of $150.00. Because they would be charging a slightly higher price under this option, variable costs as a percentage of sales drop to 40%, resulting in a relatively high contribution margin of 60% of sales. Wholesalers, who generally sell directly to the commercial users take a 15% markup. Fixed expenses will remain nearly the same as for the consumer market option, with the exception of marketing and distribution costs. None of the promotional activities, such as displays, seasonal discounts, sweepstakes, or advertising, will be used in the commercial market. Instead, the size of the sales force will be increased to 30 to handle the lengthy sales calls necessary to golf courses. In addition, $100 000 has been set aside for free samples to be distributed to potential customers by the sales force. Finally, distribution costs decrease if the commercial market is chosen because demand tends to be slightly less seasonal. Thus costs for freight, warehousing, and storage decrease to $225 000 under this option.

EXHIBIT 13-2 Allocation of Marketing Budget for Consumer Market Launch

Marketing Task	Total Expenditure (Estimates)
Seasonal Discounts	$225 000
In-Store Displays	$ 92 000
Magazine Advertising	$104 000
Newspaper Advertising	$ 84 000
Sweepstakes	$ 50 000

THE DECISION

The three founding partners of Stone Age Marketing Consultants were in the conference room discussing the results of their research and analysis. As Karen Jonestone pointed out, "A strong case can be made for both target markets! Each has its own advantages and limitations." Rob Sommerstone countered with the fact that HydroCan was a start-up business. "Their financial resources are extremely limited right now. They cannot increase their production capacity for at least two years, and if they hope to acquire expansion capital to increase their total capacity, they need to show a profit as early as possible." Cari Clarkstone was considering a more creative solution—targeting selected parts of either or both the consumer and commercial markets. Before the group could begin to assess the viability of HydroCan and its product, StaGreen™, they had to decide on which market to target, how to position StaGreen™ in that target market, and then they had to develop a viable marketing strategy for the launch year. The final pressure for the group was the fact that HydroCan needed to launch in February—just prior to the peak selling season—thus the consultants knew there was no time to acquire additional market research. The decision had to be based on the information at hand.

ENDNOTE

1. Source: *Maclean's*, Volume 109, April 22, 1996, pages 62–63.

DEPARTMENT

OF HEALTH

James Agarwal and Dorothee Feils

Canada's health care system is well known for its high quality and universal access. The health care system has traditionally been funded by the federal and provincial governments. However, rising health care costs and budgetary constraints at the federal as well as the provincial level have led health care providers to look for non-government-based supplementary financing. According to Health Canada figures, in 1994, total health expenditures in Canada amounted to 9.7% of the Gross Domestic Product ($72.5 billion), down from 10.1% in 1992 and 1993. Of this amount, 37.3% was spent on hospitals, 14.2% on physicians, 12.7% on drugs, and the remainder on other institutions and medical professionals. Drugs represented the fastest growing category of health care expenditures, growing at 3.8% in 1994. Similar growth rates are predicted for the future.

Joan Smith, Vice President, International Marketing Division, at the Department of Health,[1] has identified a comprehensive set of different health administrative databases (hereon referred to as health database) collected over the years by her organization as one promising alternative source of funding. Joan has been in this department for about two years and has already earned a reputation of being a talented, dynamic, and creative visionary. Trained as a computer scientist, she has a flair for clear and logical thinking and is a fairly quick decision-maker. She also has an innovative entrepreneurial spirit of trying new concepts and methods. Joan sees a tremendous potential in the health database and compares it to a "gold mine." At the same time, there are several ethical and distribution-related challenges in the marketing of health data that she must successfully address.

Currently, parts of the health database are made available to select clients for medical research projects on a cost-recovery basis. The North American health data industry has an

The authors of this case are James Agarwal and Dorothee Feils, Faculty of Administration, University of Regina, Regina, Saskatchewan, S4S 0A2. Please direct all correspondence to James Agarwal. Reprinted with permission.

ample supply of usable health data. However, much of this data has not been organized or promoted for marketing. The demand for health data has increased as regulatory bodies have demanded more rigorous and systematic methods of assessing safety and cost-effectiveness in the areas of drug utilization and drug efficacy. There is, therefore, a critical need to effectively customize and market health data to suit individual clients' needs. While many clients desire raw data sets, others require aggregate data sets or research projects. In order to determine the appropriateness of the product, Joan examines the strengths of the database as compared to competing databases.

THE HEALTH DATABASE

The Department of Health has collected a comprehensive health database for the entire population of the province including, but not limited to, information on health insurance registration, outpatient prescription drug data, physician services data, hospital separation data, and vital statistics data. The data have been collected since the 1970s for a defined geo-political population. Thus, the database provides an excellent source of information for medical and pharmaceutical research. The database is considered to be one of the best in the world in terms of its coverage, representativeness, longitudinal tenure, stability, validity, drug exposure, and diagnostic information.

It is one of the few databases in the world that is population-based and contains drug and diagnostic information. Other databases in this category are mostly American-based and collected by the government, such as the Medicaid database, or by private health maintenance organizations (HMOs). The benefits of the Department of Health's database are obvious when compared with these competing databases. For example, the information collected by Medicaid does not represent a cross-section of the population. Medicaid is available only to people who cannot afford health care. This is important for medical research, since a link between income and health has been established. Also, the Medicaid database is not well suited for long-term studies, since many people are on Medicaid only for a short time period (they no longer qualify once they find a job). Although the Department of Health's database has a good reputation, market research indicates that clients would prefer the linking of the existing database to external databases such as Statistics Canada, demographic and lifestyle databases, and survey data on health status and health determinants.

CURRENT MARKET

The health database is used for medical research in several areas, including drug utilization and drug safety studies, epidemiological studies, and pharmaco-economics. Clients putting forth research proposals come from academic institutions, the pharmaceutical industry, private consultancy firms, and other governments. Major dollar volume comes from international pharmaceutical firms, albeit often indirectly through collaboration with the universities. In the past, demand for the health data has also come from federal governments nationally and internationally.

Joan Smith foresees an increase in demand for medical research by pharmaceutical firms in general and in the area of pharmaco-economics in particular. Pharmaco-economic studies examine the economic efficiency of drugs. Given the concern of health care providers and payers (government) with rising health care costs, they want the pharmaceutical firms to show that new drugs are more cost-efficient than existing drugs. For example, if a new drug costs more than an old drug, but reduces the time patients stay in the hospital, then it might be considered superior from a pharmaco-economic standpoint.

ETHICAL ISSUES

While Joan realizes that the database is unique and that there is demand for the database, there are several challenges in the marketing of health data products that she has to consider. In deciding which customers to pursue, ethical considerations are very important. For example, while marketing health data to medical researchers might create a positive outcome to society, marketing the same to life insurance firms could be a violation of human rights and provide a potential for abuse of personal information. Insurance companies could start discriminatory practices of differential premium rates based on medical information. Ethical factors should therefore be taken into consideration in determining the market boundaries.

Another ethical dilemma is the issue of ownership of the data. Who owns the data? The current practice with respect to data ownership is based on the common-law tradition that states that persons or organizations lawfully collecting information own the information. As such, the Department can sell the data provided certain conditions, such as informed consent and confidentiality, are met. However, there are mixed opinions on this issue and the matter is subject to debate. For example, Sweden maintains that the health data are owned by the people and thus the government cannot sell the data to any outside entity. If the people own the database, should their consent be taken before marketing it to potential researchers?

The Freedom of Information and Protection of Privacy Act stipulates that if a government institution collects personal information that is required to be collected directly from an individual, it shall inform the individual of the purpose for which the information is collected. Should the Department have to inform the individual about the additional uses of the information collected? Is this consent required if the individual's identity is not revealed? These questions are crucial for the marketability of the database, since the original data were collected for administrative purposes and not for medical or other research.

In dealing with health data, confidentiality becomes a sensitive ethical issue. The Privacy Act stipulates that personal information under the control of the government institution may be disclosed to any person or body for statistical and research purposes only when the government institution is satisfied that the objectives of the researcher cannot reasonably be accomplished without such information. In such cases, a written undertaking is obtained from the researcher stating that no disclosure will be made in a way that identifies the individual to whom it relates. In order to understand the confidentiality issue better, Joan checked with the confidentiality policy of Statistics Canada. Any information collected by Statistics Canada is also subject to the Statistics Act, which guarantees the confidentiality of the information collected. In practice, interviewers working for Statistics Canada have to pledge an oath of secrecy. Any violations of this oath are subject to prosecution. The information collected by Statistics Canada is then released only at the aggregate level, which insures confidentiality of information.

Joan believes that at the minimum, names and identification numbers of patients and physicians must be deleted from the database before it is made available to clients. However, even this precaution may not be sufficient if subsets of the database are so small that individuals could be identified. The more information is deleted from the database, the less valuable is the database to researchers.

One of Joan's colleagues, Pat Hodges, was also very concerned about the integrity of the data analysis by outside researchers. She feels that if researchers did poor research, the database's reputation would be compromised. In particular, if the data were used for a second research project that had not been approved by the Department of Health, potential problems with the integrity of the data analysis could arise.

Overall, Joan is convinced that the key to this problem is in striking a balance between protecting ethical standards and achieving research and commercial marketability. On one hand, researchers should be trusted and provided with ideal data sets for scientific progress. On the other hand, confidentiality and the integrity of data has to be preserved as well. One researcher client thinks "that the amount and depth of the information held by financial institutions and credit card companies is more than that held in the health database." Other researchers concede that confidentiality needs to be preserved and are willing to do with fewer data items in the database.

PRODUCT LINES

Joan has identified three different products that could be sold by the Department of Health. These products are raw data sets, aggregate data sets, and research projects.

First of all, the raw data sets could be made available for a fee. Most researchers would prefer raw data since they provide them with more flexibility and control in analyzing the data. Furthermore, raw data sets can be more easily provided by the Department of Health and therefore are cheaper. However, Joan needs to address two major concerns regarding the sale of raw data sets: the confidentiality of patient and physician information and the integrity of the data analysis.

As a second alternative, the Department of Health could sell data at an aggregate level, thereby insuring confidentiality. Aggregated data means that only summarized statistics pertaining to the population would be available to the clients, similar to aggregated economic indicators. However, the higher the level of aggregation of the data, the less useful the health data product would be for the individual researcher. Most researchers require very specific information that is more often than not lost when the data are aggregated. This dramatically reduces the researcher's flexibility to perform meaningful research. Past research indicates that the market for aggregated data has been rather limited.

Finally, research products could also be marketed by the Department of Health. Research products encompass the entire stages of the research project: from proposal development to research design to data analysis to report preparation and presentation. The client provides the terms of reference for a research project and the Department of Health delivers the research report complete with results, conclusions, and recommendations. This product would make it easy to ensure confidentiality, since the client would never see the raw data set and thus it would be easy for the Department of Health to ensure that no individual patient or physician could be identified. In addition, the Department of Health would control the data analysis and thus ensure its integrity. Two potential drawbacks from the clients' perspective of this health data product are the higher cost and the reduced flexibility and speed of the data analysis.

Therefore, the Department of Health could provide the database as raw data sets, aggregate data sets, or as completed research products.

DISTRIBUTION ALTERNATIVES

Another major issue to address is the best way of distributing the health data products. The traditional means of distribution has been through computer tapes and, more recently, CD-ROMs. Clients would request a specific raw data set, which the Department of Health would retrieve from the mainframe and store on the computer tape/CD-ROM. The tape/CD-ROM is then sent to the client. Thus, the client has to be very clear about the data needs, since it would be very expensive to retrieve additional data items from the database. There is an unavoidable time delay between order and delivery of the data products. CD-ROM is also highly suitable if the database contains standardized information that will be used by all clients. Despite the ethical concerns, Joan envisions some aggregate data sets that could be distributed via CD-ROM without compromising confidentiality.

If complete research projects are requested by clients, the Department of Health could then use in-house research consultants and deliver a "value-added" product. If the complexity of the project proposal increases, they could contract out to a third party. The third party can be an independent research consultant with expertise in medical research or a medical research team at an established university. The value-added product is then distributed via tape, CD-ROM, or hard copy, depending on the client's needs.

Meanwhile, Joan has been seriously thinking of another distribution method. She recently attended an Internet conference held in Vancouver and is convinced about its potential in marketing health data products. In Canada more and more firms are using the Internet as a source of data transmission, knowledge networking, information sharing, marketing, and advertising. In addition, there is networking in research, academic, and government circles. Back from her trip, Joan did some personal research and pulled out some vital information about the Internet and its potential for distribution of health data products.

THE INTERNET—THE FUTURE CHANNEL

The Internet is currently made up of 45 000 networks worldwide. Here are some interesting recent trends and statistics: the growth rate of Internet is estimated to be about 10 percent a month, and the World Wide Web could triple its size in one year. There are currently over 30 million people worldwide with some Internet connectivity. In the United States, the commercial domain forms about 65.2% of the all the Internet users, followed by the government (16.7%), organizations (8.0%), and education (7.1%). The domain distribution, however, keeps changing due to rapid growth.

Joan is excited about setting up a permanent node with a domain name including linkages to FTP (File Transfer Protocol), Telnet, Gopher, and Usenet via popular Web browsers. An online home page would have a menu of health data products and services being offered by the Department of Health. The Web pages would offer an assortment of informational files about the products/services and related subjects. Product description, pricing, and purchase information will also be included. Online order forms will allow customers to submit orders and also to provide feedback and comments. Periodical online market research could also be done effectively to better satisfy the customers. A sample of a server-based database would be offered to ease the search process of potential customers. However, Joan remarks with caution, "while marketing can be accomplished by making your Web site visible, advertising and unsolicited e-mails and postings can be very detrimental for business."

There is, however, something that concerns Joan and her marketing staff. It is the security issue. From the customers' point of view, how will customers be assured of the authenticity of the data, people, products, and the transaction in general? How can customers use credit cards for payment on the Internet? Joan believes that the monetary transactions can be solved by making offline arrangements or using secure HTTP (HyperText Transfer Protocol). Secure HTTP offers secure transactions between the user and the server when in a data-entry form. The user can click a secure submission button and the client program will generate a secure key during that session. According to reports, there are other secure transaction systems already developed, such as NetCash, DigiCash, etc. Joan reaffirms that many organizations are working on digital copyright systems using encryption to safeguard documents.

Joan is faced with the challenging task of convincing the board of directors at the Department of Health to use the Internet to promote and distribute its products. She is convinced that marketing health data products on the Internet is clearly the way of the future. This new distribution technology will connect her globally and she can attract clients from all over the world. She enthusiastically comments, "What could be a faster way to go global than the Internet?" As optimistic as she is, she fears that the board members will consider these ideas as quite revolutionary, unorthodox, and even controversial. She is faced with the enormous task of cogently addressing this complex decision. Traditionally, she would have had to deal with complex issues of confidentiality, data integrity, and other ethical aspects in marketing health data products. And now comes along the additional challenge of convincing the board to use the Internet to distribute the health data product.

ENDNOTE

1. We refer to the Department of Health at the provincial level as the concerned organization. The names of the organization and the vice-president have been disguised for reasons of confidentiality.

RESTORED VISION INC.

Brock Smith

INTRODUCTION

Restored Vision Inc. is a clinic for refractive eye surgery that is operated by a group of four doctors in Vancouver, British Columbia. We have been open for business since March of 1995 but this type of surgery has been performed in Canada since 1990. It has only recently been given approval in the United States. The surgery uses a laser to reshape the cornea of the eye, restoring vision, and freeing people from the confines of their glasses or contact lenses. Between March 1995 and January 1996, we did approximately 250 laser procedures. Unfortunately, our monthly revenues have only just begun to match our expenses. We need some help developing a marketing plan to reach our goal of 60 treatments per month in our third year.

COMPANY HISTORY

In 1990, when excimer Photorefractive Keratectomy (PRK) laser eye surgery first became available in Canada, two of us initially became interested in the procedure. Rather than jumping into the market with an unproven product, we waited until there was a sufficient track record to assess the different laser technologies and the risks to our patients. In 1994, after conducting an initial business analysis, we invited two additional surgeons to join the group and Restored Vision was formed. Our group shares a common style of practice and is dedicated to quality patient care. Each of us runs our own private ophthalmology practice and works from one-half to two days a week in the clinic.

The first key decision we had to make was which of the various laser technologies to adopt. There are about fifty different makes of excimer laser machines. Visx is a brand adopted by many of the early entrants in North America. It uses a pulsing beam that shines down on the cornea and uncouples a layer of corneal tissue with each pulse. While this process is very precise and can produce good results in the low ranges of shortsightedness, it does not do farsightedness or astigmatism very well. It can also produce a side effect called "Central Islands" where fluid builds up in the centre of the cornea, causing distorted vision.

We chose a new European technology that uses a scanning beam to uncouple corneal tissue. This process distributes the beam more smoothly and evenly across the surface of the cornea, cutting down the amount of haze on the cornea. It produces a better visual outcome and seems to eliminate the "Central Islands" problem. This machine is more expensive than those using the pulse technology but it handled farsightedness and astigmatism. It also had a better maintenance record.

The price of the excimer laser scanner was about $800 000. However, we took a lease agreement where we pay $1000 to the manufacturer for each operation. We have a nominal buy-out option after 900 cases. We decided to lease our machine so we could change models when new technology became available. Some of our competitors will be hesitant to adopt new technology as they will still be paying off their first machines and these will have little resale value.

We then turned our attention to finding rental space for our office. We chose a location on a major transit route in downtown Vancouver. We have about 1600 square feet that is set up for consultation rooms, an examining room, a technical room, and a laser room. We have got a nice reception area and a very friendly receptionist. One of the doctors had a flair for office decorating and we spent about $14 000 in furnishings and fixtures (see the income statement and balance sheet in Exhibits 15-1 and 15-2).

It became apparent that none of the doctors had time to manage the business, so we hired an office manager and contracted a freelance marketing consultant. Neither of these people worked out and our anticipated opening date was delayed by a month. We hired a new office manager and an advertising agency, and finally opened our doors to the public in March of 1995.

ISSUES

As with any new company, we experienced our fair share of problems. We got off to a bad start by having to delay our opening by a month. We have also found that patient consultations, which normally took fifteen to twenty minutes in our regular practices, took up to an hour, due to the newness of the excimer laser treatment.

In the beginning, we tried to make all important business decisions by consensus. This did not work very well. To streamline the decision-making process, a subcommittee of two officers was formed and tasks were allocated more efficiently. This has cut down the amount of time we spend running the business but it still takes five to eight hours a week for the officers.

Another problem we still face is our lack of sales experience. Although we have taken a sales training seminar with Dale Carnegie, we still feel somewhat uncomfortable with selling a medical service. Up until very recently it has been illegal for doctors to advertise

EXHIBIT 15-1 Income Statement

	Restored Vision Inc. Income Statement[1]	
	Jan. 1–Dec. 31 1995	Forecast[2] Jan. 1996
Revenue[3]		
Revenue—Principal Doctors	$447 000.00	
Revenue—Assoc. Doctors	32 200.00	
Interest Income	1 300.00	
Total Revenue	$480 500.00	$88 000.00
Expenses		
Laser Rental	250 000.00	40 000.00
Office Rent	40 000.00	3 330.00
Telephone	6 000.00	280.00
Other Overhead	25 000.00	950.00
Medical/Pharmacy	15 700.00	750.00
Fees—Associates	11 805.00	2 800.00
Fees—Principals[4]	79 800.00	25 200.00
Equipment Lease	13 600.00	1 220.00
Insurance	1 233.00	70.00
Wages & Benefits	60 000.00	5 750.00
Marketing/Advertising	77 200.00	7 200.00
Travel	2 000.00	200.00
Legal/Accounting	14 400.00	450.00
Total Expenses	$596 738.00	$88 200.00
Net Income Before Taxes	($116 238.00)	($200.00)

1. Numbers in this exhibit have been disguised to protect confidentiality.
2. Based on 40 treatments per month.
3. Revenues reflect charges to clients for 250 treatments (10 months).
4. Fees ranged from $150 to $800 during startup.

in Canada. It is still considered "unprofessional" in some circles, so we must always be conscious of what the public and the College of Physicians and Surgeons might think. Consequently, we tend to undersell our services for fear of ethical and professional backlash.

Recently, we have faced additional issues. One such issue is budgeting, specifically for marketing. Initially, Restored Vision started off small, but due to high levels of spending by our competition, we have had to double our expenditures. In addition, with four doctors and one examining room, we are realizing that we need additional space or at least another set of examining equipment so patients do not have to wait very long for a consultation.

EXHIBIT 15-2 Balance Sheet

Restored Vision Inc.
Balance Sheet[1]
As at Dec. 31 1995

Assets		Liabilities & Equity	
Current Assets		Current Liabilities	
Cash	113 692.78	Accounts Payable	110 520.00
Accounts Receivable	44 851.21	WCB Payable	136.80
Prepaid Expenses	4 608.97		
Total Current Assets	163 152.96	Total Current Liabilities	110 656.80
Fixed Assets		Loans from Principals	200 000.00
Furniture & Fixture	14 403.31		
Equipment	5 652.31	Share Capital	65.59
Leasehold Improvement	4 044.31		
Computer Equipment	1 141.53	Retained Earnings	(6 089.97)
Total Fixed Assets	25 241.46	Current Earnings	(116 238.00)
Total Assets	$188 394.42	Total Liabilities & Equity	$188 394.42

1. Numbers in this exhibit have been disguised to protect confidentiality.

The business has also been stressful. Each of the doctors invested $50 000 to start the business, and operating expenses are divided among us. Our growing pains have been expensive; for example, we spent $5000 with our first marketing consultant and ended up with a logo we never used. We got off to a slow start and the bills have been piling up. Some of us are still putting $2000 more a month into the business than we are taking out. Some of the doctors are working harder than others to make the business a success and that has also created some tension in the group. We have tried to put some incentives in place to reward the people who put in more effort.

We did not get into the business to make a great profit. We wanted a way to be involved in this leading-edge technology and provide a quality service to our patients, while maintaining our general practices. The government has no plans to fund this procedure and the universities do not have the budget. We saw an opportunity to provide a community resource where other physicians could service their patients and pay us a facility fee. Hence, our goal is to have as many people as possible involved with the centre, making it easier for us to make a profit without having to do all of the treatments and cover all the overhead ourselves. Our competitors have taken a different approach. They have full-time corrective laser surgery practices. Still, we would like to recover our investment soon.

CURRENT STRATEGY

Our mission is to provide quality facilities, technical procedures, and personal services for conducting refractive laser (PRK) eye surgery. We service the general public of the Pacific Northwest and the community of ophthalmologists who would like to learn to apply these procedures to their own patients.

Our goals are to operate a profitable business and maintain a reputation of excellence. We want to be the excimer laser clinic of choice for British Columbia because of our reputation among clients for exceptional customer service and our reputation among health care professionals for excellence in treatment standards.

Our specific business objectives are:

1. Evoke the laser equipment buy-out option by the end of year 3.
2. Hold shareholder loans to $50 000 with pay-back in year 3.
3. Average 60 treatments per month in year 3.

Restored Vision differentiates itself from the competition primarily in two ways: quality of service and superior technology. First, we are positioning ourselves as the clinic with the highest quality of service. We have four experienced ophthalmologists with university affiliation operating the business who have numerous years of individual practice. Where our competitors rely a great deal upon technical help and non-medical optometric personnel, we offer a high degree of doctor–patient interaction, greater security, and a higher quality of personalized care. Our state-of-the-art laser allows us to provide a broader range of treatments than our competitors, and we achieve excellent visual outcomes.

PRODUCT STRATEGY

We offer a full-service package. This includes the pre-treatment consultation with the doctor, computerized eye measurement, the laser treatment itself, eye drops, sunglasses, and ten to fourteen follow-up visits. Our service also includes re-treatments for the two to four percent of cases that require it to get the best result.

After the pre-treatment consultation, the procedure can be done in an hour. The patient comes in, we put anesthetic drops in the eye being treated, wait half an hour, do ten to fifteen minutes of preparation in the laser room, and then do the treatment. The treatment itself takes three minutes or less. The laser is programmed to eliminate the patient's refractive error. It removes a minute layer from the surface of the cornea, less than the width of a human hair, until the correct shape for the cornea is obtained. We then put a protective contact lens on the eye, give the patient sunglasses to wear when outdoors, and instruct them on how to apply the eye drops they need to apply at home.

The patient comes back for a check-up the next day and every two or three days for a week or two after that. After about five days, we take out the protective contact lens. Sometimes the patient's vision is blurry for the first week. After about two weeks, the patient's vision should be very good. We give out our home phone numbers and patients can call us any time they think there is a problem. Our competitors do not provide this level of service.

Of the half million eyes that have been treated worldwide, there have only been about ten serious problems where a corneal transplant has been needed. While this is significant to those few people, the percentage risk is low. Less than one percent of patients experience corneal hazing and end up having poorer vision with their glasses than they had before. Everyone experiences better vision without their glasses than they had before. We cannot guarantee 20/20 vision, but worldwide success rates (at least 20/40 vision) have been in the 96% range. This means that most clients will be able to see, at least 20 feet away without their glasses, as well as perfectly sighted people can see 40 feet away.

PRICING STRATEGY

Price is an important consideration during the decision-making process; it is often the first question asked by prospective clients. As a "special" promotion during the first month, we charged $1500 per eye. Then we went with $2400 per eye, which was $100 more than our competitors. We found that clients were coming to us for the advice, then going to the competition to save the $100. So after a few months, we dropped our price to $2200. We hoped this strategy would help increase volume and broaden word-of-mouth referrals. Clients seem to find it hard to evaluate our services and perceive little differentiation. We have a flexible pricing policy for family and friends of the doctors (typically $1650 per procedure). This discount comes out of the doctor's fee (usually $700) and not the contribution to the clinic ($500).

COMMUNICATION STRATEGY

A new advertising agency took over our account in May of 1995. In June, and through the summer months, we focused on mass-market print advertising (ads) running two campaigns: "Throwing Away Your Glasses" and "You Do Have a Choice." Both were awareness campaigns that promoted the immediate benefit of laser eye surgery. Summer ads made reference to the freedom of not having glasses while "in the water, on the courts, or cruising the beach." These campaigns were placed in all the municipalities making up the greater Vancouver region.

In August, and continuing through the fall, we ran a transit campaign called "20/20" which consisted of an overhead ad and threefold brochures for take-away. This was run on Vancouver's SkyTrain system because of rider demographics: business commuters, aged 25–55, with medium to high disposable incomes; and tourists, primarily from the United States.

At the same time, we selectively placed Restored Vision brochures into fitness centres. We also placed a print ad "Eye Can See Clearly Now" in *Whistler* magazine, which targets ski enthusiasts, particularly those visiting from the US. We also targeted magazines which featured refractive laser eye surgery articles.

In the fall, we developed a more informational ad "Goodbye Glasses" and a decision-evoking ad "To Be the Best." The placement schedule was designed so that awareness ads were followed three weeks later by informational ads, and the decision-evoking ads followed three weeks after that. We have tried to assess the effectiveness of these advertisements by tracking calls and treatments (see Exhibit 15-3).

PERFORMANCE

In 1995, we lost $116 238 (see Exhibits 15-1 and 15-2). However, our revenues only reflect ten months of operation, while the expenses reflect the full year. Our forecast for January 1996 suggests that we will almost break even (on a monthly basis) and we expect to show a modest profit in 1996.

OUR CUSTOMERS

Our target market includes those people currently using corrective vision devices such as glasses and contact lenses (about 30% of the population). Originally we thought we would attract the white-collar professional crowd that has more discretionary income. Most of our clients have

EXHIBIT 15-3 Advertising Effectiveness

**Restored Vision
Advertising Tracking
June to December 1995**

	% of total calls	% of total budget	% of total consults	Treatments
Print				
daily print media	20.0%	24.0%	18.0%	
urban print media	15.0%	18.0%	11.5%	
community media	18.0%	12.0%	20.0%	
Specialized	12.0%	17.0%	11.0%	
Radio	15.0%	14.0%	23.0%	
SkyTrain	8.0%	12.0%	6.0%	
Phone book	5.0%	0.1%	4.5%	
Word of mouth	7.0%	0.0%	4.0%	
Other	0.0%	3.0%	2.0%	
Total	100.0%	100.0%	100.0%	
Marketing Generated Totals	946.0	$62 500.00	224.0	130.0
Privately Solicited Totals			113.0	120.0

Notes: Treatments can exceed consults since two eyes are usually treated with one client. Numbers in this exhibit have been disguised to protect confidentiality.

been blue-collar workers with more modest incomes. About 53% of the people we have treated are male, 50% live in Vancouver, 45% live in the Vancouver region, and 5% are from out of town. About 75% of clients are aged 26–55. Some of the benefits they might seek are:

- freedom from the hassle of glasses or contact lenses
- greater ability to participate in, or enjoy, recreational sports
- a more natural appearance without glasses
- engage in careers/activities where glasses are prohibited or inconvenient
- improving night vision
- avoiding the cost of maintenance of correctional devices
- wanting to improve self-esteem and attractiveness

Refractive surgery is limited to those clients who:

- are 18–70 years of age
- have had stable vision for one year
- have no complicating injuries/diseases

- are not pregnant or nursing
- are comfortable with the risks
- have eyes in a correctable range of vision (90% of the population)
- are prepared to pay the full cost of the elective surgery

A summation of our targeted customers follows.

British Columbia

The market for patients in British Columbia is shown in the table below:

Greater Vancouver Region   1.7 million people

- extremely active
- recreation oriented
- health and fitness conscious
- relaxed, carefree attitudes
- not very conservative

British Columbia   3.4 million people

Populations with Incomes above $25 000 (in thousands)

Age	Male	Female
25–34	274	128
35–44	444	195
45–54	366	151
55–64	205	66

Pacific Northwest

Up until very recently (1996), the refractive laser eye surgery procedure had not been approved in the United States. Consequently, American ophthalmologists have not had the same level of experience with the procedure as Canadians. With a 30% exchange rate working in our favour, we expect many Americans to elect doing this surgery in Canada.

OUR ENVIRONMENT

There are three other groups who are in direct competition with us. One such group, the Downtown Laser Centre, is located quite near us and is run by two ophthalmologists who have also retained their own ophthalmology practices. The Laser Centre has been in business for the last four years and has generated up to 40% of their business from the United States. They have performed about 500 procedures to date, and charge $2400 per eye. We estimate their gross revenues per year at over $300 000. One source of their referrals is an optometry clinic in Delta, BC, 20 minutes from Vancouver. They have used testimonials in local newspapers to their advantage and have a professional-looking information package to distribute.

Their laser equipment allows them to treat common refractive problems (myopia and astigmatism) but not other problems that are less common.

A third doctor recently separated from the Downtown Laser Centre and set up shop two blocks from us. This ophthalmologist is focusing his marketing in Asia. We do not know how well he has been doing.

A third clinic, the Vancouver Eye Surgery Centre, is located 30 minutes south of Vancouver. It is operated by an ophthalmologist who is considered a pioneer of this procedure. This doctor and his associates have been in business for four years and practise refractive surgery on a full-time basis. The Vancouver Eye Surgery Centre has been using television, radio, and print advertising to actively market their services in British Columbia and the United States. They have also been running a 30-minute info-commercial, but we do not know the reach or frequency. This group conducts seminars throughout BC and has an information package that includes a video. This group did about 2000 procedures this year (at $2275) and have done more than 5000 to date. Their laser technology allows them to treat myopia, astigmatism, and low degrees of hyperopia.

In addition to these clinics, there are competitors in Kelowna (400 miles northeast of Vancouver) and Victoria (30 miles west of Vancouver, on Vancouver Island). We expect two more clinics to open in the Vancouver area in the next year or two. We also expect a bit of a shake-out in the industry, with some clinics being taken over by large multinational health organizations.

Finally, industry observers are predicting continued acceptance, growth, and prominence of laser refractive surgery in the coming years. The safety, predictability, and superior visual correction that the technology offers will be the keys to long-term success. We expect a steady growth of refractive laser surgery in the 10–15% per year range. Some industry forecasters predict a day when glasses will no longer be worn. Advances in excimer laser technology are also expected. As the industry matures, we expect a proliferation of vendors, new product features, and lower costs to clinics such as ours.

POLITICAL CLIMATE

Our company is concerned with two major stakeholders in the macro-environment: The BC College of Physicians and Surgeons, and the general public. The College of Physicians and Surgeons self-governs the practice of medicine in British Columbia and acts as a consumer watchdog to ensure the quality of medical care in the province. Until very recently, doctors have been forbidden to advertise their services. Although the College has relaxed this rule, there is still a sentiment among our colleagues, and the general public, that it is not appropriate to aggressively promote elective surgery. Our facility is approved by the College of Physicians and Surgeons.

CONCLUSIONS

We have probably made a few mistakes along the way, but we are learning more each day about running a small business. Before we get too far into January, we need to reflect on our experiences in 1995 and come up with a marketing plan for the new year. If you were running this business, what would you do?

APPENDIX 15-A

Frequently Asked Questions

1. How long does it take?

   Laser eye surgery itself takes only a few minutes. The entire procedure including pre-operative preparation and a post-surgery eye examination, takes about an hour.

2. Do I have to go to the hospital?

   No. The surgery is performed in our clinic.

3. Will I be awake during the surgery?

   Yes. The laser procedure takes only a few minutes and clients are awake throughout. If desired, the doctor will administer a mild sedative prior to surgery.

4. Will it hurt?

   No. The treatment is virtually painless. The discomfort patients feel after treatment is minimal and pain-relieving medication is rarely needed.

5. How long does it take to recover?

   Most patients notice better vision right away, with further improvement over the next few weeks. Normal activities can usually be resumed within a few days of the treatment.

6. Can I drive home after the surgery?

   We suggest that you do not drive yourself after the treatment, particularly if you have had any sedation.

7. When can I go back to work?

   Provided you do not work in an excessively dirty or smoky environment and do not have to engage in extreme physical activity, you may return to work immediately after treatment.

8. What happens after the surgery?

   After the surgery, your doctor will monitor your progress through regular eye examinations. These check-ups will occur at approximately one day, three to five days, two weeks, one month, three months, six months, and one year after. In most cases, these appointments can be booked through your regular eye-care provider.

9. Are both eyes done at the same time?

   In most cases, each eye is done separately with an interval of several weeks between procedures. It may be possible to shorten this interval and, in exceptional cases (for example, when a patient has come from afar), both eyes may be done at the same time.

10. Will I still have to wear glasses or contacts after surgery?

    Even though everyone sees better after treatment, some patients may have to continue wearing glasses or contact lenses for specific activities, usually on a part-time basis.

APPENDIX 15-B

What Our Customers Say About Us

In the beginning I did perceive it to be a risky thing, but I wanted it badly enough that I was willing to look into it. I went to a couple of clinics and the information that I got led me to believe that it wasn't really a risky thing, but you're always kind of apprehensive about someone operating on your eyes because you only have one set of eyes. I heard about Restored Vision over the radio so I made an appointment and went down there and from day one they were very professional. They explained the procedure to me step by step. They made me feel confident that this operation would be a benefit to me.

— *Andy Peters*

I'm 58 years old. I've had 20-500 vision for most of my life and I've just been sick and tired of glasses and contacts. For about five years, I considered radial Keratectomy but I just didn't feel it was an exact enough science to do it. But then I read about laser surgery and I attended two seminars on it. I still can hardly believe that I walked into his office that morning and spent twenty minutes getting my eyes numbed and twenty more minutes in the laser room getting prepped and having a two and a half minute laser treatment. Then I got up from the chair, went into the examination room and immediately read 20-30 on the eye chart. It was unbelievable!

— *Carol Smith*

I don't know too many people who like wearing glasses and having to rely on contacts (which I never really liked) and since I play a lot of sports it's something that I'm very happy now that I did.

— *Andy Peters*

I have recommended it to many, many people. I took brochures with me to Hawaii when I went. I took them down to California when I went to my painting seminar. I carry them in my purse!

— *Carol Smith*

I would recommend the Restored Vision Clinic to all my friends because they were excellent. They were very helpful and friendly. They explained everything and answered all my questions. Very helpful.

— *Koren Jordan*

You almost start taking it for granted now that you don't have contacts or glasses. It's kind of strange actually. But you know, I'd definitely recommend it.

— *Andy Peters*

APPENDIX 15-C

Glossary of Terms

Astigmatism   Astigmatism is when both distant and near objects are blurry. This results when the eye is not spherical and symmetrical and light is focused on multiple points in front of, and behind, the retina.

Cornea   The transparent, circular part of the front of the eyeball. The curvature of the cornea determines most of the eye's refractive (light-bending) power.

Hyperopia   Hyperopia is farsightedness. As a result of insufficient curvature of the cornea or too short an eyeball, light entering the eye is focused behind the retina. Distant objects can be seen clearly but near objects are blurry.

Ophthalmologist   A medical doctor who specializes in the eye. To become an ophthalmologist, one must first obtain a Medical Degree (MD in North America) and then complete further specialty training.

Retina   The light-sensitive nerve layer which converts light images into electrical signals for transmission to the brain. The retina is analogous to the film of a camera.

WILDERNESS NEWFOUNDLAND ADVENTURES

Cori-Jane Radford and
H.F. (Herb) MacKenzie

It was a beautiful January morning in St. John's, Newfoundland, and Stan Cook, Jr. was staring out of his office window, contemplating the 1999 promotional strategy for his family's ecotourism business, Wilderness Newfoundland Adventures (WNA). He was supposed to meet with his father on Friday to discuss it. It was already Tuesday, and time was short. Many advertising and promotional items should have been placed by now. Stan Cook, Sr. would be expecting a progress report. Stan, Jr. decided to review the 1998 promotional strategy to see which items should be continued, and which should be changed or dropped for 1999.

WNA'S PRODUCT

WNA offers single- and multi-day tours, including kayak day (approximately eight hours), half-day, and sunset trips. As well, they offer weekend tours, multi-day combination-activity tours, multi-day single-activity tours, and on-site and off-site equipment rentals. Tours include instruction and interpretation on sea kayaking, mountain biking, hiking, canoeing, orienteering, outdoor camping, and wilderness survival skills. WNA offers a comprehensive program for beginner, intermediate, and expert paddlers, and adventurers of all ages.

WNA tours are all-inclusive. The adventurer is supplied with all food, camping equipment, sporting equipment, and safety gear. Participants only bring appropriate clothing and a backpack. WNA covers all sections of non-consumptive adventure tourism and caters to the traveller who is attracted to these activities. WNA also specializes in outdoor excursions that are modified for its clients.

WNA has been focusing recently on products that are thought to have national and international potential and are "market-ready." Sea kayaking is one of these products. According to the Canadian Recreation Canoe Association, sea kayaking is the fastest growing paddling activity, with an annual growth rate of 20%. Many areas of Newfoundland are ideal for this activity. Newfoundland is an island with over 10 000 miles of fascinating coastline, dotted with caves, waterfalls, sea stacks, and arches. Icebergs are abundant from May through July, and thousands of humpback and minke whales visit from late June to mid-August.

WNA mainly uses two-person, ocean-going kayaks for all trips. These kayaks are very stable and seaworthy, and all use rudders to steer. The area that the Cooks picked to run their day trips, Cape Broyle, is beautiful and quite calm. Rarely has anyone ever fallen out of a kayak, although it has happened in knee-deep water when participants were pulling the kayak up on the beach. The guide to participant ratio is 1:6, one guide kayak (single-person kayak) to every three participant kayaks. WNA's guides are all trained in safety, rescue, and first-aid techniques. Sea kayaking in these circumstances is not difficult; people of all ages and fitness levels can participate. In fact, WNA has taken an 84-year-old grandmother on one of the day trips.

HEADQUARTERS

After searching for three years, WNA decided to locate its operations in Cape Broyle, about 50 minutes south of St. John's on the province's Avalon Peninsula. The area has natural beauty (soaring cliffs, caves, waterfalls, varied topography), nature attractions (icebergs, bird sanctuaries, caribou herd), protection from the wind (7-kilometre fjord), an abundance of marine life (whales, seals, otters), proximity to a large urban population (St. John's), an historic property (85-year-old community general store), and cultural distinction (Irish Heart of Newfoundland). WNA believed this area to be a world-class area for sea kayaking, mountain biking, and hiking, and an ideal location for its site.

WNA has become the first adventure-travel and ecotourism operator to utilize the opportunity that Newfoundland and Labrador offers with its unique culture and history. WNA has leased a heritage building for $150 per month in Cape Broyle. The building is suitable for barbecues and dinners for groups of up to 30 people. Together, the adventure tours and facilities highlight the cultural and historical identity most tourists and visitors welcome, and provide a unique and memorable experience.

SHORT SEASON

Newfoundland has a relatively short summer. Therefore, WNA has a short season to generate revenue. WNA presently has twelve two-person kayaks, but is considering purchasing four more for the 1999 season. Newfoundland's summer extends from late June until mid-September. Kayaking in May and early June is beautiful, but it can be cold and uncomfortable. Late September is a great time to paddle, but the tourist trade usually drops off. As well, once children are back in school, local people lose interest in summer activities. To counter this seasonal disinterest, WNA has contacted local high schools, and has encouraged them to take their students on kayaking field trips. Biology and physical education teachers were the targets of this promotion. Biology students were invited to take a close-up look at the marine life in Newfoundland's waters, and physical education students were invited to participate simply for exercise. This promotion was relatively successful; four of 12 schools participated in 1998. On average, schools have the potential to take at least two classes of students.

TRIP BREAKDOWN

WNA's day trips run from May until early October. People can book any day they wish, but a trip is cancelled if fewer than four people book in advance. An equal number of tourists and local adventurers participate in the shorter trips. During the peak whale and iceberg period, WNA runs a 5-day kayak trip; a 7-day kayak and mountain bike trip; a 14-day kayak, mountain bike, and canoe youth trip; and several "kayak week-ends." In 1998, the numbers of participants for each of these types of trips were 12, 10, 12, and 16, respectively. Extended trips are made up entirely of tourists who come from all over the world, including Japan, Germany, the United Kingdom, the United States, and other parts of Canada. These trips often involve other areas of the province, such as Trinity Bay, Notre Dame Bay, and Terra Nova National Park. These trips begin when participants arrive at the St. John's airport, where they are met and then taken to the appropriate trailhead.

Tourists book reservations for these excursions months in advance, often by calling the WNA toll-free number. The provincial travel guide, WNA's Web page, *The Great Outdoorsman* television program, and the Outdoor Adventure Trade Show seem to be the routes of discovery to WNA for international tourists. As well, wholesalers in both Ontario and the United States have expressed an interest in representing WNA to their markets. These wholesalers take WNA's price and mark it up 10%–15% before advertising it to their customers. This requires limited marketing by WNA, and is a relatively stress-free option, although unpredictable. These wholesalers usually market trips to different locations each year.

WNA markets sea-kayaking packages to both potential tourists and to visitors who come to the province. This forward strategy provided WNA with an early introduction in the industry, and allowed it to become the premier adventure travel and ecotourism company in the province.

COMPANY BACKGROUND

In 1970, Mr. Cook introduced commercial canoeing to Newfoundland. He provided all-inclusive canoeing trips that averaged five to ten days in length. These trips included instructions on canoeing operations, trout fishing, camping skills, and orientation with maps and compass instruction. The focus of the trips was placed on acquisition of life skills that are indigenous to outdoor experience. Cooperation, self-reliance, and appreciation of the great outdoors were the main priorities with Mr. Cook. He guided and instructed both children and adults of all skill levels throughout the 1970s and early 1980s.

During the 1980s, Mr. Cook received numerous international inquiries about his abilities to coordinate and handle groups interested in canoeing and camping in Newfoundland. After joining the Marine Adventures Association of Newfoundland and Labrador in the late 1980s and becoming its secretary/treasurer, he noticed the interest that the province was generating for adventure travel. Mr. Cook believed that it was economically feasible to expand his current canoeing school, which was focused on the local provincial market, to encompass a larger, yet specific, international market interested in adventure travel and ecotourism. This would not only include the usual training in canoeing and portaging skills, but would also utilize the world-class sea kayaking and mountain biking opportunities that existed in the province and had not been properly marketed.

In 1995, Mr. Cook changed the company name from Stan Cook Enterprises to Wilderness Newfoundland Adventures, symbolizing the new focus on international business. The expanded product line was promoted to new target markets, and the business and Mr. Cook's reputation soon enhanced the Newfoundland and Labrador tourism industry.

Besides Mr. Cook, the company involved two other members of his family, and a number of seasonal workers. Stan, Jr. was responsible for the daily operations of the business. He had an undergraduate business degree, and was available to manage the business during the earlier and later parts of the season when his father was still teaching physical education at one of the St. John's high schools. Much of the success of WNA can be attributed to its first marketing plan, developed and implemented by Stan, Jr.

Mr. Cook's daughter, Cori-Jane Radford, started working with WNA in the spring of 1996, when she assumed responsibility for marketing. This allowed Stan, Jr. to get more involved with daily operations, and to address issues that had previously been ignored. Many of the marketing ideas implemented during 1997 and 1998 were her creation. In September 1998, however, Cori-Jane decided to get her MBA, and her involvement with the business diminished.

During the summer of 1998, WNA employed five seasonal employees. There were three full-time guides and one part-time guide ($10/hour), and a junior guide ($7/hour). The full-time guides averaged 40 hours of work per week, the part-time guide averaged 15 hours of work per week, and the junior guide averaged 30 hours of work per week. All guides had specific outdoor qualifications before they were hired. Before being given responsibility to lead trips, all guides had a one-week training program, followed by a weekend expedition with Mr. Cook and Stan, Jr. Guides were hired based on their qualifications, personality, and knowledge of the history and culture of Newfoundland.

For 1999, WNA plans to increase the number of seasonal employees, and it will also attempt to increase the length of the season. This is an attempt to increase revenues and to market itself as a destination in the shoulder seasons as well. However, this strategy directly hinges on the ability of WNA to attract larger volumes of out-of-province travellers. WNA wishes to expand further into the international adventure market. To achieve this goal, the company needs a larger work force, and perhaps a full-time marketing and sales person.

This person would be expected to take the marketing responsibilities from Stan, Jr., so that he can concentrate on other important matters. As well, this person would be responsible for generating individual sales, both locally and internationally. The two-day sea kayak trip sells for $250, the five-day trip is $625, the seven-day combo trip (sea kayak/mountain bike) is $875, and the 14-day youth combo is $980.

ADVENTURE TRAVEL AND ECOTOURISM IN NEWFOUNDLAND AND LABRADOR

The tourism industry in Newfoundland and Labrador has evolved to the point where traditional markets are being segmented into highly specific niche markets, such as soft and hard adventure, and ecotourism. However, in Newfoundland and Labrador, the ecotourism segment of the market is still in its developmental stages, with few quality operators. This category of tourism is particularly beneficial to the province, due to its careful use of the environment, and the tendency of nature-oriented travellers to spend more money during their vacations than recreational travellers.

Adventure travel is defined as a leisure activity that takes place in an unusual, exotic, remote, or wilderness destination, and is associated with high or low levels of activity by the participants. Adventure travellers expect to experience varying degrees of risk, excitement, or tranquillity, and to be personally tested or stretched in some way. Adventure travel is participatory, informative, interesting, unique, and in addition to excitement, it offers a wide range of challenges in an outdoor setting. A trip might be devoted to one activity or a combination of activities. The duration can be from several hours to several weeks.

Non-consumptive tourism uses the natural habitat without removing any of its resources (consumptive tourism removes resources, e.g., hunting or fishing). Non-consumptive adventure tourism can be subdivided into three areas: soft adventure, hard adventure, and ecotourism. WNA is most concerned with soft adventure and ecotourism but can offer participants hard adventure if they so desire. All three types of adventure tourism take place outdoors, involve travel to a particular natural attraction and some level of physical activity, and focus on activities that offer new or unusual experiences. Though these types of adventure tourism differ in degree of physical exertion, it is possible that all three can be combined into a single tour package.

Soft Adventure Travel

Soft adventure travel focuses on providing a unique outdoors experience or "adventure." However, it involves only a minor element of risk, little physical exertion, and no skill. It involves less physically demanding activities. All ages and fitness levels can participate.

Hard Adventure Travel

Hard adventure travel combines a unique experience in an outdoor setting with excitement and a degree of risk. It frequently demands physical exertion and a level of skill, and it often requires that the participant prepare or train for the experience.

Ecotourism

Ecotourism is purposeful travel that creates an understanding of the region's culture and natural history, while safeguarding the integrity of the ecosystem and producing economic benefits that encourage conservation. An ecotour can be either soft adventure or hard adventure, but not both.

THE APPEAL OF ADVENTURE TRAVEL AND ECOTOURISM

Adventure travel and ecotourism form one of the world's fastest growing tourism sectors. It holds appeal for travellers who are no longer happy with traditional vacations. Members of these groups are looking for the things that adventure travel and ecotourism offer: excitement, risk, unique experiences, education, and fun.

Analysts believe that the world-wide demand for adventure and ecotourism vacations will continue to grow well into the next century, with increasing demand each year. Currently, growth in this sector is leading the whole Canadian tourism industry, and it is actually out-performing the Canadian economy.

Newfoundland and Labrador are in a good position to profit from the increased demand for adventure travel and ecotourism. The province offers pristine environments, wildlife, unique flora and fauna, and exotic, challenging experiences. Almost every region of the province is trying to develop a variety of activities or products to draw visitors. However, the adventure travel and ecotourism business is highly seasonal, with few operators open all year. Despite its potential, Newfoundland and Labrador attracts a small fraction of the North American market. Clearly, there are opportunities for growth in this business. This task is not easy because inter-national competition has kept pace with the growth in demand. Today, consumers can chose from the wide variety of appealing activities and experiences available in many countries.

WNA believes its success in the international marketplace depends on both the quality of the experience it provides, and on how that experience is marketed and managed. The future success of Newfoundland and Labrador adventure travel and ecotourism will depend on how well operators are provided with tools to address challenges with informed, effective action.

TARGET MARKETS FOR ADVENTURE TOURISM

The target market includes travellers interested in visiting a specific place to engage in a new or unusual participative experience. This group of tourists has different product needs that change on a seasonal basis. Many market researchers believe the single most significant trend that will determine the nature of demand for the adventure product will be the aging baby boomers. They are wealthier, not as interested in the hard "roughing-it adventure," have less time, and yet still seek new experiences.

Some interesting statistics about adventure travellers are:

- There are 30 to 40 million Americans that are potential candidates for an adventure trip of some kind.

- There are 787 000 potential adventure tourism clients in the United Kingdom. Thirty-five percent of British vacationers seek adventure and are looking for an active holiday where they can get in touch with their daring adventurous side.

- The outdoor sports segments, totalling 1.3 million people, represent potential for adventure travel.

These potential adventure travellers fit the following three main profiles.

Casual Adventure Travellers

These are the entry-level adventurers, experimenting with newer and challenging outdoor activities. They take short trips (one or two days) to get a "taste of adventure." This market affords the greatest growth potential in the short term. Also, there is little difference between these travellers and the touring urban-based tourists. Therefore, the opportunity to attract city-touring visitors for short excursions is good, due to their closely related desires.

Committed Adventure Travellers

These travellers form the most affluent segment. They are fitness-conscious, in the middle- to upper-income brackets, 30–55 years old, well-educated, and live in urban centres. They demand and are willing to pay for quality accommodations.

Expert Adventure Travellers

These are the adventurers who are on their way to mastering a sports-related skill or knowledge about a topic (e.g., wildlife), and for whom the motivation for a trip has shifted from general growth and exploration to the fine-tuning of a particular skill. This market tends to be younger, has less disposable income, and is more inclined than other groups to "rough it."

COMPETITION

It is important for WNA to understand and cultivate its target market and to know its competition. The main competition for WNA is not within the province. Since this province has very few quality operators, the real competition is coming from operators outside Newfoundland and Labrador who are offering similar travel experiences. Many of these operators are very good and have much to offer. Therefore, WNA is working hard to create better products. By monitoring its larger international competitors, WNA has been trying to improve its products, providing better value and, hopefully, attracting more customers.

The major competition for all adventure travel and ecotourism customers comes from outside Canada. World-wide consumer demand for unique experiences and intriguing packages is fueling international competition. However, current market opportunities support WNA's products. WNA remains highly competitive with its current pricing strategy, service quality, product uniqueness (i.e., sea kayaking with whales and icebergs), wilderness environmental appeal, and current currency exchange rates.

1998 PROMOTIONAL ACTIVITIES

Stan, Jr. and Cori-Jane generated all of the ad concepts and material and decided the 1998 media plan (see Exhibit 16-1). Cori-Jane created the physical displays and then had films produced by the printer. This is quite inexpensive compared to hiring a marketing firm, although it is time-consuming. Stan, Jr. had limited involvement with the graphic design, but his involvement has been increasing due to Cori-Jane's decreasing involvement in the business.

Print Advertising

Newfoundland Sportsman Magazine

Newfoundland Sportsman magazine is a 70-page, full-colour, glossy magazine. This magazine prints 20 000 copies every two months. It has approximately 5000 subscribers and the other copies are distributed to retailers and news stands all across the province. This magazine is published in Newfoundland and marketed to adults interested in the outdoors. Most readers are between the ages of 18 and 55 years old, and include both men and women in approximately

EXHIBIT 16-1 WNA Media Budget 1998

Media	Date	Company	Form of Ad	Cost
TV	07/28/98	The Great Outdoorsman Show	½-Hour Television Show	$ 7500.00
Radio	06/30/98	OZ-FM	60 × 30 sec. spots (2 weeks)	$ 1750.00
	07/31/98	OZ-FM	60 × 30 sec. spots (2 weeks)	$ 1750.00
	08/31/98	OZ-FM	60 × 30 sec. spots (2 weeks)	$ 1750.00
Print	12/29/97	St. John's Visitor's Guide	¼-page ad (full colour)	$ 575.00
	01/15/98	NewTel Communications	Yellow Pages ⅛ page ad (1 colour)	$ 1200.00
	04/30/98	*NFLD Sportsman*	⅙-page ad (full colour)	$ 400.00
	05/03/98	*NFLD Sportsman*	⅙-page ad (full colour)	$ 400.00
	06/07/98	*NFLD Sportsman*	Full page ad (full colour) and accompanying story	$ 1300.00
	12/29/97	Provincial Travel Guide	¼-page ad (full colour)	
	04/30/98	St. John's Board of Trade	Front Cover	$ 1200.00
	03/31/98	Sterling Press Printers	Small Brochure (full colour)	$ 1350.00
Sales Promo.	06/04/98	Gift certificates	25 half-day trips for 2	$ 2500.00
Signage	05/02/98	Highway Signage	3½' × 8' signs	$ 500.00
	04/26/98	WNA Van Signage	Full-colour, 4 slides	$ 500.00
Trade Show	06/01/98	Kinetic Marketing	NFLD Sportsman Show/ St. John's (booth)	$ 600.00
	02/14/98	National Event Management	Outdoor Adventure Show/ Toronto (booth)	$ 2000.00
Total				$26 775.00

equal numbers. Both consumptive and non-consumptive approaches are represented in this publication. In 1998, WNA placed three ads in this magazine. Two were 1/6-page ads, placed for recognition, and the third was a full-page, full-colour advertisement that appeared facing an article written by the magazine on sea kayaking and, in particular, on WNA.

Newfoundland Travel Guide

The *Newfoundland Travel Guide* is a 200-page, colour brochure created by the Provincial Department of Tourism. Interested potential tourists from all over the world contact the Department of Tourism to request information. The guide is then delivered free-of-charge to anyone expressing an interest in visiting the province. A new guide is published each year, listing accommodations, events, attractions, tours, and services.

All businesses relating to the tourist industry receive a free 100-word listing under their appropriate heading. As well, the Department provides pages in the publication for businesses that wish to purchase ad space. Rates for 1999 are double the 1998 rates.

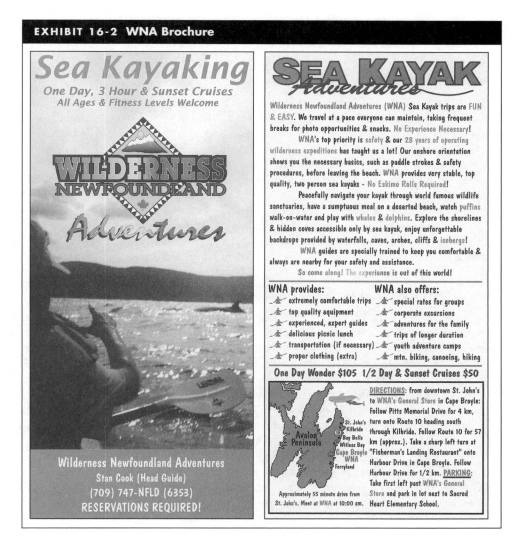

EXHIBIT 16-2 WNA Brochure

Sea Kayaking

One Day, 3 Hour & Sunset Cruises
All Ages & Fitness Levels Welcome

WILDERNESS NEWFOUNDLAND
Adventures

Wilderness Newfoundland Adventures
Stan Cook (Head Guide)
(709) 747-NFLD (6353)
RESERVATIONS REQUIRED!

SEA KAYAK *Adventures*

Wilderness Newfoundland Adventures (WNA) Sea Kayak trips are FUN
& EASY. We travel at a pace everyone can maintain, taking frequent
breaks for photo opportunities & snacks. No Experience Necessary!

WNA's top priority is safety & our 28 years of operating
wilderness expeditions has taught us a lot! Our onshore orientation
shows you the necessary basics, such as paddle strokes & safety
procedures, before leaving the beach. WNA provides very stable, top
quality, two person sea kayaks - No Eskimo Rolls Required!

Peacefully navigate your kayak through world famous wildlife
sanctuaries, have a sumptuous meal on a deserted beach, watch puffins
walk-on-water and play with whales & dolphins. Explore the shorelines
& hidden coves accessible only by sea kayak, enjoy unforgettable
backdrops provided by waterfalls, caves, arches, cliffs & icebergs!

WNA guides are specially trained to keep you comfortable &
always are nearby for your safety and assistance.
So come along! The experience is out of this world!

WNA provides:
- extremely comfortable trips
- top quality equipment
- experienced, expert guides
- delicious picnic lunch
- transportation (if necessary)
- proper clothing (extra)

WNA also offers:
- special rates for groups
- corporate excursions
- adventures for the family
- trips of longer duration
- youth adventure camps
- mtn. biking, canoeing, hiking

One Day Wonder $105 1/2 Day & Sunset Cruises $50

St. John's
Kilbride
Bay Bulls
Witless Bay
Cape Broyle
WNA
Ferryland
Avalon
Peninsula

Approximately 55 minute drive from
St. John's. Meet at WNA at 10:00 am.

DIRECTIONS: from downtown St. John's
to WNA's General Store in Cape Broyle:
Follow Pitts Memorial Drive for 4 km,
turn onto Route 10 heading south
through Kilbride. Follow Route 10 for 57
km (approx.). Take a sharp left turn at
"Fisherman's Landing Restaurant" onto
Harbour Drive in Cape Broyle. Follow
Harbour Drive for 1/2 km. PARKING:
Take first left past WNA's General
Store and park in lot next to Sacred
Heart Elementary School.

Brochures

WNA has produced two brochures. A small brochure (see Exhibit 16-2, which displays the
front and back of the brochure) was created to advertise WNA's full-day ($100/person),
half-day ($65/person), and sunset trips ($65/person). This was targeted at the local population and the tourists visiting the St. John's area. These brochures are placed throughout St.
John's, in tourist chalets, hotels, motels, restaurants, and any stores that will accept them.
These are two-sided, full-colour, high-quality brochures. They are printed on cardboard-
type paper, cut to $3\frac{1}{3}$" $\times$ $8\frac{1}{2}$".

WNA's larger brochures are mailed to people interested in extended trips. This brochure
was created and printed in 1996. In order to keep the brochure up-to-date, there is a pocket

inside the back cover that allows WNA to insert current prices and updated information. This brochure was expensive to produce, but most adventurers have been impressed by it.

Radio Advertising

OZ-FM (94.7) is a St. John's radio station that reaches approximately 182 000 people over 12 years of age each week. The target market for OZ-FM is 18 to 49-year-old adults with active lifestyles, from all socio-economic classes.

WNA ran three sets of 30-second ads throughout the summer. The duration of each set was two weeks. In conjunction with the advertisements, WNA arranged to have six pairs of free gift certificates given away on the radio during the Friday "morning drive" time slot. OZ-FM's morning drive is called the "Dawn Patrol," and has three radio personalities. WNA invited all of them to participate on a free day-trip. This proved to be a great idea as, when they gave away the free passes, they were able to make first-hand and favourable comments about sea kayaking. In fact, they continued to promote WNA and sea kayaking with personal comments throughout all of the radio advertising campaigns.

Television Advertising

The Great Outdoorsman (TGO) is a half-hour Sunday night television program on the Life Network (carried all over North America). The program host, John Summerfield, and his two-man crew travel all over the world seeking different types of adventure. John was interested in sea kayaking with whales and icebergs, and contacted Stan, Jr. after meeting him at a trade show. In July 1997, TGO came to St. John's and filmed a show. The shooting went extremely well, and both John and WNA received considerable praise. John enjoyed Newfoundland so much that he decided to return in July 1998 to film a second show with WNA (never before had he done two shows with the same company, with the same product). This show aired in October 1998, and was scheduled for two repeats during 1999.

WNA has received many benefits and much recognition from these shows, although they were very expensive. WNA paid the air travel, accommodations, and meals of the TGO team for four days and three nights, a total of approximately $2500. As well, there was a $5000 fee payable to TGO to participate in its show.

Internet

WNA first created its Web site (www.wildnfld.ca) in the spring of 1997. It enlisted a small local Web-page design firm to assist it to develop its online personality. The Web page gets updated about twice a year (before and after the regular season). WNA is currently investigating E-commerce, hoping to take both bookings and payments over the Web.

Signage

St. John's is the end-of-the-line when driving east on the Trans-Canada Highway (TCH), as it is the most easterly city in North America. The TCH is the most used route into the city and many local businesses have signs along it, advertising to incoming motor tourists.

WNA decided to strategically place three signs. The first was placed along the TCH with all the other signs. The second was put on a highly used arterial within the city. The final sign was placed along the Southern Shore Highway. This highway follows the coast from St. John's, south past Cape Broyle, and then it loops back along St. Mary's Bay to the city, a route called the Irish Loop. The signs were designed by Stan, Jr. and Cori-Jane, and were painted by an art student at Stan, Sr.'s high school

Additional signage was placed on a company van. WNA leased a forest-green, Ford AeroStar in April 1998 ($500/month). This van is used for pick-up and delivery of clients, shuttle of equipment, and transportation for the guides to and from the various sites. The WNA van is only used for 16 weeks during the summer. It requires gas about twice a week, and costs $60 per fill-up. Cori-Jane thought that WNA should take advantage of the vehicle's visibility around St. John's and that it should be incorporated in the promotion strategy. She hired a local business that specializes in auto advertising to put WNA's logo and other information on all four sides of the vehicle. The final product was quite impressive, and a number of people commented that they had seen the "Green WNA Machine" around town.

Sales Promotions

In 1998, WNA gave away 25 pairs of "Half-Day Sea Kayak Adventures for Two" gift certificates to different individuals. Some people won them on the radio, while other tickets were given to local celebrities or other prominent people. WNA wanted to get people to try sea kayaking and thought this would be a good idea, although only 11 pairs were redeemed over the summer.

Trade Shows

The Newfoundland Sportsman Show is sponsored by *Newfoundland Sportsman* magazine and is the largest show of its type in the province. It is a consumer retail trade fair with its primary focus on the outdoor industry. Many types of land, air, and marine activities are represented, and it attracts 8000–14 000 interested consumers.

A new trade show, "Outdoor Adventure Sports Show (OASS)," has been held in February in Toronto, Ontario, for the past two years. At the OASS, attendees can try climbing the Pyramid wall, and can test ride mountain bikes on a demo track, and try canoeing or kayaking in an indoor pool. As well, outfitters from all over North America show what their province/company/activity has to offer the willing adventurer.

Attendance at the 1998 OASS included 23 320 people, with 62% either making an adventure purchase there, or expressing an intention to make such a purchase as a result of the show. This attendance was 120% over the 1997 attendance, and it is expected to continue to grow for some time. WNA has participated both years. This show provides a venue for WNA to reach clients for their longer-duration adventures. These people will specifically come to Newfoundland for an excursion with WNA. Travelling, accommodation, and meal expenses amount to approximately $2000 for two people to attend OASS.

Other Methods

Excluding trade shows, the majority of WNA's personal selling has been informal. Mr. Cook and Stan, Jr. attend many local events, sporting rallies, and other activities that attract adventure-minded people. As well, WNA encourages its summer employees to promote sea kayaking on their own time by giving them a $10 bonus for every customer they bring on a full-day kayak trip, and a $5 bonus for every customer they bring to half-day or sunset trips. This encourages the guides to get a group of friends together to go out kayaking. (At the beginning of the summer, each staff member also receives three free day passes for family and friends.)

In their first two years of operation, WNA had a difficult time attracting local customers. Due to unfamiliarity with sea kayaking, many people were very nervous. The only information people had accumulated previously was on the dangerous sport of river kayaking. River and sea kayaking are completely different sports, with very different shaped vessels and different objectives. Now that people have heard of sea kayaking, they are starting to differentiate WNA from other local outfitters by both reputation and value.

St. John's is becoming a popular tourist destination. An increasing number of businesses and associations are holding annual conferences in the oldest city in North America. Exhibit 16-3 presents a list of conferences planned in 1998 to come to St. John's in the summer of 1999.

Finally, WNA is considering the possibility of hiring a salesperson. So far, little thought has been given to what the salesperson would do, how he or she would be compensated, and exactly what criteria would be important in selecting an appropriate salesperson.

Public Relations

WNA has attempted to take advantage of free publicity. Stan, Jr. has invited several local reporters to participate on a free day-trip in return for writing articles on WNA. So far, two reporters have participated, and both have written very positive articles on their experiences. The first article was printed in *The Evening Telegram* (St. John's). It was a full-page article, accompanied by five full-colour photos. The second article was printed in *Mount Pearl Pride*. Mount Pearl is a smaller city that borders St. John's. Again, it was a full-page article with full-colour photos. WNA received many phone calls following the printing of these articles.

EXHIBIT 16-3 Upcoming Conventions and Events, City of St. John's, 1999		
Date	**Convention**	**Delegates**
May 10–13	Canadian Association of Principals	500
June 1–5	Co-operative Housing Federation of Canada	700
June 11–14	Canadian Council for the Advancement of Education	250
June 13–20	Canadian Corps of Commissioners AGM '99	400
June 17–20	Air Cadet League of Canada	150
June 23–27	CAMRT/CSDMU Joint Meeting	500
July 5–9	Canadian Orthopedic Association	700
July 11–16	Offshore Mechanics and Arctic Engineering	400
August 21–26	Canada Employment and Immigration Union	325
September 19–22	Risk and Insurance Management Society	500
September 27–30	Workers Compensation Commission	100
October 1–3	International Association of Business Communicators	300

Source: City of St. John's, Department of Economic Development and Tourism. Please note that this information was accurate at the time of printing, but may be subject to change.

CONCLUSION

Before making any decisions with respect to the 1999 promotional strategy, Stan, Jr. decided to review the summary of responses to the customer satisfaction surveys collected in 1998. Each person that participated on a day, half-day, or sunset trip between May 24 and September 6, 1998, filled one out. The summary of responses is provided in Exhibit 16-4.

EXHIBIT 16-4 WNA Customer Satisfaction Survey Results, Summer 1998

Age	Total	Trip	Total	Sex	Total
10–19	48	Full Day	360	Male	332
20–29	309	Half Day	180	Female	388
30–39	239	Sunset	180	Total	720
40–49	76	Total	720		
50–59	28				
60+	20				
Total	720				

How Did You Like Our Staff and Service?

Guides

Friendly	Ratings	Total	Knowledgeable	Ratings	Total
dissatisfied	1	0	dissatisfied	1	0
	2	0		2	0
	3	0		3	0
satisfied	4	11	satisfied	4	15
	5	33		5	28
	6	73		6	55
100% satisfied	7	603	100% satisfied	7	622
Total		720	Total		720

Physical Product

Food	Ratings	Total	Equipment	Ratings	Total
dissatisfied	1	0	dissatisfied	1	0
	2	0		2	0
	3	4		3	9
satisfied	4	14	satisfied	4	12
	5	32		5	33
	6	68		6	70
100% satisfied	7	602	100% satisfied	7	596
Total		720	Total		720

EXHIBIT 16-4   WNA Customer Satisfaction Survey Results, Summer 1998 (continued)

How Do You Feel?

Would You Return?	Ratings	# of People[1]
No	1	0
	2	0
Maybe	3	38
	4	66
Definitely	5	616
Total		720

Recommend Us to Others?	Ratings	# of People[1]
No	1	0
	2	0
Maybe	3	30
	4	69
Definitely	5	621
Total		720

Where Did You Hear About Us?	# of People[1]
Brochure (large)	10
Brochure (small)	99
Gift Certificate	11
Other	7
Phone Book (Yellow Pages)	32
Radio	66
Referral (Word of Mouth)	175
Repeat Customer	53
Television *The Great Outdoorsman*	19
Travel Agency	5
Web Site	23
Magazine	
Newfoundland Sportsman	35
Provincial Travel Guide	68
St. John's Visitor's Guide	12
Road Sign	
Harbour Arterial	31
Trans-Canada Highway	19
Southern Shore Highway	17
Trade Show	
Newfoundland Sportsman	33
Outdoor Adventure Show	5

What Influenced You to Try Sea Kayaking?	# of People[1]
Advertising	148
Brochure	45
Travel Guide Ad	8
Sign on Road	8
OZ-FM Ad	44
Television Show	24
Mount Pearl "Pride"	19
Alpine Country Lodge Recommendation	15
Always Wanted to Try Sea Kayaking	33
Dept. of Tourism Recommendation	13
FAM TOUR	20
Family Recommendation	26
For the Adventure	15
Free Invitation	10
Friend of the Cooks	22
Friend Recommendation/Going with Friends	112
Good Reputation	44
Group from Work Going	55
Guide Recommendation	35
Hotel Recommendation	22
New Experience	10
OZ-FM Dawn Patrol Recommendation	55
Received Gift Certificate	16
Repeat Customer	53
Wedding Day Activity	10
Won on the Radio	6

1. Some customers responded more than once.

EXHIBIT 16-4 WNA Customer Satisfaction Survey Results, Summer 1998 (continued)

Overall Satisfaction with Your Excursion

Overall	Ratings	Total		
dissatisfied	1	0		
	2	0		
	3	0		
satisfied	4	8		
	5	24		
	6	96		
100% satisfied	7	592		
Total		720		

Stan Jr. has a tremendous amount of planning to do and decisions to make over the next few days. How successful has the 1998 promotional campaign been? What items should be retained for 1999, and what items should be changed or deleted? How should WNA set its promotional budget? Stan, Jr. knew his father would want answers to all of these questions at their Friday meeting.

SAMUEL'S FURNITURE

A Family Affair

Lindsay Meredith

In the late 1980s, approximately 10 million trips were made by British Columbians into the United States. Most of these trips were made via one of the three border crossings that served the Vancouver lower mainland. By 1991, those cross-border trips had risen to around 15.4 million. The majority of the crossings were made through the Peace Arch entry point to Washington State cities such as Bellingham and Seattle.

What caused this marked increase in cross-border travel activity by Canadians? Moe Samuel, his son-in-law Dave Cherry, and his son Elie knew the pretty obvious answer. Canadians were going south in record numbers to buy everything from gas and milk to big-ticket durables like appliances and furniture.

Some mid-market Vancouver furniture retailers were badly hurt by this exodus of shoppers to US stores. This was because much of the cross-border purchasing activity was done by consumers who had become extremely price- and quality-conscious. Experts felt this was caused as a result of the protracted recession and high taxes that were putting a lot of pressure on consumer budgets. In addition, some retail analysts suggested that Canadian consumers were also attracted to US outlets because they perceived that American stores offered a larger assortment of product choices. The ability of American stores to attract Canadian shoppers was not to be taken lightly. The Whatcom County Chamber of Commerce (located in northern Washington State) estimated that 46% of the county's total business activity originated in the retail sector and of that 46%—Canadian shoppers generated 40%.

In 1991, Moe, Dave, and Elie decided to open a large retail outlet called Samuel's Furniture. It was located approximately 17 kilometers (ten miles) south of the Canadian border, just off the US Interstate route 5 (I-5), on exit 262 at a small town called Ferndale. The location was well chosen, especially to intercept Canadians moving south to shop at the Bellis Fair mall

This case was prepared by Lindsay Meredith, Professor of Marketing, Faculty of Business, Simon Fraser University, Vancouver, British Columbia, as a basis for class discussion. Reprinted with permission.

in Bellingham. In fact, for many consumers living in the largest suburbs south of Vancouver (e.g., White Rock, Delta, Richmond, Surrey, and Langley) access to American stores was sometimes more convenient than it was to outlets in the Vancouver city core.

In addition to Canadian trade, Samuel's was, of course, intended to also draw American shoppers from surrounding Whatcom County. Based on their many years of experience in the Vancouver furniture business, the owners established a positioning strategy for the product, price, and distribution components of the Samuel's marketing mix. In addition, part of the promotional mix was also determined. (The positioning strategy of the mix is shown below).

THE POSITIONING STRATEGY

Product

This element of the marketing mix was centred around two key attributes—quality and assortment. The owners realized that consumers had in recent years become sensitized to the issue of good product quality, especially when it came to big-ticket durables. As a result, they concentrated their product line selection on brand names that were well known for their quality construction and fabrics. Brands like Henredon, Century, Bernhardt, and Mastercraft, which consumers would recognize as having a good reputation, were given priority in the product mix.

The owners' concern with also offering a wide product assortment was reflected in the full range of home furnishings displayed on their 50 000 sq. ft. (4645 sq. metre) showroom floor. A display area of this size was considered to be very large in the furniture business, but the consumer drawing power in terms of the product assortment it could hold was felt to be worth the investment. Samuel's carried bedroom, dining-room, and living-room suites, as well as smaller decorating items such as lamps, occasional tables, and art work. In addition, for those customers who wanted even greater selection, they could custom order direct from manufacturers.

Price

Price ranges reflected the broad spectrum of selection and quality choices that the company felt were necessary to attract consumers in the competitive furniture business. For example, Samuel's carried complete living-room suites that varied from a low-end price of $1165 to a high-end value in the $12 000 range (all dollar values shown here have been converted to Canadian funds). For perspective, a medium-priced suite would sell for somewhere in the $3000 to $5000 range. In the furniture market, this pricing pattern would place the store in the mid to very high end of the competitive pricing spectrum.

Distribution

Samuel's delivered to both the US and Canadian markets. Delivery charges were established at a flat rate of $65. The company also cleared all customs, tax, and import requirements for Canadian buyers at the border. For in-stock items, the average delivery time was three days.

Promotion

Since personal selling, as well as quality service, was considered by the owners to be important in the sale of mid- to high-end furniture products, a total of eight sales staff and five warehouse employees were used in the Samuel's operation. A high level of product knowledge was required of the staff so that they could clearly explain and demonstrate product quality and features to customers.

A very important part of the promotional mix was incomplete however. The owners had not decided on what media to use in their introductory advertising campaign. Nor had they decided what media schedule or message content to use in positioning their new store in the minds of Canadian and American shoppers. To complicate matters even more, the Canadian exchange rate was beginning to weaken against the American dollar, and Elie, who was to manage Samuel's, was worried that this would drive away the price-sensitive Canadian shopper.

Samuel's had a $200 000 maximum advertising budget for their first year of operation. The owners knew from experience how quickly that could disappear. One weekend of heavy advertising on just BCTV, for example, could cost $4000. The budget would be spent very quickly if they chose a concentrated campaign. On the other hand, it could be spread out over the entire year with an intermittent campaign. Pulsing or flighting techniques could make the money last longer so that seasonal purchasing patterns could be exploited. Not enough advertising, however, and the whole campaign could fail and jeopardize the store's launch—not to mention the colossal waste of money that would be incurred.

Some preliminary information had been collected on possible media sources that might be used in the ad campaign. A number of the media vehicles under consideration along with comments regarding some of their strengths and weaknesses corresponded to the following:

Television

BCTV	72*	
CBUT	66	Canadian stations covering all of British Columbia with some spillover of TV signal to the US
CKVU	68	
KVOS	53	—American station in Bellingham covering Whatcom County and Vancouver markets

*% of Vancouver market reached

Radio

CHQM-AM	— older audience/easy listening format
CKNW-AM	— older audience/news & talk show format
CKLG-AM	— teenage and early 20s audience/rock station

All above are Canadian stations with limited spillover signal to the US.

KGMI-AM	— older audience/news & talk show format. US station with limited spillover to Vancouver market.
KISM-FM	— adults aged 35+/soft rock & easy listening format. US station with extensive spillover signal to Vancouver market.

Newspapers

Vancouver Sun
Vancouver Province
} Daily papers covering all of British Columbia. Some limited regional edition media buys possible. No contract rates available for large buys because Samuel's is an American-registered company.

Delta Optimist
Surrey Leader
White Rock
Peace Arch News
Langley Times
Richmond Review
} Community papers covering specific suburbs, all south of the Vancouver core. All of these are published one or two times per week (Mon–Thurs).

Bellingham Herald — American community paper serving Whatcom County.

S/ *Experience w/ Cdn mkt → name known*
→50 000 sqft showroom →large buy comparison
→Carrying well known brand names
→Delivery to both sides of border.
→Strong cut-off location →right on Interstate.
→Staff - high level of product knowledge.

W/ *Mid-high pricing spectrum but very price sensitive consumers*
(see threats)

O/ *→15.4 will cross borders*
→perception of larger assortment among Cdn shoppers
→Good selection of media vehicles & some which cover both markets

T/ *→Weakening exchange rate*
→price sensitive consumers.

UNIVERSITY OF OTTAWA INTERCOLLEGIATE SPORTS

David S. Litvack

The phone rang in the office of Luc Gelineau, the Director of Sports Services at the University of Ottawa. He had just finished a meeting with the Sports Services Advisory Council outlining the recent budget cuts to the "Big 5" intercollegiate programs and strategies to acquire alternative funding.[1] On the line was John Goldfarb, the manager of the local branch of the Royal Bank of Canada. The bank was recently approached as a potential sponsor of intercollegiate sports, and Mr. Goldfarb was calling to update Luc on the reaction of the bank executives. He summarized the situation, "Well Luc, I've spoken to several of the executives and it seems like we might be interested in getting involved. We're excited at the possibilities and would like to sit down and discuss the details. Specifically, we would like to know what type of exposure your teams can offer us."

Mr. Gelineau understood what Mr. Goldfarb was getting at, but after recently attending a football game and being surrounded by empty seats, he realized that he could provide few of the exposure incentives that he felt the bank was looking for (see Exhibit 18-1 for attendance records). He got off the phone, turned to his MBA interns and said, "Dammit guys, we have a quality product! Our soccer team won the National Championships, our football team is ranked third in the nation, and we've produced athletes that have competed internationally at the Olympics and professionally. How come we still can't get fans out to watch these stars of tomorrow! Set up another meeting with the Advisory Council. We need to

EXHIBIT 18-1 Ticket Sales Analysis (Average Attendance for Seasons 1991–96)									
Team	**1991–92**	**1992–93**		**1993–94**		**1994–95**		**1995–96**	
Football*	970	1163	(+20%)	815	(−30%)	531	(−35%)	625	(+18%)
Hockey	103	189	(+46%)	196	(+4%)	228	(+17%)	180	(−21%)
Volleyball**	58	138	(+140%)	147	(+7%)	124	(−16%)	181	(+14%)
Basketball**	154	281	(+82%)	213	(−24%)	220	(+3%)	201	(−9%)
Total Tickets	1312	1771	(+35%)	1371	(−23%)	1103	(−20%)	1147	(+4%)

* PANDA Game not included
**Based on regular season and exhibition games only (tournaments not included)

look at intercollegiate sports and investigate ways we can increase attendance at games and make it more attractive for sponsors to become involved."

BACKGROUND

Established in 1976, Sports Services at the University of Ottawa is a subsidiary of Student Affairs. They manage and operate all of the sporting facilities on campus, including the university's gymnasiums, the hockey arena, and the football field. In addition to offering recreational, instructional, and intramural activities to students, Sports Services provides the necessary training environment for student-athletes, enabling them to represent the university on an intercollegiate level. Presently, eight men's and seven women's teams compete at Canadian Intercollegiate Athletic Union (CIAU) or Ontario University Athletic Association/Ontario Women's Intercollegiate Athletic Association (OUAA/OWIAA) sanctioned events. Of these 15 intercollegiate teams, the five highest-profile sports are classified as the "Big 5."

Historically, Sports Services has relied on money raised through their recreational, instructional, and intramural programs, along with funds from student auxiliary fees, to operate each of the intercollegiate teams effectively. The 1994–95 overall intercollegiate budget was approximately $650 000.

The budgets for the "Big 5" teams were more than adequate to run their respective programs effectively prior to and including the 1994–95 season. However, more recently, several factors have caused significant reductions to each of the team's operating budgets and have raised the need to investigate alternative methods of funding. A discussion of some of these factors follows.

Gender Equity

The issue of gender equity in sports has become a "hot" topic, not only on the campuses of Canadian universities, but across the United States as well. In March 1994, the then-Director of Sports Services, Michel Leduc, appointed a committee on gender equity to study the status of women's involvement in Sports Services. In order to establish a policy of gender equity in intercollegiate sports, the committee recommended that financing and membership in men's and women's inter-university programs should reflect the gender distribution of the student population: Women = 56%; Men = 44%. In response to the above recommendation, Sports Services granted intercollegiate status to women's soccer and reduced the ratio of men's to women's financing from 2.66 in 1994–95 to 1.96 for the 1996–97 season. This decrease in funding for male-dominated teams (e.g., football) led to a chain of events which resulted in decreases to all intercollegiate teams.

Mass Participation

Increased enrollment in sports services is transforming the traditional competitive environment into a more recreational atmosphere. That is, more participation in recreational activities is occurring instead of traditional competitive intercollegiate sports.

Financial Constraints

In January 1996, the University of Ottawa outlined proposed cuts to the 1996–97 budget that would eliminate over $7 million from university services, including a 14%, or $435 000, reduction to the budget of Student Affairs. Increases to students' tuition fees and resulting demonstrations held by the Student Federation Union Organization (SFUO) have made it unrealistic for Sports Services to increase athletic auxiliary fees to compensate for the budget cuts. In addition, recent renovations to Sports Services' athletic facilities have resulted in a further strain on funds.

ENVIRONMENT

Student Life at the University of Ottawa

The University of Ottawa, North America's oldest and largest bilingual university, is located in the downtown core of the city. Student enrollment for the 1996–97 academic year totalled nearly 25 000 full-time and part-time students (see Exhibit 18-2 for specific breakdowns). In addition, 77% of the University's graduates remain in the Ottawa area.

The university school year begins with one week of activities for the new students (freshmen). These activities are organized by senior students that serve as floor reps in the residences, and executives of the faculty associations. Recently, these activities have included games, pub crawls, talent contests, and other events. Freshmen look to their senior peers for guidance and direction. At the same time, new students are looking to maximize their freedom and explore new activities and interests. Although the transition can be rough, active involvement in student life can smooth out the bumps in the adjustment period.

At the conclusion of this week, students move to the usual routine of courses and homework. Approximately two thousand students live in the university residences. Events are sporadically planned throughout the year, arranged by various associations and clubs, coinciding with calendar events such as Halloween, Christmas, Valentine's Day, etc. A vast

EXHIBIT 18-2 Student Composition at the University of Ottawa

	Graduate	Undergraduate	Total
Full-time	2 147	14 150	16 297
Part-time	1 378	6 074	7 452
TOTAL	3 525	20 224	23 749
English program	2 363	12 350	14 713
French program	1 162	7 874	9 036
TOTAL	3 525	20 224	23 749
Female	1 759	11 985	13 744
Male	1 766	8 239	10 005
TOTAL	3 525	20 224	23 749
Graduate students	3 525		3 525
0		22	22
Freshmen		8 480	8 480
Sophomores		4 511	4 511
Juniors		4 846	4 846
Seniors		2 365	2 365
TOTAL	3 525	20 224	23 749
Faculty:			
Administration	861	2 199	3 060
Arts	500	4 873	5 373
Common Law		561	561
Civil Law	67	516	583
Education	541	1 503	2 044
Engineering	372	1 357	1 729
Medicine	232	852	1 084
Science	359	2 031	2 390
Health Sciences	152	1 781	1 933
Social Science	441	4 521	4 962
Registrar's Office		30	30
TOTAL	3 525	20 224	23 749
Average Age:			
Full-time	32.0	24.2	25.2
Part-time	35.5	33.7	34.0
TOTAL	33.4	27.1	28.0

majority of these activities are organized by the faculty associations and are extremely popular with the students. However, faculty activities are rarely directed to the intercollegiate sports program. Currently there are nine faculties at the University of Ottawa (see Exhibit 18-2 for more details), each of which has its own student association.

The school year is divided into two semesters, fall and winter. The fall semester is broken up by the Thanksgiving weekend in early October, and University of Ottawa day (where regular students have the day off and prospective students visit the campus) at some point in late October. The Christmas break ends the month of December. The winter semester is highlighted by the study break in late February, and the four-day weekend in the beginning of April, before exams. The typical student has 15 hours of class time a week, plus additional homework time. In general, students will usually have some time to participate in extracurricular activities during the week.

Activities in Ottawa/Hull Region

With a relatively small and young population, the people of Ottawa have traditionally been strong supporters of all sporting events and activities. As of 1996, the region is home to two major junior hockey teams (Hull Olympiques, Ottawa 67s); three Inter-university Athletic Programs (Algonquin College, Carleton University, University of Ottawa); a triple-A baseball team (Ottawa Lynx); and three other professional sports franchises (Ottawa Rough Riders Football Club, Ottawa Senators Hockey Club, and Ottawa Loggers Roller Hockey Club).

Although all of the professional teams have been well-supported in the past, recently they have been experiencing significant attendance problems. This decline in attendance is threatening the very existence of the 126-year-old tradition of Rough Rider Football in Ottawa. As of Monday, November 4, 1996, the Canadian Football League revoked the Ottawa Rough Riders' franchise. Although there is talk of starting a new franchise, Ottawa fans are still left without football to satisfy their gridiron needs. Similarly, after initial enthusiasm for the introduction of the Senators in 1991, filling the newly constructed 19 000-seat Corel Centre has become a problem. Many of the supporters of these teams cite the high ticket prices and poor competitive performance as reasons for their absence.

Although attendance has demonstrated a sharp decline, there is still a strong base of potential supporters in the region. Ottawa residents are very active, and according to the last census, spend more money on entertainment than the average Canadian. Thus, instead of sporting events, people have turned to other entertainment options, such as the numerous theatres, museums, and art galleries that are located in the city.

The Game Experience

The "Big 5" varsity teams compete throughout the school year, with the seasons of different teams beginning and ending at different times. The football team "kicks off" the varsity season usually with the first game taking place at the end of the first week of class. While the football season ends in November, the hockey, basketball, and volleyball teams compete throughout both the fall and winter semesters.

Getting Students to Attend

Before deciding what should be done to alleviate the problem, the group of MBA interns decided to go to a game themselves.

Jeff, the most outgoing of the group attempted to encourage some of his classmates to come. He approached them and said: "Hey guys, a bunch of us are going to the game this weekend, why don't you come?"

Tara, usually a sports enthusiast responded: "What game? I haven't heard a thing about it!"

Jeff exclaimed: "How can you say that? There are posters in every building on campus and a pep rally was held at the campus bar."

"Oh. Is that what that was?" asked Adam sarcastically. "I thought it was a little get-together for the physics club."

"O.K! O.K! So a lot of people didn't show up, but I heard other promotions such as ticket giveaways and Rowdy Challenges[2] are being attempted to bring more fans out," responded Jeff.

In an attempt to stay away from the game, Adam interjected, "I was at a game last year and although the play was exciting it just wasn't made into an event."

Jeff replied, "Well guys, Sports Services apparently hires students to run promotions during the game and they hold contests at half-time. You could win a pizza or even drive home with a new car for a year."

"Hey! I like pizza," exclaimed Tara enthusiastically. "I'm willing to give the game a chance if the price is right. What is it going to cost us?"

"Well," Jeff explained, "There are different ticket prices depending on whether you are a student or not and whether you're interested in seeing more than one game" (see Exhibit 18-3 for a description of ticket prices).

EXHIBIT 18-3 Intercollegiate Ticket Price Structure

	Students	Adults
Regular season:		
Hockey	$ 2	$ 4
Basketball	$ 2	$ 4
Volleyball	$ 2	$ 4
Football	$ 4	$ 7
Playoffs:		
Hockey	$ 3	$ 5
Basketball	$ 3	$ 5
Volleyball	$ 3	$ 5
Football	$ 4	$ 7
Season pass: (admits individual to all home games)	$20	$30

Tara replied, "You know, I've always wanted to go to a Gee-Gees game, but I never know where the games are played. Where are the games played and how do you get ..."

Interrupting Tara, Adam began to chuckle and said, "Yeah, the reason you don't know where to go is because the football games are a half-hour walk from campus."

Jeff acknowledged the distance to the football stadium but said, "All of the other teams play their games right on campus, so there's no excuse!"

Finally, after realizing that the game might be an opportunity to have a good time and meet new people, Adam agreed to go to the game with Jeff and some of his classmates.

The Game as an Event

In the Spring of 1994, a marketing survey was conducted in an attempt to understand students' perceptions of Sports Services. As part of their survey, an analysis of intercollegiate sports revealed that while the majority of students were interested in sports, only a small percentage were drawn into supporting the Gee-Gees. With regard to those students who attended football games, a majority of the respondents (31%) answered that they went to the games to be with friends. Interestingly, only 15% of the respondents who attended did so to see the game.

In addition to the above findings, an informal survey conducted by the promotions officer of Sports Services revealed that in order to make the games more attractive, more than just the game would need to be offered. In fact, this finding was consistent with past attendance records. Games with high attendance were often associated with an event outside of the game itself. The survey also identified that students have the perception that the quality of the games is poor, even though past successes are numerous.

The annual Panda Game between Ottawa and Carleton is a good example of game-related events resulting in elevated attendance. This historical game always attracts a large number of students, as events leading up to the game promote rivalries between the two universities. While attendance for the Panda game has ranged from 2000 to 5000 in recent years, Sports Services has had a difficult time carrying these numbers over to other regular-season games. In contrast, several other Canadian universities have been able to maintain a respectable number of spectators at all of their games by making them an event and part of the university tradition. However, this has not occurred at the University of Ottawa.

Sports Services' Dilemma

Back in his office, Luc was getting ready for the meeting with the Advisory Council when he turned to his interns. "You know guys, I am so damn frustrated! I have been working like mad to get a sponsorship deal with the Royal Bank and I'm not sure if it is going to happen. I would love to invite some of their managers out to the game on Saturday and show them the outstanding product that we have to offer. However, how could I if our fan support is typical of most games? They would probably no longer be interested in working out a deal! How do I get more people to attend our games?"

Luc reflected on a game he had attended at the University of Michigan between the Wolverines and the Buckeyes from Ohio State, where the stands were filled to the rafters with over 100 000 fans. He thought how nice it would be to get even a small percentage of those numbers to come out to a game. If only the University of Ottawa could cultivate this type of environment, then attaining the support of students, alumni, local residents, companies, and sponsors would be easy.

Although Luc knew what they wanted, he did not know how it should be accomplished. Out of frustration, he turned to his interns and said: "What should we do?"

ENDNOTES

1. The big five teams are basketball (male and female), hockey, football, and volleyball.
2. A Rowdy Challenge is a competition between two groups on campus, usually within residence, to see who has more spirit at a sporting event.

HEC ON THE INTERNET

Stéphane Bossé and Normand Turgeon

Mathieu Pérnier and Christine Tremblay, two Masters students at École des Hautes Études Commerciales (HEC), had been working together for a few months on their end of studies project. Specializing in information systems, they were studying the impact of new information technologies on the enterprise, in particular, the effect of the Internet. Mathieu had a passion for the Internet and he developed a site for the student associations of HEC. With the help of Christine, he wanted to present his project to the Board of Directors of the student association and to the man responsible for the HEC Web site, professor Jean Talbot.

A UNIQUE UNIVERSITY SITE ON THE INTERNET

Mathieu had been investigating the idea of a Web site for the school since his arrival in Montreal. Mathieu, from France was participating in an exchange program to finish his studies in Quebec. When he had applied to the M.Sc. program (Masters of Management Science) at HEC, he found the procedures both long and costly. One factor that contributed to the length of the process was that all correspondence was by mail, with a minimum of a week to 10 days for each mail delivery. Between the initial request for information and the final letter of registration confirmation, several months could pass. The process was also expensive, as Mathieu had to call Montreal on numerous occasions to find a research supervisor for his thesis.

Upon his arrival in Montreal, Mathieu learned that a new Web site had just been created. Curious by nature and an experienced Web surfer, Mathieu decided to explore HEC through the Internet (visit www.hec.ca). He found a wealth of information, beginning with a detailed menu.

Mathieu knew that the school was working on enhancing the site, and that the Patrick Allen Library catalogue was accessible via GOPHER, an information highway service, but he hadn't imagined the site would be so advanced. This would have made the registration procedure a lot easier for him as it contained all of the information he needed about the school. The site dealt with all subjects related to the school, including study programs, student services, personnel, education services, research, and various other topics.

Mathieu noted, however, that the subject of extracurricular activities wasn't listed, notably information on student associations. He got the idea to develop a *student associations* section. Mathieu formed a partnership with Christine Tremblay, who was equally interested in the Internet. Christine was working at establishing marketing information systems (MIS). Within her research, she envisioned the Internet as a way for the firm to get information on its own clientele, and on customers in general. She was also working on the technical aspect of computer systems and had developed an evaluation of the technical conception (programming or software) and hardware (physical equipment and peripherals).

THE PRESENT HEC SITE

Enthusiastic about the idea of developing the student associations section for the HEC site, Mathieu and Christine decided to have a meeting with the person responsible for the Web site, Jean Talbot, associate professor with education services and information technology. Talbot was very helpful and explained in detail the objectives of the HEC Internet page, and the current progress on the site.

The site was targeted to three groups of users: teachers at educational institutions, students, and the business world in general. It served, above all, as a communication tool. It allowed HEC, for a relatively low overall cost, to connect with any of the 40 million Internet users around the world who might have an interest in the university and its programs.

From a technical point of view, the school, thanks to its computer services, already possesses the equipment and specialists to create and manage a Web site. For Talbot, the site content was a problem. It was, in effect, impossible for his team (the head of the project and himself) to write and update the complete body of text, considering time, budget constraints, and the astronomic quantity of information on the site. Thus, Talbot acted as project coordinator.

The content of the Web site came from many sources within the school, and was then integrated within the site by Talbot and his team. In a cooperative spirit, Talbot continued to encourage the development of new sections. For example, in collaboration with the public relations office, publicity campaigns and press releases were added to the site. For Talbot, the principal short- and middle-term objectives were to expand and improve the site content (of which many sections were still in development), and to attract more visitors to the site. To measure the effectiveness of the Web page, the number of hits (i.e., the number of visitors) in a given period was monitored.

THE FUTURE HEC SITE

Mathieu and Christine prepared a site plan that they contemplated adding to the existing HEC Web page. The section on student associations would include the following topics:

general information, associations (history and description), calendar of events, e-mail, and a list of directors and members. Each of these topics was subdivided further. For example, the section associations was subdivided into different topics, including, Student Radio, Business Relations Society, and PROMO 95, among others.

Nevertheless, the two contributors desired to make this site as attractive as possible. They wanted to maximize the impact of the site by using all the multimedia and graphics capabilities for audio-visual elaboration. Mathieu and Christine reserved a surprise for the committee: the sale of advertising space as a method of financing the project.

THE MARKETING COMMITTEE OF THE HEC STUDENT ASSOCIATIONS

The Board of Directors of the student association decided it was necessary to create a marketing committee. This committee was composed of five members: three marketing students, one finance student, and one accounting student.

After their meeting with the Board of Directors of the student association, Mathieu and Christine presented the Internet project to the marketing committee. The Internet project was a priority for this committee because it had already planned to create one for the next academic year. Christine and Mathieu were one step ahead of the committee, and due to their expertise, they could help speed up the project.

A SUMMIT MEETING … OF THE INTERNET

Christine and Mathieu prepared a demonstration of their site for the committee. They made a simplified version of the site that they were planning to launch on the Internet.

The simulation resembled the actual site, but the information was presented in a condensed format. Christine, being technically competent, placed considerable emphasis on multimedia enhancements, including several images, a 12-second audio-visual welcome from the director of the school (taken from an official school video from audio-visual services), and a few video sequences taken from amateur filming done by the students of the school.

Following Mathieu's suggestions, Christine included a surprise element in the presentation: advertising clips comprised of logos from large enterprises, such as Bell Canada, and professional orders, such as the Quebec Order of Chartered Accountants. In effect, Christine had used the waiting moments, the bottom of pages, and presentation pages to display the advertisements. For example, within the section *list of directors and members*, there is the message, "This page is sponsored by Bell Canada," along with the company logo. According to Mathieu, who conceived the idea, the advertisements could largely finance the cost of creating and maintaining the site.

The members of the committee were impressed by Mathieu and Christine's presentation. Martine, a marketing student and a member of PROMO (a committee responsible for financing activities), was thrilled by the project. She could already picture advertising the next activities (e.g., parties, fashions shows) on the site. Advertising would permit the student association to offer added value to retailers and other potential partners. Martine suggested that Bell Canada might consider offering discounts in return for advertising on the Internet site.

Alain Laquerre, the finance student on the committee, questioned the use of a Web page to promote student associations. Alain always had the impression that the Internet was more a toy for adults than a promotion tool. Also, he was opposed to making the creation of the site a priority over the other tasks facing the committee. Alain believed that the Internet was simply a passing fad. Further, he questioned whether the school would permit the use of its Web site to announce parties, and to promote beer. According to Alain, students were not the only Internet users. He thought it would be inappropriate if a businessperson visited the site and was exposed to a beer promotion. In Alain's view, HEC was a superior educational establishment and not a student bar.

Claire Pothier, one of the marketing students, didn't agree with Alain. She also viewed the school as a superior educational institution, but she thought the financing of the project by selling advertising was appropriate, particularly in a school that taught business. She did not believe that they should have to limit and censor the advertising content simply because the site belonged to a university. The other two members of the committee put forward their opinions and the group engaged in a mini-debate on advertising on the Web site.

ONTARIO RUTABAGA COUNCIL

Jane Funk and Thomas Funk

In June of 1996, Smithfield Communications was retained by the Ontario Rutabaga Council (ORC) to develop a new promotional campaign for Ontario rutabagas. This was a fairly unusual account for the medium-sized agency, which specialized in agriculture. The average Smithfield client had a promotional budget of $4 million. The firm's clients included a number of organizations in the fertilizer, chemical, feed, and seed industries. They also handled a few industrial accounts, the largest of which was the $6 million Warren ("Windows to the World") Window account.

The agency was established in 1972 by Simon Smithfield, a former sales representative for Massey Ferguson. Smithfield had started by working with equipment accounts, but as the business prospered and the staff expanded, the firm moved into other areas of agri-business and industrial products. The agency remained fairly conservative in its approach. Smithfield's own specialty was slogans, but the real agency emphasis was on "quality" promotion designed to inform customers. Though Smithfield himself had no formal marketing training, he was a great believer in hiring account executives with a marketing background because he recognized that ad executives couldn't work in a vacuum.

"We have to work on behalf of the client! We have to look at their strategy or help them develop one. Otherwise they may as well toss their money down a rat hole for all the good a flashy ad campaign will do! What's more, we gotta have the guts to tell them their ideas stink! We owe them that honesty!"

This philosophy was still at work at Smithfield, though Simon had retired. Every junior account person was thoroughly versed in the philosophy and history of the company.

Though the agency dealt mainly with agri-business accounts, Smithfield had never been in favour of hiring only those with an agricultural background. As Simon often said, "Too narrow-minded! If he grew up on a hog farm in Simcoe, then basically he thinks he has the last word on hogs! In this business you need a wide range of experience and a quick, open mind."

Most of Smithfield's junior ad people came right out of university. One of the latest additions was Ted Banner, a graduate of the Ontario Agricultural College. Ted had been with Smithfield for two years. He learned fast and was quite ambitious. To date, his greatest success had been the brochure for Farnum Feed. On the basis of his past performance, Smithfield executives felt he was ready to take on the ORC account.

Ted realized this was his big chance. The ORC account was expected to increase to around $300 000 for 1996/97 and he planned to make the campaign a real landmark. First, however, he knew he must do his homework, so he began studying all the background material he had collected on the ORC.

RUTABAGA INDUSTRY IN CANADA

Canadian rutabagas were originally used as feed for sheep which were bound for New England markets in the mid-1800s. In those days, rutabagas were called turnips. The sheep buyers themselves tried the vegetable and ordered more for their own consumption. These early turnips were a far cry from the sweeter-tasting turnip developed in the 1930s and known as the Laurentian. This variety became known officially as the rutabaga in 1967. The rutabaga is large and globular in shape, with yellow flesh and a purple top. Usually it is waxed to preserve it during shipping and storage. Rutabagas vary in size from one to three pounds and cost anywhere from 25 to 30 cents a pound.

Ontario is the centre for Canadian rutabaga production, though some Canadian competition comes from Quebec and P.E.I. The Ontario industry supports 130 growers plus a number of shippers and packers. In 1988, the farm value of rutabagas in Ontario was $5.9 million, making it the eighth highest for vegetables grown in Ontario. Rutabagas reach the consumer by way of the following channel: Farmer → Packer → Shipper → Wholesaler → Supermarkets and Fruit and Vegetable Stores.

A large share of the Ontario rutabaga crop is shipped to the United States; in fact, rutabagas account for approximately 15 to 20 percent of the value of all fresh and processed vegetables exported to the US from Canada. Rutabagas are also grown in the US, but Ontario rutabagas are considered superior. Since there is no tariff on rutabagas, Canadian rutabagas compete effectively in price with those grown in the US.

PAST PROMOTIONAL EFFORTS

Although the ORC had coordinated promotional programs on behalf of rutabaga producers for many years, its efforts were hampered by small budgets that often varied significantly from year to year. For example, last year, the ORC had a $60 000 promotional budget, while the year before it was over $100 000. They used their budget, mainly in the United States, to promote rutabagas to homemakers as a unique and different vegetable. In the United States, most rutabagas are consumed South of the Mason Dixon Line and East of the Mississippi River, and the ORC felt that the main competition in this area was white turnips and turnip greens; hence, their program of differentiating the rutabaga.

To formulate their promotional program, the ORC hired the advertising agency of J.B. Cruikshank Ltd. This agency prepared a promotion mix consisting of magazine ads, press releases for radio, a TV video, and a video for high-school family-science teachers. All of this was developed around the persona of "June Conway," the fictional resident home economist for the ORC.

The magazine ads appeared in *Woman's Day* and *Family Circle* magazines during the months of November (the beginning of the holiday season in the United States, which is the peak period of rutabaga consumption) and April (the end of the turnip season in the United States). These full-page ads stressed new uses and recipe ideas, and featured a sample recipe and picture. They mentioned, but did not stress, nutrition, and they included a free write-in offer for a rutabaga recipe book. The agency reported that this phase of the program had received a "reasonable response" of 1000 requests per month.

Other aspects of this promotional program included press releases for radio and a short TV video. The agency hoped the radio releases would be aired in the late morning or early afternoon on women's shows. The television video, produced at a cost of $28 000 and entitled "Everything You Wanted to Know About Rutabagas—But Didn't Know Who to Ask," was distributed upon request to cable TV channels for use at their convenience. The agency felt "this scheduling gave the video excellent exposure without requiring the ORC to pay for air time." The film highlighted the growing of rutabagas and their nutritional value, and included attractive recipe ideas. In addition to this, a new video entitled "The Ontario Rutabaga in the Kitchen" was distributed to high-school family-science teachers.

The TV video, like the magazine ads, included a write-in address for recipes, but response here was not as high as for the magazines. Mr. Cruikshank explained "this doesn't indicate less interest, but rather that TV viewers are less likely to copy an address down and mail for more information than those who see advertisements in a magazine or newspaper." Mr. Cruikshank further reported that "by use, the video appears successful. All ten prints are booked well in advance." He encouraged the ORC to increase the number of video copies and increase the number of high school videos available. Board member Fred Hunsberger supported this idea, especially increasing the number of high school videos available. He felt that "We have to let those kids know what a good value tur-rutabagas are. If we get them early on, we've got them for life."

CURRENT SITUATION

ORC President, Clyde Carson, was not as excited about Cruikshank's suggestion as was Fred. He had recently seen a publication entitled "Report on the New England Market for Canadian Rutabagas," which documented a decline in rutabaga consumption in that area. Further research revealed that per capita, rutabaga consumption had been declining for the past twenty years, and growers were reducing their acreage or leaving the industry altogether. Clyde presented these depressing statistics to the ORC and suggested a new "marketing strategy" like that discussed at a seminar he had recently attended. As expected, Clyde ran into heavy opposition from other Board members, who did not understand what a marketing strategy was and who were more interested in increasing their production levels. Fred Hunsberger had been particularly adamant about keeping their current promotional program.

"Clyde, we're already telling 'em about all the vitamins and offering free recipes. Now what woman wouldn't jump at a free recipe? And that June Conway is a mighty fine woman!

The way she talks about those rutabagas just makes my mouth water. And the kids are sure to like the video. I sure would have been pleased to see videos when I was in school! That TV cable film is doing the job too. Booked solid all last year. It looks real classy to have our own TV film. Just a fluke that consumption is down. People don't know when they're well off these days. You wait! The old values will come back soon and people will see that turnips—uh—rutabagas are good solid food!"

Clyde persevered and finally got the Board to agree to a large-scale study of the North American rutabaga market. The project was funded mainly by the Ontario Ministry of Agriculture and involved two stages. The first stage was to obtain rutabaga awareness and usage information from 2000 Canadian and 6000 US households. More detailed information was obtained in the second stage on usage, attitudes, and preferences from 300 households in Canada and 800 in the US. Based on the report, Clyde was able to convince the ORC that a drastic overhaul was needed. The first thing they did was to find a replacement for J.B. Cruikshank Ltd., the ad agency responsible for "Everything You Always Wanted to Know About…." Fred Hunsberger had insisted that Smithfield Communications be hired as a replacement because, "That's a classy outfit! I knew old Sim when he was with Massey and I'll never forget his big 'Keep Pace with Case' campaign. That's what we need. A catchy slogan! It will turn the tide in a few weeks. Look at the milk people. My grand kids won't stop singing 'Drink Milk, Love Life.' Drives me crazy but they say it sells the milk. Why not tur-rutabagas too? Of course, we'll keep June Conway."

Clyde didn't argue with Fred, though he privately felt that perhaps Smithfield Communications was not the best choice and questioned the usefulness of a slogan. Fred, on the other hand, thought that Smithfield Communications' familiarity with agriculture would be an asset. The two men planned a meeting with Ted Banner, the Smithfield Communications manager assigned to the ORC account.

RESEARCH PROJECT RESULTS

Ted Banner sat at his desk in the office of Smithfield Communications. In front of him were various documents and folders containing background and past promotional programs of the ORC. On top of the pile was a manuscript entitled "Consumer Analysis of the North American Rutabaga Market," the report which presented the results of the large-scale survey done in 1995. Ted knew that this report had to form the basis of his recommendations to the ORC. In preparation for his initial meeting with Clyde Carson and Fred Hunsberger, Ted looked through the report and summarized the main points.

Common Product Names

The report revealed that the product is called by many different names, including rutabaga, swede, swede turnip, and turnip. In the United States, 78 percent of consumers referred to the product as a rutabaga, compared to only 20 percent in Canada.

Awareness and Frequency of Use

Consumers were placed in one of six categories depending on their awareness and frequency of rutabaga use. These results are shown in Exhibit 20-1.

EXHIBIT 20-1 Rutabaga Market Segments, United States and Canada

Market Segments	Percent of Canadian Households	Percent of United States Households
Non-user, not aware	11	14
Non-user, aware	16	40
Lapsed user (not used in past year)	8	14
Light user (less than 4 times a year)	23	19
Medium user (5 to 12 times a year)	25	9
Heavy user (more than 12 times a year)	16	3

The first category is relatively small and contains people who are not aware of rutabagas. The second category contains people who are aware of rutabagas but have never purchased one. This group is relatively small in Canada but large in the US. The third group contains people who have not purchased a rutabaga in the last twelve months. These are probably "lapsed users," who have discontinued use of the product. This is a relatively small group.

The last three groups are classified as current rutabaga users and account for 64 percent of Canadian consumers and 31 percent of American consumers. The heavy user segment accounts for 16 percent of Canadian consumers but only 3 percent of American consumers.

User and Non-User Profiles

Analysis of the above groups in terms of demographic characteristics revealed some distinct profiles. In Canada, rutabaga usage tends to be highest among older consumers, consumers who live in rural areas and small communities, French-speaking Canadians, families whose female head is either a homemaker or retired, and families whose male and female head have less education. US results are very similar, with rutabaga usage being highest among older consumers, lower-income families, families whose male and female heads have less education, single-person households, and blacks.

Vegetable Purchase Criteria

Consumers in the study were asked to rank six possible purchase criteria. The highest ranking criteria were quality, nutritional value, and taste preference. Price and time needed to prepare the vegetable were of some but lesser importance. Rutabaga users consistently ranked price higher than taste preference. Non-users ranked taste preference ahead of price.

Consumers in both countries responded to a series of statements designed to measure attitudes toward a number of issues related to vegetable and rutabaga usage. The following attitudes emerged:

- Consumers feel they are eating about the right quantity and variety of vegetables, but a sizable group think they should eat more and a greater variety. This is particularly true for the non-user segment.

- Rutabagas are not considered expensive in relation to other vegetables, but consumers stated that large price increases could cause some reduction in consumption.

- A large percentage of consumers increased their purchases of rutabagas when on special. Most consumers felt that rutabagas were seldom "featured" items at their stores.

- Most consumers felt that rutabagas are not conveniently located, nor attractively displayed, and frequently not available at their stores.

- A large percentage of consumers felt that rutabagas are generally too large for the size of their families. They indicated an interest in pre-sliced, ready-to-cook rutabagas or, especially in the US, ready-to-serve rutabaga casseroles.

- Most consumers judge product quality by external appearance and many felt that the rough, black or brown spots on the exterior of the rutabaga indicated inferior quality.

- Many consumers commented on the difficulty of preparing a rutabaga.

- Most consumers have little information on the nutritional value of rutabagas and would like more.

Reasons for Non-Users and Lapsed Users

Both non-users and lapsed users listed not liking the taste as the main reason for non-use. The second most frequent reply given by non-users was that they didn't know how to cook or prepare them. Lapsed users listed several secondary reasons: too much trouble to prepare, too hard to cut, poor quality, and prefer more nutritious vegetables.

Purchase and Use

Rutabaga users were asked about their purchase and use of the product. Their responses indicated that:

- Approximately one-half of all users decide to purchase the product after entering a store.

- Almost all purchases are made in supermarkets.

- The most popular methods of preparation are boiled and mashed.

- Less than 30 percent of all users serve the vegetable raw.

- The vegetable's consumers consider carrots and squash close substitutes for rutabagas.

- Most consumers consider the rutabaga as an ordinary everyday dish.

- Over 80 percent of all current users indicated that they were using rutabagas just as often or more often than five years ago.

- Most consumers obtain recipe ideas from magazines and newspapers.

TED'S REACTION

After thoroughly studying the background information and the research report, Ted knew that the problem he faced was far more complex than he imagined. His telephone conversations with Clyde Carson indicated that Carson was aware of the severity and complexity of the problem, but Carson hinted that other Council members expected a "magic cure-all" along the lines of the famous "Keep Pace with Case" campaign of a few years ago. Ted knew he would need to call on all his tact as well as his past marketing background in order to come up with a promotional campaign for the ORC. His first task, however, would be to develop a set of marketing strategy recommendations based on the research report he had just read.

C a s e

HEALTH CARE CORPORATION OF ST. JOHN'S: MEAL DELIVERY SYSTEM

H.F. (Herb) MacKenzie

This case is designed to provide some insight into the purchasing process for expensive items, and to provide students with an opportunity to actually be involved in the negotiating process through a practical simulation. There are few marketing cases that involve experiential learning within one or two classes.

BACKGROUND

On April 5, 1998, Health Care Corporation (HCC) of St. John's called for tenders for a meal delivery system to service six locations within the city: General Hospital, Grace General Hospital, Janeway Child Health Centre, Leonard A. Miller Centre, St. Clare's Mercy Hospital, and Waterford Hospital. HCC was building an off-site food production, assembly, and distribution centre that would be responsible for providing all the food requirements for the six hospitals. The meals would be delivered to the six locations by refrigerated truck three times each day, and would then be rethermalized (reheated) at each site.

Along with an advertisement in the local newspaper, the Request for Proposal (RFP) was sent to five companies. The bill of material included 48 retherm units and 144 transfer carts (99 carts holding 24 trays each, and 45 carts holding 30 trays each). The bill of material also included plastic trays with lids, 6 oz. china soup bowls with lids, and coffee mugs with lids, in sufficient quantities to fill all of the transfer carts.

When the RFP closed on April 24, 1998, three companies submitted bids; however, only two of them, Grande Cuisine Systems and Burlodge Canada, committed to making

This case was written by H.F. (Herb) MacKenzie as the basis for class discussion rather than to illustrate either effective or ineffective handling of an administrative situation. Some data and terms in Exhibit 21-1 have been disguised. Copyright ©1999 by H.F. (Herb) MacKenzie. Reprinted with permission.

on-site presentations to demonstrate their systems. A copy of the Grande Cuisine Systems quotation is shown in Exhibit 21-1.

A formal procedure was developed so that both systems could be fairly compared. Each system was tested with delivery and rethermalizing of 14 different test menus, including, for

---

EXHIBIT 21-1 Grande Cuisine—Price Quotation

For: Health Care Corporation of St. John's

RFP #1998-0445

Meal Delivery System

Description	Unit Price	Quantity	Total Cost
Double-Flow Retherm Cart – 24	14 982.00	33	494 406.00
Double-Flow Retherm Cart – 30	15 118.00	15	226 770.00
Ergosert Transfer Cart – 24	6 890.00	99	682 110.00
Ergosert Transfer Cart – 30	7 073.00	45	318 285.00
Ergoserve Insert – 24	2 830.00	99	280 170.00
Ergoserve Insert – 30	2 924.00	45	131 580.00
Trays	35.00	3726	130 410.00
8″ high heat lids	11.10	3726	41 358.60
6 oz. soup bowl (China)	4.95	3726	18 443.70
Lid for bowl	1.60	3726	5 961.60
Coffee mug and lid	3.00	3726	11 178.00
Grand Total			$2 340 672.90

Options:

48 Timers		360.00 ea.	17 280.00
48 Polycarbonate Doors for the Double-Flow Terminal		956.00 ea.	45 888.00
144 Lockable Doors for the Ergoserve		120.00 ea.	17 280.00

Special Terms and Conditions:

Buy-back for current RXCF system		185 000.00	
Estimated freight to St. John's		34 300.00	

Standard Terms and Conditions

Delivery	26 weeks from order date
Penalty for late delivery	$5000.00 per month
Cancellation charges (if client cancels order)	5% of total contract price
Warranty	3 years, parts and labour
	5 years on Double-Flow units
Terms of payment	50% with order; 50% on delivery
Inflation escalator	3% per year
F.O.B. Point	Montreal, PQ

example, a breakfast of cheese omelet and grilled ham with whole wheat toast; a lunch of macaroni and cheese with garlic bread and salad; a dinner of roast turkey, dressing, peas, mashed potato, and gravy. Other evaluation criteria that HCC used included a maintenance assessment, an ergonomic evaluation, an evaluation of warranty and service, and a formal company presentation by each of the companies. Burlodge Canada made the first presentation, followed by Grande Cuisine Systems.

Ted Mussett, the Atlantic Provinces salesperson for Grande Cuisine Systems, arranged to have one system shipped to St. John's for testing. After the test period, Nigel Myles, Vice-President of Operations for Grande Cuisine Systems, travelled from Montreal to make the presentation with Ted. The two men met with Bruce Gorman, Director of Materials Management for the Health Care Corporation, and Jean Day, Director of Food Services for Nova Services, a division of Beaver Foods Limited. Bruce's role was to ensure that the RFP was written so that several companies could compete. He also was responsible to ensure that the bidding and evaluation processes were fair to all companies that were hoping to be awarded the contract. Jean's role was to help evaluate the food delivery system as it would be employees of Nova Services that would have to use the system once it was purchased. Nova Services had the service contract from HCC to supply food services to all of its hospitals. Nova Services would manage the central food preparation facility, and be responsible for food delivery to and distribution of food within the off-site locations.

THE FOOD DELIVERY SYSTEM

The system that Grande Cuisine decided to offer was a combination of the Ergoserve (see Exhibit 21-2) and the Double-Flow Terminal (see Exhibit 21-3). The Ergoserve is actually comprised of two parts, the Ergosert, which is the outside shell, and a stainless steel insert that holds the trays. The Ergoserve is divided vertically in two sections and both sections are refrigerated when the unit is attached to the Double-Flow Terminal. Approximately 40 minutes before meals are to be served, one section of the Ergoserve is rethermalized. This heats the items on one side of the tray while keeping the items on the other side cold.

EXHIBIT 21-2 Ergoserve (Comprised of the Ergosert and Stainless Steel Insert)

The Double-Flow Terminal is a stationery unit that is kept at the six off-site locations. One of the major advantages of the Grande Cuisine system is that the Ergosert can also be kept at the off-site locations, preventing damage that might occur if the unit had to travel to and from the central food preparation site. The only items that had to be transported were the stainless steel inserts and the trays of food. When these items arrive at the off-site locations, the insert is pushed into the Ergoserve, and the Ergoserve is then connected to the Double-Flow Terminal (see

Exhibit 21-4). When the food has been rethermalized, the Ergoserve is disconnected and taken to the location within the hospital where needed. The insert is removed from the Ergoserve and trays are taken from the insert and distributed to patients. At the same time, the Ergosert can be returned to the kitchen area. This prevents staff from reloading the insert back in the Ergosert with dirty food trays and utensils that could make the whole unit unsanitary, requiring additional cleaning effort. In this way, the inserts and food trays are returned directly to the loading dock area where they go back to the central food preparation area to be cleaned and reloaded with the next meals.

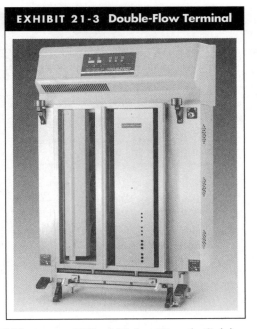

EXHIBIT 21-3 Double-Flow Terminal

NEGOTIATION SIMULATION

Your instructor will normally divide you into groups of four and one person will play each of the roles identified in the case: Ted Mussett and Nigel Myles (Grande Cuisine Systems), Bruce Gorman (HCC), and Jean Day (Nova Services). Your instructor will also provide each person with additional details of each role, with instructions. Using this additional information, the two teams are to negotiate an agreement that both agree to accept. Exhibit 21-5 is a contract that is to be completed and signed to finalize the negotiations between the two companies (a copy of the contract will be provided to the person playing the role of Bruce Gorman).

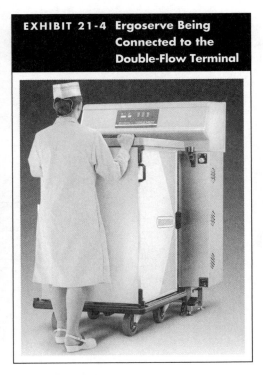

EXHIBIT 21-4 Ergoserve Being Connected to the Double-Flow Terminal

CASE PURPOSE

Negotiations play an important part in the selling of many products in business and organizational marketing (and in consumer marketing too). One of the best ways to teach negotiating skills is through role playing and similar experiential exercises. Hopefully, students will learn from the opportunity to participate in a realistic exercise such as this. Further, the exercise provides the basis to discuss various negotiation strategies and tactics appropriate for business and organizational buyers and sellers.

EXHIBIT 21-5 Final Contract

HCC Meal Delivery System

Description of final system if not completely as described in the Grande Cuisine Systems quotation:

_____

_____

_____

_____

System Price: _____

Options if taken:

    Timers: _____

    Polycarbonate Doors for Double-Flow Terminals   _____

    Locking Doors for the Ergoserve   _____

    Buy back for the RXCF system   _____

    Freight   _____

TOTAL: _____

Standard Terms and Conditions

Delivery   _____ weeks from order date

Penalty for late delivery   _____ per month

Cancellation charges (if client cancels order)   _____ % of total contract price

Warranty   _____ years, parts and labour

     _____ years on Double-Flow units

Terms of payment   _____

Inflation escalator   _____ % per year

F.O.B. Point   _____

Signatures: _____   _____

    Health Care Corporation of St. John's   Grande Cuisine Systems

PROVEL

Thomas Funk and Stephan Fleming

Dr. Bob McManus, newly appointed Manager of Provel, was in the process of preparing a marketing plan for his first product, Micotil, a very effective single-injection therapy for the treatment of Bovine Respiratory Disease (BRD). The product had just received registration for use in all non-dairy cattle in Canada. Bob knew this was a large market and the potential for Provel could be substantial. He also knew that the marketing decisions he made for this product would have long-run implications for his new company. With these thoughts in mind, Bob started to think seriously about the development of his first year's plan.

PROVEL

Provel, located in London, Ontario, is the new Veterinary Products division of Eli Lilly Canada Inc. The company was established to provide pharmaceutical products and technical services exclusively to veterinarians. Prior to the establishment of Provel, Elanco, another division of Eli Lilly Canada, acted as the distributor of all Lilly products to both the over-the-counter and ethical markets. The over-the-counter market consists of selling to farmers through a variety of retail outlets, such as feed and farm supply dealers. The ethical market, on the other hand, involves reaching end users through veterinarians. Provel was established because of the increasingly important role veterinarians play in the use of products for animal agriculture. Currently, the veterinarian market for pharmaceutical products in Canada is estimated at $60 million and expected to grow rapidly in the future. The company focuses

This case was prepared by Thomas Funk and Stephan Fleming of the Ontario Agricultural College at the University of Guelph, Guelph, Ontario, Canada. It is intended as a basis for classroom discussion and is not designed to present either correct or incorrect handling of administrative problems. Some of the data in the case have been disguised to protect confidentiality. Copyright ©1994 by Thomas Funk. Reprinted with permission.

exclusively on products for large animal, commercial agriculture, particularly beef, dairy, and swine. Its goal is to have ten products in its line by the end of the first five years. Although Provel itself is a new company, both Lilly and Elanco are well-established organizations with outstanding reputations for quality products and services.

MICOTIL

The first major product available to Provel from Eli Lilly is Micotil, a very effective single-injection therapy for the treatment of Bovine Respiratory Disease. Bovine Respiratory Disease is a term used to describe certain types of pneumonia in cattle. The North American practice of calving in the spring and weaning in the fall contributes to this problem. Calves are protected against this disease while they are nursing because their mothers' milk contains protective antibodies. At the time of weaning, they lose this protection. Unfortunately, at six months of age the calf's own immune system is not fully functional. This, combined with the stress involved in moving to a feedlot, predisposes young cattle to BRD. BRD is the most significant disease occurring in cattle that enter a feedlot. Experience has shown that approximately 35% of all calves entering a feedlot may be affected by BRD, and therefore require treatment. Mortality associated with BRD can range from 5% to 10%. In addition, cattle with BRD experience slow growth and poor feed conversion. As a result, the economic value of these losses to a feedlot operator can be substantial.

Although there are a number of markets that appear attractive for Micotil, the two largest are the veal market and the feedlot market. Veal production in Canada is concentrated in Ontario and Quebec, and is estimated to consist of approximately 400 000 animals annually. There are approximately 7500 veal producers in Canada. Most veal operations fall in the 50 to 100 animal range.

Feedlot operations are found in all regions of Canada, but are especially important in Western Canada. There are approximately 2.5 million calves entering feedlots each year, of which 1.5 million are in the West. Although the average feedlot in the country produces approximately 60 steers, there is a tremendous range in annual production. For example, there are over 2000 feedlots that have annual capacity in excess of 500 steers.

There are three types of products currently on the market for use in treating BRD. The key products, together with their manufacturers and approximate market shares, are shown in Exhibit 22-1. Exhibit 22-2 summarizes key characteristics of BRD products. Withdrawal period refers to the length of time required for all traces of the antibiotic to be gone from the animal. Treated animals cannot be slaughtered until the withdrawal period is complete. Shorter withdrawal periods, therefore, give producers more flexibility in marketing their cattle.

EXHIBIT 22-1 Competitive Products

Product	Manufacturer	Market Share
Trivetrin	Hoechst Coopers	30%
Liquamycin	PVU Inc. Rogar/STB	67%
Excenel	Upjohn	3%

EXHIBIT 22-2 Key Product Characteristics

Characteristic	Trivetrin	Liquamycin	Excenel	Micotil
Treatment or preventative	Treatment	Treatment	Treatment	Treatment
Withdrawal period	10 days	28 days	No withdrawal period	28 days
Method of injection	Intramuscular	Intramuscular	Intramuscular	Subcutaneous
Average number of injections	3.5	1.4	3.5	1.0
Single dose for a 500 lb. animal	16.5 ml per injection	25.0 ml per injection	6.5 ml per injection	7.5 ml per injection
Bottle sizes	100 ml 250 ml 500 ml	100 ml 250 ml 500 ml	80 ml 20 ml	100 ml
Requires mixing	No	No	Yes	No
Stored at room temperature	Yes	Yes	Must be refrigerated once it is mixed	Yes
Key product advantages	Broad spectrum control of many bacteria	Inexpensive	New product No withdrawal	New product Single injection Very effective on BRD
Key product disadvantages	Some bacteria becoming resistant	Large volume per injection requires more time Some bacteria becoming resistant	Must be mixed then refrigerated	Narrow spectrum of control
Length of time on market	Many years	Many years	One year	Not yet on market

VETERINARY MARKET IN CANADA

There are two channels of distribution from pharmaceutical manufacturers to end users: the over-the-counter market and the ethical market. The ethical market consists of selling through veterinarians to farmers. Use of this channel has been increasing in recent years as pharmaceutical products become more complex to use, and the advice of a veterinarian becomes more important. In fact, at the present time in Quebec, provincial law dictates that all pharmaceutical products for use in or on animals must be prescribed by a veterinarian. Most other provinces were actively considering similar legislation.

Veterinarians play a key role in commercial agriculture in Canada. Most livestock farmers have a veterinarian they deal with, much the same as most families have a doctor. The relationship between a farmer and his or her veterinarian can vary a great deal. Some farmers simply call their veterinarian when they think they have a problem, have the veterinarian inspect the animals and, if required, prescribe some treatment. In other cases, veterinarians may work on a retainer basis with farmers and manage their entire herd health program. Regardless of the exact relationship between a farmer and a veterinarian, it is obvious that the recommendations of the veterinarian are of utmost importance in deciding which pharmaceutical products to use. Although, in some cases, veterinarians actually administer products like Micotil, usually this is done by the farmer using products recommended and/or sold by the veterinarian.

At the present time, there are in excess of 600 large animal veterinary practices in Canada, employing nearly 1200 veterinarians. These practices vary greatly in size and the amount of pharmaceutical products they purchase. Exhibit 22-3 presents a geographical and size breakdown of large animal veterinary clinics in Canada. The average large animal veterinarian represents approximately $150 000 of billings per year, of which roughly one-third is accounted for by pharmaceutical products. The typical margin earned by a veterinarian on pharmaceutical products is 30%.

A number of animal health distribution organizations have emerged across Canada to act as purchasing agents for veterinarians. In some cases they are private companies, and in other cases they are cooperative organizations owned by the veterinarians they serve. The five main animal health distributors serving Canadian large animal veterinarians are:

Name of Centre	Type of Business	Location
Steere Enterprises	Private	B.C. and Saskatchewan
Associated Vet Purchasing	Cooperative	British Columbia
Western Drug Distribution Centre	Cooperative	Alberta and Saskatchewan
Manitoba Veterinary Drug Centre	Government	Manitoba
St. Mary's Vet Purchasing	Cooperative	Ontario
C.D.M.V.	Government	Quebec and Maritimes

EXHIBIT 22-3 Size and Geographical Distribution of Large Animal Veterinarians in Canada

Province	Number of Clinics	Number of Veterinarians Per Clinic				
		1	2	3	4–5	More than 5
P.E.I.	3	0	0	1	2	0
Nova Scotia	14	2	4	4	3	1
New Brunswick	12	6	3	1	1	1
Newfoundland	4	3	1	0	0	0
Quebec	193	113	25	15	20	20
Ontario	147	69	35	20	20	3
Manitoba	42	26	10	5	1	0
Saskatchewan	56	43	8	3	1	1
Alberta	100	66	19	8	6	1
B.C.	51	32	12	5	2	0
Total	622	360	117	62	56	27

None of the drug distribution centres have sales people that call on veterinarians. They serve mainly a logistics function by purchasing products from pharmaceutical companies to fill orders received from veterinarians. For most products, these organizations operate on a 12% markup on their selling price.

The buying process of a veterinarian can range from a relatively simple rebuy situation to a fairly complicated evaluation of a new product. A recent study conducted at Cornell University in New York outlined some key factors in the decision-making process of a veterinarian in purchasing new pharmaceutical products. Results of this study indicate that most veterinarians have a core set of drugs they know well and are happy with. Because these products have worked well for them in the past, they are very reluctant to make changes. There are, however, many new products coming on the market every year that may offer improvements over existing products. Veterinarians hear of these through a variety of sources, including other veterinarians, researchers, manufacturers, sales representatives, veterinary journals, seminars, and conferences. After becoming aware of a new product, the veterinarian may make comparisons with products or procedures currently being used. At this time, veterinarians require considerable information on such factors as efficacy, spectrum of control, product safety, mode of action, method of administration, ease of use, and withdrawal times. This type of information usually comes from trials conducted by the manufacturer or universities. Product price also becomes an important factor at this point because the veterinarian needs to assess the cost/benefit relationship for the customers. Products that are assessed to offer better results at a similar price, or a better price with similar results, may be tried by the veterinarian.

MARKETING PLAN

Being a veterinarian himself, Bob was quite familiar with the overall nature of the ethical market. With this as background, he began preparation of the first year's marketing plan for Micotil.

Target Market

Micotil had been given label registration for the treatment of pneumonia in cattle. Because the product cannot be used in lactating dairy cows, the main applications are for veal and feedlot cattle. Although the feedlot market is considerably larger than the veal market, Bob thought he could approach both markets in the first year. This would mean, of course, that his target would be large animal veterinarians that had at least a significant portion of their business in one of these two areas. Available statistics indicated that approximately 80% of all large animal veterinarians met this requirement. In addition, he felt he should also target the veal producers and feedlot operators themselves to create awareness and interest in the product. Finally, he thought he should also include key influencers such as university scientists, government extension people, and feed company nutritionists in his target.

Product

Micotil has been under development and testing by Eli Lilly scientists for a number of years. The product itself is a preconstituted solution of the antibiotic Tilmicosin. Tilmicosin is a member of the macrolide class of antibiotics. Although these antibiotics are extremely

effective in controlling BRD, they are painful when injected and can cause minor irrita-
tion. Veterinarians that have tried the product report that "it is always as good, and sometimes
better than what is currently on the market."

Provel planned to sell Micotil initially only in 100 ml bottles. This is because, given
the low dosage required, the cost per bottle of Micotil compared with most other products
is very high. Selling only in the smaller bottle size may reduce the impact of what Bob calls
"sticker shock." All product for Canada will be imported from the United States. Provel's
cost is $41.00 per 100 ml.

Although Micotil has many strengths, its key feature is single injection. All other competing products require administration more than once, some as often as four or five times.
Single injection has benefits to both the farmer and the animals. It means a substantial
reduction in the labour required for treatment and the stress level in treated cattle. The
reduction in labour can be significant, especially in larger feedlots where many animals
require treatment. To identify and treat one animal can take two people as long as ten minutes. Reducing stress in the cattle is also important because it translates into more rapid and
efficient weight gain.

Although Bob definitely was going to feature the single injection characteristic of
Micotil, he had not yet developed a complete positioning strategy for the product.

Price

Pricing a new product is always a difficult task. If the introductory price is set too high,
this may discourage a lot of potential users of the product; if the introductory price is set too
low, the company may be limiting its profitability. Establishing an introductory price for
Micotil is particularly difficult because there is such a wide range in prices of competing products. Current retail prices of key competitors are shown in Exhibit 22-4.

Although Bob was not sure at all what retail price he should suggest for Micotil, he felt
it would have to be in the range of $100 to $200 per 100 ml bottle.

Distribution

Distribution of Micotil, and all Provel products for that matter, has been restricted to the ethical veterinary market. As outlined earlier, this means that the product will be sold to veterinarians through veterinary product distributors across Canada. These organizations supply a
broad range of products to veterinarians and operate on a 12% margin. They carry a minimum
level of inventory of most products and, therefore, place frequent orders with manufacturers.
Most pharmaceutical companies have their sales representatives make monthly calls on the
distributors to check on inventory levels, introduce new products, and obtain orders.

EXHIBIT 22-4 Current Retail Prices of BRD Products			
Products	**Small Bottles**	**Medium Bottles**	**Large Bottles**
Trivetrin	$22.31 per 100 ml	$49.90 per 250 ml	$84.23 per 500 ml
Liquamycin	$14.25 per 100 ml	$28.49 per 250 ml	$47.50 per 500 ml
Excenel	$38.64 per 80 ml		

Promotion

The biggest problem facing Bob was in the area of promotion. He knew he had several issues to deal with in creating demand for Micotil now, and other Provel products in the future. Foremost among these issues was the question of how he should reach target veterinarians with adequate information to get them to try Micotil. There appeared to be several options available.

Sales Force

The first option is to hire salespeople to make personal calls on target veterinarians with the objective of introducing Micotil and explaining its potential benefits. In consultation with others in sales management, Bob estimated that a typical salesperson could make three to four calls on large animal veterinarians a day. On average, a sales person would have approximately 200 days a year for active selling. This means that one salesperson could make approximately 700 sales calls a year.

It would take a well-trained person to do this type of work. Ideally, the person should have a background in animal agriculture and several years of selling experience. Bob felt it would cost somewhere in the neighbourhood of $90 000 per year to attract and retain this type of individual. This figure includes a salary of approximately $65 000, and car, travel, and general expenses of $25 000.

The job of a salesperson for Provel would involve establishing new customers as well as working with existing customers. In establishing a new customer, the salesperson would make an initial contact with the veterinarian, arrange an appointment, and then visit the veterinarian to introduce him- or herself, Provel, and Micotil. It probably would take one hour with the veterinarian to accomplish these objectives. Although it was hoped that, at minimum, this call would result in a trial order of Micotil, Bob's experience suggested that not all veterinarians would be willing to even place a trial order. This was especially true for products with lots of well-established competitors. Follow-up calls would be required in cases where veterinarians were not prepared to make a purchase on the first call.

Once a veterinarian became a customer, sales calls would still be required at regular intervals. The purpose of these calls would be to check on customer satisfaction, deal with any product or service problems, and encourage increased usage of Micotil and other Provel products. Any orders generated by Provel salespeople would be channelled through the appropriate distributor.

Some competing pharmaceutical companies with extensive product lines use sales reps in the ethical market. The more aggressive firms call on vets at least once a month. Other competitors with less extensive product lines find it difficult to justify the expense of a sales force.

A few pharmaceutical companies used sales reps to contact feedlots. Only the very largest feedlots are considered of sufficient size to justify this type of activity. Bob wondered if he should consider this approach as part of his overall communication plan?

Telemarketing

A second approach Bob was considering involved direct marketing. Under this option, all contact with veterinarians would be made by telephone instead of in person. This approach had a lot of appeal to Bob because it solved the real problem of distance. Large animal veterinary practices in Canada are located in rural communities across the country. As a consequence, travel time and cost can be a significant factor using traditional face-to-face selling. To a large extent, telemarketing can overcome this problem.

Bob felt that a telemarketing rep should have essentially the same qualifications as a personal sales representative, so salaries would need to be identical. Based on the experiences of other companies with telemarketing, he figured that a rep should be able to make a minimum of 15 contacts a day. Over a 200-day year, this would be 3000 calls.

The main direct cost of telemarketing is long distance tolls. Cost data from Bell Canada revealed that a typical ten-minute call would cost approximately $6. Of course, calls within Ontario would be less, while calls to distant locations would be substantially more.

Telemarketing was new to Eli Lilly in Canada, so they decided to do a short survey of veterinarians to determine how they felt about this approach. Key results of this survey are shown in Appendix 22-1. In addition, Bob attended a seminar sponsored by the Canadian Direct Marketing Association to learn more about this method. While at this meeting he heard a presentation given by the marketing manager of the Business Products Division of Control Data Canada. Control Data had recently set up a telemarketing operation to sell computer accessories such as disks, tapes, and forms to small businesses across the country. The Control Data marketing manager mentioned that they were successful in making a sale in approximately one call in four. This success rate was about half the comparable rate in face-to-face selling. Bob wondered if he could achieve similar results with veterinarians.

In addition to using telemarketing with veterinary clinics, Bob wondered if there might be an opportunity to use the approach with some feedlots. As far as he knew, although one or two competitors were using telemarketing on a limited basis with vets, no competing firms were using this approach with feedlots.

Direct Mail

A third approach Bob was considering involved the use of direct mail. Under this option, the number of sales calls would be minimal, while the use of high-quality direct mail would be extensive. Based on input from Provel's advertising agency, Bob estimated that the cost per contact using high-quality direct mail was approximately $12.00. This included the cost of preparing and printing the direct mail piece, as well as the cost of postage and handling. Direct mail was widely used in this industry. Most competitors had extensive direct mail programs with veterinarians, and some used direct mail with larger feedlots and veal producers.

Media Advertising

A final option would be to concentrate promotional expenditures on media advertising. The strategy here would be to communicate the benefits of Micotil to both veterinarians and farmers through print advertising in veterinarian journals and farm publications. Exhibit 22-5 shows advertising rates for various publications that could be used to reach veterinarians, while Exhibit 22-6 shows similar rates for farm publications.

In addition to ads, publications could be used to distribute inserts. An insert is a brochure that normally is four pages in length and contains a significant amount of information. A sin-

EXHIBIT 22-5 Advertising Rates for Selected Veterinary Publications

Publication	Frequency	Four-Colour Rates	Circulation
Veterinarian Magazine	6 times/year	$2950 full page $3500 back cover	4426
Canadian Vet Supplies	6 times/year	$3300 full page $3890 back cover	4536
Canadian Veterinary Journal	3 times/year	$2235 full page $2900 back cover	Not available
Le Medicin Veterinarian	3 times/year	$1585 full page $2365 back cover	Not available
Compendium on Continuing Education for the Practicing Vet	12 times/year	$1775 back cover	2212

EXHIBIT 22-6 Advertising Rates for Selected Beef and Dairy Publications

Publication	Frequency	Four-Colour Rates	Circulation
Cattlemen's Corner (Grainews)	17 times/year	$7213 full page $8655 back cover	60 484
Cattlemen	11 times/year	$4428 full page $5313 back cover	33 985
Alberta Beef	12 times/year	$1860 full page $2220 back cover	13 849
Ontario Milk Producer	12 times/year	$2215 full page $2565 back cover	13 288
Le Producteur Lait Quebec	12 times/year	$2770 full page $3230 back cover	16 623

gle four-page insert in *Compendium on Continuing Education for the Practicing Vet* costs $6300. The cost of inserts in other publications are similar on a per-reader basis.

DECISION

Although it was unrealistic to expect Provel to break even in the first year with just one product, Bob was excited about the long-term prospects for the company. He knew, however, that the launch of Micotil was critical to the success of the entire concept.

Reaching target veterinarians with proper information was the main issue facing Bob. Although he felt that sales representatives could give the product the most push, he was concerned about the high cost of this approach. Media advertising, direct mail, and tele-marketing were less costly approaches, but would they give Provel the right image in the marketplace, and would they generate sufficient volume? What is a realistic promotional budget for Micotil? At what level should prices be established? These were key questions Bob would have to answer prior to the launch in a few months.

APPENDIX 22-1

Market Research Results

1. Nearly 40% of veterinarians felt that telemarketing gives a company a negative image, an additional 40% felt it has no effect on a company's image, and only 20% felt it gives a company a positive image.
2. Key factors associated with a negative image:
   - Personal contact is needed to relay information and to build relationships.
   - Telemarketing conjures up an image of a cheap, "fly-by-night" operation.
   - Telemarketing is a waste of a veterinarian's time.
   - Telemarketing provides a difficult atmosphere in which to promote products.
3. Key factor associated with a positive image:
   - Telemarketing provides more information at the convenience of the veterinarian.
4. When asked to rank three selling approaches, the response of veterinarians was that personal selling is first, direct mail is second, and telemarketing is third.
5. A similar ranking was found when veterinarians were asked to rank the three methods in terms of best use of their time and which method gives the most product information.
6. A small percentage of the veterinarians indicated that they had been serviced by another animal health company using telemarketing. In general, this amounted to 15% to 20% of the veterinarians.
7. Where telemarketing has been used in the animal health industry, it has been used for order taking, inquiry follow-up, and informing veterinarians of specials and promotions.
8. Almost all veterinarians believe that the use of telemarketing to veterinarians will increase in the future.
9. Although direct mail is seen as the second best approach to personal selling, it is not widely read by veterinarians. It is estimated that only about 40% of all direct mail received in a veterinary clinic is ever read by a veterinarian. In many cases, direct mail is opened by a secretary or animal health technician who screens this and selects what to pass on to the veterinarian.
10. The main reason given by veterinarians for not reading direct mail is because it is seen to be too long and would take too much time to read.

SMITHS INDUSTRIES MEDICAL SYSTEMS (SIMS)

Case

Opportunity in Winnipeg

Robert Young and David Large

It was June 10, 1996, and Bob Young, a sales territory manager for SIMS Canada, was working in his home office in Ottawa when the phone rang. He picked up the receiver.

"Bob Young here!"

"Hi Bob, it's Faith. I've just received a copy of a fax from the Manitoba Community Intravenous Therapy Program. It's the request for product information on infusion pumps for the home care program."

Faith West was the Product Manager for the Deltec CADD® (Computerized Ambulatory Drug Delivery) pump line manufactured by SIMS. The two had met with the Manitoba program staff as recently as the fifth of June and had been expecting the request. The Intravenous (IV) Therapy Program was considering the use of IV pumps in the home care setting to deliver antibiotics to their patients. For Young it was another step in his efforts to establish the CADD® pump as the accepted mode of intravenous medication delivery in home care in the province of Manitoba.

"Bob, I'll fax you a copy right away. We have to give them a response by June 24, 1996. Take a good look at it and give me a call if you need any help. I expect you already know how you will address this, but I can supply you with any other information that you require."

They had previously discussed the options that SIMS had, and it was time to develop an organized approach; the request simply formalized what they knew they had to do. Although pump prices weren't necessary at this point, the request was a competitive situation and they were in a quandary; their competitors had a new generation pump capable of being used in different infusion modes (e.g., continuous flow, intermittent flow based on time intervals, flow upon patient demand). SIMS had been developing such a pump, but it was not expected on the market until late in 1996. However they did have a pump, the CADD-Plus®, which would handle the intermittent mode required for antibiotic infusion, and the CADD-Plus® was the market leader for this use. The Manitoba program was going initially to evaluate the pumps for IV antibiotic infusion. The real question was how could they present the CADD® Pump not only to secure an evaluation, but to ensure that it would be considered the pump of choice.

"That's great Faith! I'll start working on the request as soon as I receive it. I probably will have to run some things by you before we submit this. Where can I get a hold of you over the next few days?"

As he hung up the phone, Young realized that the SIMS presentation would have to be good. His sales territory extended from the western part of the province of Quebec through to Kingston and Ottawa, all across Northern Ontario and Manitoba to the Manitoba/Saskatchewan border. He knew the various provincial systems and he knew that the competition was knocking at the door. Winning the Manitoba Home IV program (based in Winnipeg) pump contract would probably ensure winning most of the province for all of the home care IV pumps.

SMITHS INDUSTRIES PLC.—COMPANY BACKGROUND

Smiths Industries Plc. was a major international company based in London, England. This organization was a key player in its chosen markets, categorized by the three distinct operating groups: Industrial, Medical Systems, and Aerospace & Defence. Altogether there were more than 12 800 employees working in the Smiths Industries (SI) groups worldwide.

Smiths had its humble but historic beginnings in 1851 when Samuel Smith founded a family clock and watch business in London at Newington Causeway near the Elephant & Castle, "an area crowded with shops interspersed with several splendid gin palaces." Interestingly, the same skills required for watch and clock making were considered appropriate for working on the new instrumentation requirements stemming from the emerging motor industry. Consequently, in 1901 Smith's grandson, continuing in the traditional family business, invented the mileometer which was in fact an early odometer.

During a conversation with King Edward VII, the King asked Smith why he couldn't design a measurement device that was also capable of measuring the speed of travel, and in 1904 the first British speedometer, made by Smith, was installed in the King's Mercedes. The company was granted a Royal Warrant and subsequently started to evolve a part of its business into motor accessories. On July 15, 1914, S. Smith & Son (Motor Accessories) Ltd. was formed as a public company.

With England soon involved in the First World War, Smith's instrumentation manufacturing expertise was put to good use manufacturing instruments such as "tankometers," kite balloon wind indicators, shell fuses, and spark plugs, amongst other things. In 1917, Smiths made a particularly significant acquisition of an invention for measuring airspeed and one of their airspeed indicators was installed in the Vickers Vimy bomber used by Alcock and Brown in their epic trans-Atlantic flight of 1919.

From this point on over the next seventy-five years and particularly during the war years, Smiths grew as a company involved in both the motor and aviation industry. The Smith KLG spark plug was used in the Rolls Royce Merlin engine which powered aircraft such as the Spitfire, Hurricane, Mosquito, and Lancaster bombers, and in the American B17 bomber. They were also mass-producing speedometers, clocks, and other instruments and mechanisms.

The year 1958 bought two significant events under Smiths' policy of diversification. First, Smiths Aviation and Marine Division was created. Then a company that would be the foundation of the future core Medical Systems Group was acquired when Smiths purchased a controlling interest in Portland Plastics, and its subsidiary Surgical Plastics. In 1967 Portland Plastics became "Portex," a medical plastics company which pioneered and became a leader in the manufacture and sale of single-use (disposable) medical products, such as endotracheal tubes, tracheotomy tubes, and epidural trays for anesthesia. Further diversification in 1960 saw Smiths forming the Industrial Division, which was mainly concerned with industrial instrumentation.

Other acquisitions in the 1970s and 1980s cemented Smiths Industries firmly as a leader in the aerospace, marine, industrial, and medical markets. In 1984 the company was finally re-organized into the three core business groups previously mentioned. By this time, Smiths Aerospace and Defence Group had become a major subcontractor of products for Boeing Aircraft as well as several other British and European aviation companies. The Industrial and Medical Groups had also evolved through the acquisition and divestment of different companies. However, the early 1990s saw new challenges to the Aerospace Group, with a worldwide reduction in defence spending and financial problems for many of the leading airlines. A subsequent shift in focus resulted in the Medical Systems Group becoming the leading SI profit contributor in 1993, for the first time; this position was further strengthened in 1994 with the acquisition of the US company, Deltec, for $150 million (see Exhibit 23-1).

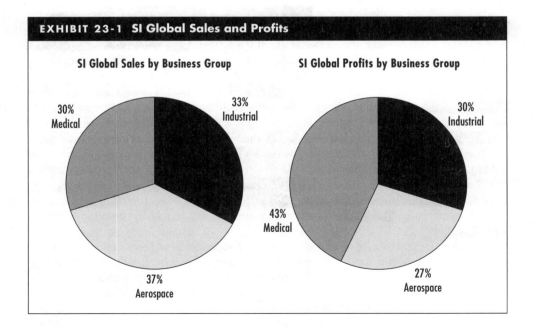

EXHIBIT 23-1 SI Global Sales and Profits

SI Global Sales by Business Group

- 30% Medical
- 33% Industrial
- 37% Aerospace

SI Global Profits by Business Group

- 30% Industrial
- 43% Medical
- 27% Aerospace

SMITHS INDUSTRIES MEDICAL SYSTEMS OF CANADA LTD. (SIMS CANADA)

Smiths Industries first established itself in Canada in early 1960, when it hired a direct sales representative for both its automotive and medical business. It was realized very early that Smiths' biggest strength in Canada would be its medical business and thus, Portex Canada was formed in 1962–63 as a separate company. Portex quickly positioned itself as the leader in the sale of quality medical disposables for anesthesia, respiratory, and intensive care medicine in Canada.

The company continued with a period of major growth that started in the UK and filtered rapidly through to its North American operations. Important new disposable devices were added to the sales product portfolios in anesthesia and critical care (epidural anesthesia trays and thoracic drainage devices). During the late 1970s and early 1980s, SI acquired Concord Labs, Downs Surgical, and Eschmann Bros. Walsh Ltd: companies which contributed to an added breadth and depth in the existing product lines. The Canadian operation grew concurrent with these acquisitions and Downs Surgical was amalgamated with Portex in 1984. By 1986 SIMS Canada employed more than 30 people.

SI UK subsequently sold off Downs Surgical but followed up quickly on this divestment with several major acquisitions which substantially increased their presence in the medical markets (see Exhibit 23-2). The most significant of these additions was without a doubt the purchase of Deltec from Pharmacia Plc. (now Pharmacia-Upjohn). Deltec was and continued to be the pioneer in the development, manufacture, and sale of venous access devices and infusion devices for use in home care and in the hospital for the infusion of antibiotics and chemotherapy agents, as well as morphine and its derivatives (for pain control). The CADD® (computerized ambulatory drug delivery) pump was the "flagship" product of the infusion devices division.

In 1996 SIMS Canada had about 25 employees, of whom nine were in direct sales, with two product managers to support the salespeople and carry out product marketing activities (see Exhibit 23-3). In addition to this staff, SIMS Canada also engaged two distributors located in the Maritime provinces and the Western provinces. Each had different and exclusive rights to the sale of certain SIMS products in their respective areas.

What is interesting is that the Canadian sales force was trained in and successfully sold all SI medical products, whereas in the US, SI used several sales forces (depending on the product), numbering close to 170 people to do the same job. The Canadian sales group were undoubtedly technically knowledgeable, highly skilled, and well-motivated with their product lines.

The SIMS approach to their clients was on a direct sales basis. Because many of the SIMS products were repeat business based on long-term contracts or pricing agreements, a SIMS salesperson tended to develop long-term relationships with his or her customers. New business leads came from various sources: advertising in trade magazines, displays at many medical conferences, referrals from current customers, and especially from the old-fashioned cold call.

A cold call was a sales approach whereby the salesperson would make an initial contact with a potential customer, qualify the business opportunity (if possible), and outline what benefits the SIMS product had to offer. The main goals of a cold call were to establish the customer's interest in the product and to meet person-to-person with the customer.

Because the Deltec line was relatively new to the SIMS sales force, they had to either follow up on existing leads passed on from the previous business, and/or develop new customer

EXHIBIT 23-2 Smiths Industries Medical Systems: Major Acquisitions and Divestments

1958: Took controlling interest in **Portland Plastics & Surgical Plastics**—manufacturers of medical tubing and sheeting; endotracheal tubes for anesthesia

1967: Company renamed "Portex" after trademark registered in 1940

1970s: Thoracic drainage and epidural analgesia products added to product line

1979: Purchased **Concord Labs** (USA)—manufacturer of arterial blood gas kits and other procedural kits for respiratory, ICU, and anesthesia

1984: Acquired **Downs Surgical Ltd.** (UK)—manufacturers of surgical instruments

Acquired **Eschmann Bros. Walsh Ltd. (UK)**—manufacturers of ostomy and incontinence products, autoclaves, sterilizers, and operating room tables

1989: Sold **Downs Surgical Ltd**.

Acquired **RSP Ltd.** (USA)—manufacturer of temperature monitoring and respiratory support products for respiratory and anesthesia

1992: Acquired **Intertech Ltd.** (USA)—manufacturer of disposables for respiratory, anesthesia, ICU, and emergency departments

1994: Acquisition of **Deltec Ltd.** (USA)—manufacturer of venous access devices and ambulatory infusion pumps for oncology, palliative care, infectious disease treatments, and other medication therapies

1995: Acquisition of **Level 1 Inc**. (USA)—manufacturer of IV fluid/blood warming units and infusers for the operating room, recovery room, and emergency department

EXHIBIT 23-3 SIMS Canada Ltd.

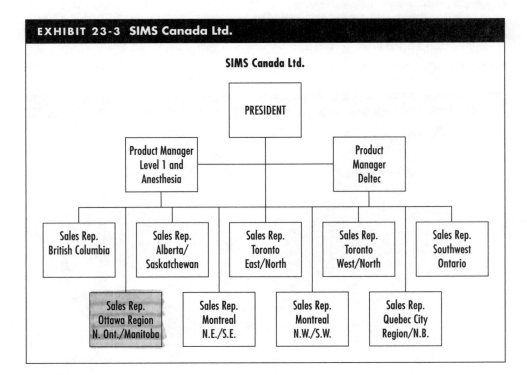

contacts through a process of research and investigation and, again, cold calls. Once a sales-person had qualified the business opportunity, then these contacts were further cultivated through extensive pre-sales support up to the point of product sale and followed up closely with post-sales assistance. Their successes with the CADD® pump and the related dispos-ables quickly and significantly added to SIMS's bottom line at year end (see Exhibit 23-4).

THE CADD® PUMP

In 1982 two US companies, Pharmacia and Newtech amalgamated as Pharmacia to manu-facture and sell a revolutionary new venous-access device called the Port-a-Cath®. This consisted of a subcutaneous medication reservoir (for implantation in the chest) with a venous catheter attached. The catheter was threaded through the sub-clavian vein into the supe-rior vena-cava. By use of a special needle, medications could be repeatedly introduced into the reservoir over a long period (more than six months) and infused directly into patients' veins, vastly facilitating antibiotic and chemotherapy administration for a sick patient.

Recognizing that one way for a hospital to lower costs was to get patients into home care, Pharmacia formed an alliance with Deltec to develop a home intravenous (IV) infusion pump capable of delivering medications through a Port-a-Cath® or other IV access devices. In June of 1985, the first two CADD® pumps came on the market; these were the CADD-1® (for chemotherapy) and the CADD-PCA® (for pain control). Shortly after this, Pharmacia and Deltec merged as Pharmacia Deltec.

By the early 1990s the CADD® pump was accepted as the standard infusion device for IV infusion in the home care market. At the time that SIMS acquired Deltec, there were five different configurations of the CADD® pump. Each one addressed a specific medical need(s) that was differentiated by the medication required and its related protocol of infu-sion (see Exhibits 23-5 and 23-6).

For example, the CADD-PCA® (patient controlled analgesia) Model 5800 was designed to meet the rigid restrictions necessary for the safe and secure "unsupervised" administration

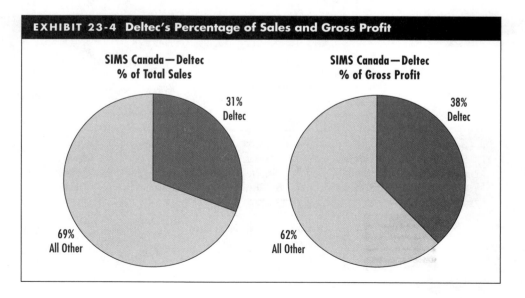

EXHIBIT 23-4 Deltec's Percentage of Sales and Gross Profit

SIMS Canada—Deltec
% of Total Sales

31% Deltec

69% All Other

SIMS Canada—Deltec
% of Gross Profit

38% Deltec

62% All Other

EXHIBIT 23-5 The CADD Pump Family

Pump	Functions and Medications
CADD-1 Model 5100	• Programmed to provide a continuous flow rate over a 24-hour period. • Used extensively for infusion of chemotherapy agents for cancer treatment, Desferal for iron chelation, heparin for deep vein therapy, and other regimens requiring continuous flow.
CADD-Plus Model 5400	• Can infuse on an intermittent basis; administers a programmed volume over a specified time duration and at a defined frequency (20 min. to 12 hrs.10 min. cycles or on a 24 hr. cycle). Optional delay start or keep vein open (KVO) rate between cycles. Can also be programmed with a continuous hourly rate. • Used with antibiotics and other anti-infectives. Can also be used for same applications and medications as the CADD-1.
CADD-TPN Model 5700	• Highly specialized functioning for infusion of total parenteral nutrition (TPN). Infused at regular intervals through a permanent venous access device. Capability of high flow rates lends itself to hydration. • Administers special nutrition formulations to patients with inability to process solid food or liquids. Hydration agents used for palliative care patients (when they become dehydrated).
CADD-PCA Model 5800	• Can be programmed to provide continuous 24 hr. flow rates and patient- or clinician-activated doses. Can be programmed volumetrically or by concentration (e.g. mg./ml.). • Used extensively for palliative, chronic, and post-operative pain control. Can securely administer morphine and its derivatives as well as other analgesics. Patient can only dose within pre-programmed parameters. Also has a continuous flow rate capability and can be used for same functions as CADD-1.
CADD Micro Model 5900	• A miniature syringe driver-type pump. Capable of being programmed to provide up to 24 individual doses of same or different volumes to be infused over same or different time durations. Infusion times, therefore, are all in real time. Also has provision for patient- or clinician-delivered doses. • Can deliver at increments of 0.002 ml. Used for fertility drugs, Desferal, morphine and its derivatives, as well as other analgesics, heparin, some regimens of chemotherapy infusion (Interferon A), as well as other applications. Capable of "pulsatile" delivery.
CADD Prizm VIP Model 6100	• Versatile pump that can function in the following modes: continuous, PCA, intermittent, and TPN. Has all of the functions of the CADD 5100, 5400, 5700, and 5800 pumps. Also has event memory and patient history registers. User-friendly with over 2000 "help" screens. Event memory and patient history can be downloaded onto a PC or printed out direct to a printer. Telecommunications ability allows for remote access, programming, and downloading of historical information. Has many other sophisticated features. • Used in all the applications and for all the medications specified for the four pumps noted.

of morphine and its derivatives for use in the relief of pain in palliative, chronic, and post-operative care. The concept was simple and proven in research; a patient controlling his or her own pain relief would use only sufficient amounts of analgesia to ease their pain, if and when it was experienced.

The CADD-PCA® was pre-programmed by a clinician to infuse a continuous base rate of medication to provide analgesia over a known therapeutic range of pain. The clinician could also pre-program control parameters for a patient to self-administer a single "bolus" or dose for those periods of "break-through" pain, wherein the base-rate of medication was not

EXHIBIT 23-6   CADD-PLUS® Ambulatory Infusion Pump

CADD-PLUS®
Ambulatory Infusion Pump   Model 5400

...for intermittent delivery
of antibiotics and continuous
delivery of chemotherapy

Flexibility
- Programmable dose ranges allow physician to select a variety of drugs and concentrations
- Accessories allow large volume delivery
- Delay start allows programmed delay of first dose for clinician and patient convenience

Safety
- MEDICATION CASSETTE™ Reservoir for drug security and simple attachment to pump
- Three programmable lock levels to control patient/pump interaction
- Visual and audible alarms alert clinician and patient of conditions that require attention

Convenience
- 48-hour drug supply allows reservoir changes to be made every two days for many antibiotics*
- Automatic delivery minimizes patient interaction and maximizes patient compliance
- Reporting function displays drug delivered for evaluation of patient compliance
- Compact, lightweight design permits patient mobility

Dependability
- Programmable doses and intervals automatically deliver programmed dose volumes at pre-selected intervals

Support
- Service and support includes 24-hour access to clinical and technical information
- Educational materials for both clinician and patient
- Reference materials and instructional support to assist in economical use of the CADD-PLUS pump

*Refer to the manufacturer's product literature and other references for information on drug stability.

effective. The pump also had provisions to record patient demands for pain relief that were outside of the limits allowed by the pump so that the clinician could measure whether or not the patient was receiving sufficient analgesia. A digital code number could be "keyed" into the pump by the clinician to electronically lock or unlock the pump for either patient operation or clinician programming respectively, thereby attaining the desired levels of safety and security. This "electronic key" was common to all CADD® pumps.

Other similar designs and concepts were embodied into each of the other pumps. This imparted a high level of consistency to this product line when one considered that the same home care staff were usually implicated in patient care with two or more of the different CADD® pumps.

The CADD-Plus® (for use with antibiotics) also fit into a highly specialized niche in the home care market. It had the capability to infuse a specific amount of medication over a programmed time duration and at a specified daily frequency. Further, the pump could be programmed to start this infusion at a later time, such as 2:00 A.M., eliminating the need for nursing supervision when the infusion started. These features had important implications for the administration of antibiotics.

The benefits realized were as follows:

• they forced compliance (i.e., the patient couldn't "forget" to take medication—the pump did it for them);

• they allowed for the administration of less expensive, narrower spectrum antibiotics (thereby more effectively attacking the specific "bug" and decreasing the possibilities of increasing patients' resistance to the medication);

• by utilizing antibiotics with longer stability periods, the need for costly, daily nursing visits decreased.

Even in 1994 when SIMS acquired Deltec, Deltec was developing a new infusion device that would combine all of the functions of all of their previous pumps, thus allowing for extreme flexibility in utility. This device was to be based on the best aspects of the older CADD® pumps but would use updated, more user-friendly approaches to programming, such as a more intuitive keyboard (e.g., using "enter" instead of "set/clear" and "next" instead of "select mode"), and immediate clinician support via 2000 on-board "help" screens.

This pump would also incorporate such advances as patient history and event screens, telecommunications capability, and the ability to download information to a printer or PC. This pump was dubbed the Prizm® and would be available as the PCS (pain control system) or the VIP (variable infusion profile). The VIP could be programmed for pain relief, chemotherapy, and antibiotic administration, and for TPN or hydration, as well as having an added telecommunications capability. The PCS version could be upgraded at a later date (at nominal cost) to the VIP version. The SIMS sales-staff anxiously awaited the arrival of the Prizm®, which would be available on the Canadian market sometime after September 1996 (see Exhibit 23-7).

VALUE ADDED: HOW IMPORTANT IS IT?

Deltec acknowledged the significance of the value-added component in complementing quality products. Thus from inception, Deltec built the business with customer support occupying a position of prime importance. In recognition of the effectiveness of this approach,

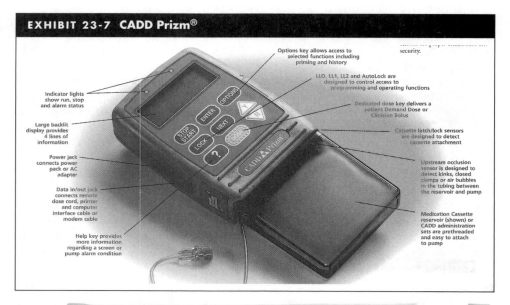

EXHIBIT 23-7 CADD Prizm®

Options key allows access to selected functions including priming and history

LLO, LL1, LL2 and AutoLock are designed to control access to programming and operating functions

Indicator lights show run, stop and alarm status

Dedicated dose key delivers a patient Demand Dose or Clinician Bolus

Large backlit display provides 4 lines of information

Cassette latch/lock sensors are designed to detect cassette attachment

Power jack connects power pack or AC adapter

Upstream occlusion sensor is designed to detect kinks, closed clamps or air bubbles in the tubing between the reservoir and pump

Data in/out jack connects remote dose cord, printer and computer interface cable or modem cable

Medication Cassette reservoir (shown) or CADD administration sets are prethreaded and easy to attach to pump

Help key provides more information regarding a screen or pump alarm condition

they were awarded the MIE100 Award for Excellence in Quality and Service for both 1992 and 1993. Sponsored by the Medical Industry Executives, the recipient of this award was selected by the customers of the industry.

It is easy to see how Deltec accomplished this. First, they developed and published extensive and comprehensive clinician and patient support literature and videos, available to customers and potential customers upon request. This was part and parcel of the sale of the various products, whether it be used in the pre-sales or post-sales phase. They had more than 80 publications and 35 videos available for customer support.

One of the more significant publications was a much sought after *Pharmacy Handbook* containing stability tables for different concentrations and doses of various antibiotics. The values listed therein were calculated by SIMS Deltec's own staff pharmacists and the book was continually updated as new medications came on the market.

Deltec also published a Clinician Support telephone number for its customers. The 800 number was staffed by several clinical nurse specialists, pharmacists, and biomedical technicians. During daylight hours they could respond immediately to any client requests, with after-hours they guaranteed call return to the clinician within 20 minutes. On top of all this, Deltec (SIMS) provided its clients with extensive financial support for educational pursuits. With their quality products came unsurpassed client support.

THE CANADIAN MEDICAL SYSTEM

In the mid to late 1980s, the various provincial governments in Canada learned of the approaching crisis in the funding of health care in each of the provinces; up until then the spending had seemed to go on unchecked, contributing significantly to provincial deficits and debt. By the 1990s there was not a week that went by that there wasn't some reference to health care problems in the news media.

The dilemma was the conflict between maintaining the principles of Canada's Health Care System versus the concomitant funding required to run the system at the required levels.

The five fundamental principles of the Canada Health Act were detailed in the Liberals' 1993 election "manifesto" or promises to the Canadian people called the *Red Book*, and it was their intent not to divert from this act.

The Act stated that health care must be universally available, reasonably accessible, medically comprehensive, publicly funded and administered, and portable between provinces. Unfortunately the very ideal of these principles, coupled with the "negligence" of successive governments in addressing the problems, had spawned the rampant spending that produced the crisis; naturally most of the people expected nothing less than free, subsidized quality health care as part of their rights as citizens of Canada. Consequently health care was a big piece of the provincial spending pie.

The results of the crisis had been many-fold and ongoing since the early 1990s. There had been regular yearly spending cuts in health care by all of the provinces, with their ensuing program cuts, staff layoffs, and hospital closures. Other "mechanisms," such as Ontario's "Rae Days" of 1993–94, had been instituted to further cull extra dollars, much needed to balance provincial budgets. There was a distinct move towards centralization of common hospital services, such as purchasing, laundry, food services, laboratories, and biomedical engineering. Significant savings could be realized when hospitals organized under geographic groups with a common administration. For example, ten hospitals would have more purchasing power than one or two hospitals, and the cost of administering the purchasing function would be reduced. A smaller hospital, as a member of such a group, could realize significant savings. There was evidence of these trends right across Canada.

Saskatchewan reacted early to the financial pressures when it closed more than sixty hospitals in 1992; this province had been next only to Quebec with the total number of individual hospitals. As part of the reforms in Saskatchewan, three separate centralized purchasing authorities were formed, one for each of the cities of Regina and Saskatoon and one for the entire province.

In Alberta drastic measures were taken by the Klein government in 1993. They closed and restructured hospitals, and initiated the formation of centralized group management of hospitals within delineated geographic regions. This included the concepts of centralized group purchasing, a single, "super" administration for the individual groups of hospitals, and the centralization of other common hospital services for each group.

Quebec had formed 18 Régie Régional or geographic groups of hospitals and related health care services in December 1991, and the reformation was still taking place. Manitoba was in the process of moving to centralized group alliances with the recent (1996) formation of twelve geographically organized hospital groups. Ontario had made early efforts at forming purchasing groups, but these would probably be supplemented in the future by geographic strategic alliances similar to those formed in Quebec and Manitoba.

In a nutshell, none of Canada's provinces were without the quandary of reforming and streamlining its health-care system, while at the same time looking to radically cut the costs of operating the system.

THE MARKET, THE CADD® PUMP, AND THE COMPETITION

Medicine, pharmacology, biotechnology, and technology had been co-evolving at mind-bending rates over the last decade. One only had to consider the huge bounds that were being made in the fields of genetic engineering and computer chip technology, both of which figured integrally in many of the most recent medical products and advances at that time.

Besides improved methods of diagnostics and therapeutics, technology had also made possible many of the important trends that were occurring in the medical field. The move to get patients on their way to faster recovery had been ongoing now for more than five years and the resultant freeing of hospital beds was one way of cutting costs, insofar as another patient could be treated sooner. For instance, a laparoscopic cholecystectomy (removal of the gall bladder) could be done using a small telescope with a television camera attached, and required only two small incisions instead of the muscle-cutting procedures of the past; rather than a three-week recovery, patients were ambulatory and back home within days.

The most important trend and of prime interest in the context of this case had been the furtherance of home care as practicable for the treatment of medical problems. There were two considerations. The first was that of returning the patient to his or her home for active treatment, thereby eliminating the cost of a hospital bed occupancy (and incidentally improving the patient's quality of life somewhat). The second was reducing, to a minimum, the number of attendant visits by a home care nurse for a specific patient, again providing financial economies to the system. The use of computerized ambulatory pumps for home care IV infusion facilitated both of these economies and was becoming more of a part of home care in Canada.

A salesperson in this field had to be adept at seeking out all the key stakeholders in a specific area or region; this diversified approach was very effective because the influencers were many and they gave much weight to the final decision. The sales procedure was also a highly educative process, with the salespeople devoting much of their time to conducting in-services on the pump operation, often long before the sale was actually made. This same in-service method was continued well after the sale; the salesperson had to be prepared to persevere and follow up constantly with the customers. This very fertile market could be quite lucrative to an experienced and well-trained salesperson.

It is important to note that the provincial home care systems differed widely and were not necessarily standardized, even within the province from one region to the next. They required careful consideration when sales and marketing strategies were being formulated. Ontario was a case in point. The general organization of the home care system is shown in Exhibit 23-8. When the patient was discharged from the hospital, a Homecare case worker liaised with the discharge planner to decide on the patient's requirements, and based on certain priorities and criteria, whether or not they could receive provincially subsidized home care. It is noteworthy that in Ontario, "Homecare" was by name an actual provincially funded organization that could fall under the auspices of the municipality, a hospital, or in some cases, the Victorian Order of Nurses (VON).

Having decided on the level of care that the patient required, Homecare then assigned the job of patient care or supervision in the home to one of several different domestic nursing organizations. At the same time, Homecare decided whether or not any assistive equipment was required and arranged the rental of the same from a designated home care equipment supply company. If medication was also required for the patient (especially in the case of IV therapy), a pharmacy was contracted to supply the drugs. In some cases, the pharmacy was also the "home care equipment" supplier in that they rented out the IV pump to the patient as well. Through subsidization from the government, Homecare "paid the bills."

It was estimated that the CADD® pump had about 95% of the Ontario home care IV infusion pump market. In Ontario, sales efforts for the CADD® pump were directed at

EXHIBIT 23-8 Ontario Homecare System

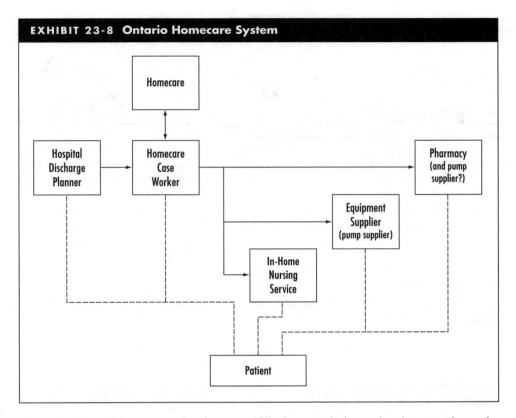

Homecare, the visiting nurses, the pharmacy (fills the prescription and perhaps purchases the pump), and/or the home care equipment company (purchaser). In a few cases, the hospitals (nursing and pharmacy) were also involved. All of these groups took part in the decision process, but Homecare tended to have the most input as they controlled the purse strings. The sales cycle was anywhere from a few months (where business was already established) to two years (where the sale had to be developed). In Ontario, once initial sales and acceptance of the CADD® pump were accomplished, their use tended to spread out geographically within the province because of referrals amongst the practitioners. There was also a strong tendency to standardize products, even though there hadn't been any formal agreements to do so. Ontario was a very solid market for the CADD® pump.

Quebec, on the other hand, had a more simplified home care system; they had organized their health care into 18 regions, each composed of the hospitals therein (centres de santé) and CLSC (Centre Local de Services Communautaires). Sales approaches varied from region to region but generally were similar to sales efforts in Ontario. The CLSC (who would supervise patient usage of the pump) and the hospital (who would buy the pump and dispense the medication cassettes) were the two targets. Attention was also given to biomedical engineering, who often had some influence in the decision. Education was again the goal with the CLSCs and hospitals, but it helped to get a pump or two into the hospitals for field evaluation.

The CADD® pump enjoyed about 65% penetration in the Quebec market; this was partially due to the standardization of infusion pumps by geographic region within the province. For example, Quebec City and eastern regions of the province used the CADD®-Plus only. Montreal areas principally used the CADD® pump. The Laval region chose the Abbott Aim™ pump as its basic infusion device in 1995, and the Abitibi region had recently (1996) standardized on the Sabratek® Homerun™ pump. It was significant that both of these pumps had a multi-therapy infusion mode capability, while the Prizm VIP™ with comparable functioning characteristics wouldn't be available until December 1996.

The move towards a flexible, multi-therapy infusion pump was not confined to Quebec. Calgary had been using the Abbott pump for 10 years, so it was a natural progression for them to shift over to the Abbott Aim™ pump. A recent requirement for 40 PCA pumps almost automatically went to Abbott. Edmonton, on the other hand, was not initially committed to the Abbott pump. They did, in fact, like the CADD® pump and its features and were using the CADD-TPN® in their home care program. Unfortunately, Edmonton also decided on the Abbott Aim Plus™ for use in the home care program, mainly because of its multi-therapy capability. The SIMS salesperson involved learned that had SIMS's new VIP been available, then there would have been more likelihood of the order going to SIMS.

In the United States, there was a proliferation of multi-therapy pumps on the market (at least six others), and there was a genuine concern at Deltec for potential loss of market share. Exhibit 23-9 shows the breakdown by both market share and market share of new acquisition in the US. For the first time in recent history, Deltec's 1995 share of new ambulatory pump placements had fallen below their established market share.

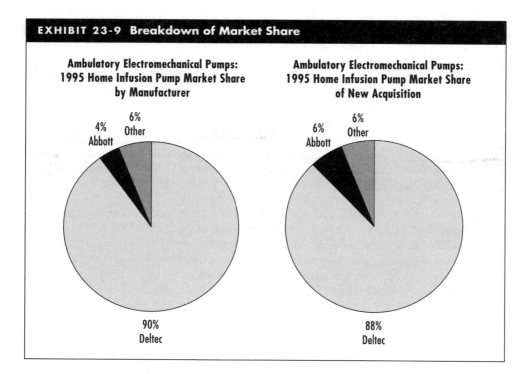

EXHIBIT 23-9 Breakdown of Market Share

Ambulatory Electromechanical Pumps: 1995 Home Infusion Pump Market Share by Manufacturer

- 4% Abbott
- 6% Other
- 90% Deltec

Ambulatory Electromechanical Pumps: 1995 Home Infusion Pump Market Share of New Acquisition

- 6% Abbott
- 6% Other
- 88% Deltec

It was only logical that the Canadian operation faced the same concerns as their US counterparts. SIMS's Canadian sales force were mainly confronted by the two previously named competitors. There were several other multi-therapy pumps being sold, but they had a much diminished presence in the market, mainly due to inadequate or no representation in Canada. Exhibit 23-10 outlines the competitive similarities and differences between the main competitive products in Canada, the Abbott Aim Plus™, The Sabratek® Homerun™, and the CADD Prizm VIP™.

Abbot
+ Sabratek
p MGD

EXHIBIT 23-10 Ambulatory Infusion Pumps—Competitive Profiles

Feature	Sabratek®	Aim Plus®	CADD-Plus®	CADD Prizm VIP®	Comments
Size	4.7" × 3.9" × 2.3"	6.0" × 4.0" × 1.5"	6.4" × 3.5" × 1.1"	5.6" × 4.1" × 1.7"	Without reservoirs
Weight	16 oz.	21.2 oz.	15 oz.	20 oz.	
Accuracy	±6–10%	±5%	±6%	±6%	
Batteries	Two 9V Alkaline	Five 9V Alkaline	One 9V Alkaline	One 9V Alkaline	
Battery Life	25 hrs. @ 125 ml/hr	68 hrs. @ 50 ml/hr	25 hrs. @ 150 ml/hr	25 hrs. @ 150 ml/hr	
Battery Pack	Optional	Optional	Optional	Optional	All are rechargeable
AC Power Supply	Optional	Optional	Optional	Optional	
Digital Display	2 lines— 16 characters/line	4 lines— 16 characters/line	Basically one line of 3 characters	4 lines— 21 characters/line	
Keypad	16 Keys	22 Keys	7 Keys	9 Keys	
Security Lock Levels	3	5	3	3	Security levels
Access Codes	8	1	2	3	
Delivery Modes	PCA, Continuous, TPN, Intermittent, Circadian	PCA, Continuous, TPN, Intermittent, Circadian	Continuous, Intermittent	PCA, Continuous, TPN, Intermittent	Circadian— based on awake/sleep patterns
Medication Reservoirs	100 ml. Reservoir and IV bag adapter	Can only use a special administration set with IV bags	50 ml. & 100 ml. cassettes; IV bag adapters (3)	50 ml. & 100 ml. cassettes; IV bag adapters (3)	
Help Screen	None	Yes—limited access and numerical only	None	Over 2000 screens— variable access depending on lock level	
Event Log	Very limited information	512 Event memory—can erase all info.	None	500 Event memory— cannot be erased	
Remote Communications	Yes	Yes	No	Yes	Can program remotely and download memory

continued

EXHIBIT 23-10   Ambulatory Infusion Pumps—Competitive Profiles (continued)

Feature	Sabratek®	Aim Plus®	CADD-Plus®	CADD Prizm VIP®	Comments
Air in Line Detector	Yes—adjustable	Yes—three settings	No	Optional—fixed setting	
Data Output	Yes	Yes	No	Yes incl. pump-to-pump	To printer or PC
Occlusion Alarm	Upstream, Downstream	Downstream only	Downstream only	Downstream only	
Stop/ Start Button	One switch— positive	Two switches— can turn pump on/off accidentally	One switch— positive	One switch— positive	
Language Options	English, Spanish	English, French	English, French, Spanish, German	English, French, Spanish, German	
Durability	Moderate	Low	High	High	
Reliability	Unknown— no history	Unknown— no history	High— long history	Expected to be high	
Clinical Support	Some—limited	Good— 800 number	Excellent— extensive	Excellent— extensive	
Representation	One Quebec distributor	National— manufacturer	National— manufacturer	National— manufacturer	
Pump Price	$4000–$5000	$4000–$5000	$4800	$5800	
Disposable Price	$18–$20	$13 Each	$21–$35	$21–$35	

THE MANITOBA SITUATION

Exhibit 23-11 shows the home care infusion pump usage and programs in other provinces. In 1993–94, Manitoba presented what could only be described as a "virgin market" for IV infusion devices used in antibiotic administration. Outside of Winnipeg, there had been little thought or effort given to establishing any home antibiotic infusion programs. That is not to say that the CADD® pump wasn't recognized; several rural hospitals had, in fact, purchased the CADD-PCA® for use mainly in palliative care. Most of these locations had learned of the CADD-PCA® through referrals from the Health Sciences Centre (HSC) in Winnipeg. HSC owned and actively used about 12 of the CADD-PCA® pumps for home palliative and chronic pain therapy and were responsible for many of the leads for CADD-PCA® sales in the rural areas.

The only established program for home antibiotic infusion at this time was the provincially subsidized program based in the pharmacy at St. Boniface General Hospital in Winnipeg. From the late 1970s on, St. Boniface had operated such a program with patients who could self-care or self-administer (infusion by gravity) their medications unsupervised in the home setting. Being able to self-administer the medications did not necessarily mean acceptance into the program as it had the severe limitation of being able to treat only 10 patients per day at any one time. In a city of close to a million, this was woefully inadequate and consequently many potential home care IV patients had to be hospitalized for their therapies. This naturally was an added financial burden on the Manitoba and Winnipeg health care systems.

EXHIBIT 23-11 The Use of Infusion Pumps in Home Care: Other Provinces

Newfoundland	Virtually no usage of, or penetration for any manufacturer's pumps.
Nova Scotia	Home care is not yet organized. Home care infusion of antibiotics utilizing pumps is non-existent. PCA pumps are used but on a regional basis and not everywhere. Where used, they are generally owned and administered by the hospitals (pharmacies) with VON involvement in the home. The CADD-PCA® has about 90% of the PCA market.
New Brunswick	Home care is well developed. Pumps are owned and administered by the hospitals with central pools of pumps in various regions. Cassettes are either filled by hospital or private pharmacies. Extramural Extendicare is an independent, non-profit nursing agency (similar to VON) with 700 nurses in the field. In Sept.1996, they will also fall under hospital jurisdiction. CADD-PCA® enjoys 95% of the pain control market and CADD-Plus® has about 30% of antibiotic infusion market, with Abbott having most of the rest of the market.
Prince Edward Island	Home care is government-controlled. Pumps are controlled by the hospitals and hospices; cassettes are filled by the hospital pharmacies. The VON tends to the patients in the field. The CADD-PCA® has 100% of the market, but use of pumps for antibiotic infusion has not started here.
Saskatchewan	The CADD-PCA® has 100% of the market for pain control. The province has not started antibiotic infusions yet. When it does, all of the market will go to Abbott due to long-term contract with the hospitals; hospitals must give first option to Abbott because of agreement between the province and Abbott upon locating manufacturing there.
British Columbia	CADD-PCA® pumps had achieved 99% penetration of the BC palliative care market and the CADD-1® took about 48% of the chemotherapy market. A multi-disciplinary approach has been organized in BC, with close affiliations between the various hospitals, specialists, clinicians, and BC Homecare. This is a provincial government-operated agency and in different situations is either affiliated directly with a large-centre hospital or a smaller-centre hospital with some regional affiliation. The CADD-Plus® and the home IV antibiotic programs are only starting to develop (Jan., 1997).

Previous to SIMS's 1994 acquisition of Deltec, the Pharmacia salesperson for this region had been making exploratory efforts towards sales of the CADD-Plus® pump; therefore, there was some awareness of the pump and its capabilities on the part of the St. Boniface home IV infusion group. In addition to this, the Pharmacia salesperson had identified the home care nursing agencies and companies that could potentially be implicated in a home IV infusion pump program (VON, We Care) and had made some progress in apprising them of the possibilities presented by the CADD-Plus®.

This was the situation when SIMS took over the sales of Deltec in Canada in October of 1994. Sales territory manager Bob Young immediately picked up the leads from Pharmacia and approached each of the contacts that had previously been identified. It was essential for him to clarify the whole situation before proceeding with any focused sales efforts. He quickly ascertained that any decisions regarding initiation of a pump program would come from the provincial government, based directly on recommendations made by the Winnipeg Home IV Program staff and/or director. The fact was that they were the only ones with any authority or backing to mount a program. Young already had a relationship with the purchasing department at St. Boniface, selling other SIMS products, but he established that the IV program staff would deal with any new products for the IV program directly (although purchasing would initiate the final purchase order). He was similarly advised by the IV program staff that biomedical engineering was well acquainted with the CADD® pump and had, in fact, recommended it as a product to consider when the time came. Consequently, Young spent little time with them. The question for Young at this point was how could he facilitate the progress of pump sales for home care antibiotic infusion?

During this time, the Manitoba Health authorities were up to their necks in various problems. They were undergoing the restructuring of the health system, reorganization of district or regional health care groups (geographically), and centralization of purchasing within the city of Winnipeg. To top it all off, the provincial government was starting to focus its efforts towards an upcoming provincial election. Thus it was quite difficult for Young to establish any influential contacts within the provincial group. However, through continual contact and follow-up with the various nursing agencies, the IV Program staff, and other allied health care professionals whom he encountered during his day-to-day business dealings, he was able to keep abreast of any upcoming changes in the situation. Thus he decided that the emphasis of any sales endeavours had to be directed towards the Home IV Program group.

His first big break came from an unexpected source. Until June of 1995, Young had also dealt with an oncologist based at the MCTRF Cancer Clinic at St. Boniface Hospital. His efforts here were towards sales of the basic CADD-1® pump to be used for longer-term home IV infusions of chemotherapy agents. The physician involved had talked about the possibilities of establishing such a program, but the funds were not available and he had been unable to gain the required support. SIMS had a number of obsolete pumps that were in working order and that could do the same job as the CADD-1®. Young suggested that the physician could conduct a long-term trial using these pumps, loaned for purposes of evaluating the effectiveness and economy of pump operation with his patients. In a quick about turn, the oncologist rallied support from the nursing director of the clinic. She was under pressure to do more with less money, and she immediately decided that the results of a trial study were the only way to wake up the bureaucrats to the potential savings of such a program.

The decision was made to do the trial, and by July of 1995, the nursing staff and pharmacist at the clinic were trained in the use of the pump. Six pumps were subsequently put into operation in home chemotherapy infusion, under the nursing supervision of the Cancer Clinic. Although independent from St. Boniface, the pharmacist in the satellite pharmacy of the cancer clinic worked directly for the director of the hospital pharmacy, the same director involved in the Home IV Program. This was a big plus; although it was only a trial situation, Young felt that events were now moving in a positive direction.

A second break came in October of 1995, when he learned of a planned, two-phase expansion of the Manitoba Home IV Program slated for the following year. In February of 1996, the first phase would see an increase in the number of patients it would handle (going from 10 to 35 patients), as well as acceptance of patients who were not capable of self-care. These patients would require periodic supervision by visiting nurses trained in IV therapy. The second phase in the fall of 1996 would expand the scope of the program's therapy options. Home care IV therapy using portable pumps was to be instituted at this time; the thinking was that the resultant decrease in nursing visits would more than defray the outlay of capital costs for procurement of the pumps. There were also two additional considerations. There were certain areas in Winnipeg where it was questionable for visiting nurses to venture after dark; the use of pumps would partially alleviate this problem. Probably more important but less considered were the consequent quality-of-life issues that a patient could enjoy through therapy in the home.

It was at this point that it suddenly became easier to gain an audience with the director and IV program staff, and several meetings ensued between February and June 5, 1996. With help from Faith West, a product manager having extensive experience with the CADD® pumps, Young was able to present the features and benefits of both the CADD-Plus® and the CADD Prizm VIP™ (they had a working prototype) and of SIMS's product support program. The program director and program staff, as well as a provincial government representative for home care, attended the presentation. It was not so much that the seed was sewn as that it had already started to grow. He learned that the long-term objective of this group was to develop a cost-effective, viable program that used all the different IV therapy means as required, including disposable, mechanical pumps and electronic/electric pumps such as the CADD®.

They also stated that their program would probably be expanded to cover the whole province and would likely have jurisdiction over the pain pump program as well as the home chemotherapy program. These points were to prove important in the final consideration of which pump would best suit their needs. So when the request for pump information was received on June 10, 1996, some very quick and astute actions and decisions were required. Upon examining the request (see Exhibit 23-12), Young could see the possibility of some flexibility in how it was completed. He decided that one last phone call to the program was required.

EXHIBIT 23-12 Request Letter and Questionnaire

St-Boniface
June 9, 1996

SIMS Canada Ltd.
Bob Young, Territory Manager
301 Gough Road
Markham, Ontario
L3R 4Y8

Dear Bob,

The Manitoba Community Intravenous Therapy Program is a home infusion program presently utilizing a gravity system for the administration of intravenous anti-infective agents.

An expansion phase has recently taken place. As a result, we are presently investigating the use of a pump delivery system for an expanding list of intravenous medications and hydration solutions.

The attached questionnaire is being sent to a number of different companies. We hope that the information obtained from the questionnaire will help us to select a number of product(s) that can be used in a trial. Upon completion of the trial, we will choose those product(s) that best meet the program's needs for use throughout the province of Manitoba.

Once again, kindly fill out the attached questionnaire and return to Manitoba Community Intravenous Therapy Program by June 24, 1996. Please do not hesitate to contact us at 1-(204) 555-5555 for further information.

Thank you in advance for your cooperation and expedient reply.

Sincerely,

Glenna Germaine
Nurse, Manitoba Community
Intravenous Therapy Program

EXHIBIT 23-12 Questionnaire (continued)

MANITOBA COMMUNITY INTRAVENOUS THERAPY PROGRAM

REQUEST FOR PRODUCT INFORMATION (INFUSION DEVICES)

The Manitoba Community Intravenous Therapy Program is considering electronic and non-electronic infusion devices for use by patients and nurses in delivery of medications in the home.

Please complete for each device you have available:

Product name: _____   Model Number _____

Circle the applicable response(s):

The rate control mechanism is: electronic   tubing size   other

Comment: _____

The power source is: electricity   battery   elastomeric   spring   other

Comment: _____

The device is: reusable   disposable

Please respond to the following questions using one of the response codes.

1. Available on the current model.
2. Currently under development, will be available on the next model upgrade (to be available within 6 months).
3. Currently under development, will be available on the next model upgrade (to be available within 1 year).
4. Not currently available and no plans for inclusion on the next model upgrade.
5. Not applicable.

1.0   FEATURES

1.0.1   Can the device provide the following infusion types?

    a) intermittent infusion

    b) pre-programmed intermittent infusion

    c) continuous infusion

    d) intermittent bolus

1.0.2   Is there a signal which indicates an infusion is in progress?

1.0.3   Is there an alarm to indicate?

    a) infusion complete

    b) air in line

    c) low battery

    d) high pressure

EXHIBIT 23-12 Questionnaire (continued)

    e) low pressure

    f) other (comment)

1.0.4   Is there a lock out security feature?

1.0.5   Where does the accuracy rate fall?

    a) $\leq$ 5%

    b) > 5%, $\leq$ 10%

    c) > 10%

1.0.6   Can the device handle a volume of:

    a) $\leq$ 10 ml

    b) > 10 ml $\leq$ 25 ml

    c) 50 ml

    d) 100 ml

    e) 200 ml

    f) 250 ml

    g) 350 ml

    h) 500 ml

    i) 1000 ml

    j) > 1000 ml

1.0.7   Can the device handle a rate setting:

    a) < 0.5 ml/hr

    b) < 1 ml/hr

    c) < 25 ml/hr

    d) 25 ml/hr

    e) 100 ml/hr

    f) 250 ml/hr

1.0.8   Is there a bolus feature?

1.0.9   Can a bolus rate be programmed?

1.0.10 How many medications can it infuse simultaneously?

    a) 1 only

    b) 2

    c) 3 or more

1.0.11 Is there a memory record of functions performed?

1.0.12 Is the device available with French programming?

EXHIBIT 23-12 Questionnaire (continued)

2.0   MAINTENANCE & SERVICING

2.0.1   If battery operated, are the batteries rechargeable?

2.0.2   If battery operated, state the battery life.

2.0.3   Are replacements provided when servicing is required?

2.0.4   Comment on device servicing and service contracts.

3.0   PHARMACEUTICAL QUESTIONS

3.0.1   Are drug stability data and references provided to support use of medications with the device as prescribed?

3.0.2   Are there any medications which cannot be delivered due to interactions with the device components?

4.0   AUXILIARY SUPPLIES

4.0.1   Is there special tubing which must be purchased for use with the device?

4.0.2   Does the tubing have luer lock connections?

4.0.3   Can the tubing be used with a needleless system?

4.0.4   The volume of the tubing is:
   a) ≤ 0.2 ml
   b) ≤ 0.5 ml
   c) ≤ 1 ml
   d) > 1 ml

4.0.5   Is the tubing available with an in-line filter?

4.0.6   State micron size, particulate matters and air.

4.0.7   Must special reservoirs be ordered to hold the medication solution? Explain.

4.0.8   What is the recommended life of tubing and reservoir?
   List which part or parts are reusable and for how long.
   Please comment on recommended number of doses, duration of viability.

4.0.9   Can device be frozen?
   Can tubing be frozen?
   Can reservoir be frozen?
   Provide guidelines on freezing.

4.0.10   Is there any other equipment required to operate the device (e.g., special computer software)? Explain.

EXHIBIT 23-12 Questionnaire (continued)

5.0   OTHER CONSIDERATIONS

5.0.1   State the device's dimensions.

5.0.2   State the device's weight.

5.0.3   Is there a case for patients to carry the device in?

5.0.4   Itemize and cost out supplies required to provide:
           Drug A in 100 ml NS per dose. Doses every 6 hours for 1 week.

5.0.5   Is your product environmentally friendly? Comment on biodegradability.

Please provide a current client name and contact number which may be used as a reference.

His question was simple. He asked Glenna Germaine, the nurse involved in the program, what their short-term goals would be with the actual pump trial.

"We actually have three goals Bob." Glenna answered. "We want to demonstrate the potential savings from using these pumps. We want to evaluate the best pumps before making the decision, and we want to ensure that the visiting nurses and patients can all function well with the pumps."

This was all the information Young felt that he needed. He pulled out the request form and pen and started to work.

24

SUE JONES

H.F. (Herb) MacKenzie

Sue Jones didn't notice the heat and humidity. She sat in her car with her hands on the steering wheel, the engine running, and the air conditioner operating. She didn't realize that she had been sitting in that position for nearly 20 minutes, and she was unaware that several people inside the coffee shop where she was parked had noticed and were beginning to wonder whether there was something wrong.

BACKGROUND

Sue Jones was one of those people everyone liked. She was cheerful and optimistic; she was smart, both in intellect and dress; she was gregarious and loved to talk to people. With these personal qualities, it was no surprise when she finally got a sales position with one of Canada's largest transportation companies.

Sue had always wanted to be a salesperson. Her father had been a manufacturer's agent and had spent most of his life travelling across Western Canada. He represented eight manufacturers and had developed his business "from a briefcase to a million dollars in one year," and to over five times that amount 10 years later. Sue loved her father, and while she was growing to womanhood, she and her father would frequently walk for hours while he told her his selling secrets and what made "super salesmen." Before Sue finished elementary school, she had already decided that she wanted to grow up to be "just like daddy." During high school, Sue helped her father, sending direct mail flyers to his accounts, calling customers to make appointments for him, typing correspondence to both customers and to the manufacturers that he represented, and occasionally, travelling with him to visit his accounts when she did not have to attend classes.

By the time she completed high school, Sue decided she wanted to work. She left home and got a job in Mississauga, Ontario, as a receptionist in a small office that provided temporary personnel services in and around the Toronto area. Her pleasing telephone personality was appreciated by many of the firm's clients, and Mrs. Thompson, the General Manager, eventually encouraged Sue to visit some of the major clients when she was not too busy, to help develop closer relationships with them.

Sue was quickly hooked on selling. She decided that she needed some formal training. She first thought about attending some professional seminars, but her father convinced her to get a degree in business and he offered to finance her education. Sue declined his financial help; she liked her independence. Sue decided to take her program on a part-time basis while continuing to work. At the same time, she searched for and found a full-time job in sales, selling transportation services for a Toronto-based trucking company. She loved her job and she was very successful, doubling sales in her territory over her first two years.

The job gave her some flexibility to complete her degree. While she certainly worked more than 40 hours per week, she did not have to follow a strict nine-to-five schedule, and she frequently took a day or two off when exams approached. Just before her graduation, a major Canadian trucking company advertised for a salesperson to assume an established territory in Calgary. Sue applied for the job, and the National Sales Manager was impressed enough with her that he hired her in March, but kept her in the Toronto area until she completed her courses a few months later. In June, Sue transferred to the Calgary office where she was the junior salesperson among six others, all men.

During her first week there, which she was supposed to spend in the office learning about her territory and planning her account strategy, one of the more senior salespeople, Joe Kirwan, suffered a severe stroke and had to be hospitalized. None of the more senior salespeople wanted Joe's territory as they did not want to give up their current customers.

Alan Best, the Sales Manager, decided it would be better to reassign Sue to Joe's territory as he had already been covering what was originally to be Sue's territory for several months, and he had developed some close personal relationships there. He felt he could continue to cover it until another salesperson was hired.

Joe's territory was one of the better territories. Joe had serviced it very well and he had a lot of loyal customers. In fact, Calgary Structural Contractors (CSC) was in Joe's territory, and it was the largest and most profitable account they had in Alberta. Sue spent her second week in the office studying a new territory and a new group of accounts. She decided that because CSC was her most important account, she should visit them as quickly as possible. On Friday morning, she called Bim Hadley, the Traffic Manager, and made an appointment to see him early Monday morning. She explained to Bim that she was new to the territory. Because his account was very important to her company and she would be responsible for servicing it, she wanted to spend some time understanding what CSC did, what their transportation needs were, and how she could best serve them. Bim told her he would give her a tour of the plant, and she could see the material they used, how it was unloaded, where it was stored, and the finished products that they manufactured, so she could understand their transportation needs for both incoming and outgoing shipments.

THE INCIDENT

When Sue appeared on Monday morning, she was looking forward to meeting Bim and getting a tour of CSC. Over a coffee in Bim's office, the two discussed the history of the relationship between their two companies, and what was important to CSC when it came to selecting a transportation service. Bim finally offered to take Sue on the tour he had promised. First, they visited the shop where the manufacturing was done; then they went outside where the structural steel inventory was stored. There were thousands of tons of steel, in all shapes and configurations. She remarked, "I don't think I have ever seen so much steel in one place." Bim replied, "We are the largest structural steel fabricator in the province, and next year is going to be even better for us. We are planning a major expansion as we have just been awarded three new multi-million dollar contracts."

As they returned to the building, Bim motioned to a side door. "Let's take that one, Sue. It's a shortcut to my office." He held the door open for her and followed her inside. Sue noticed that she was in a long narrow office with a doorway at the far end. She turned to Bim to verify that she should proceed to the doorway when she suddenly felt his hand under her skirt. For the first few seconds, Sue was stunned. She could not believe that this actually was happening, but then she realized that it was, and it was not an accident.

After she left CSC, Sue pulled into a nearby parking lot and parked in front of a coffee shop. She was still shaken. She still could not believe what had happened. She didn't know what she should do. As one of the employees from the coffee shop approached her car, Sue got out and headed for the entrance. She entered, ordered a coffee, and took a table away from the other customers so she could think. She didn't feel like talking to anyone. Sue needed to compose herself, and to decide what her next actions should be.

SOME ETHICAL DILEMMAS IN BUSINESS-TO-BUSINESS SALES

H.F. (Herb) MacKenzie

The following were actual situations experienced by the case writer during more than 15 years in business-to-business sales and sales management. The names of firms and individuals have been disguised due to the nature of the material in this case.

HALCO MANUFACTURING

Dave MacDonald was excited when he got the unexpected phone call from Nicki Steele, a senior buyer from Halco Manufacturing.

"I know it's a year since we bought that prototype reel from you, but we just got a contract from the government to build ten more 'bear traps' and we desperately need to hold our price on these units. Could you possibly sell us 10 new reels at the same price you charged last year?" Nicki inquired.

"I'll see what I can do and call you back today," Dave replied.

Dave immediately retrieved the file from the previous year and saw that they had supplied the reel for $6990.00 F.O.B. the customer's warehouse. There was a breakdown of the pricing on the file:

Manufacturer's list price	$4000.00
Special engineering charge (25%)	1000.00
Total list price	5000.00
Distributor discount (20%)	1000.00
Distributor net cost	4000.00

Estimated Currency Exchange (8%)	320.00
Estimated Duty (22½%)	972.00
Estimated Freight	245.00
Estimated Brokerage	55.00
Estimated distributor cost, F.O.B. destination	5592.00
Markup (25%)	1398.00
Selling Price, F.O.B. destination	$6990.00

There were some notes on the file that Dave reviewed. The reel was designed as part of a "bear trap" on Canadian navy ships. These bear traps would hook onto helicopters in rough weather and haul them safely onto landing pads on the ship decks. The reel was really a model SM heavy duty steel mill reel, except some of the exposed parts were to be made of stainless steel to provide longer life in the salt-water atmosphere. There was a special engineering charge on the reel as it was a non-standard item that had to be specially engineered. The manufacturer had suggested at the time they quoted that Dave could keep the full 20 percent discount as they thought there was only one other manufacturer capable of building this unit, and their price would likely be much higher.

When Dave got a price from the manufacturer on the 10 new units, he was surprised they quoted a price of only $3200.00 each, less 40/10 percent. When he asked for the price to be verified, the order desk clarified the pricing. First, there had been a 20 percent reduction in all SM series reels. That made the manufacturer's list price only $3200.00. Then, because there was a large quantity, the distributor discount was increased to less 40/10 percent instead of the 20 percent that was given on the original reel.

As Dave estimated his cost, things got better. The original reel was imported from the United States at 22½ percent duty as "not otherwise provided for manufacturers of iron or steel, tariff item 44603-1." In the interim, the company Dave worked for got a duty remission on series SM steel mill reels as "machinery of a class or kind not manufactured in Canada, tariff item 42700-1," and the duty was remitted (and the savings supposedly passed on to the end customer). The currency exchange rate also improved in Dave's favour, and the estimated freight and brokerage charges per unit dropped considerably because of the increased shipment size. Dave estimated his new cost as follows:

Manufacturer's list price	$3200.00
Distributor discount (40/10%)	1472.00
Distributor net cost	1728.00
Estimated Currency Exchange (2%)	35.00
Estimated Duty (remitted)	0.00
Estimated Freight	85.00
Estimated Brokerage	14.50
Estimated distributor cost, F.O.B. destination	$1862.50

Now that he had all the figures, Dave had to decide what the selling price should be to his customer.

CROWN PULP AND PAPER LTD.

Bill Siddall had been promoted to the position of salesperson, and he was pleased when he received an order for nearly $10 000 for stainless steel fittings from the new pulp mill being built in his territory. Unfortunately, he quoted a price that was 40 percent below his cost.

"We have to honour the price quoted," Bill insisted.

"I know if you let me talk to Rory, he'll let us raise the price," replied Dave MacDonald, the Sales Manager. "Rory used to be the purchasing agent at one of my best accounts before he came to the mill."

"No. You gave me responsibility for this account, and I want to build a good relationship with Rory myself. He gave us the order over two weeks ago. He can't change suppliers now because he needs the material next week, and I don't want to put him on the spot now because it would be unfair. Since this is our first order, I would like to supply it without any problems. We'll get back the money we lost on this order many times if we can get their future business. This material is needed for a small construction job, and they haven't even started to consider their stores inventory yet."

After much discussion, it was agreed that the order would stand, but Dave would call the fitting manufacturer's Sales Manager, Chuck Knowles, as the two men were good friends.

"We need some help on that last order we placed with you. Bill sold it at 40 percent below our cost," said Dave.

"How could that happen?" Chuck seemed amazed.

"Well," replied Dave, "you give us a 25 percent distributor discount and we gave 10 percent to the customer due to the size of the order. What we forgot was to double the list price because the customer wanted schedule 80 wall thickness on the fittings instead of standard schedule 40. This was Bill's first large inquiry and he made an honest mistake. He doesn't want me to get involved with the customer, and I don't want to force the issue with him, so I'm hoping you can help us on this one order. We expect to get a lot of business from this account over the next few years."

"I'll split the difference with you. What you're selling now for $0.90, you're paying $1.50 for, and if I give you an additional 20 percent discount, your cost will come down to $1.20. Can you live with that?" Chuck asked.

"It's a help. We appreciate it. We'll see you on your next trip to our territory, and I'll buy lunch."

"A deal. See you next month." The conversation ended.

When it was over, Dave was feeling reasonably satisfied with himself, but he still felt somewhat uneasy. He promised not to call Rory, and he promised not to interfere with the account, but he still thought something could be done.

On Saturday morning, Dave went to the Brae Shore Golf Club. He was confident Rory would be there. Sure enough, at 8:00 A.M., Rory was scheduled to tee-off. Dave sat on the bench at the first tee and waited for Rory to appear. Promptly, Rory arrived with Bob Arnold, one of his senior buyers. The three men greeted each other pleasantly and Rory asked who Dave was waiting for.

"Just one of my neighbours. He was supposed to be here an hour ago but I guess he won't show."

"Join us. We don't mind. Besides we might need a donation this fall when we have our company golf tournament. We'll invite you, of course, and we'll invite Bill if he plays golf."

"He doesn't play often, but he's pretty good. Beat me the last time we played. How is he doing at your mill? Is everything okay?" Dave asked.

"Checking up on him? Sure. He's fine. He made a mistake the other day when he went to see our millwright foreman without clearing it through my office first, but he'll learn. He'll do a lot of business with us because we want to buy locally where possible, and you have a lot of good product lines. I think he'll get along well with all of us as well. He seems a bit serious, but we'll break him in before long. We just gave him a big order for stainless fittings a few weeks ago, but we told him to visit at ten o'clock next time and to bring the doughnuts."

"I know," replied Dave. Unfortunately, we lost a lot of money on that order."

"Your price was very low. I couldn't understand it because I knew your material wasn't manufactured offshore. Did you quote the cheaper T304 grade of stainless instead of the T316 we use?"

"No. We quoted schedule 40 prices instead of schedule 80. The wall thickness for schedule 80 is twice as thick, and the price should have been double as well."

"Heck. Double the price. We'll pay it. I'll make a note on the file Monday. I know you're not trying to take us and I can appreciate an honest mistake. At double the price, you might be a bit high, but you know we want to place the order with you anyway because you're local. Eventually we'll want you to carry some inventory for us, so we might just as well make sure we're both happy with this business."

STRAIT STRUCTURAL STEEL LTD.

Dave MacDonald was sitting in the outer office waiting to see Stan Hope, the purchasing agent for Strait Structural Steel, a new account that had just begun operations in a remote, coastal location about forty miles from the nearest city. Stan had telephoned Dave the previous week and had an urgent request for four large exhaust fans that were required to exhaust welding fumes from enclosed spaces where welders were at work. The union had threatened to stop the project unless working conditions were improved quickly, and although Dave didn't sell fans at the time, he found a line of fans and negotiated a discount from the manufacturer, along with an agreement to discuss the further possibility of representing the fan manufacturer on a national basis.

When Stan gave the order to Dave for the fans, the two men discussed other products that Dave sold. Dave sold products for a company that was both a general-line and specialty-line industrial distributor. Included in the general-line products were such items as hand and power tools, cutting tools (drills, taps, dies), safety equipment, wire rope and slings, fasteners (nuts, bolts), and fittings (stainless steel, bronze, and carbon steel flanges, elbows, and tees). Included in the specialty-line products were such items as electric motors and generators, motor controls, hydraulic and pneumatic valves and cylinders, rubber dock fenders, and overhead cranes. When the men finally met, they were almost instantly friends, and it was obvious that the opportunities for them to do further business were great. "One item that really interests me," said Stan, "is PTFE tape. We need some and we will be using a lot of it."

"We have the largest stock of PTFE tape in the country," replied Dave. We import it directly from Italy, but it's high quality and is the same standard size as all others on the market; $\frac{1}{2}$ inches wide, 0.003 inches thick, and 480 inches long. How much are you interested in?"

"Let's start with 400 rolls," Stan suggested.

PTFE tape was a white, non-adhesive tape that was used as a pipe thread sealant. It was wrapped around the threads of pipe or fittings before they were screwed together to make a leak-proof seal. The tape first came on the market in the late 1960s at prices as high as $3.60 per roll, but since then prices had dropped considerably. North American manufacturers were still selling the tape for list prices near $1.80, and were offering dealer discounts between 25 and 50 percent depending on the quantities that dealers bought. Dave was importing the tape from Italy at a landed cost of $0.17 per roll.

"We have a standard price of $1.00 per roll as long as you buy 200 rolls," Dave offered.

"No question. You have an excellent price. How much would you charge M H Sales?"

"I don't know. Who is M H Sales?" asked Dave.

"A small industrial supply company located in my basement. The "H" is for Hope. I share the company with Bruce Malcolm, the "M," and he's in purchasing at Central Power Corporation. M H Sales is a small company and we are looking for additional products to sell. Between Strait Structural and Central Power, we could sell several thousand rolls of PTFE tape each year."

MCCORMICK GLEASON LIMITED

Dave MacDonald telephoned Clarey Stanley, a Senior Buyer at McCormick Gleason Limited. "Clarey, I'm calling about that quote we made on Lufkin tapes. Can we have your order?"

"Sorry. Your price was high. I gave the order to Ken Stafford. You need a sharper pencil."

"How much sharper?" Dave asked.

"I can't tell you that. But you were close." Clarey replied. "By the way, Kenny called me from the stores department this morning and he has a large shipment of electric relays that was delivered yesterday. They weren't properly marked and he can't identify the ones with normally open contacts from the ones with normally closed contacts. Do you want them returned, or can someone see him and straighten it out here?"

"Tell him I'll see him immediately after lunch. I can tell them apart and I'll see they get properly identified."

When the conversation ended, Dave made a note to see Clarey about the tapes. There was a problem somewhere. Dave knew his cost on Lufkin tapes was the lowest available, and he quoted 12 percent on cost because he really wanted the order. The order was less than $1500, but it meant that Dave could place a multiple-case order on the manufacturer and get the lowest possible cost for all replacement inventory. That would increase the margin on sales to other customers who bought smaller quantities. There was no possibility that Stafford Industrial, a local, one-person, "out-of-the-basement" operation that bought Lufkin tapes as a jobber, not as a distributor, could match his price.

That afternoon, while waiting to see Ken MacKay, the Stores Manager, Dave noticed a carton from Stafford Industrial Sales being unloaded from a local delivery van. Although he knew that Stafford supplied quite a few maintenance, repair, and operating (MRO) supplies to this customer, Dave decided to play ignorant.

"What do you buy from Stafford Industrial?" he asked the young stores clerk who was handling the package.

Opening the carton, the clerk read the packing slip. "It says here we ordered 144 measuring tapes, ¾ inch wide by 25 ft. long."

"Are those things expensive?" Dave asked.

"Don't know. There's no price on the packing slip. Clarey Stanley in purchasing ordered them. You could talk to him." The clerk continued to unpack the shipment. As he did, Dave noticed the tapes were manufactured offshore and were poor quality compared to the Lufkin tapes that he sold, and that he quoted to Clarey Stanley the previous day.

"Aren't those supposed to be Lufkin tapes?" Dave asked.

"Not that I know. The packing slip just says tapes. Wait and I'll haul our copy of the purchase order." The clerk went to a filing cabinet next to his desk and returned with a carbon copy of the purchase order. "No, it just says tapes. It doesn't specify any brand."

There was something wrong, and Dave was determined to get an answer.

POWER & MOTION INDUSTRIAL SUPPLY INC.

H.F. (Herb) MacKenzie

It was 7:00 P.M. on Sunday evening when Hal Maybee returned to his office. He had spent the afternoon golfing with one of his customers, and he now had to decide what he was going to tell head office on Monday morning with regard to new salaries for the sales staff at his branch.

Hal had just been appointed Atlantic Region District Manager for one of Canada's largest industrial distributors. His appointment was made only two weeks before, following the sudden death of Fergie McDonald who, at 48 years old, had been in charge of the company's most profitable branch. About 70 percent of the sales in Atlantic Canada, including the four most profitable product lines, were for manufacturers that the company did not represent on a national basis. There were many manufacturers in Ontario and Quebec that served central Canada with their own sales forces, and used distributors for the east and west coasts due to the distances from their head offices and the geographical dispersion of customers in those regions. Although Power & Motion had sales agreements with over 400 North American manufacturers, only about 100 manufacturers were involved in 80 percent of the sales.

It was a complete surprise to Hal when he was promoted, and he knew there were people at the branch who expected they deserved it more. Exhibit 26-1 shows the performance evaluations that Fergie had completed on the six sales people just before he died. Head office had intended to send only five forms to Hal, but one of the secretaries mistakenly included Fergie's evaluation of Hal as well.

EXHIBIT 26-1 Evaluation of Salespersons

Salesperson	Evaluation Criteria	Far Worse Than Average			About Average		Far Better Than Average	
Dave Edison	Attitude	1	2	3	4	⑤	6	7
	Appearance and Manner	1	2	3	4	5	⑥	7
	Selling Skills	1	2	3	4	5	⑥	7
	Product Knowledge	1	2	3	④	5	6	7
	Time Management	1	2	3	④	5	6	7
	Customer Goodwill	1	2	3	④	5	6	7
	Expense / Budget	1	2	3	④	5	6	7
	New Accounts Opened	1	2	3	④	5	6	7
	Sales Calls / Quota	1	2	3	④	5	6	7
	Sales / Quota	1	2	3	4	⑤	6	7
	Sales Volume	1	2	3	④	5	6	7
	Sales Growth	1	2	3	4	⑤	6	7
	Contribution Margin	1	2	3	4	5	6	7
	Total Score: 61							

Comments: Current salary $52 000. Territory is Cape Breton Island and the city of Moncton, N.B. Needs more product knowledge, but has learned a lot since hired. A bit aggressive, but he has developed some excellent new accounts through attention to detail and follow-up support.

Salesperson	Evaluation Criteria	Far Worse Than Average			About Average		Far Better Than Average	
Arne Olsen	Attitude	1	2	③	4	5	6	7
	Appearance and Manner	1	2	③	4	5	6	7
	Selling Skills	1	2	③	4	5	6	7
	Product Knowledge	1	2	3	④	5	6	7
	Time Management	1	2	③	4	5	6	7
	Customer Goodwill	1	2	③	4	5	6	7
	Expense / Budget	1	2	3	4	⑤	6	7
	New Accounts Opened	1	2	③	4	5	6	7
	Sales Calls / Quota	1	2	3	4	5	⑥	7
	Sales / Quota	1	2	③	4	5	6	7
	Sales Volume	1	2	3	④	5	6	7
	Sales Growth	1	2	③	4	5	6	7
	Contribution Margin	1	2	③	4	5	6	7
	Total Score: 46							

Comments: Current salary $44 500. Has been calling regularly on his existing accounts in southern New Brunswick (except Moncton). Although he has increased the number of sales calls as agreed at our last review, sales have not gone up accordingly. Some concern with product knowledge. Arne knows all of our major product lines very well, but has not shown much effort to learn about many of the new lines we have added that may become our best product lines in the future. Further concern with his contribution margin. This is the fourth year in a row that it has dropped although it is almost the same as last year.

EXHIBIT 26-1 Evaluation of Salespersons (continued)

Salesperson	Evaluation Criteria	Far Worse Than Average			About Average		Far Better Than Average	
Hal Maybee	Attitude	1	2	3	4	⑤	6	7
	Appearance and Manner	1	2	3	④	5	6	7
	Selling Skills	1	2	3	④	5	6	7
	Product Knowledge	1	2	3	4	⑤	6	7
	Time Management	1	2	3	4	5	⑥	7
	Customer Goodwill	1	2	3	4	5	⑥	7
	Expense / Budget	1	2	3	④	5	6	7
	New Accounts Opened	1	②	3	4	5	6	7
	Sales Calls / Quota	1	2	3	④	5	6	7
	Sales / Quota	1	2	3	4	⑤	6	7
	Sales Volume	1	②	3	4	5	6	7
	Sales Growth	1	2	3	4	5	6	7
	Contribution Margin	1	②	3	4	5	6	7
	Total Score: 52							

Comments: Current salary $38 500. Although still the Office Manager, Hal has taken over Newfoundland as a territory and travels there four times a year. Hal also travels to northern New Brunswick with me occasionally due to his expert product knowledge on electric and pneumatic products, which we sell to the mines and pulp mills in the two areas. Hal is very focused and successful with the big sales, but needs to develop knowledge of and interest in some of the lower sales volume, less technical products as they are generally higher margin items. Hal has a lot of respect in the office and our efficiency has improved greatly, as has the general work atmosphere within the office.

Salesperson	Evaluation Criteria	Far Worse Than Average			About Average		Far Better Than Average	
Tanya Burt	Attitude	1	2	3	④	5	6	7
	Appearance and Manner	1	2	3	④	5	6	7
	Selling Skills	1	2	3	4	⑤	6	7
	Product Knowledge	1	2	③	4	5	6	7
	Time Management	1	2	3	4	⑤	6	7
	Customer Goodwill	1	2	3	4	⑤	6	7
	Expense / Budget	1	2	3	④	5	6	7
	New Accounts Opened	1	2	3	4	⑤	6	7
	Sales Calls / Quota	1	2	3	4	⑤	6	7
	Sales / Quota	1	2	3	4	⑤	6	7
	Sales Volume	1	2	3	④	5	6	7
	Sales Growth	1	2	3	4	⑤	6	7
	Contribution Margin	1	2	3	4	⑤	6	7
	Total Score: 59							

Comments: Current salary $36 000. Very impressed with her performance. Has good knowledge of product pricing and sourcing, but needs to learn more about product applications. Tanya sells mainly maintenance and operating supplies, but she has a number of accounts that buy large annual volumes, as her territory is the Halifax-Dartmouth area surrounding our warehouse. Tanya is dedicated and dependable. She has opened many new accounts for us, and I predict good success for her as she continues to develop her knowledge and selling skills.

EXHIBIT 26-1   Evaluation of Salespersons (continued)

Salesperson	Evaluation Criteria	Far Worse Than Average			About Average		Far Better Than Average	
Jim Stanley	Attitude	1	2	③	4	5	6	7
	Appearance and Manner	1	2	③	4	5	6	7
	Selling Skills	1	2	③	4	5	6	7
	Product Knowledge	1	2	3	④	5	6	7
	Time Management	1	②	3	4	5	6	7
	Customer Goodwill	1	2	③	4	5	6	7
	Expense / Budget	1	2	③	4	5	6	7
	New Accounts Opened	1	②	3	4	5	6	7
	Sales Calls / Quota	1	2	3	④	5	6	7
	Sales / Quota	1	2	3	4	⑤	6	7
	Sales Volume	1	2	3	④	5	6	7
	Sales Growth	1	2	3	4	⑤	6	7
	Contribution Margin	1	2	3	4	⑤	6	7
	Total Score: 46							

Comments: Current salary $42 000. Jim seems to be performing quite well, but there is concern with his behaviour. I hope that a salary increase and some direction from me will improve his performance next year. He has been making some suggestions that he might like to move back to Office Management because everyone thinks I will be promoting Hal to full-time sales and letting him take over my territory as well as Newfoundland. I really do not want Jim back in the office, and I think he should be a good salesperson. His sales and contribution margin are good, but part of his sales increase this year came from a new customer that has a manufacturing plant in his region, but actually buys from an office located in Tanya's territory. Tanya and Jim have agreed to split the credit for the sales as Tanya must do the selling, but Jim has to service the account.

Salesperson	Evaluation Criteria	Far Worse Than Average			About Average		Far Better Than Average	
Buck Thompson	Attitude	1	2	3	④	5	6	7
	Appearance and Manner	1	2	3	④	5	6	7
	Selling Skills	1	2	3	4	⑤	6	7
	Product Knowledge	1	2	3	4	5	⑥	7
	Time Management	1	2	3	④	5	6	7
	Customer Goodwill	1	2	3	④	5	6	7
	Expense / Budget	1	2	③	4	5	6	7
	New Accounts Opened	1	②	3	4	5	6	7
	Sales Calls / Quota	1	2	③	4	5	6	7
	Sales / Quota	1	2	3	④	5	6	7
	Sales Volume	1	2	3	④	5	6	7
	Sales Growth	1	2	3	④	5	6	7
	Contribution Margin	1	2	3	④	5	6	7
	Total Score: 51							

Comments: Current salary $49 000. Sells in Pictou County, N.S., where we have a very established customer base and a variety of industries. Buck knows all of his customers very well as he has lived in the area all of his life. He has very good selling skills and product knowledge and has been the main reason we have done so well in his territory.

Nearly three weeks previously, Fergie and Hal were making some joint calls on some pulp mills in Northern New Brunswick, the territory that Fergie kept for himself, even though head office wanted him to stop selling and spend more time on sales administration. During the trip, Fergie told Hal that he was given six percent of the total sales staff salary to be divided among them for the coming year. This was the customary way of giving salary increases at the branches as it gave head office the discretion to decide the total increase in the salary expense, but it gave the district managers responsibility for allocating salary increases. Fergie was told that nationally, sales increases would average about three percent, but his branch was among the lowest paid in the company and had been the best performing branch for several years.

Hal did not want to express his opinions as he knew he and Fergie would disagree. However, he did allow Fergie to express his own thoughts on the staff. There were two sales-people that Fergie had a real problem with. He viewed Jim Stanley as his biggest problem. Jim actually had seniority at the branch. He had been hired as shipper, order desk salesperson, and secretary when the branch was only large enough to support one person other than Bob Laird, the first salesperson the company had in Atlantic Canada. Bob and Jim operated the branch for almost two years when Bob decided to hire Fergie as a salesperson to help develop the territory. When Bob retired, Jim thought he would get the position as District Manager as he had seniority, and he had experience with all aspects of the business including managing the office and warehouse, which had grown to include seven people. He was very disappointed when head office gave the position to Fergie as he had no experience other than sales.

Within a year, Jim decided he wanted to get into sales. He was finally resigned to the fact that office management was a dead-end job, and the only possibility for advancement was through sales. Now, after five years, Jim was not performing as well as he should. In fact, he hated selling and spent an increasing amount of time drinking while away from home. He hinted that he wanted to get back into the office. However, when these rumours started to spread, the staff let it be known that they did not want to work under Jim again if there were any alternatives.

Fergie was thinking about giving Jim a good salary increase. First, it might make him appreciate his job more and maybe he would put more effort into selling. Second, it would make the position more attractive than a possible return to the office as he would not want to take a tremendous salary cut.

The other problem was Arne Olsen, the other senior salesperson. As the territory developed quickly, the branch hired a secretary just after Fergie was hired. A month later, a warehouseman was hired and Jim was promoted to Office Manager. Jim immediately hired Hal Maybee as an order desk salesperson. Within a year, another salesperson, Arne, was hired, along with a second secretary. The branch growth slowed, but was steady from that point on. Arne was always an average salesperson. He never really had much motivation to perform, but he always did whatever he had to do so that he was never in any serious trouble as far as his job was concerned. Lately, he was starting to slip a bit, and rumour had it that he was having at least one affair. He also recently bought a Mazda Miata that he drove on weekends as he was not allowed to drive anything but the company car through the work week.

Dave Edison was with the company for just under one year. If he had a few more years with the company, Hal knew he would have probably been the new District Manager. He came to the company from the life insurance industry, and rumour had it that he was slated for a national sales manager position within the next year as the company was rumoured to be taking on a new line of capital equipment from Europe that would be sold nationally, but would have one person at head office responsible for national sales.

Tanya Burt was also in sales for only a year. She had been hired as a secretary, but it soon became apparent that she had exceptional telephone skills. She was promoted to order desk salesperson within a year, and three years later, she requested and was given an outside sales territory. There was some concern with her product knowledge, but no concern with her attitude or sales ability. Tanya was the first and only woman to be promoted to one of the company's 80 outside sales positions.

Buck Thompson had a very solid, established territory. He needed little direction as he was doing most things very well. Fergie was a bit concerned that he was not making enough sales calls, but he certainly was performing well.

As Hal reviewed the performance evaluations, he agreed that Fergie had been very thorough and accurate in his assessment of each of the individuals. Hal wondered about the amount of salary increase he should give to each person. While he had to make this decision immediately, Hal realized there were other important decisions he would have to make soon. He recognized some of the problems Fergie had trying to decide salary increases, and these were more important for Hal, as he had to get the support of the sales staff before he could hope to overcome some of these problems. He also had to start thinking about hiring another salesperson to cover Newfoundland and northern New Brunswick, as head office was determined that he give up responsibility for all accounts in the region. He would, however, be allowed and encouraged to call on customers with the sales staff.

Case

AGF

Eleanor Humphries, Tom Wolfer, and Tony Schellinck

MARKETING STRATEGY FOR AGF

On July 30, 1997, Lisa Bowens, Marketing Manager responsible for AGF Management Group's Canadian Equity Fund, was directed by her immediate superior and V.P. of Marketing, to develop a marketing strategy for the 1998 RRSP season and beyond. Lisa was asked to consider several factors in developing her strategy. The Canadian Equity funds market in Canada had grown rapidly in the last twelve months—AGF's Canadian Equity Fund hadn't. Only months earlier, Mackenzie Financial Corporation, a key rival, had been widely publicized for its Ivy Canadian Fund's number one ranking on a risk-adjusted, three-year return basis. AGF's Canadian Equity Fund consistently ranked below industry average in this respect. More sophisticated Canadian fund buyers looked to be moving away from independent dealers and brokers, while AGF only sold its Canadian Equity Fund through independent dealers and brokers. Changes to the Bank Act provided an opportunity to market through Canadian Banks. Doing this might cause channel conflict.

A MUTUAL FUND

A mutual fund is a pool of savings contributed by many investors, invested on their behalf by a professional money manager in company stocks and bonds.[1] Mutual funds spread investments over an assortment of companies that can vary according to size, degree of

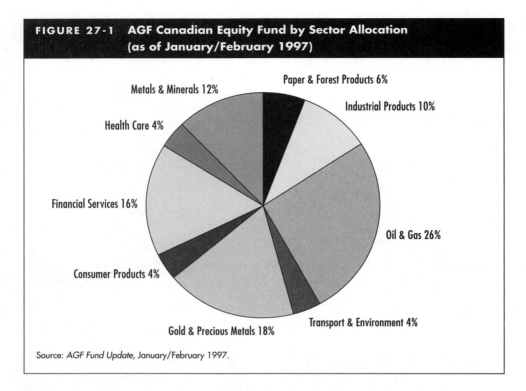

FIGURE 27-1   AGF Canadian Equity Fund by Sector Allocation (as of January/February 1997)

Paper & Forest Products 6%

Industrial Products 10%

Metals & Minerals 12%

Health Care 4%

Oil & Gas 26%

Financial Services 16%

Consumer Products 4%

Transport & Environment 4%

Gold & Precious Metals 18%

Source: *AGF Fund Update*, January/February 1997.

risk, and sector of the economy (see Figure 27-1). Through this diversification, investment risk to individuals is much lower relative to purchasing bonds or shares in individual companies on the stock market.

The most important aspect of a fund is its investment objective. The fund's objective tells investors the goals the fund seeks to achieve, and outlines how it intends to achieve them. Funds with different investment objectives have varying levels of risk that are reflected in the composition of companies in their portfolio. With "growth funds," the overall mix of companies invested in will be riskier to suit individuals placing a premium on achieving higher returns. "Income funds" comprise a group of less risky companies to meet the needs of fixed income earners seeking a stable level of return on their investment. The performance of a mutual fund is reflected in its net asset value. This value is the total market value of the securities in the fund, including cash, less any liabilities or amounts owing due to such things as the redemption of funds by investors.[2]

FACTORS AFFECTING MUTUAL FUND PURCHASES

A person's stage in life is a critical determinant of their savings and investment goals. Investors tend to save for the purchase of a home in their younger years, invest for their children's future as they approach middle age, and increasingly focus on saving for retirement as they reach their mid-fifties[3] (see Figure 27-2). These varying goals have an impact on the levels of risk and expected rates of return that are acceptable to investors in mutual funds. Well-educated persons in higher income brackets are most likely to invest a portion of their savings into a mutual fund[4] (see Figure 27-3).

| Figure 27-2 | Reasons for Saving (Other than Retirement) by Canadians (%) | | | | |

Reasons for Saving	Age Category of Respondent				
	18–24	25–30	31–34	35–54	55 and over
No Reason	9	15	6	24	32
Children's Education	4	15	36	24	10
Financial Security	17	16	16	15	17
Travel Fund	10	7	10	11	12
Home Purchase	20	20	18	5	2
For Family/Children	4	3	12	7	13
Emergency Fund	8	10	4	7	5

Source: Survey conducted by Angus Reid Group for Ernst & Young, June 1997.

| Figure 27-3 | Demographics of Fund Owners (%) | | | | | | |

Have You Ever Purchased a Mutual Fund?	Education				Income		
Response	Less Than High School	High School	Some Post-Secondary	University Graduate	Under $30K	$30K to $60K	Over $60K
Yes	41	56	60	67	42	60	70
No	57	43	38	32	57	39	29
Don't Know	2	1	2	1	2	1	1
Total (%)	100	100	100	100	100	100	100

Source: Survey conducted by Angus Reid Group for Ernst & Young, June 1997.

INDUSTRY TRENDS

From 1991 to 1995, the average annual asset growth rate had been 32% for the mutual fund industry, outpacing growth in other financial sectors of the Canadian economy.[5] In 1991, the fund holdings market totalled approximately $25 billion and increased to over $180 billion by 1996.[6] Between June 1996 and June 1997, the net asset value of Canadian Common Shares (Canadian Equity) type funds grew from $45.9 billion to approximately $76.1 billion.[7] The number of Canadian equity member funds on the market totalled 217.[8]

The growth in mutual funds investment is in large part due to the increasing number of Canadians reaching the age of 45 and older, a segment of the population otherwise known as the "baby-boomers"[9] (see Figure 27-4). Canadians only begin to start saving once they reach their forties and fifties. At this point, they reach their peak income-earning years and have the highest level of disposable income due to fewer financial obligations such as mortgage payments and the expense of raising children.[10] There is a high correlation between age and concern with savings—the higher the age, the more concern about saving for retirement.

Historically, retirees in Canada relied upon three sources of income for retirement—personal savings, Government of Canada funded pensions (CPP and OAS), and employer-

Figure 27-4	**Canadian Population Distribution by Age (1000s)**					
Year			**Age**			
	35–39	**40–44**	**45–49**	**50–54**	**55–59**	**60–64**
1996	2 657	2 377	2 146	1 667	1 327	1 209
2001	2 723	2 716	2 399	2 140	1 651	1 300

Source: Statistics Canada, 1996 Census Data.

sponsored pension funds.[11] Federal legislation to reduce the Government of Canada's contributions to the Canada Pension Plan (CPP) and "claw-back" OAS and CPP benefits have significantly reduced the amount of support seniors can expect from these sources. Traditional sources of retirement investments no longer provide the desired returns. For example, annual rates for both GICs and Canada Savings Bonds in 1996 were less than 5% (about 4% for GICs and slightly more for Canada Savings Bonds).[12] This is well below the expected minimal rate of return of 5–7%, and is not expected to change in the near future.[13] Recognizing this, Baby-boomers are turning to mutual funds as an alternative means to generate the income necessary to provide for retirement. Between 1989 and 1995, the number of adult Canadians with investments in equity mutual funds jumped from 10% to well over 40%.[14]

LOAD VS. NO-LOAD FUNDS

Load funds account for approximately 60% of the market, about 85% of which are so-called "redemption funds."[15] Load funds involve a sales charge being added to the net asset value of a mutual fund in order to calculate a public selling price.[16] The load, or sales charge, is paid to the selling brokerage firm, which in turn pays out much of it to the individual broker as a commission. If a fund's shares are worth $10 and the load fee is 5%, the offering price to the public is $10.50—with the 50 cents representing the broker's commission on sale. Load funds are typically distributed through brokers and other indirect channels.

There are four types of load fee structures: front-end load fees (a percentage fee charged at the time of the initial investment), rear-end load fees (a fee charged, on a declining balance, at the time funds are withdrawn), no-load funds, and a choice of front or rear load fees. The most popular type of load fee is a rear-end load. This form of fee decreases over a number of years to zero, and does not have to be paid provided the investor doesn't switch mutual fund companies. As of January 1997, over 75% of commissioned mutual fund sales were made using a rear-end load fee.[17] In addition to the service fee, a management fee is levied against the fund's earnings on a set basis (monthly, semi-annually, or annually). Given that management fees are incorporated into the fund and fund performance rates, they are often not perceived as a charge by consumers.

With no-load funds, no fees are applied at redemption, meaning no commission opportunity for dealers or brokers. As a result, this segment of funds is typically distributed direct by fund companies and represent the remainder of the Canadian market. Investors in no-load funds tend to leave their money with the companies they invest in, and do not jump from one fund or company to another very often. This is in large part due to their "perceived" physical difficulty of making a switch: writing a letter to authorize a redemption, sending it or taking it in personally to the fund company, and then waiting for the cheque to be mailed or deposited in an account so that the money can be transferred.[18]

DISTRIBUTION CHANNELS

There are over 74 companies registered with the Investment Funds Institute of Canada. They deliver some 1300 mutual funds to consumers via three distinct channels: independent brokers/dealers, banks and financial institutions, and fund companies. Of these 1300 funds, 217 are Canadian Equity member funds.[19] Independent brokers/dealers distribute approximately 45% of the total asset value of mutual funds managed in Canada. According to the Investment Funds Institute, there are over 600 independent brokers and dealers (see Figure 27-5).

Channel members evaluate which fund companies to deal with according to several criteria. One such measurement is the ability of fund companies to correct errors quickly on statements that do not reflect transactions that have occurred. The timely issuing of account statements; a ready supply of high-quality, up-to-date sales literature; easy access to the appropriate personnel; and electronic communication for accessing clients' accounts online are also identified to be of importance.[20]

A survey conducted several months earlier by Marketing Solutions Inc., a financial services marketing consulting company, measured the attitudes of fund salespeople on such things as the time they are left on hold when calling their fund company; whether the company asks for their name; the accuracy of information provided; and the frequency of transfers to the wrong person. These factors are thought to be of importance to fund-selling channel members. According to a report in the February 14, 1996, *Globe and Mail*, AGF Management Group ranked 5th in this survey, while Mackenzie Financial Corporation ranked 4th.[21]

Mackenzie Financial ranks as one of the more successful companies in establishing brand loyalty among brokers and dealers, by making it easier for them to sell funds. Mackenzie has three distinct categories of funds: the Industrial Group of Funds, the Universal Group of

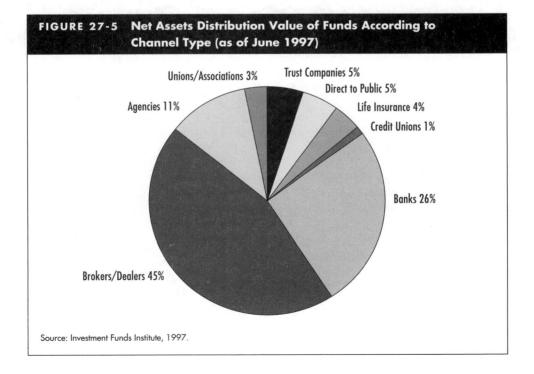

FIGURE 27-5 **Net Assets Distribution Value of Funds According to Channel Type (as of June 1997)**

Unions/Associations 3%
Trust Companies 5%
Direct to Public 5%
Agencies 11%
Life Insurance 4%
Credit Unions 1%
Banks 26%
Brokers/Dealers 45%

Source: Investment Funds Institute, 1997.

Funds, and the Ivy Group of Funds, each with varying degrees of risk and return levels. Mackenzie's "Strategic Asset Allocation Service" provides a plan for matching the investment and risk objectives of investors to one of a possible 17 portfolio options within these three fund groupings. Investment professionals recognize this service as a valuable tool for selling Mackenzie mutual funds to less-experienced investors. Mackenzie enjoys the further advantage of recently having its Ivy Canadian Fund ranked number one, as offering the highest, risk-adjusted three-year return and consistent performance.[22]

Advertising

In the 1996–1997 fiscal year, the mutual fund industry as a whole spent $78 million in advertising, with approximately 31% of this total being spent during the RRSP season in the months of January and February (see Figure 27-6). Fund companies historically spent most of their advertising dollars on campaigns to convince investment professionals to carry their products. These campaigns communicated the strength of the fund manager and fund performance, in order to provide investment professionals with confidence that particular funds would meet the investment objectives of their clients. They also heavily emphasized the fee revenues associated with a particular fund and how carrying it would enhance the dealer's reputation. All of these above variables are considered to be of importance to investment professionals. These independent brokers have traditionally been left to establish the relationship with consumers and deliver the message about how certain funds can meet their investment needs.

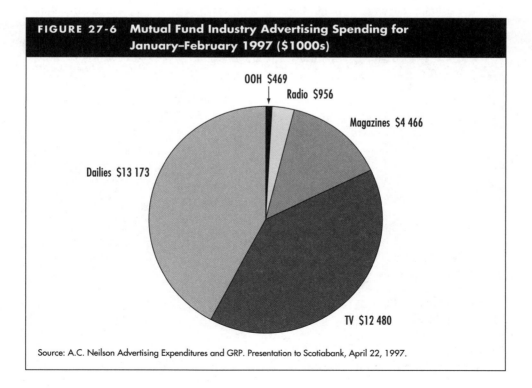

FIGURE 27-6 Mutual Fund Industry Advertising Spending for January–February 1997 ($1000s)

Source: A.C. Neilson Advertising Expenditures and GRP. Presentation to Scotiabank, April 22, 1997.

CHANGING CHANNEL ARRANGEMENTS

With the changes to the Bank Act in 1992, fund companies are permitted to market their no-load funds through banks and other financial institutions. This opens up opportunities to leverage the close business relationship banks have with consumers, given their dealings with consumers on so many other financial matters. In selling their funds on a no-load basis through banks, mutual fund companies can make it as convenient as possible for investors to purchase their funds. Doing so requires a marketing strategy to create brand recognition amongst consumers about their products. A relationship must be created directly with consumers in order to ensure they know what mutual fund to ask about when inquiring at their branch.

BANKS: MAKING CHANGES

Banks have been selling their own lines of mutual funds for several years, but only recently began to market heavily in the last four or five. Generally, bank no-load funds have lagged behind the industry in terms of net-asset growth. This is widely believed to be due to their lack of advice-giving capabilities at the investor level—something viewed as a key to success within the industry.[23] Banks have been making marked improvements in this area.

Canadian banks have invested heavily in training to ensure that they have qualified mutual fund representatives dedicated to cross-selling existing customers and attracting new ones.[24] New tools have also been developed to assist in selling funds to consumers. The Bank of Montreal, for example, has in place the "Matchmaker" strategic investment service.[25] This program involves potential clients taking a self-test which measures them according to whether they are a security-seeking, income-seeking, or growth-oriented investor. Based on these results, investors are directed to one of several combinations of Bank of Montreal funds.

TYPES OF INVESTORS

There are two extremes of mutual fund investors: the novice and the affluent.[26] The novice investor knows very little about the investment process and requires advice to this effect. They more than likely begin using the services of an investment advisor. After learning the process, they will tend to migrate to self-help, no-load channels for their future purchases. Service in this no-load market revolves around the efficient delivery of choices, "deposit ease," and clear account statements.[27] Generating high brand recognition among consumers through advertising is of paramount importance.

Affluent investors require the assistance of financial advisors for two reasons: constraints on their time and lack of expertise.[28] A recent study of Canada's top income earners indicated that only 20% feel they have any real skill in managing their money, and only half currently have a financial advisor.[29] According to a CIBC/Wood Gundy Report, a survey conducted by Dalbar Financial Services in the United States concluded that 89% of individuals investing more than $100 000 want financial advice.[30] This is a segment of the population that is likely to grow due to changing demographics.

Investors with financial advisors typically earn higher returns than those that purchase mutual funds directly. Over a 10-year period, investors with professional help posted returns five times higher than those purchasing directly.[31] Investors are much less likely to bail out of their investments when they have a personal financial advisor to help them overcome short-term emotional anxieties associated with temporary fund performance downturns.[32] The true value of an advisor is in their ability to work with, advise, re-assure, and help time-constrained and unknowledgeable fund consumers plan their investment future.

MUTUAL FUND CONSUMERS

Mutual fund investors in Canada have become much more sophisticated compared to prior years.[33] Whereas previously, consumers asked their mutual fund salesperson "What should I buy?", more and more are asking "Why should I buy it?" They have also greatly increased their knowledge about available no-load funds that can provide them with desired returns. Canadians are also feeling a high level of confidence about their mutual fund investments. More and more are opting to avoid the fees associated with using brokers and dealers by purchasing from no-load fund vendors.

Drawing on the experience of the US market, investment professionals in early 1997 were predicting that an estimated two-thirds of those who purchased load funds the first time would invest in no-load funds the second time.[34] According to a CIBC/Wood Gundy report issued on January 24, 1997, the no-load market is widely expected to be the fastest growing segment over the next three years.[35] The reality of the Canadian marketplace is also such that approximately 75% of potential mutual fund investors are already owners of mutual funds.[36] A company's best asset is its own mailing list, which can be mined to gain a larger share of each client's wallet. A poll of Canadians conducted by the Angus Reid Group for Ernst &Young in June of 1997 confirms that the next most likely investor in mutual funds is the last investor.[37] A majority of fund holders prefer to spread their investments over at least two or more fund companies.

A June 21, 1996, article in *The Globe and Mail* quoted a survey conducted that month by Marketing Solutions. The survey found that 94% of fund investors were very satisfied or somewhat satisfied with their investments.[38] Furthermore, 80% of present mutual fund holders were either very likely or somewhat likely to buy more mutual funds in the next two years.[39] If interest rates rose to 9% on GICs, however, almost half of mutual fund owners would put some of their RRSP money into these certificates.[40] Interest rates are not expected to rise to this level in the foreseeable future. Mutual fund investors prefer mutual funds to GICs as long as interest rates are 5–7%, with a minimum yield of 2.5% over GICs and Canada Savings Bonds.[41]

Returns are not the only factor of concern to investors. According to a study conducted by Dalbar Financial Services in 1996, customer service is becoming a new differentiating benchmark for investors when deciding upon which companies to purchase funds from.[42] "Service" is measured by how fast literature is sent out, how quickly an account can be opened, and the speed with which redemptions can be made over the telephone or by letter.

Despite their satisfaction with fund performance, over 40% of investors do not always believe the performance numbers posted about funds or that fund companies are always honest about disclosing investment risks.[43] One third of consumers strongly or somewhat suspect that there are hidden costs or charges incurred in their fund investments, according to a 1996 study by Marketing Solutions Inc.[44]

AGF AND ITS MARKET

AGF is the fourth largest mutual fund Company in Canada and has been in existence since 1957. It offers investors 38 mutual funds to choose from, across all major asset classes and a broad range of markets.[45] AGF defines its competition primarily as those companies that market their funds through the independent broker/dealer investment channels.[46] Mackenzie Financial, the second largest fund company in Canada by market share, is considered a major competitor and monitored closely. Other major competitors include Trimark and Fidelity Investments. Trimark is the largest fund company in Canada, with a 23% share of the overall fund market in Canada. Fidelity Investments ranks as the 5th largest with 9% of the market. AGF heavily targets pre-retirees more aggressively than other investor segments. Its mission is to become the pre-eminent independent Canadian wealth management company specializing in the retirement market.[47] Generally, this segment is looking for long-term growth as opposed to high-risk investments.[48] AGF's positioning philosophy is to focus more on the "return objectives and risk tolerance" of investors rather than their stage in the life cycle.[49] This is based on the view that there are always investors who are quite insensitive to risk, despite the fact that they may be older.

IVY CANADIAN VS. AGF CANADIAN EQUITY

The AGF Canadian Equity Fund was first introduced in 1963. Mackenzie's Ivy Canadian Fund has existed since 1993. Both funds have the same investment objective—long-term capital growth—and invest primarily in equity securities of established, high-quality Canadian companies.[50] They are both considered to be conservative in terms of risk and appeal to those seeking relative investment security. AGF's Canadian Equity Fund is sold on a strictly load basis through independent dealers and brokers.[51] Since 1989–1990, the fund has consistently ranked below the industry average for Canadian equity class funds in terms of annual returns[52] (see Figure 27-7). The only exception was the 1995–1996 fiscal year ended September 30, when it posted an annual return of 20%.[53] The AGF Canadian Equity Fund's net asset value for the fiscal year ending September 30, 1995, was over $366 million.[54] As of June 1997, the net asset value of AGF's Canadian Equity Fund totalled $716.3 million, up from $690 million in June 1996.[55] The Ivy Canadian Fund grew from net assets of $1.5 billion as of June 1996, to over $3.8 billion in June 1997.[56]

PRODUCT POSITIONING AT THE CONSUMER LEVEL

Product differentiation at both the consumer and investment professional level represents a key challenge for companies in the industry. This is often attempted through changes in the composition of funds offered and special fund themes. Changing fund compositions permit companies to position various products among different segments of the investor popula-

Figure 27-7   AGF Canadian Equity Return Rate vs. Ivy Canadian Industry

Fund	Annual Average Return (%)			
	1996–1997	1995–1996	1994–1995	1993–1994
Ivy Canadian Fund	29.5	17.1	12.6	8.1
AGF Canadian Equity Fund	25	20	3.4	5
Canadian Equity Market	32.5	18.5	6.1	7.7

Source: "15-Year Report on Mutual Funds," *The Globe and Mail.* November 1997

tion through advertising according to the risk/return spectrum. These strategies, however, can be easily copied by competitors looking to protect themselves against lost market share.

For the 1996 RRSP season, AGF employed a "branding the manager" strategy in an effort to differentiate itself from competitors.[57] Veronika Hirsch, a high-profile and respected fund manager, had been recruited from the Canadian branch of the Prudential Insurance Company in the fall of 1995. AGF aggressively marketed Hirsch in multimedia spots leading up to and during the 1996 RRSP season. This promotional effort raised her profile to one of "star status," in the process making her name synonymous with both AGF and the Canadian Equity Fund she managed. The campaign stimulated exceptional interest in the Canadian Equity Fund and resulted in net sales of around $150 million.[58] While effective, Hirsch's resignation on August 13, 1996, after the campaign, was a reminder of how risky this type of strategy is. She never signed a contract with AGF—something considered not unusual in the industry. Her departure caused a slowdown in net sales for a period of time which is just now starting to rebound.[59]

AGF's positioning strategy for the 1997 RRSP campaign took a much lower-key approach and did not involve a "star manager." More emphasis was placed on company branding, emphasizing themes such as experienced fund management, a broad range of funds, and AGF's steady presence in the industry since 1957.[60] The overall benefits of investing with AGF—such as a secure, active retirement—were emphasized instead of the features of individual funds. No emphasis was placed on either individual fund performance or an individual manager. AGF's advertising expenditures during the first three months of 1997 were an estimated $1.5 million[61] (see Figure 27-8). The campaign had been considered a success, although comparing it to the previous year is not possible, given that the markets were far more buoyant as a whole in 1997.[62]

During the 1997 RRSP season, Fidelity Investments emphasized a high-risk, high-growth theme in advertising its line of Canadian Equity Funds. Mackenzie Financial positioned its funds under a conservative theme, emphasizing consistent growth. Both Trimark

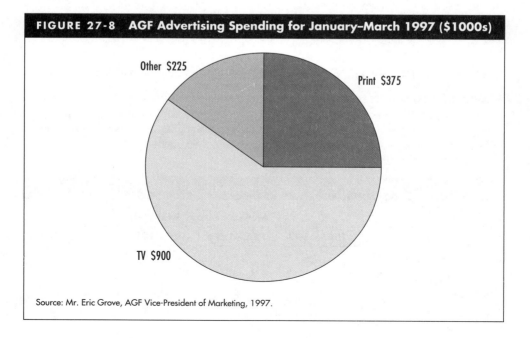

FIGURE 27-8   AGF Advertising Spending for January–March 1997 ($1000s)

Other $225

Print $375

TV $900

Source: Mr. Eric Grove, AGF Vice-President of Marketing, 1997.

and Mackenzie doubled their sales and marketing budgets from the fiscal year 1996 level, for the purposes of more heavily promoting and raising brand awareness about their funds and companies, leading up to the 1997 RRSP season.

Mackenzie groups its line of funds together into three branding categories, the Ivy, Industrial, and Universal Group of funds, rather than attempting to brand 35 separate funds.[63] In the 1997 RRSP season, Mackenzie heavily promoted the exposure given to its Ivy Canadian Fund by the media for its number one ranking in terms of risk and performance in 1996.[64] Overall, 68.1% of the $2.4 million spent by Mackenzie on advertising its groups of funds was spent in the 1997 RRSP season months of January and February[65] (see Figure 27-9). It used this opportunity to promote its Ivy Canadian Fund as offering more dependable performance and consistent growth than AGF's Canadian Equity Fund and Fidelity's True North Canadian Equity Fund. The following is a product positioning statement used by Mackenzie during the 1997 RRSP season in its advertising:

> The Ivy Canadian Fund was recognized by *Maclean's Magazine*, for providing investors with dependable performance and consistent growth, unlike AGF's Canadian Equity Fund and Fidelity's True North Fund, which adopt a higher risk strategy to investment, resulting in less dependable and inconsistent growth.[66]

THE DECISION

There is only one week to develop recommendations based on what seems to be an endless array of conflicting issues. The majority of new fund business seems likely to come from current fund investors and it appears they will be looking to no-load channels for their

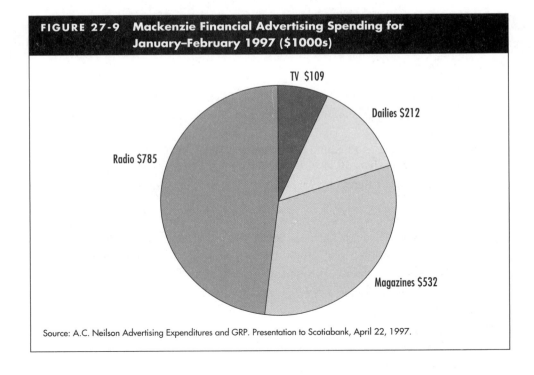

FIGURE 27-9   Mackenzie Financial Advertising Spending for January–February 1997 ($1000s)

TV $109

Dailies $212

Radio $785

Magazines $532

Source: A.C. Neilson Advertising Expenditures and GRP. Presentation to Scotiabank, April 22, 1997.

next purchase. Banks seem to be in a favourable position via load channel sellers. Their ability to mine large databases of customers and package complementary banking services is a definite competitive advantage. Banks have the proper tools and well-trained staff necessary to sell funds to increasingly sophisticated and knowledgeable consumers. Marketing no-load funds through banks, however, holds the possibility of drawing clients away from AGF's dealer network and causing channel conflict. AGF Management Group's Canadian Equity Fund is only sold on a load basis through brokers and financial planners.

Slow growth poses another dilemma. Between June 1996 and June 1997, AGF's Canadian Equity Fund grew at a much slower rate than the industry average for Canadian Equity class funds. It lagged even further behind Mackenzie Financial's Ivy Canadian Fund. Two years ago, the Veronika Hirsch campaign generated tremendous growth comparable to that experienced by the Ivy Canadian Fund. The risks involved with "branding the manager" are very high however, and successful corporate brand advertising has a longer life span.

Focusing on fund performance, features, and benefits was a possibility, given that they are so directly impacted by the needs, goals, and level of risk acceptable to investors. Mackenzie's Ivy Fund, however, continues to outperform the AGF fund. It no doubt still enjoys the advantage of last season's media recognition for its solid three-year return rate. Alternatively, focusing on fund features and benefits has the disadvantage that both can be readily copied by Mackenzie.

Using new media could perhaps resolve some of these issues. Lisa had heard much about a new "direct marketing" approach of targeting consumers with products and services. This strategy entailed using demographic and other information about consumers to identify their unique needs and purchasing behaviours on an individual basis. This information, often stored in a database, could then be used by companies to direct-mail promotional material to consumers about products customized to meet their specific needs. Experts on the subject claimed that this "one-to-one" relationship marketing approach was an effective way for companies to position their products, cultivate client loyalty, and generate repeat business.

ENDNOTES

1. Peter W. Johnson Jr., "What Is a Mutual Fund," Green Jungle Education Resources. http://www.greenjungle.com/pub/education/edartmutualfund.html#OV. December 1, 1997.

2. "Preserving Wealth ... Pursuing Opportunities," AGF Group of Funds Performance Summary. Toronto. June 30,1996. p. 5.

3. "Investment Issues," Report by Angus Reid Group for Ernst & Young. Toronto. June 1997. p. 6.

4. Ibid. p. 10.

5. "The Canadian Financial Services Sector," Department of Foreign Affairs and International Trade. http://www.dfait-maeci.gc.ca/english/menu.htm. December 1996.

6. "Monthly Statistical Summary," Investment Funds Institute. Toronto. August 30, 1997. p. 1.

7. Ibid. June 30 1996 and June 30 1997. www.mutfunds.com/ific.

8. Ibid. August 30, 1997. p. 1.

9. "Population Projections by Age Group and Sex," Statistics Canada 1996 Census of Canada Data. http://www.statcan.ca/english/Pgdb/People/Population/demo23a.htm

10. David Cork, *The Pig and The Python*. Toronto: Stoddart Press, January 1997. p. 113.

11. Ibid. p. 103.

12. Interview with Mike Wolfer, Commercial Loans Officer. Bank of Montreal. October 1997.

13. Ibid.

14. David Cork, *The Pig and The Python*. Toronto: Stoddart Press, January 1997. p. 161.

15. Eleanor Humphries, "Marketing Program Report: Dalhousie MBA Advanced Marketing Assignment #3." January 1997.

16. Peter W. Johnson Jr., "What Is a Mutual Fund," Green Jungle Education Resources. http://www.greenjungle.com/pub/education/edartmutualfund.html#OV. December 1997.

17. "The Canadian Mutual Fund Industry: The Rising Tide," CIBC/Wood Gundy Investment Research. January 24, 1997. p. 21.

18. Interview with Mr. Colin Deane, Senior Principal, Ernst &Young International Capital Markets Group. October 1997.

19. "Monthly Statistical Summary," Investment Funds Institute. Toronto. August 30, 1997. p. 4.

20. Interview with Mr. John Kaszel, Director of Academic Affairs and Research, the Investment Funds Institute of Canada. October 1997.

21. Andrew Bell, "Mutual fund firms learning phone etiquette," in *The Globe and Mail*. February 14, 1996. p. B17.

22. Ross Laver, "The Best and Worst Mutual Funds: *Maclean's Magazine* Special Edition." Mackenzie Financial Corporation Brochure. January 27, 1997.

23. "The Canadian Mutual Fund Industry: The Rising Tide," CIBC/Wood Gundy Investment Research. January 24, 1997. p. 21.

24. Ibid. p. 20.

25. Brian Lewis, "Funds Taking an Educating Approach," in *The Toronto Star*. January 21, 1996. p. D4.

26. "The Canadian Mutual Fund Industry: The Rising Tide," CIBC/Wood Gundy Investment Research. January 24, 1997. p. 22.

27. Ibid. p. 22.

28. Ibid. p. 22.

29. Ibid. p. 22.

30. Ibid. p. 22.

31. David Cork, *The Pig and The Python*. Toronto: Stoddart Press, January 1997. p. 84.

32. Ibid. p. 84.

33. Brian Lewis, "Funds Taking an Educating Approach," in *The Toronto Star*. January 21, 1996. p. D4.

34. "The Canadian Mutual Fund Industry: The Rising Tide," CIBC/Wood Gundy Investment Research. January 24, 1997. p. 17.

35. Ibid. p. 17.

36. Ibid. p. 17.

37. "Investment Issues," Report by Angus Reid Group for Ernst & Young. Toronto. June 1997. p. 13.

38. Andrew Bell, "Trust lacking for fund firms: Survey," in *The Globe and Mail*. June 21, 1996. p. B14.

39. "Investment Issues," Report by Angus Reid Group for Ernst & Young. Toronto. June 1997. p. 10.

40. Jade Hemeon, "Comfort with Funds Rising," in *The Toronto Star*. June 21, 1996. p. E2.

41. Johnathan Chevreau, "Investors are loyal, if weak on knowledge," in *The Financial Post*. June 22, 1996. p. 22.

42. Johnathan Chevreau, "Customer service seen as new benchmark," in *The Financial Post*.

43. Andrew Bell, "Trust lacking for fund firms: Survey," in *The Globe and Mail*. June 21, 1996. p. B14.

44. Ibid. p. B14.

45. AGF Fund Update. January–February 1997. p. 3.

46. Interview with Mr. Eric Grove, Vice-President of Marketing, AGF. December 1, 1997.

47. Ibid.

48. Ibid.

49. Ibid.

50. AGF Group of Funds Simplified Prospectus Package. January 1, 1997. p. 6. Mackenzie Financial Investor Guide and Simplified Prospectus. November 20, 1996. p. 12.

51. Interview with Mr. Eric Grove, Vice-President of Marketing, AGF. November 4, 1997.

52. "15-Year Mutual Fund Review," in *The Globe and Mail*. November 29, 1997. p. F8.

53. Interview with Mr. Eric Grove, Vice-President of Marketing, AGF. December 1, 1997.

54. AGF Canadian Equity Funds: 1996 Annual Report.

55. Ibid.

56. Interview with Mr. David Farwell, Mackenzie Financial Corporation Marketing Services. December 1, 1997.

57. Interview with Mr. Eric Grove, Vice-President of Marketing, AGF. November 28, 1997.

58. Interview with Mr. Eric Grove, Vice-President of Marketing, AGF. December 1, 1997.

59. Ibid.

60. Ibid.

61. Ibid.

62. Ibid.

63. Mackenzie Financial Investor Guide and Simplified Prospectus. November 20, 1996.

64. "Ivy Canadian Fund: A number one choice in triplicate!" Mackenzie Financial Brochure.

65. Eleanor Humphries, "Marketing Program Report: Advanced Marketing Assignment #3." January 1997. Appendix E.

66. Eleanor Humphries, "Marketing Program Report: Advanced Marketing Assignment #3." January 1997. p. 5.

PARKER INSTRUMENTS LTD.

Philip Rosson

Parker Instruments Ltd. (PI) is a British firm that operates as a manufacturer and an importer/distributor. Its field is electronic instruments, and the imported products account for about 75 percent of sales. One of the companies Parker Instruments represents in the United Kingdom is Electro Industries (EI), a Canadian precision instrument firm. PI and EI have been working together for about 10 years. The relationship between the two companies was good for a number of years. Then things started to go wrong, and this was accentuated by an accident a year ago that robbed EI of its top two executives. George Parker feels strong ties to EI but is increasingly worried by the Canadian company's seeming indifference to its international operations in general and to the relationship with PI in particular.

George Parker locked the door of his car and walked across the parking lot toward the station entrance. Although it was a sunny spring morning and the daffodils and tulips provided welcome colour after the grayness of winter, Parker hardly noticed. Within a few minutes, the train from London would be arriving with Bruce MacDonald, the export sales manager for Electro Industries. Parker would be spending the day with MacDonald, and he wondered what the outcome of their discussions would be.

PARKER INSTRUMENTS LTD.

George Parker was managing director of Parker Instruments Ltd., part of a small, family-owned UK group of companies. The company gained its first sales agency in 1923 (from an American manufacturer), which made it one of the most well-established international trading firms in electronic instruments. PI sales were the equivalent of about $1 million, with

---

This case was prepared by Philip Rosson, Professor of Marketing, Dalhousie University, Halifax, Nova Scotia, as a basis for class discussion. Reprinted with permission.

75 percent coming from imported distributed items, and 25 percent from sales of its own man-ufactured items. The company had a total of 15 employees.

PI was the British distributor for 15 manufacturers located in the United States, Canada, Switzerland, and Japan. Like many firms, it found that the 80/20 rule held true: About 80 per-cent of its import sales of $750 000 were generated by 20 percent of the distributorships it held. With current sales of $165 000, the Electro Industries distributorship was an important one.

ELECTRO INDUSTRIES

Electro Industries was a younger and larger organization than its UK distributor. Located in southern Ontario, it was founded in the mid-1950s and had current sales of $4 million and a workforce of 90 employees. EI had developed a strong reputation over the years for its high-precision instrumentation and testing equipment, and this led to considerable market expansion. The company had moved in a number of new product directions. The original prod-ucts were very precise devices for use in standards laboratories. From this base it had more recently established a presence in the oceanographic and electric power fields.

As a result of this expansion, 80 percent of its sales were now made outside Canada, split evenly between the United States and off-shore markets. In the United States, the com-pany had its own direct-sales organization, whereas indirect methods were used elsewhere. In the "best" 15 off-shore markets, EI had exclusive distributors; in 30 other markets, it relied on commission agents.

WORKING TOGETHER

EI and PI first made contact in New York City, and the two companies agreed to work together. George Parker was on a business trip in the United States when he received a cable from his brother saying that a representative of EI wanted to get in touch with him. Parker and his wife met the senior executive in their hotel room and, after initial introduc-tions, settled down to exchange information. At some point, Parker, who had had a hectic day, fell asleep. He awoke to find that PI was now more or less EI's UK distributor, his wife having kept the discussion rolling while he slept.

The two firms soon began to prosper together. The distributorship gave PI a product line to complement those it already carried. Furthermore, the EI instruments were regarded as the "Cadillacs" of the industry. This ensured entry to the customer's premises and an interest in the rest of the PI product line. As far as EI was concerned, it could hardly have cho-sen a more suitable partner: PI's staff was technically competent, facilities existed for prod-uct servicing, and customer contacts were good. Moreover, as time passed, George Parker's long experience and international connections proved invaluable to EI. He was often asked for an opinion prior to some new move by the Canadian producer. Parker preferred to have a close working relationship with the firms he represented, so he was happy to provide advice. In this way, PI did an effective job of representing EI in the United Kingdom and helped with market expansion elsewhere.

As might be expected, the senior executives of the companies got along well together. The president and vice president of marketing—EI's "international ambassadors"—and George Parker progressed from being business partners to becoming close personal friends. Then, after nine successful years, a tragedy occurred: the two EI executives were killed in an airplane crash on their way home from a sales trip.

The tragic accident created a management succession crisis within EI. During this period, international operations were left dangling while other priorities were attended to. Nobody was able to take charge of the exporting activities that had generated such good sales for the company. Although there was an export sales manager, Bruce MacDonald, he was a relative newcomer, having been in training at the time of the accident. He was also a middle-level executive, whereas his international predecessors were the company's most senior personnel.

From Parker's point of view, things were still not right a year later. The void in EI's international operations had not been properly filled. Bruce MacDonald had proved to be a competent manager, but he lacked support because a new vice president of marketing had yet to be appointed. A new president headed the company, but he was the previous vice president of engineering and preferred to deal with technical rather than business issues. So despite the fact that MacDonald had a lot of ideas about what should be done internationally (most of which were similar to George Parker's ideas), he lacked both the position and the support of a superior to bring about the necessary changes.

While the airplane accident precipitated the current problems in the two companies' relationship, Parker realized that things had been going sour for a couple of years. At the outset of the relationship, EI executives had welcomed the close association with PI. Over time, however, as the manufacturer grew in size and new personnel came along, it seemed to Parker that his input was increasingly resented. This was unfortunate, because Parker believed that EI could become a more sophisticated international competitor if it considered advice given by informed distributors. In the past, EI had been open to advice and had benefited considerably from it. Yet there were still areas where EI could effect improvements. For example, its product literature was of poor quality and was often inaccurate or outdated. Prices were also worrisome. EI seemed unable to hold its costs, and its competitors now offered better value-for-money alternatives. Other marketing practices needed attention, also.

THE OCEANOGRAPHIC MARKET

One area where EI and PI were in disagreement was the move into the oceanographic field. George Parker was pleased to see EI moving into new fields, but wondered if EI truly appreciated how "new" the field was. In a way, he believed the company had been led by the technology into the new field, rather than having considered the fit between its capabilities and success criteria for the new field. For example, the customer fit did not seem even close. The traditional buyers of EI products for use in standards laboratories were scientists, some of whom were employed by government, some by industry, and some by universities. By and large, they were academic types, used to getting their equipment when the budget permitted. As a result, selling was "gentlemanly," and follow-up visits were required to maintain contacts. Patience was often required, since purchasing cycles could be relatively long. Service needs were not extensive, for the instruments were used very carefully.

In contrast, the oceanographic products were used in the very demanding sea environment. Service needs were acute, due not just to the harsh operating environment but also to the cost associated with having inoperable equipment. For example, ocean research costs were already high but became even higher if faults in shipboard equipment prevented taking sea measurements. In such a situation, the customer demanded service today or tomorrow, wherever the faulty equipment was located. The oceanographic customer was also a difficult type—still technically trained but concerned about getting the job done as quickly as possible. Purchasing budgets were much less of a worry; if the equipment was good, reliable, and with proven back-up, chances were it could be sold. But selling required more of a push than the laboratory equipment.

When EI entered the oceanographic field, a separate distributor was appointed in the United Kingdom. However, the arrangement did not work out. EI then asked George Parker to carry the line, and with great reluctance he agreed. The lack of enthusiasm was due to Parker's perception that his company was not capable of functioning well in this new arena. Because PI was ill equipped to service the oceanographic customer, it was thought that there could even be repercussions in its more traditional field. Parker was unwilling to risk the company's established reputation in this way. However, while he preferred not to represent EI in the oceanographic field, he worried about a "one market, one distributor" mentality at EI.

THE CURRENT VISIT

George Parker had strong personal sentiments for EI as a company. In his opinion, however, some concrete action was required if the business relationship was to survive, let alone prosper.

Parker recognized the good sales of EI products, but also took note of shrinking profit margins over the last few years due to the increased costs PI faced with the EI product line. Since EI was slow to respond to service and other problems, PI had been putting things right and absorbing the associated costs more and more frequently. However, these costs could not be absorbed forever. Parker had been willing to help tide EI over the last difficult year but expected a more positive response in the future.

George Parker hoped that Bruce MacDonald would bring good news from Canada. Ideally, he hoped to drop the oceanographic line and rebuild the "bridges" that used to exist between his firm and the manufacturer. A return to the close and helpful relationship that once existed would be welcomed. However, he wondered if EI's management wanted to operate in a more formal and distant "buy and sell" manner. If this were the case, George Parker would have to give more serious thought to the EI distributorship.

MURRAY INDUSTRIAL LIMITED

H.F. (Herb) MacKenzie

Murray Industrial Limited (MIL) was advertised as Newfoundland's most complete industrial supplier, and sold to industrial accounts throughout Newfoundland and Labrador from three locations across the province. Products sold included hydraulic hose and fittings, bearings, conveyor products, hand and power tools, fasteners (nuts, bolts, etc.), chain, packing, and general mill supply items.

According to Dave Rowe, "Our success has been largely due to our customer service strategy. We aim to provide superior service with a well-trained, motivated staff and a broad inventory of quality products. We have an ongoing commitment to in-house training and product seminars, and we have a 24-hour emergency service for all of our accounts."

Prior to 1991, MIL was a sub-distributor for Snowden Rubber, a Gates Rubber distributor located in Dartmouth, Nova Scotia. In 1991, an opportunity arose to become a distributor for one of North America's largest and best-known manufacturers of hydraulic hose and fittings when its Newfoundland distributor, Newfoundland Armature Works, became bankrupt.

Industrial distributors that sold hydraulic hose and fittings usually bought the more popular sizes and types of hose in full reel lengths and then cut it to fit particular customer applications. Frequently, distributors would attach hydraulic fittings or other special attachments to the shorter hose lengths as required by customers. When distributors bought full length reels of hose (that varied in length depending on the size of the hose) or full box quantities of fittings (that also varied depending on the size and style of fitting), they paid a standard distributor price for their inventory. If they desired to buy a cut-to-length piece of hose or a small quantity of fittings for special applications that might arise infrequently, they paid a 10 percent surcharge on the distributor price. For shipments that were needed urgently, manufacturers would often guarantee shipment within 24 hours, but charged a $10 special order handling charge.

At the time negotiations between MIL and the manufacturer began, the manufacturer had a distribution centre in Dartmouth, Nova Scotia, and prepaid shipments from there to distributors throughout Atlantic Canada. It offered a prompt payment discount of 2%–25th following, and co-op allowances to share promotion costs with distributors. Within a month (and before an agreement was signed), the Dartmouth warehouse was closed and the salesperson was let go. Shipments were still prepaid but came from Toronto, and the salesperson that serviced the Atlantic Provinces operated from Quebec. After about three months, the manufacturer's policy changed, and shipments became F.O.B. Toronto, and the prompt payment discount was eliminated.

MIL increased sales by establishing sub-distributors in remote regions, and hydraulic hose eventually accounted for about 8 percent of the company's total sales, and helped increase sales for complementary products. The largest customer MIL had was Royal Oak Mines, a gold mine located about 1½ hours from Port aux Basques, and accessible only by air or water. It accounted for 35 percent of MIL's hydraulic hose sales.

Within a year, MIL began to have problems getting inventory. Back-order rates increased. The manufacturer closed its Toronto and Edmonton distribution centres in 1993, and decided to supply the Canadian market from the US. The manufacturer sales force was reduced from six to two representatives in Canada. Distributors were reduced from 140 to 40 (MIL was the 22nd largest at the time). All co-op policies were eliminated, and the Canadian price sheets were removed, so that Canadian distributors had to purchase from US price sheets and add exchange, duty, brokerage, transportation, and whatever markup they needed.

"Our biggest problem," said Dave Rowe, "was that they didn't plan for the change to the distribution system. Service continued to worsen from Toronto as inventory that was sold from there was not replaced, and we were told we couldn't order from the US until July 1, 1993, when it would be organized to serve us. We haven't seen a salesperson since early 1993, and any contact we have had with them since then has been initiated by us. Service started to affect our relationships with our customers. We eventually lost the Royal Oak Mines account, and they started buying Gates Rubber products. We were stuck with about $50 000 in inventory that we stocked specifically for them. When we approached the manufacturer, they refused to help us beyond their normal return goods policy. They were willing to take back up to 2 percent of our annual purchases as long as the material was still in new condition and was still a standard item listed in their catalogue. We had to pay return freight and a 15 percent restocking charge. It was also their policy not to accept return of any hose products after one year, as hose quality deteriorated with time. While their pricing and inventory management practices were standard for the industry, we felt they had an obligation to help us as they were largely to blame for our lost customer."

SYNDCOM LIMITED

Thomas Funk and Michael Atkinson

Debra Gray, radio manager for Syndcom, a small radio and television syndicated producer in Toronto, Ontario, was browsing over the latest quarterly financial reports. For the past two years, station numbers and the overall profile of BizRap, Syndcom's sole radio product, were well below her expectations. BizRap had been marketed by Trirad Enterprises, a representation firm located in Western Canada. At the end of the month, Syndcom's contract with Trirad Enterprises was up for renewal. This provided Debra with an opportunity to reconsider this distribution relationship. She was looking at the possibility of either selling directly to radio stations or seeking better representation.

BACKGROUND OF SYNDCOM AND THE BROADCAST INDUSTRY

Syndcom is a small firm that specializes in business programming for the major television networks across Canada. Their well-established expertise in the television industry recently allowed them to expand into radio. Syndcom now produces and provides radio programming features for simultaneous broadcast on stations across Canada. In many cases, a radio program is the same as a TV program with the absence of video. For example, a business report that is produced for television can easily be transformed into a radio feature by dividing the video and audio signals during transmission. The audio signal is cut out and produced as a separate feature designed for radio. It contains similar broadcast and commentary material as the television feature without the visual contents.

This case was prepared by Thomas Funk and Michael Atkinson of the University of Guelph. It is intended as a basis for classroom discussion and is not designed to present either correct or incorrect handling of administrative problems. All data have been disguised to protect confidentiality. Copyright ©1993 by Thomas Funk. Reprinted with permission.

Syndcom's sole radio product is BizRap, presently the leading syndicated radio feature across Canada with approximately 123 subscribing stations. It is a daily feature that is available to stations at half past the hour from 4:00 p.m. to 12:30 a.m. central time, for a total of 56 feeds per week. In the past, the feature has commented on such issues as the investment implications of the Free Trade Agreement, the impact of the G.S.T. on small business, and the effects of G.A.T.T. negotiations on agriculture. It is designed to update the listener on the changing environment of business. The feature is two minutes in length plus an additional 30-second spot required for the national sponsor. The current national sponsor is Organizer Limited, a company that specializes in computer and stationery supplies for small and medium-size companies. Organizer is quite pleased with the feature and with the amount of awareness and audience reach gained through BizRap. In fact, Organizer's advertising objectives have been met and exceeded consistently during the entire campaign with BizRap. As a result, Organizer finds the $13 500 per week for the national spot to be a worthwhile expenditure, given the exposure it receives. Although Syndcom has no other radio properties, plans for expansion of the product base are in progress.

In the syndicated radio market served by Syndcom, there is a potential reach of 515 stations across Canada. Although this market has grown in the past few years, it is expected to decline in the future, given the increased popularity of pay television and satellite services. Consequently, the radio syndicated market is highly competitive and it is difficult to increase the number of subscribing stations. Many stations in larger markets have begun producing features in-house. As well, other syndicated radio firms have placed greater emphasis on business programs to cater to those stations moving towards formats with more talk and less music. Larger radio stations have little loyalty towards syndicated features as they generally cover the necessary business material with their own resources. Smaller stations, on the other hand, tend to be more loyal to syndicated features because they lack the resources and finances to produce and provide the variety of programming necessary for their listening audience.

Within the broadcast industry, there are two main payment options that are used. Currently, most stations and syndicators prefer a barter arrangement. Syndicators produce a program and distribute it to all subscribing stations. In exchange for the program, stations agree to relinquish programming time and to air the feature in its entirety so that the national advertisement is kept intact. The national sponsor pays the syndicator a set contractual fee per week in exchange for the exposure and audience reach gained.

Pay-per-day is a second payment option that is beginning to gain increasing popularity. Pay-per-day places the onus of payment on each subscribing station. Each station pays the syndicator a set fee for each feature feed. This effectively removes the need for a national sponsor. A radio station is then free to recruit a local sponsor that may be more consistent with their target and format. This enables the station to generate its own revenue, part of which is used to pay the syndicator.

DISTRIBUTION SYSTEM FOR SYNDICATED RADIO FEATURES

The distribution network for syndicated radio products typically consists of a three-member channel. This arrangement ensures that each party's competitive advantage is utilized by allowing them to focus on specialized activities.

Radio shows are produced by a syndication company and made available to a satellite distribution company via a network of fibre land-line cables. The satellite distribution company then transmits these signals to subscribing radio stations so they are received clearly, with little static. Representation houses have the responsibility of attracting and securing subscribing radio stations. In addition, the syndicator normally relies on representation houses for assistance in developing new product concepts and features consistent with audience trends.

Exhibit 30-1 shows the typical distribution system in the Canadian syndicated radio industry.

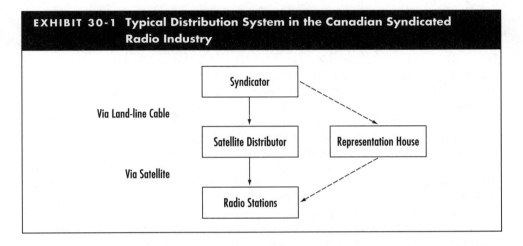

EXHIBIT 30-1 Typical Distribution System in the Canadian Syndicated Radio Industry

REPRESENTATION FIRMS

A typical representation firm handles the complete product line of a syndicated company. The representation firm normally receives 25% of all revenue for marketing and promoting the syndicator's radio features. Most representation firms appoint two or three salespeople for each product within the product line. Promotional packages are often created to add value and increase salability. As well, syndicators often expect representation firms to provide information on audience and market trends. Syndicators also expect some assistance and consultation with new product development and future programming concepts.

All revenues are collected by representation firms and returned to syndicators, minus the 25% commission. In addition, all station contracts and affidavits are prepared and monitored by representation houses. Affidavits indicate the number of times a particular radio station aired the feature. These affidavits are of crucial importance to the national advertiser because most contracts stipulate a minimum number of guaranteed airings per week for the agreed advertising cost. These affidavits are then used to compare reach and frequency estimates with actual levels so national advertisers can determine the effectiveness of their radio advertising spots. Affidavits must be carefully monitored and organized so they can be made available to the advertiser on demand.

As mentioned, to increase a feature's attractiveness the representation house often produces and distributes some promotional material. These packages outline and describe the concept of the features and emphasize the quality and ability of the syndicator to gather up-to-date business stories and events. The promotional material used by representation houses includes video clips, brochures, and direct mail.

SATELLITE DISTRIBUTION FIRMS

In the Metro Toronto area, there are three satellite distribution companies that possess varying degrees of satellite transmission capabilities. Depending on their size, up to a total of 10 channels can be used to broadcast syndicated features. The average Toronto satellite distributor has four channels.

Satellite distributors are responsible for accurate and timely delivery of all audio feeds to subscribing stations. This requires each subscribing station to be cleared and encoded by the distribution company so they can receive the signal. As well, the satellite distribution firm provides the radio stations with a daily advisory. This highly valued service is made available to all radio stations via land-line cable or satellite. Its purpose is to notify stations of programming changes, broadcast channel availability, and special event programming. The advisory's most important function, however, is to update stations on feed times so each radio station can calculate how the feature will fit into its allotted programming time. To receive this valuable service, radio stations generally pay a contractually set fee to become an affiliate of the satellite distribution company. This affiliation is considered valuable because satellite distribution companies also have their own news collection and production facilities that can provide live news footage to all subscribing affiliates. This footage can then be used in the stations' own news programs.

The satellite time required for transmission of the radio feature is paid by the syndicator. Generally the satellite transmission company and the syndicator enter into a contract that establishes a payment schedule for the duration of the contract. It is usually advantageous to enter into such an agreement because transmission costs often decrease over the contract period.

RADIO STATIONS

Currently, there are 515 radio stations in Canada. These stations are regulated by the Canadian Radio-Television and Telecommunications Commission (CRTC), a federal government agency. The CRTC recently stipulated that all radio stations must devote a certain amount of their programming time to news and talk formats. In order to fulfill this news content requirement, a majority of radio stations receive their satellite services from one or more satellite distribution firms. This affiliation ensures that each radio station has wide accessibility to a variety of programming and news services. For many stations, it also reduces operating costs because they can receive news programming from their affiliate satellite distribution company without the expense of in-house production. Although each satellite distribution company would prefer to have individual stations on an exclusive basis, this is not feasible given the competitive pressures and demands of the industry. This can pose an obvious problem to syndicators that decide to affiliate with only one of the satellite distributors in that it effectively reduces the number of stations across Canada that can be reached. This is especially true if their chosen satellite distributor is not subscribed to by all stations in the major demographic markets.

The recent trend of network ownership has posed some additional challenges for both syndicators and distributors. Several smaller radio stations have been acquired by larger radio stations within the same geographical area. A single owner may possess as many as ten radio stations of varying formats and audience targets. This network arrangement enables one station within the group to subscribe to the syndicated radio feature and down-link the feature to all its network affiliates. As more stations begin to simulcast programs from their "sister" stations, a number of complications arise.

The first major challenge is the difficulty of regulating and monitoring the number of stations using a program, and the frequency with which those programs are used, because of the lack of affidavits from all stations. Secondly, network ownership has caused problems for product fit and compatibility. Not all stations owned by one central organization are similar in programming format and target. In fact, many networks desire both target and format variety to cover the broad requirements of each demographic group. Consequently it is increasingly difficult for syndicators to develop programming that caters to the needs of all radio stations within a network. About the only advantage of these types of networks is from a representation house's point of view, in that it decreases the number of contacts they need to make.

SYNDCOM'S DISTRIBUTION

Syndcom relies on one representation house to reach a total of 123 stations. The representation house used by Syndcom is Trirad Enterprises, a small rep house located in Winnipeg. Syndcom and Trirad have been working together for the past two years, and have maintained a good relationship during this time. Previously, Syndcom worked with Globalnet, another small rep house, until they went into receivership. The relationship with Trirad has proven to be beneficial for both parties. When Globalnet went into receivership, the station list for BizRap was only 88 subscribers. During the past two years, Trirad has been able to maintain these original stations and recruit an additional 35 for the present total of 123. In the original contractual agreement, Trirad was granted a 30% commission on all net advertising revenues from the national sponsors. Syndcom thought the additional 5% above the industry standard would give Trirad a greater incentive to push Syndcom's product offering.

The satellite distribution agency used by Syndcom is Newscast Cable Limited, a large delivery agent serving the same geographical market as Syndcom. Newscast has four available satellite channels, with BizRap broadcast on Newscast's Channel 3. Channel 3 is the premier audio syndicated channel in the industry. It is a highly desired channel due to its excellent quality and accessibility, so Syndcom is very pleased with this arrangement. However, there is an indication that space for future programming may be a problem on Newscast Channel 3 because of its popularity. In addition, of the 515 stations across Canada, only 263 stations are current subscribers of Newscast's services. A renewed contract with Newscast has set satellite transmission costs for three years. The contractual transmission costs are $151 180 for the current year, with a 5% decrease each year for the remaining two years.

Among the 123 radio stations that currently subscribe to BizRap, 105 stations pay for the feature on a barter arrangement, while the remaining 18 stations have agreed to pay based on a pay-per-day format. The current rate is $150 per station for 56 feeds per week. As mentioned, the pay-per-day format removes the need for sponsorship, and allows each individual radio station to generate its own revenue from local sources. Therefore, the 18 radio stations on pay-per-day are not required to broadcast Organizer's advertising spot, and Trirad collects the broadcast fee and forwards 70% to Syndcom in the normal manner. The current contractual agreement between Organizer and Syndcom, guarantees a minimum of

100 stations airing the spot 56 times per week for the agreed upon fee of $13 500. Should additional stations adopt the pay-per-day arrangement, it will be necessary to re-negotiate Syndcom's contract with Organizer.

TRIRAD'S PERFORMANCE AND ABILITIES

Although the current distribution system and representation by Trirad was working fairly well, Debra Gray was thinking about making a major change. The current station list seemed adequate, but Debra sensed that Trirad had underachieved in many of the key market areas. Presently, Debra was contemplating the elimination of a representation firm altogether, with Syndcom taking over responsibility for marketing their own radio properties. She was, however, well aware that Syndcom lacks expertise and knowledge in this area because past activities had focused exclusively on production of syndicated features rather than marketing. Should Syndcom require any marketing support, there was a possibility of hiring either a consultant or RadioResults, another smaller representation house on a limited, short-term contract basis. This assistance could aid in the maintenance of existing station lists, the acquisition of new stations, and the development and introduction of new products during the transition to direct distribution.

This decision to re-evaluate the current distribution strategy was prompted by a number of considerations that supported Trirad's underachievement in several critical areas. First, Trirad had failed to achieve some of the objectives outlined in their current two-year Action Plan, casting doubt on whether the radio syndication potential of Syndcom had been fully maximized. Trirad's Action Plan included the goals of establishing a network of 175 stations by the end of the first year, and 195 by the end of the second year. Syndcom has yet to see fulfillment of these objectives. As well, their Action Plan included an objective that they would assist Syndcom in developing and launching two additional features by the end of the contract period. To date, Trirad failed to provide any assistance in this area.

A second concern was that Trirad has been unable to attract an adequate number of stations in the key market areas of Vancouver, Edmonton, Winnipeg, Calgary, Toronto, London, Hamilton, Montreal, and Halifax, all areas that are important to a national sponsor. As a result, BizRap's attractiveness to national advertisers was hindered and Syndcom was unable to secure higher-paying sponsors. Although Syndcom presently receives $13 500 per week from their national sponsor, it is well below the industry average of $17 500 per week for similar shows. It is quite possible that if BizRap were to have better coverage in these major markets, Syndcom could attract a higher-paying sponsor. Moreover, these markets represent tremendous growth opportunities for both their present and future radio products.

A third concern was the fact that Trirad has yet to appoint a second person to represent Syndcom. Currently, only one person is responsible for the marketing and promotion of BizRap. This led Debra to wonder whether Trirad considered BizRap to be a high-priority activity. As a result, it seems doubtful that Trirad could achieve Syndcom's objective of building a greater presence in the radio syndication market by increasing the value of BizRap and by expanding the program base.

Debra was also concerned about the financial stability of Trirad. The current contract allowed Syndcom to have access to Trirad's financial audit. The most recent audit revealed a very high level of debt and overall financial difficulty. Debra wondered if this lack of financial strength may in part be responsible for the poor achievement of Trirad.

One last consideration was the lack of information available on the syndicated market. Trirad had done a poor job of providing feedback from subscribing stations on changes in audience composition and preferences. This made it difficult for Syndcom to anticipate future programming needs of the existing stations. Debra had repeatedly asked Trirad for this type of information, but had received very little to date.

MARKET RESEARCH

Prior to making a final decision on how to distribute BizRap, Debra decided that some market research should be conducted. Information on the needs of sponsors and stations was the main emphasis of the research.

The market research consisted of telephone interviews with a random sample of advertising agencies and stations that currently subscribe to BizRap. The important findings of this study are:

- In deciding what syndicated properties to air, radio stations examine the length of the report, with two minutes or less being preferred.

- The current trend in payment options is towards pay-per-day rather than barter syndication. Pay-per-day removes the need for a national sponsor, and allows each radio station to attract their own local sponsor. Radio stations are beginning to prefer this approach because it allows them to localize sponsorship.

- National advertisers need stations in the major market areas of Vancouver, Edmonton, Winnipeg, Calgary, Toronto, London, Hamilton, Kitchener-Waterloo, Oshawa, Montreal, and Halifax. Within each of these 11 market areas, a specific radio station should rank within the top 10 based on the rankings of the Average Quarterly Hour Reach (AQHR) study.

- Many radio stations in the larger markets are considering a change in news service from Newscast Cable Limited to Allcast Limited, Newscast's main competitor. Allcast represents the interests of more radio stations in the larger markets and can provide access to over 325 stations.

- A majority of radio stations said that it did not matter who represented syndicated features as long as the programming is consistent with their local target audience, and as long as the national sponsor does not conflict with any local interests.

- Several national advertisers do have reservations regarding direct distribution. Some advertisers feel that the quality of the syndicated feature may be compromised if the syndicator takes on the two roles of production and distribution.

- Some radio stations in the past have encountered difficulties with Trirad Enterprises in terms of contract dealings and affidavits. Although most difficulties were minor, some radio stations were frustrated with broadcast clearance problems and overall coordination. An example is poorly coordinated feed times resulting in some subscribing stations not being properly and accurately encoded to receive the feature. This proved embarrassing, especially when the station had promoted the feature during the preceding week.

OPERATING CHANGES

The change in strategy to direct distribution was thought to affect several areas of Syndcom's operations.

The first area that would be affected was staffing. The expanded responsibility of Syndcom to both produce and market radio properties would require the hiring of additional people. First, it would require the appointment of an experienced Station Relations Manager who would monitor and coordinate station lists and contracts, bill all advertisers and stations for revenue owing, and be responsible for working with current national sponsors as well as recruiting new ones. This manager would report directly to the radio manager, Debra Gray, and would provide some input with regards to new programming concepts and development. To provide information and direction for future programming, the Station Relations Manager would also be responsible for market and trend research. The base salary for an experienced person would be $75 000 per year.

The promotional budget would also be affected by the proposed change in distribution. Syndcom would now become the primary marketer of its products, so it would be required to develop promotional material. Debra felt that an initial promotional budget of $45 000 per year would be required. Most promotion would take the form of circulating flyers and advisories to all available stations across Canada. As well, miscellaneous budgeted items were expected to increase from the present $6000 per year to approximately $10 000 to allow for unexpected incidental costs associated with this greater involvement.

As mentioned earlier, Trirad had appointed only one salesperson to the BizRap account for the purpose of marketing and selling the feature. Most representation firms felt it necessary to appoint at least two salespeople for each syndicated radio property. To successfully increase Syndcom's portfolio and presence in the syndicated broadcast market, Debra knew that additional salespeople would have to be recruited; however, she was unsure of the exact number. Debra felt that her salespeople would have to be responsible for maintaining strong relationships with current stations, as well as attracting new stations. She felt that all subscribers of BizRap should receive a personal sales visit quarterly to maintain a strong working relationship. As well, she realized that new station subscribers may require additional sales calls to reinforce and strengthen the new relationship. Given the responsibilities and travel associated with the sales representative position, Debra estimated that each sales rep would cost approximately $100 000 in salary and expenses.

Current salaries for Syndcom's two radio commentators are approximately $120 000. As well, last year's production costs amounted to nearly $40 000. Syndcom's production costs are generally lower than competitors because of their ability to transfer resources from television to radio production.

Two new products are in the development stage. If these products reach the market, Debra estimates that each will have a similar cost structure to BizRap.

DECISION

Debra had arranged for a meeting with the president and vice-president of Syndcom for the end of the week. This meeting would determine the final decision on Syndcom's distribution strategy. Other scheduled items for discussion were the quarterly financial reports. Although Debra would be advocating the direct distribution option, Murray Phillips, the vice-president, disagreed with her about the merits of direct distribution. He felt that the additional manpower and responsibility would be too much to handle, given the limited size of the company. As well, he voiced his concerns with regards to Syndcom's limited knowledge and expertise in marketing and promotion. Tom Bradshaw, the president, was somewhat unclear as to what the future direction of Syndcom should be in terms of distribution. He could, however, see the value of gaining greater control over the selling and handling of their radio properties. All of them wondered if there were other alternatives that should be considered.

Although Debra was in favour of the change in distribution, she had some reservations. First, she questioned Syndcom's ability and expertise in marketing and promotion. Until now, all energies within the company focused mainly on the production of high-quality syndicated features. She was also concerned with the increase in staff that would be required for direct distribution.

Second, rumours in the industry indicated that BusTech, another major syndicator of business programs, was attempting to develop an exclusive arrangement with CHAT Radio FM 106.1. CHAT Radio was the first radio station in the Toronto market to convert to an all news/talk format, and was ranked second according to the most recent AQHR study. If successful, this arrangement would exclude Syndcom from providing any business products to this very important station. Debra was extremely concerned about this potential development because she felt this could be the beginning of a major trend in the industry. To date, Trirad had been unsuccessful in negotiations with CHAT. She wondered whether Syndcom might be more successful in negotiating this type of arrangement on its own.

Third, there was some concern about the increasing competitiveness of the entire broadcast industry. Several other radio syndicators were beginning to provide more business-oriented syndicated features, and thus would become direct competitors. As well, both radio syndicators and stations presently face increasing pressure for audience as more people rely on television for their news/business information. The recent introduction of satellite services and home movie channels also exacerbates this problem of audience attractiveness.

Fourth, the industry trend away from Newscast Cable Limited to Allcast Limited implies that other syndicators will have greater access to more radio stations across Canada. As well, Allcast is known to represent more stations in the markets that are considered necessary for attracting good sponsorship. Debra felt she had to at least evaluate additional satellite distribution by Allcast in an attempt to increase Syndcom's station base.

The last and most important reservation Debra had was how to handle the termination of Trirad as Syndcom's representation firm. Trirad had been retained during a period when Syndcom was experiencing financial hardship and thus some of Syndcom's staff had a certain feeling of indebtedness. In addition, the current three-year contract included a termination clause which stated that the party who terminated the relationship prior to its three-year term would be subject to a penalty of 10% of all net advertising revenues for the past twelve months. Because there was still another year left on the contract, this would be a substantial penalty for Syndcom.

NATURE-PLUS LIMITED: US EXPANSION?

Joseph J. Schiele

On August 1, 1998, Brian Reis, President of Nature-Plus Canadian Operations, located in Toronto, Ontario, faced the following problem. The number of new distributors that were joining the company each month had been steadily declining. After reviewing a proposal to expand Canadian operations into the US, Brian wondered what action he should take next.

INDUSTRY OVERVIEW

The Direct Selling Association estimated that 1996 United States and Canadian total retail sales by direct selling sources amounted to $US20.84 billion. The percentage of sales by major product groups was as follows: home and family care products (cleaning, cookware, and cutlery, etc.) 33.6%; personal care products (cosmetics, jewellery, and skin care, etc.) 29.2%; services and miscellaneous, etc. 18.3%; wellness products (weight loss, vitamins, and nutritional supplements, etc.) 13.1%; and leisure items (books, toys, and games, etc.) 5.8%.

The total North American market for wellness products, including direct selling sources, was highly fragmented and rapidly growing. For the US market, 1996 sales were US$6.5 billion compared to US$5.0 billion in 1994. This rapid growth was due to a number of factors, including increased interest in healthier lifestyles, the publication of research findings supporting the positive effects of certain nutritional supplements, and the aging of the "baby boom" generation, combined with the tendency of consumers to purchase more wellness products as they age.

Prepared by Joseph J. Schiele, Ph.D. Program, Richard Ivey School of Business, University of Western Ontario. Support for the development of this case was provided by the Direct Selling Foundation of Canada. Copyright ©1998 by the Direct Sellers Association. Reproduced with permission.

NATURE-PLUS: GENERAL COMPANY BACKGROUND

Nature-Plus was a network marketing company that was established in June 1995 by Brian Reis and his wife, Christine Cook, to pursue the expanding market for wellness products in North America and internationally. Mr. Reis directed his talents towards examining the nutritional requirements of the human body and developing products that would help improve the health and quality of life for individuals. The products that Nature-Plus developed, packaged, and marketed, included nutritional supplements, antioxidants, and weight-management products. The company was a privately held organization incorporated under the laws of the Province of Ontario. The registered office of the company was located in Toronto.

CANADIAN AND US OPERATIONS

Nature-Plus had an established Canadian network of distributors who actively marketed and sold the company's products to individuals across the ten provinces. (Company sales presence throughout Canada can be found in Exhibit 31-1.)

The company only recently expanded activities into the US. In order to do this, Brian recruited Alex Harkins as Nature-Plus National Sales Manager to start up a network marketing organization in the US, with a small office and distribution warehouse in Southern California. Additionally, Canadian distributors saw the US market as a golden opportunity for new business. Consequently, many Canadian distributors had begun developing their own downline sales organizations into the US.

PRODUCTS AND NEW PRODUCT DEVELOPMENT

Existing Products

The line of Nature-Plus products consisted primarily of consumable products that were designed to target the growing consumer demand for natural health alternatives for nutrition and wellness. In developing its product line, the company had emphasized quality, purity, potency, and safety.

EXHIBIT 31-1 Company Sales Force Presence in Canada

Province	Approximate Number of Distributors	Approximate Percentage of Overall Revenue
Maritimes	500	8
Quebec	200	5
Ontario	3 000	55
Manitoba	500	10
Saskatchewan	250	10
Alberta	250	5
British Columbia	300	7

Source: Internal company documents.

Nature-Plus created a simple four-step system for better health: Step 1—Cleanse and Detoxify; Step 2—Restore and Protect; Step 3—Nourish; and Step 4—Balance. Included within this system were Revive™, a product that helped the body maintain normal regularity and rid itself of accumulated digestive waste, that had been found to contribute to fatigue and sickness; Renew™, a product that helped the body eliminate unwanted parasites, that had been found to cause symptoms including stress, fatigue, and general poor health; Repel™, a product that helped protect the body from free radicals, that had been shown to cause cancer, stroke, Alzheimer's, and Parkinson's disease; Exfat™, a product that helped the body control body fat by breaking down existing fat, reducing the formation of new fat, and reducing food cravings; and Essentials Plus™, a natural vitamin and mineral dietary supplement.

New Product Development

Nature-Plus expanded its product line through the development of new products. New product ideas were derived from a number of sources, including trade publications, scientific and health journals, the company's management and consultants, and outside partners. Nature-Plus did not maintain its own product research and development staff but relied upon independent research, vendor research, research consultants, and others for such services. When the company, one of its consultants, or another party identified a new product or concept, or when an existing product had to be reformulated for another market, the product or concept was generally submitted to one of the company's suppliers for development. The company did, however, own the proprietary rights to most of the product formulations.

MANUFACTURING AND RAW MATERIALS

Nature-Plus purchased its vitamins, nutritional supplements, and all of its other products from third parties that manufactured these products to the company's specifications and standards. Nature-Plus did not have any long-term supply agreements with any single vendor. The company believed that it could establish alternate sources for most of its products and that any delay in locating and establishing relationships with alternative sources would not result in significant product shortages and back orders.

Raw materials were purchased from reliable sources, and back-up sources were available. Most of the raw material suppliers were large, well-established North American companies. Raw materials represented approximately 50% of the cost of goods sold for the company.

The company sought the highest-quality ingredients from competitive sources. These products were encapsulated and packaged by licensed pharmaceutical companies. All nutritional supplements, raw materials, and final products were subject to sample testing, weight testing, and purity testing by independent laboratories.

COMPANY STRUCTURE

General Workforce

As of December 31, 1997, the company employed six people. There were no collective bargaining agreements in effect at that time. The company enjoyed good ongoing relations with employees. Employees received competitive benefit and compensation packages.

General Management

Nature-Plus was managed by Brian Reis, President; Christine Cook, Vice-President, Marketing; and Alex Harkins, National Sales Manager.

Brian Reis—President

Brian Reis had been with Nature-Plus as a co-founder since its inception. His primary responsibilities included the regular administration of the company's operations, oversight and negotiation of sales and purchasing for the company, and the development of the company's business. Mr. Reis had over 11 years of related industry experience and had run several large network marketing organizations, including the Canadian operations for Body Wise from 1991–1994. He was a director of the Multi-level Marketing International Association and a member of the Direct Sales Association's Strategic Committee that dealt directly with Health Canada. Mr. Reis had received his Honours Business Administration Degree from the University of Western Ontario in 1986.

Christine Cook—Vice-President, Marketing

As co-founder of Nature-Plus, Ms. Cook had over eight years of network marketing experience on two continents. From 1989–1993, she was the marketing manager for Vita-Max Inc. of Carlsbad, California, where she oversaw the advertising and marketing activities for this international nutrition company. Her duties included the coordination of advertising efforts on behalf of the company, the development of advertising strategies, consumer research, managing the advertising budget, and acting as liaison with divisions in China, the United Kingdom, and Canada. Ms. Cook received her Honours Bachelor of Science degree from the University of Loughborough in England in 1989.

Alex Harkins—National Sales Manager

Prior to his appointment at Nature-Plus, Mr. Harkins had been an independent marketing and advertising consultant responsible for projects that included marketing director for Endless Health Products Inc., where his responsibilities included the design and creation of advertising materials and direct-response programs, the development of special training programs, and the creation of product sales efforts for Links Golf Company. From 1994–1996, Mr. Harkins was the Director of Marketing for Nu-Ideas in Travel of Irvine, California. From 1993–1994, he was the National Marketing Director for Mega-Merger Bancorp, a financial services company in Irvine, California. Mr. Harkins received his Bachelor of Arts Degree from the University of California, Irvine, in 1983.

Company Advisory Council

In order to assist in the implementation of its marketing strategy, Nature-Plus created a six-person Advisory Council. Members of the Advisory Council were available to provide the company with ongoing support with their views on new products, potential development plans, and trends within the industry. Members of the Advisory Council were selected according to their knowledge of and experience within the nutrition industry.

Sales and Marketing

Nature-Plus established three primary marketing objectives for its company:

1. to produce a strong distribution network for the sale of its products;

2. to develop a comprehensive and regular customer base;

3. to establish an expanding network of distributors across North America.

Distribution

The company's products were distributed through a network marketing system consisting of approximately 5000 distributors who serviced about 20 000 customers. Distributors were independent contractors who purchased products directly from the company for their own use and resale to retail consumers.

Nature-Plus created an environment that valued people first, that brought health and opportunity to all people through a network marketing system that enabled distributors to become involved on a part- or full-time basis. Nature-Plus concentrated its efforts on encouraging individuals to develop their own business, at their own pace, without the costly expense inherent in franchise operations or other start-up enterprises. Network marketing gave individuals the opportunity to go into business without significant risk, yet offered them significant upside potential, albeit wholly dependent upon their own efforts.

Network marketing used word-of-mouth advertising to grow and capture market share. It was people talking to other people, sharing something they believed in. In addition, network marketing allowed an individual to leverage his or her time, talent, and energy to earn commissions from sales to all the people that were introduced to the business.

There were three major marketing plans that were common to network distribution organizations: (1) stair step, (2) uni-level/matrix, and (3) binary system. Management believed that because the binary system, which was employed at Nature-Plus, provided greater contact between the company and the consumer, this system would dominate the network marketing industry in the future.

The development of these marketing networks was most commonly achieved through word-of-mouth. Classified advertising was also used. Most of the distribution occurred through home-based distributors. These organization methods had proven to be a simple and effective distribution model.

The compensation plan developed at Nature-Plus for its distributors provided several opportunities for distributors to earn money. Each distributor was required to purchase and sell products in order to earn any compensation. Therefore, the distributor could not simply develop a down-line sales organization or receive payment based upon the recruitment of new distributors.

The first method of earning a commission was through retail markup on product sales. Distributors purchased product from the company and resold the product at retail prices to consumers. The difference between the price paid by the distributor and the retail price was a distributor's profit or compensation.

The second method of earning money through the distribution of the company's products was by receiving commissions on sales volumes generated by the distributor's sales organization, which consisted of as few as two additional distributors introduced to the company by the distributor, and by meeting certain personal sales volumes.

The company's ability to increase sales was significantly dependent on its ability to attract, motivate, and retain distributors. The company utilized a marketing program that it believed was superior to programs offered by other network marketing companies. The program provided financial incentives, distributor training and support, a low-priced starter kit, no inventory requirements, and low monthly purchase requirements. Management attempted to reach new distributors through various advertising initiatives, the company's World Wide Web site, teleconferencing, and regional sales meetings.

In an effort to continue to motivate distributors, Nature-Plus developed several programs. Some of these programs included the Car Advantage Program, which made car payments of up to $3000 per month for qualifying distributors; the Personal Recruiting and Sales Campaigns, which were developed to assist distributors in developing their downline distribution networks and increase sales; 24-Hour Teleconference and Voice-mail, that provided access to a weekly recorded teleconference call to its distributors, including interviews with successful distributors, up-to-date product information, announcements, and current product specials offered by the company; *Health and Wealth Trends* and *Living Well* magazines, that provided information on network marketing and the company (developed to recruit new distributors by answering the questions most commonly asked by potential new distributors); Product Literature, that was produced for its distributors, including comprehensive and attractive catalogues and brochures that displayed and described the company's products; and Toll-Free Access, for the placement of orders, customer service assistance, and faxing of orders and inquiries.

Competition

Nature-Plus competed with many companies marketing products similar to those sold and marketed by the company. It also competed directly with other network marketing companies in the recruitment of distributors.

Not all competitors sold all the types of products marketed by Nature-Plus. Some competitors marketed products and services in addition to those offered by Nature-Plus. For example, some competitors were known for and were identified with sales of herbal formulations, others with household cleaning and personal care products, while others were known for and identified with sales of nutritional and dietary supplements.

Another source of competition in the sale and distribution of health and nutrition products was from direct retail establishments, such as large retailers, independents, and non-category stores (e.g., drug stores). The most prominent retailer was the General Nutrition Center (GNC), which had a number of retail stores located both in the US and in Canada.

There were also many network marketing companies with which the company competed for distributors. Some of the largest of these were Amway, Herbalife International Inc., Rexall Sundown Inc., Market America Inc., and Relive International Inc. These companies were substantially larger than Nature-Plus and had access to far greater resources. The company competed for these distributors through its marketing program that included its commission structure, training and support services, and other benefits.

MANAGEMENT INFORMATION SYSTEMS

The company maintained a computerized system for processing distributors' orders and calculating commissions and bonus payments that enabled it to remit such payments promptly to distributors. The company believed that prompt remittance of commissions and bonuses to distributors was critical to maintaining a motivated network of distributors.

The company's computer system made available to the company's distributors a detailed monthly accounting of sales and recruiting activity. These statements eliminated the need for substantial record keeping on behalf of the distributor. The computer system was also integrated with the company's reporting system that generated monthly reports, invoices, and payroll.

The company's objective was to handle service inquiries made by distributors and customers immediately. However, only about 50% of all telephone inquiries were being handled in this manner. The current system was reaching capacity limits and would require upgrading as sales from business increased. Brian estimated that these upgrades would cost approximately CDN$50 000 for additional hardware and software. An effective information system impacted directly on the profitability of the company. Communication between the company and its distributors was central to the growth and development of the company's business.

COMPANY FINANCIALS

Overview

The financial performance of the company showed steady improvement despite its short history, and a significant increase in net income from 1995 to 1997. (Comparative financial statements for 1995 to 1997 can be found in Exhibit 31-2.)

EXHIBIT 31-2 Comparative Financial Results from 1995 to 1997 (in Canadian Dollars)

	Year Ended 1997	Year Ended 1996	Year Ended 1995
Income Statement			
Sales	$1 559 055	$1 207 462	$173 539
Less Cost of Sales	993 728	775 911	111 817
Gross Margin	565 327	431 551	61 722
Gross Margin (%)	36.3%	35.7%	35.6%
Less Expenses	455 211	408 314	103 373
Net Income/(Loss) Before Tax	110 116	23 237	(41 651)
Balance Sheet			
Total Assets	$ 240 839	$ 194 794	$113 887
Working Capital	59 698	(44 171)	(69 270)
Shareholders' Equity	105 371	(18 288)	(41 524)

Source: Internal company documents.

Inflation

Inflation could affect the cost of raw materials and goods and services purchased by the company. The competitive environment limited the extent to which the company could raise prices to recover costs. Generally, overall product prices had been stable and the company expected to recover increased costs through improved productivity and cost containment programs. The company had not been subject to material price increases by its suppliers and inflation was not expected to have a significant effect on operations in the next twelve months.

FUTURE OUTLOOK

The company believed that its success to date was due to its reputation and commitment to provide a wide range of premium-quality, innovative health and nutritional products, and an appealing business opportunity for persons interested in establishing a direct sales business.

The company's primary objective for the future was to capitalize on its operating strengths in order to become a leading distributor of consumer products in each of its markets. The company intended to do this by introducing new products, opening new markets, attracting new distributors, and increasing brand awareness and loyalty.

SITUATION

New Distributors

During the last six months, the number of new distributors joining the firm each month had been declining. This indicated that business in Canada was slowing down. Because the network marketing industry was essentially a cash business, where money was received when product was sold, as the number of new distributors declined, so did the cash flow for the business. New distributors and renewed distributors were critical to the success of any network marketing operation. This was a key indicator of the overall health of a network marketing company. Essentially, if distributor growth declined or levelled off, something had to be done.

Payments to Suppliers

As a result of this decline and subsequent slowdown in cash flow, Brian found himself behind on some of his payables. Suppliers had been expressing concern over the timing of late payments and Brian knew that if this continued, they could ultimately cut off his supply of products. This would have very serious implications, and could result in the cessation of the business. Brian owed suppliers approximately CDN$100 000 in past due payables.

US EXPANSION

Rationale for Expansion

Brian felt that the US would provide access to the new distributors needed to sustain his business for the long term. Expansion into the US seemed to represent a logical progression since the company had successfully demonstrated its viability and the quality of its products in the Canadian market. The company believed that it had refined its marketing strategies and procedures to be able to capture a profitable portion of the US market. Past experience within the market had achieved some success and, therefore, indicated the possibility for greater opportunity. (Financial forecasts for 1998 to 2000 for the US and Canada can be found in Exhibit 31-3.)

Strategic Plan

Management developed a strategic plan, whereby the company intended to establish an effective distribution network for the sale of its products in the US. As a result, the company would be concentrating on marketing all of its products, and developing and expanding its market penetration in these markets.

The expansion plan also encompassed a comprehensive training and educational program designed to teach distributors the specific methods and procedures for the marketing and distribution of its product line.

The company intended to expand its distribution network through the use of increased distributors. Southern California was selected as the base of American operations for several reasons. This area represented one of the largest markets for health and nutritional products. Network marketing systems were generally more accepted in California. In addition,

EXHIBIT 31-3 Company Sales Forecasts for the US and Canada from 1998 to 2000 (in Canadian Dollars)

	Year Ended 1998	Year Ended 1999	Year Ended 2000
Income Statement			
Sales			
Existing Products	$1 700 000	$4 900 000	$16 000 000
New Products	300 000	5 100 000	4 000 000
Product Literature	80 000	400 000	800 000
Other Income (net)*	48 000	249 000	480 000
Less Cost of Sales			
Products and Literature	314 000	1 568 000	3 140 000
Commissions & Other	910 000	4 660 000	9 320 000
Gross Margin	$ 904 000	$4 421 000	$ 8 820 000
Less Expenses			
Operating (net wages)	483 000	1 636 000	2 283 000
Wages	220 000	1 425 000	2 000 000
Net Income (Loss) Before Tax	$ 201 000	$1 360 000	$ 4 537 000

* Other Income (net) includes freight and miscellaneous less returns.

Assumptions
1. Gross Margin was expected to improve because of larger production runs and greater cost savings due to volume purchasing.
2. Commissions for 1998 were expected to be lower than 1997 because of adjustments to the compensation plan.
3. The geographical breakdown for revenues was estimated to be 70/30 between Canada and the US in 1998, and 40/60 for 1999–2000.

Source: Internal company documents.

the company believed that a number of positive marketing features for distributors were inherent to southern California, such as rallies, seminars, and incentive plans, all of which could be administered through the company's US office.

Additional Resources Required

At this point, the company had leased approximately 1200 square feet of office and warehouse space. However, Brian believed that he would need an additional 1800 square feet of space if he were to commit to the US expansion. Brian had estimated that this additional space would cost Nature-Plus an additional US$1000 per month.

Management also anticipated that its facility in the US would require a contemporary and attractive design and décor. The company was contemplating retaining an interior design consultant to assist in the layout of these offices, which would include a well-appointed reception area. This feature was essential since this area would convey the first impression to prospective distributors. Two meeting rooms would also be included. Remodelling costs were estimated between US$30 000 and US$40 000.

Existing information systems in Canada would be insufficient to meet the needs of the US market. In order to develop an integrated operation, the US would require computer upgrades in hardware to link the company's offices and their operations. These hardware costs were estimated at US$25 000.

In addition to hardware upgrades, Brian would have to purchase additional software to effectively handle the dramatic increase in business that was expected. This software would cost approximately US$100 000.

In order to run the US operations effectively, additional personnel would be required. Similar to the Canadian Operations, two administrative staff and a US Sales Manager would be required. The cost for these additional personnel would be approximately US$40 000, and US$50 000, respectively. These costs would include base pay and basic benefits, but not performance bonuses. Brian was not sure if he could manage both the Canadian and US operations at the same time. He estimated that a General Manager for the US would cost approximately US$60 000.

To effectively launch Nature-Plus products and attract new distributors to the company, Brian had estimated that he would need approximately US$100 000 as an annual budget for advertising and promotion in the US.

Opportunities for Fund-Raising

In order to meet anticipated funding requirements for expansion into the US, Brian identified six sources for funds:

1. Brian had calculated that for a CDN$2 000 000 public offering, he would be able to raise approximately CDN$1 700 000 net of fees and charges. In order to complete the public offering, Brian would have to undergo an extensive audit going back three years. This audit would cost approximately CDN$20 000. He would also have to prepare a detailed business plan for potential investors, and arrange for an investment banker.

   It could take anywhere from six to twelve months to complete the offering. The offering would require Brian to give up 49 percent ownership of his company. Also, there was no guarantee that the offering would be successfully completed since it ultimately depended on the public's interest in the company as a viable investment. However, taking the company public could raise the credibility and public awareness of the company, thereby stimulating more growth in new distributors.

2. Brian could also raise funds through a private offering. Similar to the public offering, he would have to undergo an extensive audit, develop a business plan, and arrange for an investment banker to handle the private offering. Brian would offer potential investors a 50 percent discount on the share price identified for the public offering. Brian believed that he could raise approximately CDN$150 000 to $200 000 this way. The offering could take anywhere from one to six months to complete, depending on investor interest.

3. Brian could go to the Canadian Business Development Bank (CBDB) where he would get a CDN$250 000 secured (against company and Brian's personal assets) loan at 15% interest. This loan would be repayable over a five-year period. It would take approximately one to two months to secure the loan from the CBDB.

4. In one to two weeks' time, Brian could obtain a personal bank loan for CDN$50 000 at 12% interest over five years.

5. Various members of Brian's family had offered to invest CDN$75 000 into Nature-Plus. They would have the money for him in two to three weeks. However, he was not sure what they would expect as a return on their investment, or when they would expect repayment.

6. As a last resort, Brian believed that in about one week he could come up with CDN$50 000 of his own money. This represented the bulk of Brian's net worth, and he was not really sure that he wanted to risk the investment.

US Regulation

Although the company confined its activities to marketing and distribution, the manufacturing, processing, formulation, packaging, labelling, and advertising of the company's products in the US were subject to regulation by federal agencies. The company's network marketing system was subject to governmental laws and regulations generally directed at ensuring that product sales were made to consumers of the products, and that compensation and advancement within the organization were based upon sales of the products rather than investment in the organization by distributors.

However, the company did not believe that these laws or regulations would have a material effect on its products or operations. Nutritional and dietary supplements such as those sold by Nature-Plus, for which no therapeutic claim was made, were not subject to Federal Drug Administration approval prior to sale. Also, the company did not anticipate developing any new products that would fall under this regulation in the future.

DECISION

Having gathered the key information that he felt was relevant, Brian wondered what action he should take next.

EJE
TRANS-LITE INC.
H.F. (Herb) MacKenzie

In early 1994, Paul Edison, Marketing Director of EJE Trans-Lite Inc. (http://www.eje-translite.com), was trying to decide what to do concerning the price of the Digi-Lite, the company's principal product. Paul helped design the original Digi-Lite soon after he joined EJE in 1989. His technical background was in radio operations and electronic communications. He completed a course in this at Red River College in Winnipeg before spending eight years in the off-shore oil industry immediately prior to joining EJE.

When the Digi-Lite was introduced in 1990, it was the world's smallest rescue light; it measured 4.2 × 5.0 cm. and weighed only 33 grams (see Exhibit 32-1). It could be tied or sewn on any survival system (life jacket, survival suit, or life raft) by means of a plastic tie, or specially designed patch. The light was visible for 1.2 nautical miles, and the lithium battery, when activated, would last 12 hours, 50 percent longer than competitive products. The Digi-Lite was the only product that operated automatically when in contact with water, a great advantage in marine applications where the user could be unconscious or seriously injured.

Sales growth was rapid, and by 1993, it was sold through approximately 45 independent distributors in 40 countries. EJE had a sales agent in the United States, who sold to the distributors there. Sixty percent of sales were to the US, and 97 percent of sales were outside Canada. Two of the largest distributors that EJE had were Unitor and Jotron, both Scandinavian-based companies that sold a broad range of products to the marine industry. Unitor advertised daily delivery to 837 ports throughout the world, and it had offices and warehouses in many of these ports. Jotron sold mainly to independent distributors throughout the world, and it had EJE manufacture Digi-Lites for them with the Jotron brand name.

Besides distributors, EJE sold direct to cruise lines and manufacturers of water survival clothing. Both were considered original equipment manufacturers (OEM) accounts, and the volume justified lower pricing. In fact, price was the major decision criterion among OEM accounts, followed by availability of inventory. For distributors, the decision criteria varied depending on the size of the distributor. The larger distributors placed more emphasis on price as they often sold to smaller distributors, and sometimes to large user accounts. Smaller distributors generally sold in small quantities to final customers such as fishermen or recreational users, and price was less important as the final customer was not so price-sensitive. Availability was often the most important purchase criterion, along with the convenience of being able to purchase many items from a single source of

EXHIBIT 32-1 Digi-Lite Personal Rescue Light

supply. In some instances, for example, EJE and Jotron sold to the same distributors. EJE had the price advantage when large orders were involved, but Jotron had the advantage when smaller quantities were involved as it could offer the convenience of a broad range of items that could be bought at one time.

Paul estimated that his 1993 North American market share was 35 percent, and his market share in the rest of the world was 46 percent. There were two main competitors, ACR Electronics in the US, and McMurdo in the UK. Both had larger units, required manual operation, and were slightly higher priced. ACR Electronics sold about the same number of units as EJE in North America, but its total annual sales were at least ten times greater due to an expanded product line. It also sold strobe lights, buoy lights, search and rescue transponders, electronic positioning devices, and other electronic equipment.

The original unit, model A-12M, was for marine applications. In 1993, Paul introduced model A-12A, a similar model for aviation applications, and had sold one trial order of 500 units. Government approval for general sale was expected at any time, and Paul expected to sell 6000 units in 1994. A final model was the A-12EWS, identical to model A-12M, but with a copper wire attached to it to ensure contact with the water in the event it was on an inflatable life jacket and was too high from the water to be activated automatically. The Canadian Coast Guard purchased 3600 units in 1993, and were expected to buy another 4800 in 1994. Paul also expected to sell 7200 units of model A-12EWS to the UK in 1994. Paul estimated the world market would grow by 20.4 percent in 1994, but his own unit sales should increase by 23 percent because of expected increases in sales of models A-12A and A-12EWS.

All Digi-Lites, while designed by EJE, were assembled by another firm in St. John's, and sold to EJE in lots of 10 000 units. Exhibit 32-2 shows the sales and profit data for 1993.

EXHIBIT 32-2 EJE Sales and Profit Data, 1993

Model	Units Sold	Cost	Selling Price	Contribution/Unit	Contribution/Total
A-12M	90 871	7.74	13.16	5.42	492 520.82
A-12A	500	7.74	13.16	5.42	2 710.00
A-12EWS	3 600	8.94	15.20	6.26	22 536.00

In January 1994, Paul was contacted by one of his major distributors and informed that unless he dropped his price by 12.5 percent, the distributor would have to buy elsewhere. Both competitors had dropped their prices, and although the distributor preferred to buy EJE Digi-Lites, the price differential was too great.

After a careful assessment, Paul determined that he stood to lose 27 percent of his 1994 projected sales; that is, he would only sell 84 274 units in total. He thought that he would maintain proposed sales of model A-12A as these would be domestic sales, and there was no competitive product. He also thought he would maintain proposed sales of model A-12EWS in Canada, but would probably lose the UK order. Model A-12M would account for the balance of lost sales.

Paul was trying to decide what to do. This was the first major pricing decision he had to make. He really didn't want to lower his price as he worked on a 70 percent markup over cost, and had used this markup for every product and every distributor since the company started in business. EJE had just designed a unit with a slightly smaller, lighter lens that would be cheaper to produce, but, unfortunately, approval to design changes would take about a year, and production would delay introduction another six months.

Another alternative Paul had was to introduce units identical in size and appearance to the present units, only with flashing bulbs. These could be available in one month, would extend battery life to 40 hours, and would be the only flashing units on the market. It would cost about $15 000 for engineering and production set-up; otherwise, the additional cost per unit would be $0.60 to EJE. If they were introduced in 1994, and Paul kept his full markup on all models, he expected that his sales would still be 22 percent below his 1994 projections. He also anticipated sales for model A-12A would change totally to flashing units due to the extended battery life; sales of model A-12EWS would remain totally with regular bulbs as many users were uncomfortable with flashing bulbs as they believed they might be less visible due to wave action that could hide them at times. For model A-12M, Paul thought that 30 percent of his sales would be for flashing units.

FORTRON INTERNATIONAL INCORPORATED

Marvin Ryder

When entering foreign markets, Fortron International Incorporated, a Hamilton, Ontario-based producer of sport whistles, had planned to use renewable sales-agency agreements granting exclusive distribution rights to a country-specific distributor. The first such agreement, with Allzweck-Sportartikel, a German wholesale catalogue store specializing in soccer equipment, was set to expire in October 1991. Steve Foxcroft, general manager of Fortron International, believed that the German market could be better exploited and was looking for alternative arrangements.

PRODUCT HISTORY

A conventional whistle produced its shrill "trill" through the movement of a small pea (a cork or a plastic ball) in its interior. The pea alternately covered and uncovered a hole through which air was released, producing a rapid cycle of sound and silence. Unfortunately, the pea would often stick, especially if overblown or if water and debris got into the interior.

Ron Foxcroft and Joe Forte, professional basketball referees, perceived a need for a better, more dependable whistle. Along with dependability, they maintained that a new whistle should have a louder, more penetrating sound that could be heard over the noise of a crowd. In short, they wanted a whistle that would perform under any conditions.

With the aid of an industrial designer, three and a half years of extensive development and testing, and $150 000 in start-up capital, the Fox 40 whistle was introduced in 1987 as the only whistle without a pea. It had three air chambers, and, when it was blown, these created three different frequencies. As the frequencies were out of phase, they were alternately reinforced and cancelled, resulting in a louder, piercing, intense vibrato. The Fox 40 whistle worked in all weather conditions and also floated on water. Patent protection for twenty years, from those firms that would try to copy the technology, was sought and received worldwide.

The whistle was introduced at the Pan-American Games in Indianapolis, Indiana. By 1991, the Fox 40 whistle was used in seven Olympic sports, the National Football League (NFL), the Canadian Football League (CFL), the World Basketball League (WBL), National Collegiate Athletic Association (NCAA) Basketball, and the National Basketball Association (NBA). Many police departments and safety-oriented organizations adopted the whistle. The US Cavalry and the Royal Life-Saving Society endorsed the Fox 40 as their whistle of choice.

Originally designed for a professional referee, the Fox 40 whistle was available in three models. The "Classic" was sold in eight colours (red, orange, yellow, green, blue, pink, black, and white), as was the "Mini-Fox." A referee model came in black, with a convenient finger grip.

COMPANY HISTORY

Fortron International Inc. was created in 1987 by Ron Foxcroft and Joe Forte to market the Fox 40 whistle. It was a lean organization with a staff of three executives—including Foxcroft's son, Steve, as general manager—who shared responsibility for marketing and financial decisions, and one secretarial assistant. For a dollar each, a nearby company, Promold Plastics, manufactured the whistle using injection moulding equipment and state-of-the-art ultrasonic welding. In 1991, two million Fox 40 whistles would be sold worldwide, and sales were expected to double in 1992. Revenue in 1991 exceeded $5 million and profits crossed the $300 000 threshold.

Fortron International's first overseas sales agent was Allzweck-Sportartikel in Trechtingshausen, West Germany. Exclusive distribution rights for West Germany were granted in a three-year licensing agreement signed on October 8, 1988. Under the agreement, Fortron sold the whistles for $3.45 to Allzweck. Though Allzweck was free to negotiate discounts for volume purchases or promotional purposes, the suggested retail selling price was $5.95.

Allzweck was a wholesale catalogue store specializing in soccer equipment. It distributed 5000 catalogues annually within Germany, and had four sales representatives. In addition, it operated a small booth at the most important sporting-goods trade show (ISPO), which was held annually in Munich. Allzweck's sales of Fox 40 whistles are presented in Exhibit 33-1. All of these sales were to customers from West Germany, and most were from an area thirty kilometres around Frankfurt, including Trechtingshausen.

Exhibit 33-1 Sales of Fox 40 Whistles by Allzweck-Sportartikel

Year	Number of Whistles Sold
1989	9 340
1990	19 610
1991	29 850

COMPETITION

Conventional "pea" whistles retailed for half the price of the Fox 40. A number of small manufacturers that produced these whistles were located in Southeast Asia. Their whistles were perceived to be a lower quality, low-price choice, and were not used in sporting events. Instead, they were used recreationally, and were common gifts for children.

The leading sporting whistle was made by Acme Whistles of Birmingham, England. This company had manufactured whistles for more than a century, and held the original patents for the British bobby's whistle (registered in 1884) and the original pea whistle (1895). Acme's sales director did not feel that the Fox 40 posed any threat to its major sports whistle—the Acme Thunderer. "If you wish to imply that the Fox 40 is about to sweep Acme into liquidation, I think that's not the case." Nonetheless, it was rumoured that Acme was attempting to develop its own line of pea-less whistles.

There were no whistle manufacturers in Germany.

A UNIFIED GERMANY

The breaking of the Berlin Wall in November 1989 was the beginning of German reunification. On October 3, 1990, 45 years after being separated, West Germany (the Federal Republic of Germany (FRG)) and East Germany (the German Democratic Republic (GDR)) were reunited under the former's name. The new FRG covered 356 945 square kilometres and supported a population of 79 million. Of that, 18 million lived in the former GDR.

While more than three-quarters of Germans favoured reunification, 1991 was a difficult year of adjustment. Forty percent of West Germans believed their financial health had worsened due to higher taxes, increased interest rates, inflation, and higher rents. The unemployment rate rose to 11.3% when inefficient East German plants were closed.

The national currency was the deutsche mark (DM). During reunification, the currency of East Germany (the DRR-Mark) was revalued to equal the DM. One DM was worth approximately CDN$1.33. In 1990, prior to unification, the GNP of West Germany increased by 4.5% to DM1.6 trillion. The GNP for a unified Germany was expected to grow by 3.1% in 1991 and 1.6% in 1992. This was the second-highest growth rate among the seven largest industrial nations. Inflation in West Germany was 2.7% in 1990. In a unified Germany, inflation was expected to be 3.5% in 1991 and 3.8% in 1992. These rates were among the lowest of the seven largest industrial nations. Under unification, the trade surplus was expected to decline. West Germany had a trade surplus of US$71.9 billion in 1990. A unified Germany would have trade surpluses of US$15 billion in 1991 and US$20 billion in 1992.

In 1991, over DM90 billion (US$50 billion) had been allocated for improving social security, roads, schools, and hospitals, and merging military forces in the former East Germany. This amount was more than 3% of the new Germany's GNP. Another DM90 billion would be spent over the next decade to move the federal government from Bonn to Berlin. Other spending included DM115 billion between 1991 and 1994 for the Germany Unity Fund, DM21 billion in 1991 for privatization of East German state firms, and DM50 billion for payments to the Soviet Union for the withdrawal (by 1994) of Soviet forces from East Germany, and their resettlement.

The process of unification also involved sport and sports organizations. The old East German state bodies and associations, from the National Olympic Committee (NOK) to

Exhibit 33-2 Sports Participation in East Germany During 1988*

Sport	Number Participating	Individuals in Training
Football (Soccer)	575 667	39 207
General Sports	513 453	35 265
Gymnastics	408 476	26 542
Track and Field	180 605	15 583
Handball	152 975	13 225
Volleyball	134 924	12 454
Table Tennis	126 376	12 084
Swimming	83 509	6 911
Total	3 782 892	263 512

*These are the most recent statistics available.

Exhibit 33-3 Sports Participation in West Germany During 1989*

Sport	Number of Males	Number of Females
Football (Soccer)	4 320 440	484 144
Gymnastics	1 226 507	2 669 562
Tennis	1 217 265	879 301
Hunting/Shooting	1 060 089	263 758
Table Tennis	534 391	179 876
Handball	515 514	257 824
Track and Field	452 437	364 950
Swimming	286 413	273 658
Volleyball	196 449	185 358
Judo	173 239	66 198
Total	11 604 189	6 817 754

* These are the most recent statistics available.

the German Gymnastics and Sport Association (DTSB), were dissolved and incorporated into the corresponding West German structure (the German Sports League). Many of the special sport schools for children and adolescents in East Germany were closed, as a decentralized sports movement was favoured. All sport budgets were dramatically cut, and hundreds of full-time coaches and trainers were dismissed.

In 1988, 21% of the East German population participated in sports. Of this number, only 7% were in training for national and international competition (see Exhibit 33-2). In 1989, 30% of the West German population participated in sports. Interestingly, nearly twice as many males participated as females, and the largest group of participants was made up of people 24-years-old and older (see Exhibits 33-3 and 33-4).

Exhibit 33-4 Participation in Sports by Age and Gender in West Germany During 1989*		
Age Group	**Number of Males**	**Number of Females**
Under 15	2 009 208	1 567 630
15 to 19	1 094 193	687 183
20 to 23	811 568	465 439
24 and Over	7 689 220	4 097 502
Total	11 604 189	6 817 754

* These are the most recent statistics available.

OTHER GERMAN MARKETS

As well as pondering the sports market, Foxcroft wondered about the safety, fashion, and education markets. Two blasts of a whistle were recognized internationally as an emergency signal. Since the Fox 40 whistle got louder the harder one blew on it, and since it operated under any weather conditions, it was an ideal whistle in an emergency. With the reunification in Germany came increased attacks on the poor, and racist assaults on new immigrants. Community groups were being formed to protect citizens and make neighbourhoods safer. As everyone knew how to use a whistle, translation of instructions was not required.

In the preceding decade, sportswear had become prevalent in high fashion. The Fox 40 whistle had the potential of becoming a very fashionable, safety-oriented accessory item. But the extent to which whistles could penetrate the sportswear industry was limited, and other markets remained to be explored. In hunting, fishing, hiking, camping, skiing, cycling, and boating, safety was of particular concern. Interestingly, the more consumers spent on apparel for a sport, the more likely they were to buy a whistle to go with it. After someone had spent DM2000 on ski clothing and equipment, the price of a Fox 40 whistle would seem negligible.

In 1991, there were 7.1 million students enrolled in German schools; 2.6 million of these were enrolled in polytechnic schools. A safety-education program, coordinated by teachers and school administrators, could increase awareness of the Fox 40 whistle and lead to sales.

THE GERMAN CONSUMER

The *Guide for Canadian Exporters: The European Community* informed its readers that punctuality, politeness, and a degree of formality were essential when dealing with German consumers. Also, it advised, exporters needed to have a thorough knowledge of delivery periods, shipping costs, service requirements, and performance characteristics. As holidays were very important to German workers, sales visits in July or August were to be avoided. Exporters would also find a list of references useful.

By far the best sales vehicle for the German market was the trade fair. Germany had more world-class specialized industrial trade fairs than any other country. Because of this, many non-German companies attended them; such fairs presented firms with a good opportunity to extend their marketing opportunities.

INTERNATIONAL OPTIONS

Generally, there are five levels on which a company can become involved in international marketing. The first is casual exporting, which is the most passive; it involves exporting only occasionally—when surplus or obsolete inventory is available. This choice often leads to losses and a fear of export markets.

Once a firm is making a continuous effort to sell its merchandise abroad, it moves to the second level: active exporting. This is usually accomplished through sales-agency agreements. A manufacturer grants a distributor in a foreign country either exclusive or non-exclusive rights to sell its product in a particular geographic region. The manufacturing company thus gains access to a market, but has little information about the business environment there. The distributor, however, uses its knowledge of distribution channels, consumer behaviour, and local promotion to earn a healthy margin on each item sold. Fortron had such an agreement with Allzweck-Sportartikel. The spectrum of potential sales agents ranges from importers and wholesalers to department stores, mail order houses, and buying co-operatives.

Licensing, the third level, involves a firm making a formal agreement with a foreign company to produce the firm's merchandise. Again, the firm gains access to a market but no information about its business environment. The licensee is not usually made responsible for sales of the product and so, often, a sales agency agreement is also required before a product can be distributed. Rather than making money through production, the licenser earns royalties on either a lump-sum or per-unit basis. Licensing is favoured for either elementary technology or products with short life cycles, since the potential is considerable for licensees to copy new or advanced technology or to keep using a technology after the agreement has ended. Historically, about 50% of all licensing agreements manage to satisfy both parties.

At the fourth level, a company maintains a separate sales and marketing operation in a foreign country. Its product can be made at home or by foreign contract manufacturers, but the company controls foreign sales either through its own sales force or by supervising a group of local sales agents. This path is often used when a company wants to gather information about a country before it considers launching its own production facility. It can be an especially attractive learning experience if the company can protect its technology with patents, and thus give itself time to grow slowly.

Of course, the ultimate level of involvement occurs when a company both produces and markets its product in a foreign country. A new plant can be built or an existing plant can be acquired. A foreign plant would cost Fortron $1 million, and would require management time to establish and operate. Another option at this level, however, would be a joint venture with a foreign firm. For Fortron, while this path offered the advantage of cutting in half the $1 million investment and reducing the commitment of managerial resources, there were some disadvantages. One was that profits would have to be shared. A second was the lack of control the company would have over the strategic and operational decisions that affected the joint venture. Perhaps the biggest drawback was the lack of a potential joint-venture partner. One could, no doubt, be found, but how long would the process take?

THE EUROPEAN COMMUNITY

If Fortron established a stronger presence in Germany, then Germany could become a base for expanded operations into the European Community. The European Economic Community (EEC) came into being in Rome in 1957, when a treaty was signed by Belgium, France, West

Germany, Luxembourg, Italy, and the Netherlands. In 1973, when Denmark, Ireland, and the United Kingdom joined, the EEC became a group of nine. Greece joined in 1981, and the EEC reached twelve-member status when Spain and Portugal joined in 1986. It was then that the name was shortened to the European Community (EC) to reflect the new integration goals of the group rather than the original economic ones. In 1990, the EC decided that a reunified Germany would retain EC membership. The EC represented one of the largest potential consumer markets, as the combined population of its member nations was 340 million.

The EC was striving to: (1) end inter-country customs checks; (2) create uniformity and mutual recognition of technical standards, university diplomas, and apprenticeship courses; (3) create a common market in goods and services, including a single broadcasting area; and (4) create an equal excise and national-value-added-tax system. As of January 1989, the standard value-added-tax rate in Germany was 14%. Value-added taxes paid on a product in one EC country could be reclaimed if it entered another EC country.

The positive consequences of the EC have included the overall improvement of economic conditions in member countries and easier and less costly access to member markets. Patents registered in one member country are automatically registered in all EC countries. For Canadian firms, the EC has posed some threats including: (1) intensified competition in EC markets as European firms have become more efficient and the interest of non-European firms in the EC has increased; (2) more competition in North American markets and non-EC markets as the EC has become more unified; and (3) the fact that another major bloc in the globalized world economy has been established.

The EC 1992 agreement was a major concern. It eliminated all barriers between member countries so that people, capital, and goods could move freely. The agreement also raised fears, outside the EC, that as internal barriers were lowered, external barriers would be raised—sometimes on very short notice. The worst possible outcome would be for a wave of protectionism to sweep the EC, creating "Fortress Europe." This would mean that trade between EC countries would be stimulated at the expense of trade with non-EC-member countries.

THE DECISION

As Steve Foxcroft reviewed the information before him, he needed to make several preliminary decisions. Should Fortron be selling whistles in the German market? If so, what level of international marketing involvement was appropriate? Did existing management and financial resources preclude some forms of involvement? If Foxcroft resolved not to renew the Allzweck licensing agreement, would it mean a reduction in the number of whistles being sold? Could Fortron do better if it took control of all sales activities? Could a production centre, or other arrangement, be justified on the basis that it would give Fortron a foothold in the EC?

Clearly, any decision Foxcroft made would need to be followed up with more research before it could be implemented. Still, he could not afford to have his limited managerial staff pursuing non-viable options.

AIRVIEW
MAPPING INC. Kris Opalinski and Walter S. Good

In early March 1994, Rick Tanner, the president of Airview Mapping Inc., started drafting plans for the upcoming summer season. For Airview, late winter typically involved making calls on the company's established and potential clients for the purpose of determining the anticipated demand for their services, and drafting sales projections for the upcoming year.

Airview, which had historically dominated the aerial surveying markets of Central and Eastern Canada, had recently faced increased competition from other air surveyors from across Canada in its traditional markets. The protracted recession of the early 1990s, combined with anti-deficit measures introduced by all levels of government, had reduced the demand for geomatic services in Canada, producing significant overcapacity in this industry.

This situation had already reduced Airview's profits, but the real threat lay in the fact that new competitors, once established in the company's domain, could permanently capture a significant share of the Central Canadian regional market. These competitors, typically larger than Airview, could expand their market coverage, even if it meant creating a temporary operating base in a distant central Canadian location. At the same time, their home markets were extremely difficult for small companies from other regions to penetrate, due to the fierce price competition.

Rick realized his company might face difficult times if he could not direct his attention to some new opportunities. His view was that these opportunities had to be found in international markets. He had already gathered some marketing information on several foreign markets which looked promising from the company's perspective. It was now time to review

Prepared by Kris Opalinski, under the direction of Walter S. Good of the University of Manitoba, as a basis for classroom discussion rather than to illustrate either effective or ineffective handling of an administrative situation. The names of the company and its officers have been disguised. Support for the development of this case was provided by the Centre for International Business Studies, University of Manitoba. Reprinted with permission.

the firm's situation and decide whether to attempt to penetrate any of the identified foreign markets, and, if so, what entry strategy to choose.

THE COMPANY

Airview Mapping Inc. was incorporated in November 1979 by a group of former employees of Aerosurvey Corporation Ltd., with Tom Bruise and Rick Tanner as the principal shareholders of the new entity. For the first two years, the company operated without an aircraft, providing mapping services based on externally developed photogrammetric images to clients in central Canada. Airview's initial success provided sufficient capital to acquire an aircraft and a photographic processing laboratory, which, in 1981, was initially operated under the company's subsidiary, Airtech Services Ltd. The two operations were amalgamated in November 1983 under the parent company's name.

When Tom Bruise retired in 1990, Rick took over his duties as President. He acquired Tom's shares in the company and offered 40% of them to his employees.

Airview's sales grew steadily throughout the 1980s, from an annual level of $500 000 in 1981 to $1.2 million in 1989. Sales stabilized during the 1990s at a level of just over $1.1 million.

Airview had traditionally maintained an advanced level of technical capabilities, investing in the most up-to-date photographic, film processing, data analysis, and plotting equipment. This, combined with the technical expertise of the company's staff, had enabled them to develop an excellent reputation for quality, reliability, and professionalism of its services.

PRODUCT LINE

With its extensive technological capabilities, Airview provided a range of services associated with the development of spatial images of terrain, referred to (in Canada) as geomatics. The company's primary specialization was to make, process, and analyze airborne photographs of the earth's surface.

The major groups of services provided by Airview included the following.

Aerial Photography and Photogrammetry

Aerial photography occupied a pivotal place in Airview's business. The majority of the complex services provided by Airview were initiated by taking photographs from the air. However, aerial photography was also a separate product, which, depending on the light spectrum applied in taking the photograph, could provide information on forest growth and diseases, the quality of water resources, wildlife migration, land erosion, and other physical features.

Photogrammetry involved a number of image-processing techniques using aerial photographs as a basis for the development of maps, composite views, or spatially referenced databases. Photogrammetry was distinguished from aerial photography by its capability to identify three-dimensional coordinates for each point of the captured image.

Aerial photography/photogrammetry was very capital-intensive, requiring a specially prepared aircraft with specialized cameras, and sophisticated photo-laboratory equipment. Airview was considered one of the best-equipped aerial photography companies in Canada. Its Cessna 310 L aircraft, with 25 000-foot photo ceiling, was capable of producing photographs at scales of up to 1:10 000. A recently (1992) acquired Leica camera represented the latest in optical technology, meeting all calibration and accuracy requirements set by North American mapping agencies, and accommodating a wide variety of specialized aerial film. Finally, Airview's photo laboratory, which was certified by the National Research Council, processed all types of aerial film used by the company.

Aerial Surveying

Aerial surveying involved taking photographs with the purpose of defining and measuring boundaries and the configuration of particular areas on the earth's surface for a variety of uses, such as establishing ownership rights (cadastre); triangulation[1]; locating and appraising mineral resources, forests, and wild habitat; and detecting earth and water movements.

Mapping

This service group comprised the development of maps from either internally or externally acquired photographic images. Before the 1980s, map making had largely been a manual process of drawing the terrain's contours and elevations, and then inserting the accompanying descriptive information. From the early 1980s, however, the process was increasingly computer-driven. This resulted in a reduction in manual labour required and increased accuracy of the images produced. The new technology also permitted the storage of maps in an easily accessible, digital format, which created demand for converting maps from the traditional, analogue format into a computer-based one.

CADD

This area also dealt with map making, but was based on computer-operated scanners supported by CADD/CAM (Computer-Aided-Design and Drafting/Computer-Aided-Mapping) software. With this technology, the digitizing of analogue images, such as existing maps or photographs, was fully automated. The scanners interpreted the subject image as a series of dots identified by their coordinates, colours, and illuminance, and then produced their digital presentation. The computer-stored images could then be enhanced by adding descriptive information, using a process still performed manually by the CADD operators.

Consulting

Over its 15-year history, Airview had developed a multidisciplinary team of specialists, whose expertise was also employed in providing consulting services associated with the planning and execution of comprehensive mapping projects. Consulting involved advising clients on the optimal method of gathering spatial information, the interpretation of client-provided data, and supervising data-gathering projects conducted by the client or his or her subcontractors.

Data capture (aerial photography/photogrammetry) and data processing (mapping and CADD) projects had traditionally generated (in equal proportions) around 90% of Airview's sales. The remainder had come from consulting projects (9%) and surveying (1%).

By 1994, this distribution of sales did not reflect the changing structure of the marketplace, where data capture had become a relatively small part of the overall scope of geomatic activities.

CUSTOMER BASE

Airview Mapping Inc. provided services to a variety of clients locally and nationally. The majority of the company's sales had traditionally come from the public sector. Over the period of 1991–93, government agencies (both federal and provincial), local municipalities, and regional utilities in Ontario, Manitoba, and Saskatchewan accounted for between 65% and 75% of the company's total dollar sales.

Energy, Mines, and Resources Canada, Transport Canada, the Department of Indian Affairs, Manitoba Hydro, and Manitoba Telephone System were Airview's most significant clients. Procurement by public tender, the significant size of individual contracts (from $50 000 to over $100 000), and clear specifications of requirements, characterized these clients' approach to project management.

The private sector, accounting for the remaining 25% to 35% of sales, was represented predominantly by clients from the mining sector (such as Hudson Bay Mining and Smelting Company, Inco, Delcan, Noranda and Placer Dome), whose contracts were typically in the range of $20 000 to $40 000. Companies representing such diverse areas as construction, recreation, and environmental protection provided projects valued at up to $20 000 each. Companies from the private sector did not apply a rigorous procurement procedure, and frequently needed guidance in defining (or re-defining) project requirements.

GEOGRAPHIC COVERAGE

Airview concentrated its activities within a 1200-mile radius of its Brandon, Manitoba, headquarters. This was the area where the company was able to deal directly with its clients and had a cost advantage over its competitors from other provinces. It included northwestern Ontario, Manitoba, Saskatchewan, and Alberta, each contributing equally to the company's revenues.

The company had never attempted to expand beyond the national market, even though the sizable market south of the US–Canada border was well within its defined geographic radius. In the past, this was justified by the abundance of opportunities available in Canada and restrictions on foreign access to the US market. However, this situation had recently changed on both counts, which caused Rick to consider changing his company's geographic orientation.

ORGANIZATION AND STAFF

The production process associated with the services provided by Airview involved grouping activities into three functional areas; airplane operation and maintenance (two staff members), film development (two), and image processing/output (ten). Managerial, marketing, and administrative activities required four additional staff.

Each production area (aircraft operations, photo lab, data capture, and data conversion) was assigned a coordinator, responsible for quality assurance and overall coordination of the workload. These coordinators also provided expert advice to their staff and were responsible for individual projects within their respective production areas.

Airview's production activities were characterized by the relatively small number of concurrent projects (four to six) and their modest size. This, combined with the well-trained staff (13 out of 18 had completed post-secondary education in geomatics-related fields), enabled the company to apply a skeleton project-management structure.

Coordination of project work among different production areas was the responsibility of the Production Coordinator, Sean Coleman. Garry Howell was in charge of marketing. Tim Connors, who occupied the position of Vice President, also acted as the General Manager responsible for all projects. Rick, who was the company's President, oversaw general administration and communication with customers.

PRICING

Each price quotation was based on Garry Howell's assessment of the scope of work required to complete it. This was broken down by category of activity (aircraft operation, film processing, digitization of images, or image analysis). For each of these activity categories a budget hourly rate was developed, based on historical cost figures (both direct and fixed), the budgeted number of hours for a given planning period, and the company's profit targets. Recently, rates had ranged from $25 for digitization of images to over $900 for aircraft flying time, with an overall average of $70.

The initial price was determined by multiplying the estimated number of hours required in each category by its budgeted rate, and then adding these figures for all activity categories involved in the project. This price was later adjusted by Rick's assessment of the competitive situation (in the case of a tendered bid) or his negotiations with the customer.

Generally, Airview's budgeted rates, and—consequently—prices, were within average values prevailing in Canada. This situation reflected their general knowledge of the cost structure of the industry. Any undercutting of price tended to raise suspicions of lower standards. This being the case, the competition between bidders had severely squeezed profit margins, with many firms trying to survive by quoting their services on a break-even basis.

FINANCIAL RESULTS

In the late 1980s and early 1990s, Airview had acquired advanced photographic and mapping equipment, and computer hardware and software with a total value of close to $900 000. Financing for these acquisitions had been provided by bank loans and capital leases at interest rates ranging from 12.25% to 17.25%.

During the past two years, the cost of servicing this debt load had created a real strain on the company's cash flow, requiring an annual outlay of $200 000, split evenly between interest expenses and repayment of the principal. This was extremely difficult for a company traditionally only generating a free annual cash flow in the range of $100 000 to $150 000.

Airview's operating cost structure was characterized by a high proportion of fixed costs. Currently, some 75% of direct costs and 83% of total costs did not vary with changes in their sales level. This cost structure might seem surprising for a business with some 60% of its direct expenses associated with wages and salaries. However, considering the unique nature of the professional qualifications of the company's staff, it was extremely difficult, if not impossible, to vary the number of staff in line with fluctuations in sales levels.

This situation reduced the company's profitability at their current sales level, but, at the same time, created significant profit potential with the possibility of a sales increase. It was estimated that the company, barely breaking even at its current sales of $1.1 million, could make over $200 000 in profits by increasing sales to $1.4 million.

OVERALL STRATEGIC PROFILE

Viewed from a strategic perspective, Airview could be characterized as a locally based company with strong technical capabilities, but limited expertise in marketing, particularly outside its traditional markets. Rick recognized the importance of having a clear view of his company's current position, as well as its goals for the next few years.

Analysis of Airview's structure and performance led him to develop the corporate profile presented in Exhibit 34-1.

Exhibit 34-1 Airview's Corporate Profile—Current vs. Target (Five-Year Perspective)

	Current	Target
Rank & size	$1 100 000 sales $0–$25 000 profits 18 employees Medium aerial surveying company No export sales	$2 000 000+ sales $300 000+ profits 30+ employees Medium-size GIS company $700 000+ export sales
Product line	Aerial photography—40% Mapping—30% Surveying—1% CADD—20% Commercial—9% 5–10 concurrent projects	Aerial photography—30% GIS—40% Mapping—20% Commercial/Consulting—10% 3–5 concurrent projects
Geographic coverage	Canada—100%	Canada—60% International—40%
Performance goals	Maintenance of cash flow Profit margin Protecting market share	Sales/profit growth Market penetration Technology adoption New product development Productivity
Strengths	Customer goodwill Technological expertise • aerial photography • digital imaging	Customer goodwill Active marketing Geographical diversification Flexible offer Technological expertise • digital imaging • aerial photography • system development
Weaknesses	Marketing Narrow product line Balance sheet	International exposure
Strategy	Passive	Active

INDUSTRY TRENDS

The term "geomatics" was widely used in Canada to describe a variety of fields that acquired, managed, and distributed spatially referenced data. The term was applied to generally refer to several disciplines, including the following:

- aerial photography;
- ground-based (geodetic) and aerial surveying; i.e., assessing and delimiting boundaries of land;
- mapping; i.e., cartography (map making based on ground measurements) and photogrammetry (converting photographic images and measurements into maps);
- Geographic Information Systems (GIS); i.e., computer-based systems for the storage and processing of spatial information; and
- remote sensing; i.e., satellite-borne images and measurements; quite often, airborne images were included in the remote sensing category.

The use of this general term, however, was limited to Canada. In other countries, these disciplines were referred to by their individual names. On the other hand, the term "remote sensing" was frequently used to describe all satellite and airborne observations of the earth's surface, regardless of their purpose and techniques applied.

Although traditionally distinct, these disciplines were becoming increasingly integrated due to the commonality of the computer tools employed to acquire and process spatial information, and generate the final product.

The emergence of satellite-based remote sensing had also affected the geomatics industry worldwide. Its impact on air-based services had been largely positive, despite the fact that both technologies served the same user segments. Advances in satellite technology had received a lot of publicity, which sensitized users of geomatic services to the cost advantages of remote sensing in general, and aerial photography/photogrammetry in particular. Consequently, those users who could not use satellite-based services turned to airborne imagery. In many cases, satellite trajectories limited the frequency at which information on a particular earth location could be gathered. This problem was further exacerbated by the prevalence of cloud cover over certain territories. It was expected that, despite recent plans to increase the overall number of remote-sensing satellites, aerial photography/photogrammetry would maintain its advantage in applications requiring high-resolution capabilities (aerial images could produce resolutions in a 2–3 inch range vs. a 10 m. range available from most satellites) and full-colour capabilities.

AIRVIEW'S MARKETS

In the first half of the 1990s, the Canadian geomatics industry was comprised of over 1300 firms from all geomatic disciplines, employing some 12 000 people. The largest number of firms were located in Quebec and Ontario, followed by British Columbia. The distribution of primary activities within the industry was as follows:

Major Line of Business	% of Establishments	% of Billing
Geodetic (ground) surveying	65%	53%
Mapping	9%	16%
Remote Sensing	5%	11%
Consulting	10%	4.5%
GIS	7%	12%
Other	4%	3.5%

The vast majority (86%) of geomatic firms were small establishments generating sales of less than $1 million. However, the remaining small number of larger firms generated the majority (68%) of the industry's revenues. Airview belonged to the growing category of medium-size businesses (10% of all establishments) with sales of between $1 million and $2 million.

The overall market size in Canada was estimated at $630–$650 million, and was dominated by local companies. The industry also generated some $120 million in foreign billings (mainly GIS hardware and software). Interestingly, export of services had traditionally been directed outside of North America and Europe, and concentrated in Africa, Asia, and the Middle East.

COMPETITION

Competition in the Canadian geomatics industry was on the increase. The overall economic climate, characterized by fiscal restraint in both the private and government sectors, had reduced the growth rate of the demand for services provided by the industry. As a result, geomatic companies, with their increased production capacities and reduced costs, had become more active in competing for the constant volume of business. This had resulted in a decrease in profitability. Overall industry profit levels were the same as in the early 1980s, despite a doubling of overall industry demand.

GLOBAL OPPORTUNITIES OVERVIEW

By March 1994, Rick had spent considerable time reviewing global market opportunities for his company. He had taken a general look at several foreign markets, identifying such major factors as their overall size and growth prospects, political stability and entry barriers, competition, and the availability of funding for geomatic projects.

This step had resulted in rejecting the possibility of entering Western European markets, which despite their size, were characterized by ferocious competition and limited growth prospects. Eastern Europe was felt to be too unstable politically (the countries of the former USSR), lacked funding, and was fragmented along national borders.

Rick also felt that the distances associated with dealing with markets in Southeast Asia and Oceania would put a significant strain on the company's financial and human resources, particularly in view of increasing competition from locally based companies. On the other hand, other Asian markets either lacked the size or the financing required to support Airview's long-term involvement.

Finally, he decided that Sub-Saharan Africa, although in dire need of the services offered by Airview, was either dominated by companies from their former colonial powers, or could not afford any significant level of geomatics-related development, particularly in view of the declining level of support received from international financial institutions like the World Bank.

On the other hand, Rick found the characteristics of some of the remaining regions quite interesting. Consequently, he decided to concentrate his deliberations on these markets, which included North America (the US and Mexico), Latin America, and the Arab World (North Africa and the Middle East).

American Market

The US market was somewhat different from its Canadian counterpart in that it had a larger proportion of geodetic and GIS firms among the 6300 businesses in its geomatic industry. The larger proportion of geodetic firms in the US was due to its higher population density, which increased the need for cadastral surveying. At the same time, faster adaptation of computers in a variety of industrial applications in the US had stimulated demand for GIS applications and related services.

On the other hand, in view of the relative size of the US and Canadian economies, the Canadian market was disproportionately large. The American market was estimated at $3 billion in 1994; only five times the size of its Canadian counterpart, or only half the relative difference in the size of the economies between the two countries. This disparity could be largely attributed to structural differences between the economies of the two countries. Canada's economy was largely dependent on the mineral and forestry sectors, both industries that supported a high level of geomatic activity.

The demand for geomatics services in the US market was growing at a 15% annual rate, and was particularly dynamic in the areas of airborne photography and (satellite) remote sensing, digital conversion of existing data, and consulting.

Access to US Markets

In 1994, there were few tariff obstacles when entering the US market. Previously existing barriers related to licensing and local presence requirements were being removed as a result of the passage of the North American Free Trade Agreement. In some cases, Canadian companies who had succeeded in penetrating the US market, indicated that it had been easier for them to cross the national border than to overcome provincial barriers within their home country.

Although there had been some opportunities in the US geomatics market during the 1980s, Canadian firms had traditionally been reluctant to pursue them. For aerial surveying companies like Airview, one of the reasons was the fact that American aircraft maintenance and licensing requirements were much more lenient in the US than they were in Canada. As a result, a company operating an aircraft out of Canada was not able to compete with American firms on price if there was any significant amount of flying time involved. Although these differences still remained, the recently falling value of the Canadian dollar had all but nullified the cost advantage previously enjoyed by US companies.

In general, the level of competition in the US was not much different from that in Canada except that the American firms, particularly the larger ones, marketed their services much more aggressively than their Canadian counterparts.

User Segments

It was estimated that local and state governments accounted for some 25% of the total US market for geomatics products and services, and that close to half of all local/state budgets allocated to the acquisition of geomatic services was allocated for data capture purposes.

The greatest potential lay with the 39 000 municipal/county governments. A trend to modernize land records and the registration systems which document the 118 million land parcels in the United States was the most significant factor in stimulating the demand for data capture, their conversion into a digital format, their subsequent analysis, and graphical presentation.

The average contract performed for local/state governments ranged from $60 000 to $190 000 for aerial photography/photogrammetry services. Although the northeast, southeast, southwest, and states bordering the Pacific Ocean accounted for the greatest demand, there was also an abundance of opportunities in the states closer to Airview's base, such as Minnesota (3529 local government units), North Dakota (2795), and South Dakota (1767).

Federal government agencies represented the second largest user sector, amounting to slightly less than 25% of the total US geomatic market. Digital mapping was the major area of demand within this segment. This corresponded closely to Airview's principal area of expertise.

Contracts with the federal government ranged from $30 000 for surveying projects to $1.5 million for data-digitizing projects. On average, they tended to be larger in size than those with state and local governments, and were typically awarded to larger firms. As a result of the US federal government policy of decentralizing the contracting for services, the demand from this user sector was spread across the country.

The third largest segment in the US geomatic market was the demand from regulated industries, such as communication firms and gas and electric utility companies, which traditionally generated between 20% and 25% of the overall US demand for geomatic services. Customers from this category were interested in more cost-efficient management of the large infrastructure under their administration. Consequently, they had been among the early adopters of GIS technology, and their major thrust was in implementing AM/FM (Automated Mapping and Facilities Management) systems, which combined digital maps with information on the operation of their facilities.

The utilities market for geomatic services was spread across the United States, with the size closely related to the population density of individual regions. These regional markets were dominated by large companies, such as Baymont Engineering and AT&T, which—due to economies of scale—became very price-competitive in catering to the utility sector.

Finally, the rest of the demand for geomatic services came from the private sector, with the most significant segments being the resource industries, namely mining and forestry. The rate of adoption of GIS technology in this sector was rather slow, and the remote sensing of data and basic mapping were the primary services contracted out by resource companies.

The Mexican Geomatics Market

Overview

By the early 1990s, Mexico had developed significant capabilities in geomatics. Between 40 000 and 50 000 people were employed in surveying and mapping related disciplines. Yet, in view of the country's problems with rapid urbanization, deforestation, and land use change, local demand for geomatics products and services in the early 1990s exceeded the available supply in some product and service categories.

The primary demand for geomatics services in Mexico was created by cartographic agencies of the federal and state governments. The National Institute of Statistics, Geography and Informatics (INEGI) had the primary responsibility for integrating the country's geographical data, carrying out the national mapping project, and developing the National Geographic Information System.

Each state in Mexico was responsible for undertaking and maintaining a land survey of its territory and maintaining land cadastre. Therefore, state markets were the second largest in volume after the federal market.

Several large municipalities also purchased geomatics products and services. In 1993–94, they were in the process of establishing databases of property boundaries, partly in cooperation with SEDESOL (Directorate of Cartography and Photogrammetry) under the One Hundred Cities Program.

The private sector was also a significant user of spatially referenced information. PEMEX, the state oil monopoly, was by far the largest of those users. It was also in the strongest position to acquire the most technologically advanced products and services in this area.

The total size of the Mexican market for geomatics services in 1993 was estimated at between $160 million and $200 million.

There were two cycles that affected the volume of geomatics work available in Mexico. First, there was the annual rainy season (June to September), during which the inclement weather had a negative impact on aerial surveying. Second, there was the change of Mexico's presidency every six years. As government agencies were the main purchasers of geomatic services, the political environment had a profound effect on business. In general, the first three years of any presidency resulted in minor projects, while the final three years were noted for major works.

The demand for geomatic services in Mexico was increasing. In addition, most Mexican companies competing for this business were interested in foreign participation, particularly if these relationships carried with them better technology and more modern equipment.

Mexico offered a significant operating benefit to Canadian aerial photography firms in that its weather patterns (the rainy season between May and September) counterbalanced those in Canada. This could enable Canadian exporters to utilize their aircraft and photographic equipment during the slow season in Canada (December to March).

Competition

The Mexican geomatics industry was well developed in the traditional areas of ground surveying and cartography. However, its technological and human resource capabilities in the more technical areas, such as digital mapping and GIS, were generally limited.

In the area of aerial mapping and surveying, there were about 20 companies, located principally in Mexico City. Six of these companies owned their own aircraft, and dominated the national market. The remaining 14 were quite small, did not have their own aircraft, and were fairly new to the industry.

Market Access

Public tender was the normal method for obtaining projects in Mexico. Most tenders were open to all companies, but some were by invitation only. The tendency was for contracts to go to those companies that had their own aircraft and the proper equipment. Sub-contracting was a popular way for smaller companies to obtain a portion of larger projects.

If a foreign company was awarded a contract, it had to obtain permission from the state geography department and from the Mexican Defense Department. In addition, until 1996, foreign companies were not allowed to operate aircraft over Mexican territory without local participation.

The Latin American Geomatics Market

In the early 1990s, the geomatics market in Latin America was at an early stage of transition from traditional to digital technologies for data capture, analysis, and storage. Although general awareness of GIS and remote sensing was widespread, their adoption was largely limited to international resource exploration companies and some public institutions.

The market for geomatics products and services was dominated by the public sector on both the supply and demand sides. However, the private sector was becoming the primary growth area, particularly the resource sector (agriculture, forestry, mining, and energy), where significant investment programs created demand for cadastral surveying, mapping, and GIS. This demand potential, in turn, was providing a growth opportunity for the local surveying and mapping industry. This industry had traditionally been dominated by government organizations (mostly military-controlled), which, over the previous few years, had gained a significant degree of business autonomy and were actively competing in both local and international markets.

International Financial Institutions (IFIs), such as the World Bank and the Inter-American Development Bank, were very active in Latin America. Their major concern was economic development of the region; thus they concentrated on the less-developed nations of the region. The IFIs recognized the importance of infrastructure projects and their geomatics components and provided financial support for such basic services as topographic and property mapping and cadastral information systems. As a result of this fundamental focus, the geomatics contract activity was not confined to the more economically advanced countries of the region. From the point of view of foreign-based geomatics companies attempting to enter the Latin American market, the IFI-sponsored contracts provided a very attractive opportunity since they were open for public tender.

It was anticipated that the Latin American market for geomatics products and services would grow significantly in the near term. Over the 1993–98 period, the total demand for geomatics products and services in the region was anticipated in the range of US$650 million and US$1500 million (the low and high estimates).

The provision of spatial information and its conversion to a digital format, as well as the delivery of GIS applications and the provision of training to local staff, constituted the major demand area, expected to comprise three-quarters of the region's market.

Geographic Distribution

Brazil was by far the largest market for geomatics products and services, with an estimated 50% of the total demand in the region.

Argentina, with the second largest territory and population in the region, was also the second largest market for geomatics products and services, accounting for 20% of the Latin American demand.

Chile, with its significant resource sector, was the third significant geomatics market in the region, with a 5% share of total demand.

Interestingly, Bolivia, with its relatively small population and economy, had a disproportionately large market for geomatics products and services (4% of the overall demand).

The other 13 countries of the region shared the remaining 21% of the Latin American market, with Venezuela and Colombia leading the group.

Competition

By the 1990s, Latin American companies had developed substantial capabilities in the areas of surveying and mapping. The mapping sector in the region had originated from the military and, until recent years, had been protected from foreign competition by trade barriers. Consequently, the capabilities of local firms were significant, particularly in larger countries such as Brazil and Argentina. More significantly, larger surveying and mapping companies had already invested in digital mapping technology and remote sensing. With their developed expertise and low labour and overhead costs, these firms had a significant advantage over their competitors from North America, Europe, and Australia. Their knowledge of the local market was an additional factor placing them ahead of competitors from other continents.

Larger Brazilian and Argentinean firms had used this advantage to penetrate the markets of the smaller countries of the region. Since each national market was characterized by wide fluctuations in demand, the markets in other countries provided them with an opportunity to stabilize and, possibly, expand their sales.

In view of this situation, service firms from outside the region had to compete on the basis of their technological and managerial advantage. Large-scale projects, possibly involving digital imaging, provided the best opportunity to compete with local companies.

Despite all these impediments to foreign participation in the Latin American market, European companies had succeeded in capturing a significant share of the region's business. Their success was built on the strong business network established in the region by their home countries. Their penetration strategy was to establish their presence initially (through international assistance programs and the provision of training and education), and then to develop ties with local government agencies and companies from the private sector. European firms were also characterized by their ability to form consortia to pursue larger contracts. These consortia combined European technology and equipment with local labour and market experience.

American firms had obtained a significant degree of penetration of these markets for GIS hardware and software. However, their presence in the other sectors was less pronounced, probably due to their uncompetitive cost structures.

Australian geomatics firms involved in Latin America were typically affiliated with Australia's mining and forestry companies active in resource exploration activities in the region.

The Arab World (North Africa and The Middle East)

Countries of the Arab World were characterized by the dominance of their oil and gas industries as the market for geomatics-related projects. Their economies and political systems were relatively stable and provided a good foundation for establishing long-term penetration plans by a foreign geomatics company. In terms of economic development, countries in this region were less dependent on international aid than was the case of the countries of Latin America. Consequently, their approach to the development of topographic, cadastral, and administrative mapping was based more on long-term planning.

With generally higher levels of resource allocation, countries of this region had developed their own companies, typically originating from the national cartographic agencies. In the early 1990s, these agencies still dominated the industry in the region, employing from 30% to 60% of the total number of personnel working in the geomatics field. However, their role had steadily declined over the past few years.

At the same time, the level of saturation of the industry with locally based manpower differed significantly among individual countries. Egypt, Iran, Jordan, Kuwait, Lebanon, Qatar, Syria, and Tunisia each had a substantial number of local specialists in the field (relative to their populations and territory), whereas Algeria, Libya, Iraq, Saudi Arabia, and Yemen had rather limited geomatics capability. Even more significantly, this latter group also had a relatively low proportion of geomatics specialists with university education.

The combined market size for geomatics services in the region was estimated at between $400 million and $600 million in the commercial sector. Some of the markets restricted foreign access. Libya and Iraq, for example, were not open to Canadian companies. Also, Syria, with its militarized economy, was of limited attractiveness to Canadian companies.

Iran was the country with the best opportunity for geomatics firms. The climate for Canadian firms was favourable due to Canada's position as a politically non-involved country and the technological advancement of the Canadian geomatics industry.

Major opportunities in Iran were associated with several national development programs in the areas of energy production (construction of hydro-electric and nuclear power stations and upgrading the country's power distribution system), expansion of the mining industry (production of iron ore, copper, aluminum, lead, zinc, and coal), the oil and gas sectors, and construction of the country's railway system.

Kuwait and Saudi Arabia had traditionally been the target markets for several Canadian geomatics firms. The expansion of the two countries' oil production and refining capacity had triggered major investment outlays in both countries (for a total of over $20 billion between 1992 and 1994) and would continue (albeit at a slower rate) for a number of years. These two national markets were dominated by American companies, and any penetration effort there would require cooperation with Canadian firms from the construction, mining, or oil and gas sectors.

Tunisia represented an example of a country which had developed its own expertise in the area of cartography, which, in turn, had created demand for external assistance in the provision of more sophisticated products and services, such as digital mapping and GIS applications.

Egypt represented yet another type of geomatics market in the region. Its major thrust was now on environmental concerns. The country had developed an environmental action plan which addressed problems with water and land resources management, air pollution, marine and coastal resources, and global heritage preservation, all of which had a significant geomatic component. The cost of implementing phase 1 of the plan was estimated at some $300 million over the period of 1993–1995.

Egypt also provided opportunities created by a $3 billion power generation and distribution project, and some $2 billion in construction projects associated with the expansion of the country's gas production and oil processing capacity. Although the majority of work in the geomatics-related field was conducted by local companies, sub-contracting opportunities were significant.

Egypt was also a significant market from another perspective. Historically, Egypt had exported its geomatics expertise to other Arab states. Consequently, penetration of this market could be used to leverage access to other markets in the region, particularly in conjunction with Egyptian partners.

Market Evaluation

In order to evaluate each of the four geographic regions from Airview's perspective, Rick developed a summary of the primary characteristics of each market under consideration. This summary is presented in Exhibit 34-2.

Exhibit 34-2 Market Review

Markets Characteristics	The US	Mexico	Latin America	North Africa and The Middle East
Economic and Political Environment	Stable	Stabilizing	Stabilizing	Fluctuating
Access Restrictions	None	Local agent required No flying in Mexico	All mapping on-site in Brazil	Language Culture
Market Size	Large	Small	Medium	Medium–large
Entry and Operating Costs	Low	Medium	Medium	Medium–high
Growth	Slow, stable	High	High	High
Financing	Cash, immediate	Transfer, delays	Transfer problems IFIs	Ranging from cash to IFIs financing
Contract Procurement	Transparent, fair	Ambiguous, improving	Frequently ambiguous	Ambiguous
Major Products	Digital mapping, GIS	Cadastral mapping, GIS	Topographic and cadastral mapping	Topographic mapping Surveying
Long-Term Advantage (technology, expertise)	Limited advantage	Diminishing, but not disappearing	Slowly diminishing	Sustainable
Primary Customers	State and municipal governments	Federal and state governments	Federal governments Resource sector	Central cartographic agencies Resource sector
Pricing	Competitive, but based on high local costs	Competitive, based on low local costs	Extremely competitive, based on low local costs	Relatively high
Competition	Local, very high	Local, US, high	Local, international, extremely high	Local, international, moderate
Entry Strategies	Direct bidding, local partner	Local partner or subsidiary	Network of agents or local partner IFIs projects	Local partner or agent IFIs projects
Strategic Advantages	Close, similar to the Canadian market	Entry to South America, Technological advantage Active during Canadian slack	Technological fit, Active during Canadian slack	Technological advantage Growing Less competition Long-term prospects
Expansion Opportunities	GIS consulting systems integration	Acquisition of local subsidiary	Training	CIDA project Libya after restrictions

He also reviewed several ways of establishing Airview's presence in the regional/national markets, as indicated in Exhibit 34-3.

Exhibit 34-3 Airview—Entry Strategies

Project-Oriented Penetration

This is a strategy suitable for small, niche-oriented firms. The company would have to target a specific area and seek a specific contract. Involvement would be limited to the scope of the specific contract. The main barrier to this approach could be associated with local presence requirements.

Establishing a network of local agents in the countries of interest in the region may provide access to information on upcoming tenders and allow for participation in the bidding process. Bidding for local contracts may serve as a foundation for establishing the company's presence in the region and could be treated as part of an entry strategy.

Subcontracting to Local Firms

This strategy offered the advantage of overcoming local presence restrictions.

Strategic Alliances

An alliance with a Canadian or foreign partner can work quite effectively, provided the firms complement one another in resources and business philosophies.

Establishment of Branch Office

This could be an effective way of overcoming local presence restrictions, provided the firm was sufficiently financed to undertake the costs of setting up such an operation. The choice of location would also be crucial in determining the success of such a venture.

A Corporate Buy-Out

This seemed a somewhat risky proposition, requiring both adequate financing, business acumen to succeed, and lack of restrictions on foreign ownership of local companies. If successful, however, the result would be an immediate presence in the selected market.

Establishment of Head Office Outside of Canada

Although this could enable a company to access the selected market, this possibility could only be considered for large and stable markets, such as the US.

Foreign Ownership

Like the strategic alliance option, this can offer opportunities, particularly with US firms, provided this route is in keeping with the long-term goals of that firm and the two firms are compatible.

Alliances with Local Geomatics Firms

An alliance with a local partner could be beneficial if based on the combination of local experience and inexpensive labour with Airview's equipment and data-processing and mapping capabilities.

Joint Ownership of a Local Company

Acquiring a local company in partnership with another Canadian company may provide some advantages if the partners' product lines complement each other. A provider of GIS software or system integrator may be a good candidate for joint ownership with Airview.

DISCUSSION

Regarding the choice of Airview's optimum target area, Rick assumed that once he had arrived at a sensible, coherent marketing plan, Airview could apply for financial support from the government. In fact, he had already discussed this possibility with Western Economic Diversification (WED) and the Federal Business Development Bank (FBDB). In addition, he could expect some assistance from the Program for Export Market Development if he chose to establish an office or participate in bidding for projects in a selected market. This assistance could cover 50% of the cost of travel and setting up a permanent foreign office.

His overall concerns included not only the immediate costs of implementing his marketing plan but also the process he should use to select the best market in view of its salient characteristics and the company's goals.

Rick's view of the American market was generally positive. His major concern was with price competition from local firms and possible fluctuations in the exchange rate, which over a short period of time might undermine Airview's cost structure. At the same time, he felt that Airview's technological advantage in the US was less significant than in other markets. Finally, he assumed that his best opportunity south of the border would be in GIS-related areas, which would require either a substantial investment in obtaining greater expertise in this area or a joint effort with a GIS company.

The Mexican market was also viewed positively, particularly after the flight restrictions are lifted in 1996. However, Rick felt that due to the high cost of his staff, Airview would probably be competitive only in complex projects involving both data capture and their conversion into a computer format. At the same time, he was attracted by the operating advantages of having the company's flying season extended beyond the current few summer months.

Latin America seemed to be too competitive to support Airview's solo entry. On the other hand, the region's fragmentation into many small national markets, could prove challenging from an operating point of view. Rick felt that seeking an alliance with Canadian mining and resource companies, thereby successfully establishing their operations, might prove to be attractive, particularly if Airview's entry could be supported by the provision of some elements of GIS. As in Mexico's case, the countries of Latin America provided the possibility of operating the company's aircraft during the Canadian off-season.

Finally, Rick regarded the markets of the Arab world with particular interest. Airview would definitely have a technical advantage over its local competitors in these markets. At the same time, pricing in this region seemed to be generally less competitive than in the other areas, whereas the similarity of the individual national markets, in most cases based on the demand created by the resource sector, would allow for gradual penetration of the region. As well, Rick realized that Airview's lack of experience in international markets in general, and in the Arab world in particular, would create a very challenging situation for the company's staff.

ENDNOTE

1. A specialized technique for defining an accurate three-dimensional coordinate system for determining the location and dimensions of objects on the earth's surface.

35

THE RIVERSIDE MOTOR INN

Ian Spencer

October 1, 1997

TO: Heidi Smith
             Senior Lounge Hostess

FROM: Ronald Veinot
             General Manager

SUBJECT: Chapters Lounge

Welcome to the staff of the Riverside Motor Inn. Your six years experience at The Little Brown Jug lounge in Lunenburg, your infectious enthusiasm, and your strong customer/service orientation all suggest great promise for success. I am looking forward to working with you. By the way, I just moved to Bridgewater myself in March, so the whole operation is relatively new to me as well.

    As we discussed at your interview, in time I want you to regard Chapters Lounge as your own business. For at least the first nine months, however, I'd like to work closely with you and review and approve your plans. If everything goes well, independence, profit sharing, and promotion to manager could be just around the corner. To assist you in understanding Chapters' situation, I have assembled the following summary of operations, recent results, and recent strategies. I hope you don't mind point form.

This case was written by Ian Spencer, Professor of Marketing at St. Francis Xavier University. Copyright ©1998. Some disguise has been introduced but the essence of the decision-making situation is uncompromised. Reprinted with permission.

- The Riverside Motor Inn was built in 1975 and has 34 rooms on two floors, all within one building. For the fiscal year ended November 30, 1996, occupancy totalled 7800 room nights at an average rate of $55.00. The Inn operates at capacity (almost) during July, August, and September. Our 50 seat dining-room, The Sou' Wester, is open daily from 7:00 a.m. to 2:00 p.m. and 5:00 to 9:00 p.m. Sales last year were $175 000 and will be about the same this year. The Sou' Wester, as you may recall, is across the lobby from Chapters Lounge.

- This summer the owners invested over $250 000 creating a new front entrance and lobby area, and dramatically renovating both Chapters and The Sou' Wester. Unfortunately, as I think I mentioned, Chapters had to close for almost all of May and June to accommodate the renovations.

- Chapters Lounge contains 30 seats and is open Monday to Saturday from 4:00 p.m. to 12:30 a.m. During the past three fiscal years, sales have been $63 300 (1994), $75 700 (1995) and $66 700 (1996). Cost of goods sold has been constant at 36% of sales and direct labour has been constant at about $18 000.

- Chapters Lounge offers a quiet, comfortable, relaxing alternative to "the bar scene." The seating is padded bar stools, armchairs, loveseats, and a couch. The lounge's seven square tables are solid wood. The colour scheme is burgundy and forest green, with pastel accent colours, dusty rose, and pale green. This summer we began using the slogan, "Conversation Without Shouting" to promote Chapters Lounge to guests of the Riverside Inn (signs in the lobby and notices in guests' rooms) and to residents of the community (three ads in the local weekly paper). By virtue of its name, décor, size, rich colour scheme, and overall ambiance, Chapters Lounge is unique in the area.

- In fiscal 1996, sales from drinks were beer 69%, liquor 30%, and wine 1%. Gross profit margins (markups) were beer 60%, liquor 73%, and wine 50%. Average retail prices were beer $3.00, liquor (including cocktails) $3.75, and wine $3.25. Sales from drinks was 95% of total revenue. The other 5% was packaged food items (peanuts, chips, etc.), prepared food items (from our kitchen), and cigarettes. I suspect these figures are pretty much the same this year.

- Happy Hour at Chapters now runs from 4:30–8:00 p.m. (it used to run from 5:00–7:00 p.m.). Beer is $2.80 per bottle and liquor (excluding cocktails) is $3.25 per 1½ oz. shot. The three largest bars/taverns in the area also have Happy Hours:
  - Len's Place—A country and western bar/lounge (seating for 125); 4:00-7:30 p.m.; beer $2.75, liquor $2.75.
  - Chevy's—A rock 'n' roll (50s–60s) bar/lounge (seating for 200); 4:00-9:30 p.m.; beer $2.75, liquor $2.75.
  - Pirate's Pub—Turn-of-the-century pirate theme, German cuisine (seating for 400); 4:00–7:00 p.m.; beer $2.75, liquor $2.75.

  All have dance floors, "pub food" type meals, and feature live entertainment on a fairly regular basis.

- Chapters' revenue by month in calendar 1996 was:

Jan.	$ 5 055
Feb.	5 133
Mar.	5 146
1st Qtr.	$15 334
Apr.	$ 6 345
May	6 486
Jun	7 405
2nd Qtr.	$20 236
Jul.	$ 6 071
Aug.	4 843
Sept.	5 273
3rd Qtr.	$16 187
Oct.	$ 4 902
Nov.	4 673
Dec.	5 327
4th Qtr.	$14 902

- Revenue in 1997 has been disappointing. During the seven months Chapters was open every day (January to April and July to September), revenue averaged $3140 per month. I think most of the decrease can be traced to the departure of "D.J.," a longtime bartender who moved to Calgary in December 1996, and to the hype surrounding the opening of Pirate's Pub in January 1997.

- Volume improved modestly in August ($3708) and September ($4350), but is still well below the same months in 1996. Recently, newspaper ads have urged the public to rediscover Chapters Lounge by featuring free hors d'oeuvres (value $3–5 per table), the new 210-minute happy hour, and the new slogan. As well, we sent out about 200 flyers to local groups suggesting they consider Chapters for group outings.

- I must confess I haven't had a chance to examine the lounge in any detail, given the renovations and the need to adapt to new systems and people. It seems to me though that patrons will tend to be:

  - Overnight guests at the Riverside Inn.

  - The 50 or so local groups that rented our meeting room (capacity 20).

  - Residents who work in or near Bridgewater (about 4000 people) who may want to go out for a drink—usually in groups—after work.

  - Couples, or groups of couples, who want a social drink or two prior to or after some event in the community (banquet, concert, play, movie, sporting event); Bridgewater seems to be a very active community. I estimate that at least twice a week there's something going on with audiences typically from 100–400, but occasionally as large as 2000 for major sporting events.

- Members of area organizations, clubs, and groups (there must be 300–400 of them) who want to go out for a drink after a meeting or special event.
- Anybody else who might want a quiet drink (a rather poorly defined group I admit).
- Some additional numbers you may find helpful are:
  - The population of Bridgewater is about 7500 (2600 households); Lunenburg County (including Bridgewater) about 48 000 (13 900 households); the Bridgewater trading area about 60 000 (20 700 households).
  - About 500 000 tourists (incremental visitors) pass by or through Bridgewater every May to October.
  - Across Canada, in 1996, average annual household spending on alcoholic beverages served on licensed premises was:

	Average Expenditure per Household	Percentage Reporting Any Such Spending
Beer	$118	36%
Liquor	38	18
Wine and Cider	35	25
Total	$191	49%

Heidi, I believe we can rebuild volume with good strategies and good implementation. But, I'm realistic. The ambiance of Chapters, the availability of acceptable alternatives, and the fact that a high percentage of social drinking is party-oriented suggests a ceiling on revenue. During the next week or so, could you please spend some time thinking about what we might do to rebuild volume. I'd be willing to invest the full contribution (after labour) from October 1997 to June 1998 if you think that would be necessary and appropriate.

Do you think we could hit $100 000 in the year 2000? I look forward to your size-up of the situation, your insights, and your recommended objectives and plans.

36

PANTRY PRIDE STORES

H.F. (Herb) MacKenzie

Brenda Howley was a marketing consultant in Somewhere, Alberta. She and her husband, Cameron Porter, a prominent corporate tax lawyer, earned a combined income of over $250 000 (before taxes). They had two small children, both under five years of age.

Brenda enjoyed grocery shopping as it gave her a break from her professional and family obligations. She referred to it as "mindless" work, but she prided herself on being good at it. Brenda usually alternated between two major grocery chains in her town, Pantry Pride Stores and Freshway.

Following a series of dissatisfying experiences at one of her regular grocery stores, she decided to write to the company president. Her letter is shown in Exhibit 36-1.

When she finished writing her letter, Brenda mailed a copy to the president. She then decided to visit Pantry Pride for one of her regular shopping trips, and she took a carbon copy of the letter, intending to personally deliver it to the store manager.

EXHIBIT 36-1   Letter to President of Pantry Pride Stores

October 23, 1998

16 Eden Loch Road
Somewhere, AB
T9E 3Z8

President
Pantry Pride Stores
555 Garden Place
Mississauga, ON
L9Q 8Y8

Dear Sir or Madam:

I write you today because I have been a customer of Pantry Pride Stores for over 30 years, but I am increasingly disturbed by a series of experiences I have had at the Victoria Street location in our town.

Over the past year, I have been charged incorrect prices at the checkouts seven times —three times at your competitor, Freshway, and four times at Pantry Pride. I must say, I admire the response I received each time at Freshway, and I have left your store dissatisfied each time. Let me recount some of my experiences for you so that you might appreciate the difference between what I have experienced at both stores.

My first experience was at Freshway. I had purchased a 2-litre container of ice cream. When I went through the checkout, I was overcharged $0.50. The ice cream was supposed to be on sale for $2.59, but the scanner read the regular price of $3.09. I complained to the woman at the service desk, and she insisted that I accept a full refund of $2.59. I told her I would be happy to simply get my $0.50, but she insisted that it was store policy that when customers get charged the wrong price at the check-out, they get a full refund and get the item free of charge. She refunded my money, apologized for the mistake, and asked me to please return to the store for my future grocery needs. Since then, I have had two similar experiences at Freshway.

Now, I will recount four experiences at your store. My first experience was about a year ago. I was overcharged $1.00 on a bottle of olive oil. I took it to the service desk and advised the woman there that I had been overcharged for the item. At that point, I did not know that you had a similar policy to Freshway, and I did not care as I was perfectly willing to settle for a $1.00 refund. However, the woman on the service desk asked another employee standing nearby to check the price. The second woman seemed visibly displeased that someone should ask her to do a price check, and that may explain her subsequent behaviour. I watched her stop to talk to one of the cashiers on her way to the grocery aisle, and when she finally disappeared down the aisle and failed to return after about 10 minutes, I went to see if she were still there. She was having a personal conversation with another shopper, so I returned to wait at the service desk to see how long the whole process would take. During this period, I read your sign that explained store policy with respect to overcharged prices. Eventually, when the woman returned from doing her price check, she did not address me at all, but simply said to the woman at the service desk, "She's right. Give missus a buck." As you

EXHIBIT 36-1 **Letter to President of Pantry Pride Stores (continued)**

might expect, I was quite upset with the process at this point, and I took further exception to being called "missus." I immediately informed her that I recognized her as a long-time employee of Pantry Pride Stores, and that I would have expected her to know her store policy better than me. I told her I would be pleased to explain it to her if she had not had the opportunity to read it. I grudgingly got a refund on the item.

With respect to my second experience, I admit the error was partly mine. I saw a sign that advertised white onions on special, and I decided to buy one. When I got to the checkout, I was charged a higher price than the advertised special. I asked that the price be checked, and the cashier held it in the air and asked one of the male employees who was nearby to check the price. His comment was, "One onion! &$*%#!" I mentioned to the cashier that he appeared to be having a bad day and her comment was, "Oh. That's just Ken. He's always having a bad day." The result after the price check was that the price charged was correct. Apparently, I just took a large white onion from under the sign that advertised white onions, but I really had a Spanish onion (as were all of the others under the sign). I simply paid the price and left.

On the third occasion, which occurred less than two months ago, I noticed the service desk was very busy and, to save time, I remarked to the cashier that I should get an item free as it was scanned at the checkout at a price higher than advertised. She tried to tell me that as I had not paid for the item, she could simply adjust the price. When I insisted that was unacceptable as she did not catch the error, she called over a supervisor who asked the same question, "Did she pay for it yet?" When told no, she instructed the cashier to adjust the price. I objected again, and the store manager was called for a third opinion. He agreed with me that the store policy stated that the customer would receive any item free if it scanned at a price higher than advertised at the checkout, and he instructed the cashier to deduct the item from the sale. He remarked to the two women, "Remember, we talked about this last week." I left the store thinking that customer service improvements were about to be made.

Unfortunately, late one evening last week, I had my most dissatisfying experience. When overcharged by a young man at the cash register, he asked another cashier (who happened to be the same one I had my previous experience with) what he should do. She told him to give me $0.50 and to put a note in the cash register and someone would fix it in the morning. I informed her that I was more knowledgeable with respect to store policy than she was, and that she should get some additional training as we had already been through this about a month previously. Her remark, in front of a dozen customers, was "We were told by the manager not to mention this policy unless the customer mentions it first."

That was very unsettling. First, it indicates that this store grudgingly implements store policy, and only for those customers who know what it is and who insist on it. It further implies that employees at this store are willing to take advantage of less knowledgeable customers, or those customers who are less likely or unwilling to complain. In my view, this is very unethical marketing behaviour. It is also disturbing that someone in a management position in your company supports that employees will, unknowingly or, worse, knowingly, act in an unethical manner with respect to your customers. Those employees who realize that they are being asked to behave

EXHIBIT 36-1   Letter to President of Pantry Pride Stores (continued)

unethically may be uncomfortable doing so and, in a better economic climate, may seek employment elsewhere.

I apologize for the length of my discourse, but I want you to be aware that the problem you have at this location is not an acute one. When I talked last year to the president of one of Canada's largest hotel chains, he explained his philosophy of customer guarantees to me. I recall he commented, that for them to be effective, customers must know what the guarantees are, they must receive compensation when the company fails with respect to its promises, and employees must see that the company pays when they fail. I would suggest that you either scrap this store policy, or that you train your managers as to why it is important and why it should be implemented properly.

Sincerely,

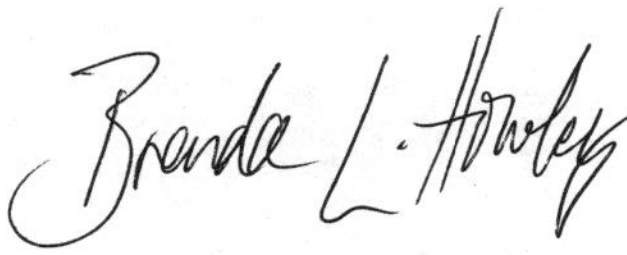

Brenda L. Howley

Brenda L. Howley

c.c.   Manager, Pantry Pride Stores
Somewhere, AB

TORONTO DOOR & TRIM

Donna Bernachi, John Blackie, and David S. Litvack

INTRODUCTION

Gerry, accompanied by his friend John, was waiting around inside his newly leased building in Markham, Ontario, surveying the layout (see Exhibit 37-1).

"What do you think? Isn't it great? I like it more than the old building in Scarborough, where I was for two years. It has the same amount of warehouse space, but it is better laid out. I can now use a forklift instead of doing everything by hand. This really saves me time. At the front there is an office and a service counter where I can deal with the contractors, and there is a large empty area in front of the counter."

"Gerry, it looks bigger than the old place."

"That's right, it is larger than the one I had in Scarborough, and of course, more expensive. The rent here is an additional $1500 per month. I'm either going to have to sell more doors or else cut costs to be able to afford this place. I thought that if I used the whole building for warehousing, then I could sell doors to more contractors. But the dividing walls in the front are well built and would be expensive and difficult to move. A contractor friend of mine estimated that the cost would be around $15 000 to remove the walls and renovate the area. What do you think John?"

"Well, it looks like the front area was used as display space by the former tenant," John replied. "Maybe you can use the area to show contractors what products you offer. Or,

EXHIBIT 37-1 Layout of New Building

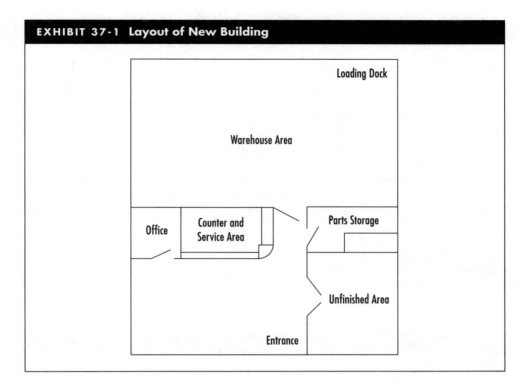

instead, concentrate on selling your doors retail and bid on a few jobs from the larger contractors in Toronto.

Gerry responded, "The retail market has some interesting possibilities. A lot of people renovate their homes themselves, especially now during this recession. John, you've just finished your MBA, you could probably come up with some good ideas. What would you do with the extra space?"

TORONTO DOOR & TRIM

Toronto Door & Trim was started by Gerry Brown in January of 1992 as a wholesale business, selling interior doors, wood trim, and casements to small contractors who build residential homes and small apartments. The product line offered consists of three categories:

1. Standard interior doors and accessories (door handles, hinges, and so on)
2. Specialty doors: French doors (solid wood and bevelled glass); closet doors (mirrored, sliding, and so on)
3. Wood mouldings and trim (required to finish the interior of residential and commercial buildings)

The doors are sold to small contractors in Toronto and surrounding areas. The new location is quite attractive, situated on the outskirts of the city across from a major nursery, which has a large clientele. It is easily reached by highway; a convenience for the customers since they can avoid travelling through the congested downtown traffic.

Gerry buys the doors and frames separately. He assembles the doors in the frames and sells them pre-hung to small contractors. This extra service saves the contractors installation time on the job site. He also offers measurement on-site, delivery, and credit for the return of leftover products. According to Gerry, it is this high level of service that differentiates him from his competitors. This service and the quality products offered are what he feels have made him successful to date.

The current gross margin on products is 33%. Gerry estimates products sold to large developers would yield gross margins of about 20% to 25%, and that retail gross margins would be 60% to 75%. (Exhibit 37-2 shows the Income Statement and the cost and selling prices of various doors.)

Although Toronto Door & Trim was opened during the recession period, Gerry's familiarity with the contractors in the area has contributed to the company's success to date. Before opening this business, he worked as a salesperson for a wholesaler of building products for ten years.

The staff consists of two employees who assemble the doors, and one commissioned salesperson who deals directly with the contractors. Most of the sales and marketing is done by Gerry himself. Should he decide to enter the retail market, an extra employee to serve at the counter would be necessary, and this would cost an additional $400 per week. He might also need to advertise to create some awareness.

Exhibit 37-2 Income Statement and Price List

Income Statement

	Standard	Specialty	Trim	Total
Sales Revenue	$850 000	$50 000	$300 000	$1 200 000
COGS	600 000	25 000	175 000	800 000
Gross Margin	250 000	25 000	125 000	400 000
Other Expenses				375 000
Net Income				$ 25 000
Total Assets	$400 000			
Total Debt	$265 000			

Note: Other Expenses includes the wage Gerry pays himself.

Price List

	Cost	Wholesale	Retail
Standard Interior Door	$ 60	$ 75	$ 80
Closet Door (Sliding Mirror)	$ 70	$105	$125
French Door (Oak & Bevelled Glass)*	$120	$225	$260
French Door (Oak & Stained Glass)	$230	—	$500

*Available from supplier of bevelled glass doors. Retail price includes finishing door.

CUSTOMERS

Most of the sales of Toronto Door & Trim are to the small contractors involved in building small apartments and residential developments. These contractors look for quality products at low prices and expect a high level of service from Gerry and his staff. However, price is the main determining factor when making a purchase.

Targeting the larger contractors, who build large apartment and row housing developments, is a feasible way for Gerry to increase sales. These customers have some similarities to his current market. However, low price becomes even more important with the larger contractors as does prompt delivery and the installation of precuts. These customers can be quite demanding at times, and they constantly seek ways to reduce costs.

The retail market consists of homeowners who are doing their own home renovations or are acting as their own contractors. Aside from quality products at a reasonable price, this group seeks service, advice, and a wide selection of products. Installation would be offered on an as-required basis.

COMPETITORS

Competition on the wholesale side of the business consists of both large warehouse-style stores and smaller specialty stores. Lumber yards like Beaver Lumber are currently serving the retail market. They can sell doors at a competitive price because their volumes are high, but they do not offer a very wide selection of products. In Scarborough and the surrounding area, there are about 15 companies other than Toronto Door & Trim that specialize in or offer doors as part of their product lines as industrial distributors to smaller contractors.

Entry barriers into this industry are minimal as a result of relatively low capital requirements to start operations, simple technology, and a relatively modest level of expertise and skills required.

INDUSTRY

Wholesale

This industry's activities have always closely followed cyclical trends in the level of new housing construction, as well as interest in do-it-yourself and contracted renovation projects. Studies have shown that the small size and urban market dependency of most companies in this industry make it especially vulnerable to competitive market forces. The ability to give close personal attention to customers' needs, especially in urban centres, is important to a firm's success.

The recession, which started in 1991, brought an abrupt decline in the number of new housing starts. As fewer homes are built, fewer contractors need Gerry's products. However, at the same time, the potential for the retail market to remain unchanged during recessionary times exists, as an interest in do-it-yourself or contracted renovations is sparked. Renovations can give your home a new look at a lower cost than buying a new home (see Exhibit 37-3).

Exhibit 37-3 Renovations Help Take Up the Slack

New kitchens and bathrooms will make up a large part of building activity over the next year. Renovation spending is on the rise, several construction forecasters predicted recently, although the outlook for housing starts across the nation remains bleak.

Peter Anderson, principal of Toronto-based Andersen & Associates, called 1993 the "worst year in this [business] cycle in terms of housing starts." He said about 150 000 new homes will probably be built this year, followed by some recovery in 1994, with a high of 168 000 forecast. Renovations are expected to increase this year and next, but figures are deceiving, Anderson said. He explained that this is because so much renovation work forms part of the so-called underground economy—cash payments permit both homeowner and builder to avoid the goods and services tax.

Canada Mortgage & Housing Corp. said last week that it projects a 3.5% increase in renovation spending to $17.5 billion in 1994 from $16.8 billion this year [1993].

But a recent study by the Canadian Home Builders Association said at least 45% of all building and renovation activity takes place in the underground economy and is not reported.

Current low interest rates are a major factor in the upswing expected in renovations, Anderson said. "People are refinancing their five-year mortgages, and with the rates [expected to be at] about 8% next spring instead of 12% in 1988, there's financing room for those thinking about redoing their kitchens or bedrooms," the real estate analyst told the recent CanaData construction forecasting conference.

Demographics may also work in favour of renovators. As people get older and their children grow up, they are more likely to make improvements to their homes. Anderson estimates about 60% of houses in Canada are more than 15 years old.

Gerry Proulx, CMHC's chief economist, agreed that as housing starts and sales of existing homes begin to increase next year [1994], renovation activity should also rise. "Home sales tend to boost the renovation market because many improvement projects are done shortly before and immediately after a house is sold," he said. This represents at least a glimmer of hope for the construction industry, which has been devastated by the collapse of the real estate market in the late 1980s.

The Canadian Construction Association estimated that 120 000 workers have lost their jobs in the past five years. Anderson said homeowners will fuel the renovation market, not work on multiple units. He added that as more people switch to working at home, he sees a niche for home-office building or refurbishing.

David Ellis, vice-president of Royal LePage Appraisal & Consulting Services, said there may be some renovation work in commercial real estate as well. "You need to keep your tenants happy or they won't stay," he said. "This bodes well for the renovation and retrofit markets, but it will be offset by the fact that 50% of office space has been built in the last 10 years."

Source: Written by Joanne Chiavello. *Financial Post*, October 6, 1993, p. 14.

Retail

The retail market is served in two ways: by large warehouse-type stores and high-end specialty stores. Nothing really exists to serve the segment between these two types of stores. The main renovation seasons are in the fall and the spring. The industry does experience price competition.

The aging population is expected to present large opportunities in all retail sectors. As children leave the home, homeowners find that they have more funds available for home renovations.

Another factor affecting this industry is the slow recovery from the current recession. Large numbers of job losses over the past few years have caused consumers to tighten their purse strings. Buyer confidence is slow to return, and this is hampering the recovery.

DECISION

John sat staring at the information he had gathered about Toronto Door & Trim, wishing he had paid more attention during his marketing courses. John wondered what recommendations he should present to Gerry.

TREMCO LTD.

Marvin Ryder

In the spring of 1991, Paul Sagar, Tremco Marketing Manager, felt that a full re-examination of Mono Foam was in order. He had been with the company since 1989 and had not participated in the first business plan for this insulating spray foam product. His objectives were to: (1) grow sales volume and market share for Mono Foam; (2) improve Mono Foam's profitability; and (3) increase the total market for insulating foams. The latter was a risky move. If he was able to cause consumers to buy more insulating foam, they could decide to buy one of his competitor's cheaper products rather than Mono Foam.

PRODUCT BACKGROUND

Tremco Ltd. manufactured and distributed protective coatings, sealants for consumers and industrial applications, roofing and flooring systems for building maintenance and construction, autobody sealants, and adhesives. The company was founded in 1928 by William Treuhouf of Cleveland, Ohio. Over time, the company grew internationally, coming to Canada in 1962. In 1979, Tremco was sold to BF Goodrich, which maintained it intact as an operating division. By 1991, the company employed 410 people in Canada, with manufacturing sites in Toronto, Montreal, and Quebec City. It also had an extensive Canadian distribution network with centres in Montreal, Calgary, Edmonton, Halifax, Vancouver, Toronto, and Winnipeg.

The Consumer Products Division was unique to Canadian operations. No consumer products were sold in the United States and only limited numbers of consumer products were available in Australia and Sweden. The first consumer product in 1962 was Tremclad rust paint, which could be applied directly to metal surfaces and effectively controlled rusting. Later in the 1960s, the company added Instant Patch—a consumer roof repair product. In 1981, it launched Mono caulking products. Each of these was a successful product in the Industrial Division applied to consumer markets.

Annually, a small executive delegation from Tremco attends the North American Hardware Trade Show in Chicago, Illinois, looking for new product ideas and monitoring competitor innovations. In 1987, while touring the cramped lower floor of the show where small companies hope to win sales of recently developed new products, Tremco's Canadian executives discovered the booth of Foam-o, a manufacturer from Norton, Ohio. It had created an insulating spray foam. Foam-o was primarily a private labeller (i.e., it had no brand of its own, opting instead to place the labels of other companies on its products). Executives quickly discovered that Foam-o had no Canadian presence and that the company would agree to give Tremco exclusive rights to distribute the product in Canada. Foam-o was even willing to add a non-competition clause which ensured that it would not try to enter the Canadian market either directly or indirectly (i.e., through an American reseller). Knowing that no Canadian firm manufactured insulating spray foam, all of these terms excited Tremco executives. The product would not be available in the Industrial Division, making it the first exclusive product for the Consumer Products Group in Canada.

Though insulating spray foam was first introduced to Canada in 1982, by 1987 there were four companies selling expanding insulating foam in an aerosol format. Insulating spray foam was used to seal drafts behind baseboards, around wall vents for dryers and fans, and to fill cracks around window installations. When sprayed, the sticky foam expanded to fill empty spaces and then dried to form a semi-rigid barrier to air flow. Three brands, Great Stuff, Foam-it, and Touch 'n' Foam, were imported from the United States, while the fourth, Sista, was imported from Germany. Tremco had followed the progress of this product line as it was given limited shelf facing in the caulking section of hardware, building supply, and mass merchandising stores. This placed it near Tremco's number one selling caulking product—Mono. However, unit volumes compared to caulking sales were less than one to twenty.

The plan was quite simple. In 1988, Tremco would import Foam-o's product. The Mono brand name was extended and the product was called Mono Foam (Mono Mousse in Quebec). This line extension was supported by a limited amount of advertising in trade publications. Distribution in retail stores was gained through Tremco's national sales force and on the strength of the Mono brand name. For Tremco, this was an easy decision. Tremco had an excellent warehousing and distribution system. It did not incur any new product development costs. There was no additional overhead other than working capital required for inventory.

Using a premium pricing system, Tremco was able to achieve a 30% contribution margin. This meant that Mono Foam sold for about $8.00 a can at retail—about the same price as Sista and twice the price of Great Stuff, Foam-it, and Touch 'n' Foam. If consumers were not willing to pay the premium price, Tremco was prepared to withdraw from the market. Nonetheless, the chance of losing money on the project was low.

THE SITUATION IN 1991

For Mono Foam, sales peaked in 1988 and over the next two years remained unchanged. Apart from some modest trade advertising and sales force support, there had been no marketing investment in the product. Communication with the consumer consisted of exposure only— through an attractive rack and an available information brochure. This approach was not unusual as no competitor supported its brand with anything more than infrequent trade discounts common to the industry. Foam-it and Touch 'n' Foam supplemented their low price approach with a manufacturer's agent who targeted smaller independent hardware stores. Sista and Great Stuff were larger competitors that were new and unknown to Tremco. Both had succeeded in getting exposure in chain hardware stores—most notably Canadian Tire.

Although positioned as the quality leader, Mono Foam placed third in market share for 1988, 1989, and 1990 (see Figure 38-1). As a result, Mono Foam's performance was seen as little more than a line extension that generated only a limited operating income. The market size, measured in the number of cans sold, also remained stable and was virtually unaffected by the introduction of Mono Foam. Perhaps the biggest problem for Mono Foam was the unwillingness expressed by Canadian Tire to put the product on its shelves. By not achieving full retail distribution, the product was not exposed to all potential customers. Canadian Tire accounted for 25% to 30% of all hardware sales to consumers in Canada.

As part of the re-examination of Mono Foam, Paul Sagar's first step was to visit Foam-o in Ohio. He discovered that in Europe insulating spray foam had a thirty-year history, though in North America the product was barely ten years old. Based on his knowledge of the use of caulking, one would expect no difference in demand for spray foam between North American and European consumers. However, Europeans were consuming five to ten times the volume of product. Foam-o convinced Paul that the market had a need for the product and that, in North America, the product could be in the primary stages of a growth cycle.

His second step was to gather market information. Sales to consumers acting as "do-it-yourselfers" accounted for 90% of volume. The other 10% was sold to small contractors. No market research was gathered on this group. In 1991, 5.2% of Canadian households bought an insulating foam product. This translated into 1 642 000 containers with a retail value of $13 million. Canisters came in three sizes: small, 350 grams (45% of sales); medium,

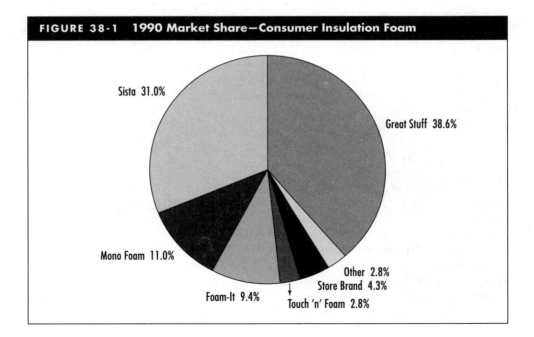

FIGURE 38-1   1990 Market Share—Consumer Insulation Foam

Sista 31.0%

Great Stuff 38.6%

Mono Foam 11.0%

Other 2.8%

Store Brand 4.3%

Foam-It 9.4%

Touch 'n' Foam 2.8%

620 grams (37% of sales); and large, 935 grams (18% of sales). (See Table 38-1 for details.) Based on some European data, Paul believed the consumer market for foam could grow at a rate of 15% per year. Future growth would be directly related to the market's incidence of purchase. If 30% of households purchased the product each year, the insulating spray foam market would be bigger than the caulking market.

Table 38-1	1990 Market Size—Consumer Insulation Foam			
Product Size	% of Households Purchasing	Total Households Purchasing*	Average Units per Purchase	Total Units Sold
350 gram	3.8%	380 000	1.93	733 400
620 gram	2.3%	230 000	2.63	604 900
935 gram	1.2%	120 000	2.53	303 600
All Sizes	5.2%	520 000	2.45	1 641 900

* Assumes approximately 10 000 000 households in Canada.

Insulating spray foam was purchased year round but sales peaked in October, November, December, and January—the months when consumers were most interested in "winterizing" their homes. Consumers also tended to purchase and then use an entire can of insulating spray foam regardless of its size. This was partly due to the product, as once the can was opened, insulating spray foam did not have the best shelf life. But this was also partly due to the multi-purpose nature of the product. Once homeowners began filling cracks and blocking air leaks, they were able to find enough to empty an entire can.

Although Great Stuff had the highest market share in 1990, it had no product in the 620-gram market and finished second behind Sista in the 935-gram market. Its sales were concentrated in the small 350-gram market. Great Stuff was positioned as the low-price foam with the same performance attributes as Mono. Sista was the first insulating spray foam in the Canadian market and Sista dominated the 620-gram market and had half the sales of Great Stuff in the 350-gram market. Sista also enjoyed a dominant position in the Quebec market, while Great Stuff fared better in the rest of Canada. Tremco identified these two companies as its key competitors.

In 1990, Mono added a 935-gram package to complement its 350-gram size. As the total number of cans sold remained constant, one could assume that some cannibalization had occurred. Nonetheless, a bigger volume of Mono Foam was sold. Revenues for 1990 were approximately $624 000 with a contribution margin of $187 000. If the market grew as anticipated, Mono Foam's sales volume would be most affected by its market share. If it could aggressively acquire share then, with its margins, it could benefit the most.

Paul's third stop was to talk directly with consumers. No competitor was undertaking any primary or secondary marketing research. Most viewed insulating spray foam as a mature product and a commodity. One competitor was quoted as likening the industry to fasteners. After all, "nails are nails."

Paul's research provided some interesting findings. Only 20% of consumers showed awareness of insulating spray foams. Awareness meant they could know the product well, have a vague idea of the product, or have no idea about the product other than recognizing the name. Approximately 25% of those aware had purchased the product (see Table 38-2 for Mono Foam sales). These people were very satisfied with the product. They had not purchased it

Table 38-2	Mono Foam Sales Volume (in Cans)		
Product Size	**1988**	**1989**	**1990**
350 gram	100 700	110 300	84 600
620 gram	—	—	—
935 gram	—	—	21 900
Total	100 700	110 300	106 500

instead of caulking and, in fact, saw the product as being completely different from caulking. They were also loyal, indicating that they would buy and had bought other Tremco products.

For the unaware group, researchers explained the product, how it was used, and the benefits it could offer. Consumers were asked to use a five-point scale to indicate how likely they would be to purchase the product. "Very likely" and "Likely" responses comprised 50% of the sample. This "top box" score was the highest of all previous products researched by Tremco. When asked what the most important factors were when buying an insulating spray foam, the top five consumer responses were: (1) high insulation/"R" value, 22%; (2) easy to apply, 19%; (3) provides a tight seal, 11%; (4) seals air leaks, 11%; and (5) seals cracks, 6 %. Given the small sample size, Paul had to make the dangerous assumption that buying behaviour would be the same in Quebec as in the rest of the country.

Paul's final step was to visit with key retail accounts (see Figure 38-2). One in four cans of insulating spray foam were acquired at Canadian Tire. This retailer was concerned about Mono's relatively high selling price. It also preferred to carry products supported by mass media advertising. In particular, it reacted better to products supported by television advertising, as Canadian Tire was a heavy user of this medium. Given the small volume of

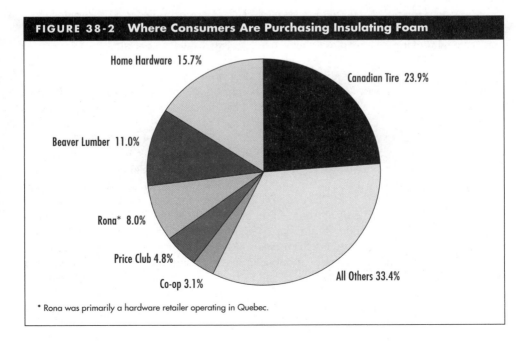

FIGURE 38-2 Where Consumers Are Purchasing Insulating Foam

Home Hardware 15.7%
Canadian Tire 23.9%
Beaver Lumber 11.0%
Rona* 8.0%
Price Club 4.8%
Co-op 3.1%
All Others 33.4%

* Rona was primarily a hardware retailer operating in Quebec.

insulating spray foam sold, it did not feel it could justify a third product listing on its shelves. A listing was important to Tremco as once granted, a product would be guaranteed exposure in all Canadian Tire stores. The retailer might be interested in private labelling Mono Foam with the Canadian Tire name. Paul was given assurances that Tremco was seen as a key supplier to Canadian Tire and there was a willingness to continue the dialogue if any major new marketing effort was expended.

NEXT STEPS

Paul tried to synthesize this information. "Mono" was a reputable and established brand name that represented high-quality products to consumers. Tremco had a good understanding of the consumer insulating spray foam market, as well as access to worldwide foam knowledge. Unfortunately, Mono Foam was not significantly different from its competition. Given the need to import from the US, the high American dollar, and the need to maintain a 30% contribution margin, Mono Foam would have to be premium-priced, thus eliminating a certain percentage of price-conscious consumers from the market.

One solution was to begin an aggressive campaign to expand the market to match European consumption trends. Marketing research seemed to support his belief that a lack of consumer communication and awareness were at the heart of the problem. If Tremco could launch a major communications initiative, it could increase the size of the market and with it, Mono Foam's market share. This strategy was not without its risks. Increasing demand for the product would undoubtedly benefit lower-priced competitors, as price-sensitive consumers turned to alternatives cheaper than Mono Foam. More of a concern, Tremco was betting that competitors would not comprehend its actions and would not change any of their marketing tactics. In particular, Tremco hoped its competitors would not launch any major communications campaigns.

A key question for Paul was how to communicate. He was limited to $100 000 for 1991 by company executives. He considered many options. Given the complex nature of the product, he could provide free samples to home owners. This would necessitate filling small trial aerosol cans with the product. These were expensive to purchase and he would be limited to 25 000 given his budget. Another possibility was in-store demonstrations. A representative could visit a retail hardware store with a small booth and, during store hours, visit with customers and show them how the product worked. This approach would cost $250 per day. A variation on this would be attendance at retailer trade shows, where no homeowners would be allowed. Rona, Beaver Lumber, Home Hardware, and Pro Hardware, to name a few retailers, held these two-day trade shows twice a year. It allowed companies, new and established, a chance to speak one-on-one with local retailers and dealers. Booth rental was only a few hundred dollars, but the big cost was the time of those who would staff the booth. Bigger retailer trade shows, like the one held in Chicago, could cost tens of thousands of dollars to attend.

He also considered advertising. As the product filled a mass consumer need, Paul considered mass media advertising. Radio was a portable medium but lacked a visual element. Magazines or newspapers could get the message across but were relatively inefficient. By having to purchase space in dozens of publications, there could be message overlap and wasted dollars. Television had broad appeal and had been used successfully with its Tremclad line of paints. Unfortunately, there were no television shows devoted to home renovation. If television was used, sports-oriented programming would have to be targeted. Finally, Paul considered in-store advertising. He had seen small television sets equipped with a built-in video cassette player. A short video could be created which would play continuously in the store to attract attention. To be successful, salespeople would have to get permission from store managers and convince them that this set-up would not be a nuisance to their operations. A past trial of this expensive system ($600 per store) indicated that only 1% of managers would permit placement.

A different approach would be to look for other elements of the marketing mix which, when manipulated, would lead to share gains. Paul considered additional sizes—medium and very small. He wondered about dropping the branded product and moving into private labelling for Canadian retailers. He could also reduce the contribution margin and lower the product's price. One key to future success would be to get a listing at Canadian Tire.

MM BAKERS, LTD.—NOUS PLAISIR

Anne T. Hale

It is late December 1996 and Laura McCullough and her partner, Jean Louis Mercier, are reviewing the launch year performance of their cookie line, Nous Plaisir (Our Pleasure). They must decide whether or not to expand the launch of their product line from Montreal to the entire province of Quebec, which has 197 major chain supermarkets. If they decide to launch, they must make additional decisions concerning possible changes in their current marketing strategy. The decision must be made quickly. The building next to their current production facility is vacant, and both partners believe that if they proceed with the provincial launch, they will need to expand their current production capacity. The owner of the building has given Laura and Jean Louis the right of first refusal on a lease to this property, but this right terminates on January 25th. Laura and Jean Louis know they must come to a decision in the next few days.

THE CANADIAN COOKIE MARKET

The total retail snack food market in Canada in 1996 was $815 900 000, of which cookies (biscuits) represented 52%. This figure had been increasing at a rate of approximately 4% per year, although industry analysts expected total sales volume to remain relatively stable over the next few years. This was primarily due to greater emphasis on health and fitness on the part of many Canadian consumers. Not included in the total market figure shown above are sales attributable to retail bakeries, such as Felix and Mr. Nortons, as well as the bakeries located within many major supermarket chains.

Prepared by Anne T. Hale, Visiting Assistant Professor of Marketing, Faculty of Business, University of Victoria, Victoria, British Columbia. While the situation contained in the case is fictitious, the market data contained in the case are factual (*Canadian Grocer*, August and November, 1994). Reprinted by permission of Anne T. Hale.

The on-shelf packaged cookie market was extremely competitive, with Christie Brown & Company, a subsidiary of Atlanta-based Nabisco Brands, Ltd., controlling 50% of supermarket sales, with nine of the top ten brands, including Oreo and Chips Ahoy. Other manufacturers include George Weston, Ltd.; Keebler, a wholly owned subsidiary of Britain's United Cookie, which entered the Canadian market in 1991; Culinar, Inc.; Dads; Dare; and Pepperidge Farm, a subsidiary of Campbell's Soup Company. Some of the reasons why competition in the on-shelf packaged cookie market was so intense include:

1. the recent entry by many powerful brands, such as Pepperidge Farm and Keebler—both with large advertising budgets and equally large sales promotion budgets;

2. the new variants of existing brands, such as Mini Oreos and Chunky Chips Ahoy, made competition for shelf space fierce;

3. the increase of private label products, such as President's Choice, and generic brands, both aimed at price-conscious consumers;

4. variety seeking on the part of the consumers. Loyalty to any one brand of cookie was rare. Rather, consumers liked a variety of different types of snack foods and generally switched between their favourite brands. This resulted in even the large, well-known brands such as Oreos, having market shares of around 9–14%.

THE QUEBEC COOKIE MARKET

Quebec is Canada's second largest province, in terms of population. Quebec's population of 6 845 000 (of which 2 980 000 or 44% live in Montreal) comprises approximately 25% of Canada's population, and over 80% of the households in this province list French as their mother tongue. It is generally recognized by consumer goods manufacturers that the Quebec market is culturally unique, and different strategies from those used in other provinces are often needed. Quebec accounts for 27.9% of the total Canadian cookie market, indicating that Quebec households have a slightly higher than average consumption rate. Most of the major brands available in the rest of Canada are also available in Quebec, with similar market shares. Most major brands offered trade promotions, in the form of price discounts to retailers four to six times per year, and offered extensive consumer promotions (in the form of contests, sweepstakes, and coupons) throughout the year. The average retail price for most branded cookies was $3.79, with private label and generic cookies selling for $2.99 per package. Retail bakery chains, such as Felix and Mr. Norton, generally charged approximately $6.50 for 10 to 12 cookies, and supermarket bakeries charged approximately $5.50 for a dozen cookies.

THE COMPANY

McCullough and Mercier first met in university and discovered a shared passion for baking. Both had several "family recipes" that had been handed down for generations, and they spent much of their free time experimenting with these formulations, as well as creating new and different types of cookies. After graduating in 1985, they formed a company named MM Bakers, Ltd. (MMB) and began selling their line of cookies to local coffee shops, cafés, and independent convenience stores and depanneurs. Their original product line consisted of two types of cookies—chocolate chip and pecan praline, which were sold in individually wrapped (in other words, one cookie to a package) packages. They did not use a brand name for their cookies. Instead, they placed their company name (MM Bakers), the type of cookie, and its ingredients on the label of each individually wrapped cookie. McCullough and Mercier acted as their own sales force, handling orders and negotiations with their distributors. They hired two production assistants who helped in the preparation of the cookies and handled other tasks such as delivery and stocking.

MMB went from an initial loss of $10 850 in 1989 to a record profit of $277 400 (after taxes) in 1994. Their cookies quickly gained in popularity, both with consumers and the cafés, coffee shops, and depanneurs that carried them. By 1994, MMB enjoyed an excellent relationship with their retail distributors, and had expanded their product line to include oatmeal-raison cookies and Scottish shortbread. In 1994, both McCullough and Mercier decided it was time to expand the distribution of their cookies. After considering several alternatives, they felt that getting their product line into the major grocery chains offered the best opportunity for sales growth. Due to capacity constraints, McCullough and Mercier felt that they should focus initially on Montreal and its surrounding communities. The launch was planned for January 1, 1996, and details of their marketing strategy for the initial year are discussed below.

Launch Year Marketing Strategy

Product and Target Market

Since MMB had been selling their cookies individually, one of their first decisions concerned the packaging for the product line. They decided to use a resealable blue and white paper bag, which would contain 18 cookies. On the front of the bag would be a picture of the cookies, together with the brand name they selected for their product, Nous Plaisir. They elected to launch their existing four types of cookies—expansion of the product line was a decision they decided to defer until Nous Plaisir had a toe-hold in the market. To maintain freshness and quality, MMB recommended to retailers that their products not be kept on the shelf for longer than one month, although they made no provision to reimburse supermarkets for unsold product.

McCullough and Mercier did not have much experience in planning marketing strategies, although they did realize that they needed to identify their target customers. They decided to target upscale households who wouldn't mind spending more for a quality cookie. Specifically, they targeted young, educated, middle-to-high-income, single- or double-career households. They estimated that their primary competition in this segment would come from local bakeries, such as Felix and Mr. Norton's, and from supermarket bakeries. Since they knew the retail price for their cookies would be higher than most other packaged cookies, they decided to position their product as a high-quality, convenient alternative to bakery-shop cookies.

Pricing and Costs

In anticipation of the increased demand for their products, McCullough and Mercier bought new equipment and increased their staff. The total fixed manufacturing expenses allocated to the supermarket distribution of their products was $425 000, with an additional $250 000 allocated for marketing communications. Variable product costs for each package of cookies came to $1.19, and they decided to use a local food brokerage firm to distribute their products to the grocery stores rather than trying to establish their own sales force. Compensation for the food brokers amounted to 5.5% of sales. MM set a manufacturer's price to the trade of $42.60 for a case of 12 packages of cookies. They anticipated that retailers would take a markup of 20–25%, which is standard for this type of product.

Advertising and Sales Promotion

McCullough and Mercier knew that they would never be able to match the large corporations in advertising or promotional spending. Their marketing budget, while substantial for such a small company, was almost nonexistent when compared to the budgets for market share leaders such as Oreos and Chips Ahoy. One aspect on which they simply could not compete was in granting retailers slotting allowances. MMB did not believe that the small amount of funds that could be allocated to slotting allowances would be sufficient to ensure favourable shelf position, so they decided to use case discounts as a means of getting retail support. MMB estimated that these case discounts would represent about 8% of total sales. They would be offered four times per year, and would allow retailers to receive 25% off the normal price of a case. Each promotion would last four weeks.

McCullough and Mercier had examined several coupon promotions, but had finally rejected the possibility of this type of consumer promotion, primarily due to the cost. Instead, they decided to use a portion of their marketing funds to insert quality check cards in each package of cookies. These cards requested basic demographic information on the consumer (including age, income, language, etc.), as well measuring satisfaction, awareness, and repeat purchase. Space was provided on the card for consumers to add any additional comments regarding MMB products. The cards were postage paid—all the consumer had to do was fill in the information and drop the card in the post box. The balance of the marketing budget would be spent on local advertising, focusing on print media and local radio stations. MMB launched with a blitz of advertising, using $\frac{1}{4}$ and $\frac{1}{2}$ page ads, and 30-second radio spots during morning and evening drive times, every day during the initial two weeks of the launch. After the blitz period, they advertised only in weekend editions of both papers, usually in the Life-Style section. Radio advertising was discontinued after the blitz period.

The ad copy communicated the company's positioning strategy—quality and convenience. They used two main themes in their ads, the first aimed at their retail bakery competition. This ad featured a couple walking through a blinding snowstorm and in the distance there was a retail bakery shop with a closed sign in the window. The ad copy stated, "You don't have to walk out of your way for quality cookies anymore. They are right at your fingertips thanks to Nous Plaisir!"

The second theme was aimed at supermarket bakeries. This ad featured two frames. In the first frame a cocker spaniel was staring at a bone-shaped dog biscuit and a supermarket cookie. In the second frame, the dog was eating the dog biscuit. The copy for this ad stated, "If your pet can't tell the difference between a dog biscuit and a supermarket bakery biscuit, then perhaps it's time you tried Nous Plaisir—quality, convenience, and something supermarket biscuits can't offer—TASTE!"

Distribution

MMB hoped to gain at least an 80% coverage of the major supermarkets in the Montreal area. They focused much of their attention on the major chains, since they represented such a significant share of the Montreal retail grocery market. MMB did not attempt to get their product into local pharmacies or discount stores, due primarily to the lack of available manpower. Expansion into these outlets was listed as a future consideration.

MMB's Launch Year Performance

MMB launched their cookie line in supermarkets during the initial days of January 1996. McCullough and Mercier collected the following information concerning their product line's performance from January 1996 through December 19, 1996.

SALES TO SUPERMARKETS

Exhibit 39-1 contains monthly case sales figures for the initial year. The four months with an asterisk (*), being January, May, September, and December, indicate those months that MMB offered a 25% reduction in case prices to retailers. MMB generally gave retailers a one-month advance notice of the planned price reductions.

By the end of 1996, the MMB product line had gained shelf space in 61 of Montreal's major supermarkets. Jean Louis had visited every supermarket in the Montreal area carrying the product line during the launch year and prepared an average retail profile for Nous Plaisir, which is contained in Exhibit 39-2. Exhibit 39-3 illustrates the typical shelf position for the cookies.

Exhibit 39-1 Monthly Sales Figures for 1996

# of Cases	January*	February	March	April	May*	June
Sold	1 307	1 483	1 943	1 872	4 168	2 472

# of Cases	July	August	September*	October	November	December*
Sold	2 155	3 391	5 722	2 296	3 214	5 263

Exhibit 39-2 Average Retail Profile

Average retail price	$4.79
Average retail price when featured	$4.29
Average monthly sales in units	28 000
Average monthly sales when featured	43 200
Average number of shelf facings	2.2
Average number of times featured	1.2 times per year
Average number of features for branded competitors	4.3 times per year
Number of times Nous Plaisir was featured in a retail ad	0.4 times per year
Average number of times branded competitors were featured in a retail ad	3.8 times per year

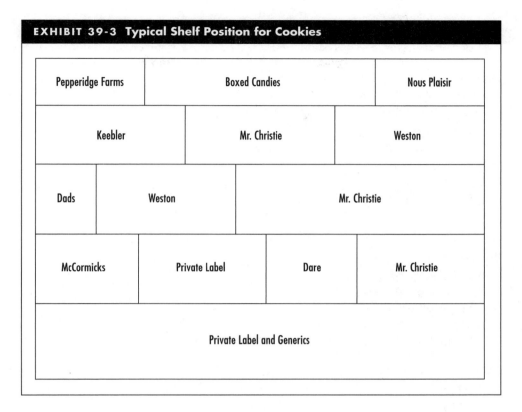

EXHIBIT 39-3 Typical Shelf Position for Cookies

Pepperidge Farms	Boxed Candies		Nous Plaisir
Keebler		Mr. Christie	Weston
Dads	Weston	Mr. Christie	
McCormicks	Private Label	Dare	Mr. Christie
Private Label and Generics			

Consumer Acceptance of the Product

By the end of 1996, MMB had received 4357 quality-check cards from purchasers of their cookies. The demographic information contained in those cards is summarized in Exhibit 39-4, and the purchase information is contained in Exhibit 39-5.

THE DECISION

MMB continued to sell their products to cafés, coffee-shops and convenience stores. Sales from this area amounted to $894 250 with a contribution margin of 42%. In fact, MMB had not changed any aspects of this distribution system. The packaging, unit price (36 cents per individually wrapped cookie), and label remained unchanged after the expansion to grocery stores. At the present time, MMB had no plans to increase the scope of their non-grocery distribution.

"Expansion of our current facilities will result in a total capacity of 1 800 000 packages (150 000 cases) per year, and I believe it is essential if we are to expand our sales to the entire province of Quebec," said Laura McCullough. "We can use the existing facility, with a capacity of 50 000 cases of cookies to continue with sales to cafés, coffee shops, and convenience stores, and use the new facility for our supermarket products. We have the additional rent, plus standard overhead expenses for our new facility, plus we will have to hire at least five more people. Just those expenses amount to an additional $515 000. Purchase of the new equipment will cost $480 000. Our marketing expenses will go up as well, especially if we

Exhibit 39-4 Demographic Data from Customers

	Entire Year
Age:	
12–20	13%
21–35	32%
36–50	24%
51+	31%
Household Language:	
French	64.5%
English	20.5%
Other	15.0%
Household Income:	
0–$10 000	8.2%
$10 001–$25 000	44.9%
$25 001–$50 000	24.1%
$50 001–$100 000	10.3%
over $100 000	5.6%
Education:	
0–12 years	12.2%
13–15 years	49.8%
16–19 years	18.4%
20+ years	0.9%
Household Size:	
1 person	35.2%
2 persons	30.1%
3–4 persons	19.4%
5–6 persons	10.4%
over 6 persons	4.5%
How Consumers Learned of MMB:	
From family or friend	12.2%
From "Dog" ad	32.5%
From "Snowstorm" ad	22.6%
Saw product in the store	3.9%
Other	28.8%

Exhibit 39-5 Purchase Data from Customers

Percent Responding	January–June	July–December
Positive Statements:		
Fresh	22%	17%
Tasty	48%	42%
Good value	18%	14%
Good variety	9%	8%
Will repurchase	34%	30%
Negative Statements:		
Stale	4%	12%
Too expensive	19%	20%
Not a good value	21%	25%
Hard to find	22%	24%
Won't repurchase	2%	14%
Satisfaction:		
Highly satisfied	25%	18%
Satisfied	50%	54%
Not satisfied	25%	28%
Total Cards Received	1655	2702

decide to advertise on regional television. We will probably have to triple our marketing communications budget. Acquiring the financing won't be a problem if we can show break-even within two years.

Jean Louis replied, "I think we would only need a 1% share of the Quebec cookie market to break-even. But, I'm not a marketing expert, and I've never been really good with numbers. I know that we have hired a former Pepperidge Farm marketing manager to assist us with our marketing efforts, but she won't be able to begin work until January 26th. This means that the two of us must seriously review our 1996 supermarket performance. I only wish that we had more time to make this decision."

"I agree. I don't think there were any major catastrophes during our first year of supermarket distribution, although there were some aspects of our marketing strategy that could have been improved. If we rush into a provincial roll-out of our cookies, we may be making the same mistakes again. If only we had time to conduct some market research!"

"Unfortunately," said Jean Louis, "that is simply not an option. We have to decide, based solely on the information from our 1996 supermarket sales, whether or not to expand distribution of our cookies, and identify areas where we should change our marketing strategy. We are going to have to review our 1996 performance very carefully."

MOTUS INC.

Kris Opalinski and Walter S. Good

In early June 1994, Greg Klassen and Phil Poetker, founders and principals of Motus Inc., were finally able to find time to discuss spring sales figures for the company in their spartan office in the industrial district of North-West Winnipeg. Since summer was a slow period for sales of gardening equipment, they were not swamped with the pressures of meeting delivery deadlines, filling urgent orders, and tracking shipments, which were typically associated with their peak sales periods in spring and fall. They were eager to use this opportunity to evaluate their progress and to re-assess the company's future.

They started with the most recent sales reports which showed significant growth over the corresponding period of the preceding year. However, as good as these results appeared, they were still not completely up to Greg and Phil's expectations. Consequently, soon after a brief examination of the sales figures, the discussion turned to a review of their overall marketing strategy.

PHIL POETKER

Phil Poetker was a phys-ed graduate with business interests. Even before forming Motus in 1992, he already had two years of experience in running his own company, Poetker Dynamics, which produced various types of specialized sporting equipment for schools and sports complexes. His limited success with the company's original product line made him think about developing a new product concept appealing to a broad consumer market. With his background and expertise in human movement, Phil focused his creative efforts on ergonomics,[1] and in 1991, developed the concept for a gripping device for various gardening and con-

---

Prepared by Kris Opalinski under the direction of Walter S. Good of the University of Manitoba, as a basis for classroom discussion rather than to illustrate either effective or ineffective handling of an administrative situation. Reprinted with permission.

struction tools, such as shovels, spades, and forks. This concept was then further developed into two products, a straight handle (closely resembling the grip traditionally attached to the shaft of a scythe), and a D-grip (shaped the same as the traditional top grip of larger shovels and spades). Both the straight handle and the D-grip, when attached to a straight-shafted tool, helped the user to work in a more ergonomical position, reducing back strain and fatigue.

With a working prototype of his concept, Phil began looking for partners, who, besides providing equity for his venture, would also offer some managerial expertise and be ready to participate in running the business on a full-time basis. With the help from the Health Industry Development Initiative (HIDI) of the Manitoba provincial government, Phil was put in contact with Greg Klassen, who was looking for new investment opportunities.

GREG KLASSEN

Greg Klassen belonged to a prominent family that owned and operated Monarch Industries, a Winnipeg manufacturer of mechanical equipment. With engineering and business degrees, he had over 20 years of business experience, first as a consultant with Ernst & Ernst and the Manitoba Institute of Management, and later as a progressively responsible manager of the family business. By the late 1980s, he was promoted to the position of Vice President Finance, and then to company President. For a brief period in 1989, he ran the $30 million company employing some 300 workers. In 1990, Greg had to leave the business after his father's half of it was sold to his brother who owned the other half.

After leaving Monarch, Greg decided to become an entrepreneur. His initial attempt to invest in an established company failed, which made him think about seeking new venture opportunities. He wanted to find a new business which, while offering significant growth potential, would also need some investment capital, and require his managerial expertise.

MOTUS INC.

In September 1992, after a few months of searching, Greg found an entrepreneurial venture meeting his criteria. Poetker Dynamics had a patented product with significant domestic and international sales potential, might be highly profitable, required a moderate amount of investment capital, and needed his business expertise. Soon after the first meeting with Phil, Greg decided to invest in the business. Under the terms of a shareholders' agreement negotiated between the two, Greg provided Poetker Dynamics (which was to be incorporated) with a $200 000 loan. He was also given a one-year option to convert a portion of the loan, defined as the greater of $100 000 or three times the first year's profits, to 50% of the company's equity.

At the same time, Phil and Greg decided that their venture should be incorporated as a wholly owned subsidiary of Poetker Dynamics, dedicated to the marketing of its proprietary products. They named the newly established company Motus Inc., after the Latin word for motion, and registered the name as a trademark in Canada and the US.

Under this new corporate umbrella, Phil and Greg quickly refined the design of the product, ordered injection moulds, negotiated a manufacturing agreement with NV Sales of Beausejour, Manitoba, and conducted mechanical tests of several prototypes. At the same time, they developed a package design for their product. The cost of this graphic design, which was in excess of $25 000, was partly financed by a $10 000 grant from HIDI. During the product-marketing phase, their recently hired sales representative, Carol Goodmanson, took prototypes to trade shows in Canada and the United States.

By early December, the D-grip and straight handle were market-ready, and the company had secured new orders from a couple of local distributors of industrial and medical equipment, and a few retail chains. On December 15, 1992, Motus shipped its first 2000 handles to Canadian Tire's Ontario distribution centre.

With the recently secured equity financing and a successfully completed product development process, Motus entered negotiations with Western Economic Diversification on a previously approved application for loan financing. In January 1993, the two sides signed a $193 000 loan agreement at a flexible interest rate 3% above the bank rate, payable in six monthly installments. The repayment schedule provided for a one-year deferral from the date of receiving the last portion of the loan, and subsequent fixed monthly payments of $10 000, covering both interest and principal.

CORPORATE PROFILE

Production

Under the long-term manufacturing supply agreement with NV Sales, Motus was guaranteed a supply of up to 2000 semi-assembled products a day. The price charged to Motus was fixed at $1.00/piece for the D-grip and $0.67/piece for the straight handle. This covered all production costs (the cost of material was estimated to be $0.20 and $0.10 for the D-grip and straight handle respectively) and manufacturer's margins. NV required a minimum production run of 1000 pieces, and an order lead time of two weeks, but was flexible enough to adjust its production schedule in case of an emergency.

Final assembly and packaging was performed manually by Phil, Greg, and Carol in the storage area at the back of their office. Since each of them could assemble and pack some 100 pieces of either product an hour, only rarely did the company need to hire additional workers at a cost of $6.00/hour.

Operations

There was no strictly defined division of responsibilities between Greg, Phil, and Carol. With his education and business experience, Greg dealt with accounting and cash management, while Phil's knowledge of plastics fabrication involved him in production. The rest of corporate activities, such as marketing, sales, and administration, were performed jointly by both partners with the assistance of Carol.

Greg, Phil, and Carol held frequent planning meetings devoted to issues of overall corporate importance, such as pricing, sales forecasting, developing marketing strategies, and the evaluation of results. The decision making process relied on obtaining a consensus between the two partners, which could lead to a stalemate in extreme situations. Nevertheless, during their relationship there had been no single occasion when their differences on any particular issue had not been amicably resolved.

Revenues and Costs

At the time of their first shipment in December 1992, Greg and Phil were very optimistic about the company's sales prospects. They felt that Motus was capable of selling 200 000 handles in the first year, and that this number could be expanded to several hundred thousand per year.

Actual sales were somewhat less, but nevertheless impressive for a fledgling operation catering to the consumer mass market.

The company sold 20 000 handles in its 1992–93 fiscal year, generating close to $100 000 in revenues. However, the high cost of the product development process significantly exceeded revenues, resulting in an overall loss in excess of $200 000. The company's goals for the second year reflected their first year results, and called for a more realistic revenue figure of $500 000 and a break-even situation.

Exhibit 40-1 presents Motus's financial statements for the 1992–93 fiscal year and its budget for 1993–94, together with the preliminary results for the first six months of the year.

Sales of Motus handles were highly seasonal in nature. Spring and fall were high-volume seasons, creating higher demand for working capital, which regularly exceeded the company's financial capacity. Obtaining a bank line of credit for a newly established venture with an unproven sales record and a significant level of long-term debt (repayment of the WED loan was to begin in August 1994) proved to be virtually impossible. To alleviate this problem, Sermelory, Greg's holding company, provided Motus with a variable loan (at prime plus 1%) for an amount equal to the value of its outstanding receivables.

Market Potential

Greg and Phil based their estimates of market potential for the Motus handles on an analysis of demographic and social trends, an examination of sales statistics for complementary products, and an evaluation of the current situation in related markets, such as garden supplies, nurseries, and home improvement.

In their initial estimates, the two partners assumed that the ergonomic advantage of using the D-Grip and Straight Handle would appeal particularly to consumers over 50 years of age. In North America, 80 million people were in this age group, creating considerable demand for products addressing their special needs. On the other hand, Greg and Phil believed that the current trend toward more active lifestyles made people interested in continuing various forms of physical activity well past retirement age. The two partners felt that the combination of these two elements created a good foundation for their marketing efforts. They also believed that these fundamental factors applied to all industrialized countries, significantly enhancing the company's sales potential.

In assessing their situation, they concluded that there had to be significant demand for the Motus handles. Trade statistics suggested that some 30 million straight-shafted implements, such as shovels, rakes, forks, and hoes were sold annually in North America. In addition, it was estimated that each North American household had accumulated an average of six such implements. Phil and Greg did not want to make any arbitrary assumptions as to the percentage of those implements to which Motus handles could be attached, but felt that the numbers spoke for themselves.

Finally, Phil noticed a growing interest by many employers in the application of ergonomics to reduce losses resulting from injuries caused by the use of improperly designed tools. The scale of the problem could be appreciated by looking at the example of CN, where annual losses resulting from absenteeism and compensation caused by lower-back injuries were in excess of $18 million. This suggested that the Motus handles, which reduced or even eliminated lower-back injuries associated with shovelling and similar tasks, could be promoted to industrial customers as a very profitable investment.

Exhibit 40-1   Financial Statements for Motus Inc.

Motus Inc.—Statement of Earnings (Loss)

| | | 6 Months Ending 03/31/94 | | |
	Year Ended Sept. 30, 1993	Actual YTD	Budget YTD	Budget Year
Revenue				
Sales	$ 95 061	$242 000	$250 000	$500 000
Cost of sales:	$ 52 340	$152 797	$150 000	$300 000
Gross margin	$ 42 721	$ 89 203	$100 000	$200 000
Expenses				
Salaries and benefits	$ 81 078	$ 49 555	$ 50 000	$100 000
Trade shows and travel		$ 21 192	$ 22 000	$ 41 000
Interest and bank charges	$ 9 838	$ 6 106	$ 6 200	$ 14 400
Rent and property tax	$ 19 685	$ 5 963	$ 6 000	$ 12 600
Utilities	$ 1 211	$ 2 152	$ 1 700	$ 2 400
Phone and fax	$ 7 399	$ 3 274	$ 3 000	$ 6 000
Promotion*	$ 47,918			
Materials		$ 6 437	$ 3 000	$ 5 000
TV test		$ 6 600		
Postage and delivery		$ 1 049	$ 1 000	$ 2 000
Office and shop supplies	$ 7 820	$ 2 064	$ 1 600	$ 3 300
Professional fees	$ 48 967	$ 4 724	$ 5 000	$ 10 000
Insurance	$ 1 823			$ 1 500
Business tax	$ 1 986			$ 1 000
Research and development	$ 51 442			
Depreciation	$ 8 386			
Miscellaneous		$ 289	$ 500	$ 800
Total expenses	$287 533	$109 405	$100 000	$200 000
Net income (loss for the year)	($244 832)	($ 20 202)	0	0

* Promotional expenses in the year 1992–93 include trade shows and travel.

continued

Exhibit 40-1 Financial Statements for Motus Inc. (continued)

Motus Inc.—Balance Sheet as at September 30, 1993

Assets

Current assets:

Cash		$ 22
Accounts receivable		$ 18 674
Inventories		$ 34 000
Prepaid expenses		$ 4 000
Total current assets		$ 56 696

Fixed assets	Cost	Accumulated depreciation	
Moulds and dies	$14 366	$ 7 183	
Shop equipment	$ 5 780	$ 822	
Office equipment	$ 3 809	$ 381	
Total	$23 955	$ 8 386	$ 15 569

Other assets

Patent application costs	$ 10 548
Deferred financing costs	$ 15 382
Total assets	$ 98 195

Liabilities

Current liabilities:	
Accounts payable	$ 24 594
Long-term liabilities	
Long-term debt	
Western Economic Diversification	$158 423
Sermelory Holdings Ltd.	$160 000
Total liabilities	$343 017

Deficiency in Assets

Share capital	
100 Class A common	$ 5
100 Class B common	$ 5
Total shareholders' equity	$ 10
Deficit	($244 832)
Total	$ 98 195

Competitors

Phil and Greg identified two other products offering similar functions to the Motus handles. Both were manufactured in the US by large producers of shovels and other similar implements. "Handle-It" and "Upper Hand" were the brand names of these competing products. They had been introduced to the US market in the late 1980s, but failed to attain significant sales volumes. Greg attributed their apparent failure (he estimated annual US sales of Handle-It at no more than 50 000 pieces) to their primitive design: both were steel-fabricated, heavy, visually unattractive, and difficult to fasten to the implement's shaft (both had an attaching mechanism consisting of split, ring-shaped clamps, coupled by bolts).

Both competing products were distributed through retail hardware stores (different from those selected by Motus), which made Phil and Greg believe that they were not in direct competition with the Motus handles. Handle-It sold for a retail price of $9.99 vs. Upper Hand's $12.99.

MARKETING STRATEGY

Target Customers

Motus handles could be applied in a variety of situations. The primary application was associated with the use of straight-shafted implements, such as shovels, rakes, hoes, brooms, and mops. However, the handles could also be applied in different environments and by different customer groups. Company promotional materials provide an insight into some potential customer groups who might use the product (see Exhibit 40-2). Suggested applications in the Motus brochure clearly identify several market segments: households, home care applications, sports, and industrial users. Another flyer (see Exhibit 40-3) suggests yet another application, gardening.

Phil and Greg felt that their products had strong sales potential in each of the above markets. However, their assessment of the marketplace suggested that the household and gardening segments were by far the largest and most promising. Consequently, they decided to concentrate their marketing efforts on customers in these two segments.

Their knowledge of these prospective customers was largely based on two sources of information: published demographic statistics and interviews with visitors to their booth at trade shows. They believed that the typical end-user of Motus handles could be characterized as male, 30 to 55 years of age (actually, older users were their primary target category), working-class, middle-class, or from the farming community. At the same time, their review of available statistical information suggested that females were responsible for 65% of all retail purchases of consumer products. Since practically all customers from these segments used the Motus handles as attachments to shovels and other similar implements, Phil researched consumer behaviour as related to the purchase of such tools. What he discovered was that the consumer's decision to purchase a shovel, spade, or rake was made without much prior consideration or planning; typically occurring immediately before or in the middle of work requiring such implements.

At the same time, Greg and Phil saw opportunities in the home care and industrial segments where they had recently noticed growing concern over injuries resulting from the use of improperly designed equipment and tools. These two segments involved both institutional and individual buyers. Motus attempted to approach both buyer groups within each of these segments.

EXHIBIT 40-2 Motus Inc. Promotional Flyer: Suggested Applications of the D-Grip and Straight Handle

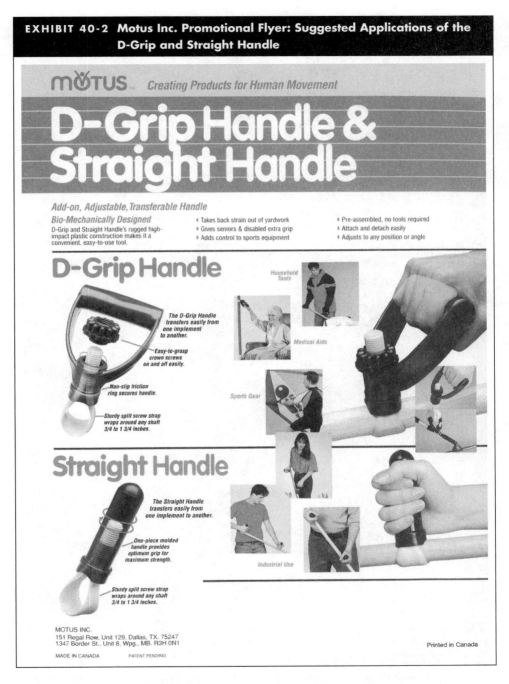

MOTUS... *Creating Products for Human Movement*

D-Grip Handle & Straight Handle

Add-on, Adjustable, Transferable Handle
Bio-Mechanically Designed
D-Grip and Straight Handle's rugged high-impact plastic construction makes it a convenient, easy-to-use tool.

- Takes back strain out of yardwork
- Gives seniors & disabled extra grip
- Adds control to sports equipment

- Pre-assembled, no tools required
- Attach and detach easily
- Adjusts to any position or angle

D-Grip Handle

The D-Grip Handle transfers easily from one implement to another.

Easy-to-grasp crown screws on and off easily.

Non-slip friction ring secures handle.

Sturdy split screw strap wraps around any shaft 3/4 to 1 3/4 inches.

Household Tools

Medical Aids

Sports Gear

Straight Handle

The Straight Handle transfers easily from one implement to another.

One-piece molded handle provides optimum grip for maximum strength.

Sturdy split screw strap wraps around any shaft 3/4 to 1 3/4 inches.

Industrial Use

MOTUS INC.
151 Regal Row, Unit 129, Dallas, TX. 75247
1347 Border St., Unit 8, Wpg., MB. R3H 0N1

MADE IN CANADA   PATENT PENDING

Printed in Canada

Phil made several sales calls to institutional customers in the industrial segment, such as larger corporations (CN and Manitoba Hydro) and departments of municipal, provincial, and federal governments. He stressed increased productivity and the possible reduced absenteeism resulting from the use of Motus handles. He also approached officers of the Winnipeg

EXHIBIT 40-3 Motus Inc. Promotional Flyer: Gardening Applications

and Toronto branches of the Workers Compensation Board, and received their endorsement of the products. He hoped that this endorsement would boost the interest of industrial safety inspectors in all larger organizations in the province. However, his efforts with these institutional customers were typically quite frustrating. His presentations were received warmly by purchasing agents, but his efforts to close sales encountered an insurmountable wall of rigid purchase policies, group decision making, and budgetary constraints.

Individual buyers from the industrial segment consisted mostly of owners of small businesses, whose purchases of tools were made in hardware distribution centres. Phil and Greg did not make a deliberate effort to develop the interest of this group in Motus handles, but hoped for some crossover effect from their promotion (especially in-store displays) to attract some of these customers.

Motus handles were also sold to the home care segment, almost exclusively to individual consumers. However, besides listing the D-Grip in a few home care catalogues, the company did not apply any differentiation strategy to reach this customer group. The following quote from an article promoting the Manitoba health care industry summarized the company's approach: "Although clearly a health care product, Motus is marketing the add-on handles in hardware stores because [Phil] Poetker feels the segregation of health care products in specialty shops is coming to an end as the population ages. 'They're going to be everyday consumer products,' he predicts."[2]

Product

The product development process was not finished after their first shipment to Canadian Tire in December 1992. Some of the handles from these early shipments broke after a few months of intensive use. Phil soon associated this problem with a phenomenon called "environmental stress cracking." Following the recommendations of an expert in the plastics field, he ordered laboratory tests of different formulations of plastics, solving the problem within a few weeks. For the next couple of months, one of every 50 handles was subjected to a range of strength tests while heated to higher than normal temperatures (higher temperatures accelerated the aging process, previously responsible for the material's breakdown). After this problem was rectified, there were no further cases of customer dissatisfaction with the product reported to Motus.

The major patent claim registered by the company in Canada, the US, and under the Patent Cooperation Treaty, concerned the mechanism for attaching the handle to the tool or implement. This consisted of a flexible plastic split screw, contoured flange, and nut. This mechanism permitted attaching the handle to implements with a wide range of shaft diameters (from $3/4$ to $1 3/4$ inches). Greg and Phil felt that their patent prevented potential competitors from offering products serving the same basic function.

Motus defined its two products in terms of convenience, safety, and efficiency. The company's brochure suggested that "Motus handles significantly improve leverage and promote proper kinetic movement, thereby improving work efficiency and substantially reducing back pain, blisters, fatigue, and other repetitive stress injuries" (see Exhibit 40-4). These benefits provided to the customer were determined through a kinematic assessment of the handles conducted at the University of Manitoba. User perceptions of the importance of each of the above factors were not entirely clear. Neither was customer assessment of the Motus handles, although Phil's conversations with visitors to his booth at trade shows suggested that consumers were satisfied with the two products.

The list of potential areas of human activity where the Motus handles could be applied was long. However, Motus had never attempted to investigate which groups of end users were principally purchasing its handles now.

The Motus handles were manufactured in a variety of colours, depending on the preferences of retailers and distributors, and packaged in individual cartons featuring colour photographs of the products, as well as user instructions. Depending on the order size,

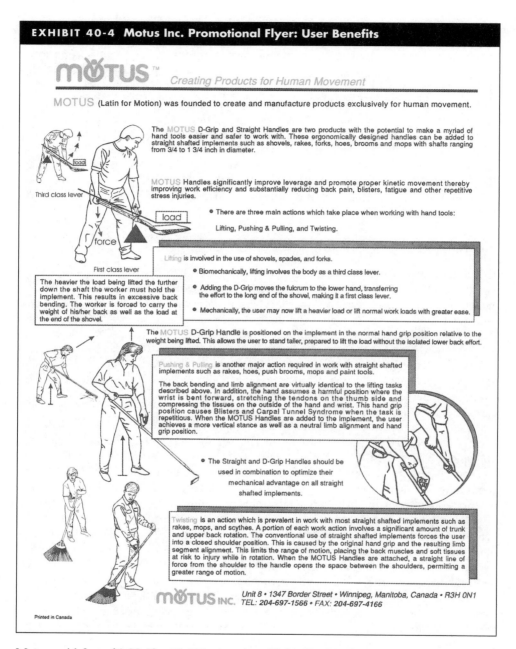

EXHIBIT 40-4 Motus Inc. Promotional Flyer: User Benefits

Motus paid from $0.23 (for 50 000 pieces) to $0.30 (for 20 000 pieces) for each D-Grip box, which was larger than the Straight Handle box which cost less than $0.25.

Motus also developed a 22" × 66" × 16" (W × H × D) cardboard display containing 32 D-Grip and 16 Straight Handle packages. The display, which was delivered free to all retail outlets (it cost $10) carrying Motus handles, was intended as a means of in-store advertising, and was to be featured in the hand tools section of the store.

Price

The average total unit cost (including packaging) was estimated at $1.50 for the D-Grip and $1.00 for the Straight Handle. Even after adding the cost of shipping and order-processing (from $0.20 to $0.30 depending on order size), the total variable unit cost was low.

Greg and Phil believed that Motus should base its pricing strategy mainly on marketing considerations. Their suggested retail prices were related to the price of shovels and other similar implements, which were typically within the range of $10 to $20 in both Canada and the US.

Based on an average $10 price point for implements, it was initially decided to suggest retail prices of $9.99 for the D-Grip and $6.99 for the Straight Handle, both in the US and Canada in their local currency. Retailer margins, which ranged from 35% to 56%, were similar in Canada and the US. This meant that the US market was much more profitable for the company than its Canadian counterpart.

Based on recent discussions with sales reps, Phil and Greg decided to reduce prices. Their new suggested retailer prices were in the range of $5.95–$7.50 for the D-Grip and $3.95–$4.99 for the Straight Handle in both Canada and the US. It was hoped that this move would increase the overall level of profits, even though it reduced unit margins. It was an established industry practice for retailers to receive an extra 10% introductory discount and a 2% advertising fee. Typical payment terms were 2% 10, net 60, but strict enforcement of large retailers' compliance with the stated terms was close to impossible for a small company like Motus. Consequently, Phil and Greg had to tolerate late payments from larger customers without revoking the 2% discount.

Motus handles offered through catalogues were typically priced much higher than those offered through retail outlets. The D-Grip offered in catalogues commanded prices in the range of US$12–$20, while the corresponding prices for the Straight Handle were US$8–$14. This pricing reflected the extremely high margins commonly commanded by catalogues, the low response rate (defined as the proportion of the number of unit sales to the number of circulated copies of the catalogue), and the higher manufacturer's price ($5.00 for D-Grip), reflecting the higher unit cost of order processing. In some cases, the price of Motus handles resulted from the price range assumed for all products offered through a given catalogue.

Promotion

Motus employed a large arsenal of promotion methods, including co-op advertising with retailers, personal selling, sales promotion, and publicity. The selection of a given method of promotion was determined based on its cost, target audience, and the demands of distributors.

The company received some attention from the media at the time of its inception. In December 1992, a feature article on the company appeared in the *Winnipeg Free Press*. Motus handles were then reviewed in editorials published in several specialty magazines, such as *Canadian Living*, *Manitoba Business*, and *Hardware Merchandising*. This publicity created some awareness among consumers, but its impact on sales was rather limited outside of Winnipeg. However, these editorials provided the new company with some degree of credibility when making contact with the purchasing agents of major retail chains.

Personal selling, particularly during trade shows, was the major component of the company's promotional effort. Between January 1993 and June 1994, Phil, Greg, and Carol participated in 10 hardware, gardening, and home-care trade shows in Canada and the US.

Participation in trade shows provided Motus with a multitude of benefits. While allowing the company to approach distributors, it was also a source of marketing intelligence, an inspiration for new marketing ideas, and a means of obtaining customer feedback. Preparation for a trade show included mailing invitations to representatives of distributors, with telephone follow-up, the development of product demonstrations, and preparing product pamphlets for distribution during the show. Personal selling was also used in prospecting outside of trade shows. Greg, who owned a distribution company in Dallas, Texas, had established strong connections with a number of US mass merchandisers. He used these contacts to establish relationships with potential distributors. Finally, the company's representatives in the US called on both existing and potential accounts.

Motus was not very active in the area of sales promotion. In practice, the use of sales promotion was largely determined by the retailers. Major incentives provided by Motus were a 10% introductory discount and cooperative advertising financed through an additional 2% discount.

Motus did not use extensive advertising to communicate with potential end users. Its co-op advertising was the result of an established industry practice rather than a reflection of the company's advertising strategy. Some TV advertising was conducted in cooperation with a US promotion firm utilizing direct-response marketing (i.e., airing an ad soliciting telephone orders through a 1-800 number). Motus and the promotion firm shared the CDN$12 000 cost of developing a video clip, which was then aired 40 times over the period of one week. The video, however, did not produce the expected results. This was attributed to the improper scheduling of the ad. Greg and Phil estimated that it only appeared three times in the time slots with a large audience of their principal target market—gardeners. They planned to edit the video (at a cost of $3000), and use it as a commercial clip.

In-store advertising was organized around the cardboard display, which was to be located in the hand tools section of retail stores. However, Motus's record of securing cooperation from retailers was mixed. In some cases, these displays proved too large for the space-conscious retailers, who removed them from their stores. In addition, space limitations in the hand tool section sometimes forced retailers to move the boxes of Motus handles to less-desirable shelf space.

Distribution

Motus concentrated its marketing effort on the US market, which accounted for 80% of its sales. The remaining sales were divided between Canada (15%) and overseas (5%).

Greg estimated that 90% of sales were made to retailers, 5% to manufacturers of implements (OEM), 3% to catalogues, and 2% directly to institutional customers.

The US

In the US, the company secured access to a number of mass merchandisers and national hardware chains, including Ace Hardware, HWI, Builders Square, and Home Depot. It signed a master representation agreement with Mike Farrell, a principal in a distribution company with 20–30 sales reps who called on retail chains across the country. Farrell received 10% of gross sales for his services. For Greg, dealing with retailers through such a representative was the only sensible way to do business in the US market. However, this arrangement was not without flaws as it limited the flow of information from retailers to

Motus. As a consequence, Greg and Phil were not acquainted with the selection criteria applied by specialist buyers in deciding to list a new product. They were also afraid that the lack of direct contact with retailers might limit their understanding of consumer reaction to the Motus handles.

The Motus handles were also listed in 20 catalogues representing a circulation of 18 million copies across the US. Starcrest, Signatures, and Handsome Rewards were examples of large leisure catalogues offering Motus handles. Museum of Modern Art and Improvements were large home-improvement catalogues, and Memorial Home Care, AliMed, Sammons, and North Coast Medical specialized in home-care supplies. Catalogue sales were characterized by small order sizes, deliveries on consignment, and very low effectiveness (defined as the proportion of unit sales to circulation), which was typically close to 0.1% for newly introduced products, and seldom reached more than 0.5% for established ones. Sales to catalogue distributors were handled by three representatives, one of whom specialized in home-care catalogues.

Greg was also interested in the opportunity associated with cooperating with original equipment manufacturers (OEM), who, in his opinion, could derive some competitive advantage from selling their implements together with the Motus handles. Initially, he found OEMs very conservative in their approach to new products in general, and the Motus handles in particular, but his perseverance in soliciting cooperative sales was starting to pay off. He was currently having discussions with several US OEMs, including Ames, Melnor, True Temper, Union Tools, and Yeoman & Company.

Canada

Canadian sales were handled by two regional representatives. By June 1994, the company had established a number of retail accounts, which included several hardware chains (Canadian Tire, Home Hardware, Pro Hardware) and mass merchandisers (Cotter Canada and Federated Co-op). Greg was also negotiating with several OEMs, including Melnor Canada, Rite Way Industries, and True Temper Canada.

Overseas

Greg explained that the company's interest in overseas markets was largely related to an attempt to prevent overseas manufacturers from copying Motus's proprietary product concept. He wanted to evaluate the sales potential in a number of regional markets, and then decide whether to extend patent protection to those markets. With this objective in mind, in 1993 and 1994, Phil and Greg participated in hardware trade shows in Cologne, Germany, where they attempted to develop contacts with European distributors and retailers. Ironically, Motus found its European representative in Winnipeg. In 1993, a retired executive of Dutch origin walked into Motus's office and made an offer to Greg to assist the company in developing sales in Europe. He teamed up with a Holland-based associate who soon began calling on customers in several countries. Their activities, which included placing an ad in a European business magazine, *DIY in Europe* (at a cost of DM750), resulted in some sales to hardware retailers in England, Holland, France, and Norway.

As a result of contacts developed during the trade shows in Toronto, Chicago, and Cologne, Motus also sold a small number of its products to customers in Australia and New Zealand.

THE DISCUSSION

Phil and Greg spent all morning reviewing the fundamental elements of their current marketing strategy. In order to obtain a clearer picture of their present situation, and to define their goals, they drafted strategic profiles outlining how they saw their situation now and in the future (see Exhibit 40-5). Subsequently, they also reviewed the newly acquired summary of a marketing survey of the gardening market in the US (see Exhibit 40-6) and business statistics characterizing the operations of hardware stores and retail centres (see Exhibit 40-7). Their discussion then turned to the relevance and the implications of this new information to Motus's strategy.

By lunchtime, they were ready to evaluate their overall marketing strategy and decide on possible changes to it. Trying not to lose the momentum, they decided to continue their discussion without a lunch break.

Initially, they concentrated on reviewing the principal factors determining their marketing strategy. They agreed on such key elements as the large size of the potential market, the low level of product awareness among customers, the very high degree of acceptance among those who learned about the product, and the lack of direct competition. They also observed that, in terms of its position in the product life cycle, the Motus handle, which had already started to generate increased sales, was probably at the end of the introduction stage. Finally,

Exhibit 40-5   Motus Inc.—Strategic Profile

	Current	Target (in 2 Years)
Rank and size	$500 000 sales Break-even 3 employees Small marketing company	$1 000 000 sales $200 000 profits 5+ employees Small marketing and R&D company
Product line	D-Grip: 70% Straight Handle: 30%	D-Grip: 40% Straight Handle: 20% New product(s): 40%
Geographic coverage	Canada: 15% US: 80% Overseas: 5%	???
Evolution	Entrepreneurial company	Entrepreneurial company
Organization	Informal	Informal
Performance goals	Sales/profit growth Market development/penetration	Maintenance of market share New product development
Strengths	Novelty consumer product Limited competition Patent protection Established sales force Secure financial backing	Wide acceptance of the D-Grip and Straight Handle Strong distribution Innovative new products Internally financed
Weaknesses	Resource limitations Narrow product line Increased competition	
Strategy	Focus on sales	???

Exhibit 40-6 Summary of the Survey of US Gardeners and Selected Characteristics

Survey Summary*

Market

61 million gardeners (one in three adults) spend over $9 billion annually on gardening materials, equipment, and supplies

Age

59% of gardeners are aged 35–64 vs. 47% of the entire population

Distribution

50%: urban areas of 500 000 or more people

20%: urban areas of 50 000–499 999 people

30%: smaller communities

Income level

Annual median household income of $35 000 vs. $30 000 for all households

House ownership

87% of gardeners own their own home vs. 64% of all households

Education

58% of gardeners have at least one year of college vs. 44% of all adults aged 18 or older

Major types of gardeners

Dabblers: the least experienced (60% of the market)

Decorators: interested primarily in ornamental horticulture (19%)

Cultivators: love to grow and eat vegetables (18%)

Masters: most sophisticated, fully devoted to their hobby (3%); the easiest group to reach (look for information in gardening books and magazines) and the group with the most potential for spreading the message

Shopping

58% of gardeners shop at lawn-and-garden centres

53% of gardeners shop at discount department stores

13% shop by catalogue

Big-city gardeners shop more frequently than rural gardeners at lawn-and-garden centres, nurseries, and hardware or building supply stores

Rural gardeners are more likely to buy products at discount department stores or by mail

Regional differences

Western gardeners: the best educated

Southern gardeners: own the most land

Westerners and Southerners put more hours per week into their hobby than Northeasterners and Midwesterners

Gardeners in colder climates do not have to spend as much time conditioning soil or controlling pests

Exhibit 40-6 Summary of the Survey of US Gardeners and Selected Characteristics (continued)

Selected Characteristics of Gardeners by Cluster Type

Characteristic	Total	Dabblers	Decorators	Cultivators	Masters
Total (in thousands and percent)	60 555 100%	32 829 60%	11 487 19%	11 110 18%	1660 3%
Average age	47	45	49	50	53
Average number of years gardening	13.9	13.2	14.6	15.0	16.0
Percent female	56.1%	59.7%	59%	47%	54%
Percent in large urban areas (population over 500 000)	48.1%	50.5%	51.3%	37.1%	45%
Percent asked for advice on gardening	42.2%	36.9%	45.9%	52.5%	63%
Percent mail-order expenditures	9.6%	9.0%	8.9%	11.8%	13.5%
1991 median annual household income	$35 081	$36 896	$37 159	$27 939	$28 287
Average annual gardening expenditures	$156	$128	$237	$140	$271
Aggregate gardening expenditure	$9.4 billion 100%	$4.7 billion 50%	$2.7 billion 29%	$1.5 billion 16%	$0.5 billion 5%
Average number of hours in a week spent on gardening	6.9	5	7.5	11	15
Division of time between types of gardening		V**: 50% O***: 50%	O: 67%	V: 70%	V: 50% O: 50%

* Based on the results of the Gardening in America Survey conducted by NFO Research, Inc. for Organic Gardening, and presented in the April 1993 issue of *American Demographics*, vol. 15(4), pp. 44–48.
** V = vegetable gardening
***O = ornamental gardening

Exhibit 40-7 Selected Retail Statistics: Hardware Stores and Home Centres*

Hardware Stores

Department	Gross Margin (%)	Sales to Inventory Ratio	Sales per Sq. Ft. ($)	Percentage of Net Sales	Percentage of Sales Floor	Percentage of Inventory
Hardware	44.6	3.71	123.73	14.3	14.5	15.9
Hand Tools	37.7	3.65	124.67	6.2	6.3	6.7
Power Tools and Accessories	30.1	3.39	149.64	4.8	4.1	5.6
Plumbing, Heating and Cooling	42.6	4.37	128.35	13.5	129.9	13.1
Electrical Supplies	40.5	4.43	145.75	10.1	8.7	9.7

Exhibit 40-7 Selected Retail Statistics: Hardware Stores and Home Centres* (continued)

Department	Gross Margin (%)	Sales to Inventory Ratio	Sales per Sq. Ft. ($)	Percentage of Net Sales	Percentage of Sales Floor	Percentage of Inventory
Paint and Home Decorating	38.3	4.58	142.02	13.8	12.7	13.0
Lumber	30.0	3.67	106.81	1.0	0.8	9.7
Building Materials	35.7	3.99	132.43	1.4	1.4	13.0
Lawn and Garden	34.5	3.89	140.69	12.8	12.5	1.0
Housewares	33.5	4.33	100.67	6.9	9.5	1.3
Automotive Supplies	34.7	4.08	101.34	3.0	3.9	3.1
Major Appliances and Home Entertainment	27.3	3.41	144.04	2.5	2.1	2.8
Sporting Goods and Outdoor Living	32.3	4.17	99.19	2.9	4.1	3.4
Miscellaneous Goods	36.5	4.41	103.70	6.8	6.4	5.2

Home Centres

Department	Gross Margin (%)	Sales to Inventory Ratio	Sales per Sq. Ft. ($)	Percentage of Net Sales	Percentage of Sales Floor	Percentage of Inventory
Hardware	41.8	6.13	191.68	7.6	12.7	8.9
Hand Tools	36.5	4.44	136.15	2.9	5.9	3.0
Power Tools and Accessories	27.7	4.31	173.45	2.6	5.4	3.9
Plumbing, Heating and Cooling	39.5	5.19	154.71	6.1	11.1	8.0
Electrical Supplies	38.1	5.22	118.19	4.1	9.5	4.8
Paint and Home Decorating	37.3	5.67	161.49	7.6	12.3	8.3
Lumber	22.9	8.99	491.80	25.3	10.2	24.6
Building Materials	26.1	10.04	440.81	24.4	9.8	20.5
Lawn and Garden	33.5	5.65	148.11	5.2	9.0	5.1
Housewares	34.0	4.92	140.31	1.9	3.7	2.6
Automotive Supplies	34.4	5.36	155.61	0.9	1.1	0.6
Major Appliances and Home Entertainment	20.4	5.47	NA	1.6	1.9	2.7
Sporting Goods and Outdoor Living	29.9	5.42	129.71	1.3	2.0	1.0
Miscellaneous Goods	31.2	10.65	288.15	8.6	5.4	5.2

* Compiled from *The 1993 Management Report, Detailed Cost-of-Doing-Business Data for Hardware Stores and Home Centers,* Published by the National Retail Hardware Association and Home Center Institute (US).

they recognized the constraints resulting from the small size of their company, including those limiting their choice of promotion methods, their access to sources of market information, and the limited control they could exercise over their sales force and distributors.

Phil and Greg attempted to summarize the company's current strategy in terms of its market coverage and marketing mix. They concluded that it could be characterized as follows:

- undifferentiated marketing (essentially, an identical offering for several identified segments);

- a new-to-the-market, multi-functional product, with patent protection restricting competition, providing the benefits of health and work efficiency;

- perceived-value pricing (based on the consumer's assumed perception of value of the product and not on its cost), generating high margins;

- a push approach to creating sales (promotion concentrated on distributors rather than consumers);

- multi-channel, one-level distribution; dispersed geographic coverage.

Having clarified their understanding of the current strategy, they moved to discussing the possibility of varying some of these elements.

In terms of their approach to market coverage, they could continue to operate in several segments of the market, but differentiate their marketing mix to better fit each of these segments. This differentiated marketing strategy would entail a significant financial and organizational effort, but could generate substantial sales growth over an extended period of time.

On the other hand, the company could utilize a concentrated marketing approach by allocating all their resources to one carefully selected market segment. Although Phil, Greg, and Carol felt that the limited resource requirements of this alternative would be more consistent with their capabilities, they were apprehensive about the inherent risks associated with it. Their selection of a single target market segment would have to be perfect; otherwise Motus, with no support from other products, could face serious problems.

Each of these two alternatives would entail changes to some elements of their marketing program. In either case, the image conveyed by the product would probably have to be altered, the pricing system adjusted, and the marketing channels modified. In the case of concentrated marketing, a pull strategy would definitely have to replace the currently utilized push process for creating sales.

Instead of radically changing their current strategy, Motus could also decide to merely fine tune it. Under this alternative, their recent change in prices could be viewed as a prelude to other adjustments, such as a decision to allocate some resources to consumer advertising and introduce new distribution channels. The attraction of this alternative lay mostly in its relatively low cost and the limited risk it entailed.

As the day passed, Phil, Greg, and Carol discussed the influence of the company's internal and external environment on their choice of the most suitable alternative. They also attempted to evaluate the potential impact each alternative strategy could have on the company's future strategic profile.

Late in the evening, they finally arrived at a clear understanding of the strategic choices they faced. However, after more than 12 hours of a continuous discussion, they were too exhausted to make rational decisions. They decided to leave this discussion to the following afternoon.

ENDNOTES

1. "Ergonomics is an analytical mechanism of simply trying to assign science and mathematical tools to designing jobs to fit workers rather than force-fitting workers into jobs. It is more an art form than a science." Quoted from Dr. Roger Stephen, an industrial engineer and senior ergonomist with the Department of Labor Occupational Safety & Health Administration in the US. *Material Handling Engineering*, January 1992, p. 30.

2. From "Leaders in Excellence—Manitoba's Thriving Health Industry," Special Supplement to *Manitoba Business*, October 1993.